Preface

Welcome to the world of System Analysis and Design, where the intricacies of technology and the art of problem-solving converge to create powerful solutions that drive the modern world. This book is crafted to provide a comprehensive, yet engaging journey through the fundamental concepts, methodologies, and tools that are pivotal in the field of System Analysis and Design.

In today's fast-paced digital era, the demand for efficient, reliable, and scalable systems is greater than ever. From the software that runs our smartphones to the complex databases that power global corporations, systems analysis and design are at the heart of technological innovation and operational excellence. This book is tailored for students, aspiring system analysts, and seasoned professionals seeking to deepen their understanding and enhance their skills.

What Makes This Book Unique

This book stands out in its ability to blend theory with practice. We believe that the best way to learn is by doing, and thus, we incorporate real-world examples, case studies, and practical exercises throughout the chapters. You will not only learn the essential theories but also see how they are applied in actual scenarios, preparing you to tackle real-life challenges with confidence and expertise.

A Journey Through System Development

Starting with the foundational concepts, this book takes you step-by-step through the system development life cycle (SDLC). You will explore the various phases of SDLC, including planning, analysis, design, implementation, and maintenance. Each chapter delves into the specific tasks, techniques, and deliverables associated with these phases, providing a clear roadmap for successful system development.

Emphasizing Modern Methodologies

In an ever-evolving field, staying current with the latest methodologies and best practices is crucial. This book places a strong emphasis on contemporary approaches such as Agile, Scrum, and DevOps, which are revolutionizing the way systems are developed and managed. We also cover traditional methodologies like Waterfall and V-Model, offering a balanced perspective that equips you with the flexibility to choose the right approach for any project.

Tools and Technologies

To be effective in system analysis and design, familiarity with the right tools and technologies is indispensable. This book introduces a variety of software tools that aid in Modelling, designing, and documenting systems. From Unified Modelling Language (UML) diagrams to computer-aided software engineering (CASE) tools, you will gain hands-on experience with the technologies that are shaping the future of system development.

Fostering Analytical Thinking and Problem-Solving Skills

System analysis and design is as much about analytical thinking and problem-solving as it is about technical skills. This book encourages you to think critically, question assumptions, and approach problems methodically. Through structured exercises and thought-provoking scenarios, you will develop the ability to dissect complex problems and devise effective, efficient solutions.

Table Of Contents

Chapter 1: Introduction to System Analysis and Design

In this chapter you will learn about:
- Types and characteristics of systems
- Principles of successful systems
- Phrases: Analysis, design, development, implementation, maintenance
- System analyst role and qualifications.

1.1 Understanding System

In the world of system analysis and design, it's essential to understand what a system is.

What is a System?

A system is like a puzzle made up of many pieces that work together to perform a specific task or achieve a common goal. Think of it as a group of parts or components that interact with each other to produce a desired outcome.

Types of Systems

There are different types of systems. Some systems are manual, meaning they rely on people to operate them, like a filing system in an office. Others are automated, where machines or computers handle the tasks, like an online banking system.

Characteristics of Systems

Systems have certain characteristics:

1. Interconnection: Parts of a system are connected and affect each other.
2. Purpose: Systems have a specific goal or purpose they are designed to achieve.
3. Boundaries: Systems have boundaries that define what is inside and outside the system.
4. Inputs and Outputs: Systems take inputs, process them, and produce outputs.
5. Feedback: Systems often receive feedback, which helps them adjust and improve.
6. Environment: Systems exist within an environment that can influence their operations.

Real-life Examples

In everyday life, we encounter various systems:

1. A transportation system helps people move from one place to another.
2. An ecosystem is a natural system where plants, animals, and the environment interact.
3. A computer system includes hardware, software, and users working together to perform tasks.

Principles of Successful Systems

Successful systems share certain principles:

1. Efficiency: They achieve their goals with minimal waste of resources.
2. Reliability: They work consistently and predictably.
3. Flexibility: They can adapt to changes or new requirements.
4. User-friendliness: They are easy to use and understand for the people interacting with them.

The System Development Lifecycle

The System Development Lifecycle (SDLC) is like a roadmap that guides us through the journey of creating and maintaining a system. It's a step-by-step process that helps us build effective and efficient systems.

1. Analysis:

In the first phase, we analyse what the system needs to do. We talk to users, gather their requirements, and understand their needs. It's like figuring out what ingredients we need to bake a cake.

2. Design:

Once we know what the system should do, we design how it will do it. We create blueprints or plans that show how the system will look and work. It's like sketching a blueprint before building a house.

3. Development:

Now it's time to build the system based on the designs we created. Developers write the code, create databases, and put everything together. It's like constructing a building based on the blueprints.

4. Implementation:
Once the system is built, we put it into action. We install the software, train users on how to use it, and make sure everything is working smoothly. It's like opening a new store and welcoming customers for the first time.
5. Maintenance:
Even after the system is up and running, it needs regular check-ups and updates. We fix any problems that arise, make improvements, and keep the system running smoothly. It's like taking care of a garden to ensure it stays healthy and beautiful.

Benefits of SDLC:
- Helps ensure that the system meets the needs of users.
- Provides a structured approach to system development.
- Helps manage risks and control costs.
- Allows for better communication and collaboration among team members.

1. Roles and Responsibilities in System Development
In system analysis and design, different people have specific roles and responsibilities to ensure the successful development of systems. Let's look at some of these roles and what they do:

Systems Analysts:
Role: Systems analysts are like detectives. They investigate and understand what users need from a system.
Responsibilities: They talk to users, gather information, and figure out what the system needs to do. They also design how the system will work and help to make sure it's built correctly.
Programmers:
Role: Programmers are like builders. They take the designs created by the systems analysts and turn them into computer programs.
Responsibilities: They write the code that makes the system work according to the design. They also test the programs to make sure they work correctly.
Project Managers:
Role: Project managers are like captains of a ship. They steer the project in the right direction and make sure everything stays on track.
Responsibilities: They plan the project, assign tasks to team members, and make sure everyone knows what they need to do and when. They also keep an eye on the budget and timeline to make sure the project stays on schedule.
Quality Assurance/Testers:
Role: Testers are like inspectors. They check the system to make sure it works the way it's supposed to.
Responsibilities: They run tests on the system to find any problems or mistakes. They report any issues they find back to the programmers so they can fix them.
Users:
Role: Users are the people who will actually use the system once it's built.
Responsibilities: They work with the systems analysts to make sure their needs are understood and met. They also provide feedback on the system during development to make sure it's meeting their needs.

1.4 Trends and Challenges in System Analysis and Design
Trends:
1. Agile Methodologies: This is like breaking big tasks into small pieces, making it easier to manage and adapt to changes.
2. DevOps Practices: Combining software development (coding) and IT operations (managing systems) for faster and more reliable software releases.
3. Continuous Integration/Continuous Deployment (CI/CD): Automating the process of testing and releasing software updates frequently.

Challenges:
1. Keeping Up with Technology: Technology changes quickly, so staying updated can be tough.
2. Managing Complexity: Systems can become very complex, making it hard to understand and maintain.
3. Security Concerns: With more data being stored and shared, keeping it safe from hackers and other threats is a big challenge.

4. Adapting to Change: Businesses and their needs change over time, so systems must be flexible enough to adapt without breaking.

Summary

1. Understanding Systems: Learn about different types of systems and how they work.
2. System Development Lifecycle (SDLC): Understand the step-by-step process of creating systems, from planning to maintenance. First, you plan, then you design, build, put it into action, and keep it running.
3. Roles and Responsibilities: Discover who does what in system development, especially the role of systems analysts.
4. Trends and Challenges: Explore current trends like agile methods and challenges faced in building systems today.

Glossary

1. System: A collection of interconnected components working together toward a common goal.
2. SDLC (System Development Lifecycle): A structured process consisting of phases like analysis, design, development, implementation, and maintenance, guiding system development.
3. Systems Analyst: Investigates user needs, designs system functionality, and ensures alignment with organizational goals.
4. Agile Methodologies: Adaptive approaches to system development, emphasizing flexibility, collaboration, and iterative improvements.
5. Quality Assurance/Testers: Responsible for testing systems to identify errors or defects, ensuring reliability and functionality.
6. DevOps Practices: Integrates software development (coding) and IT operations (managing systems) for streamlined and efficient software delivery.
7. Security Concerns: Challenges related to safeguarding data and systems from unauthorized access, cyber threats, and breaches.

1.5 Project

1.5.1 Solved Project

Title: Digital Library Solutions Project: A Comprehensive Upgrade

You are tasked with developing an integrated software solution for a local library. The library wants to improve its membership and lending services, including an online catalogue and booking system. The project will cover all aspects of system analysis and design, encompassing the understanding of systems, the system development lifecycle, roles and responsibilities, and contemporary challenges.

Approach:

1. Project Initiation

Objectives:

1. Enhance library membership and lending services.
2. Develop an online catalogue and booking system.

Key Activities:

- **Stakeholder Meetings:** Conduct initial discussions with library management and patrons to understand their needs and expectations.
- **Project Charter:** Create a project charter that outlines the project scope, goals, stakeholders, and resources needed.

2. Requirements Gathering

Objectives:

1. Collect detailed requirements for the new system.

Key Activities:

- **Surveys and Interviews:** Gather data from library staff and users through surveys and interviews to identify pain points and desired features.

- **Requirement Workshops:** Conduct workshops to define detailed functional and non-functional requirements.

3. System Analysis and Design

Objectives:

1. Design a system that meets the gathered requirements.

Key Activities:

- **System Architecture:** Define the system architecture, including hardware and software components.
- **Data Modelling:** Create data models to define how data is stored and accessed.
- **Prototype Development:** Develop prototypes for key parts of the system, particularly the user interface, to gather early feedback.

4. System Development

Objectives:

1. Develop the system according to the specifications.

Key Activities:

- **Coding:** Begin coding using the selected programming languages and frameworks.
- **Agile Methodology:** Utilize Agile development practices to allow for iterative testing and feedback.
- **API Integration:** Integrate external APIs for additional functionalities like SMS notifications and social media updates.

5. Testing

Objectives:

1. Ensure the system is stable, secure, and meets all user requirements.

Key Activities:

- **Unit Testing:** Perform unit testing to ensure individual components function correctly.
- **System Testing:** Conduct comprehensive system testing to verify that all components work together seamlessly.
- **User Acceptance Testing (UAT):** Facilitate UAT with real users to confirm the system meets their needs and is easy to use.

6. Deployment

Objectives:

1. Successfully deploy the system to the library environment.

Key Activities:

- **Deployment Planning:** Plan the deployment phase, including timelines and resources.
- **Training Sessions:** Conduct training sessions for library staff to familiarize them with the new system.
- **Initial Launch:** Implement a phased rollout, if necessary, to mitigate risks.

7. Maintenance and Support

Objectives:

1. Provide ongoing support and maintenance to ensure system longevity and relevance.

Key Activities:

- **Feedback Collection:** Establish mechanisms for users to provide feedback on system performance and usability.
- **Regular Updates:** Schedule regular updates to incorporate new features and security patches.
- **Help Desk Support:** Set up a help desk to assist users with any issues they encounter.

8. Evaluation and Refinement

Objectives:

1. Continuously improve the system based on user feedback and changing needs.

Key Activities:

- **Performance Metrics:** Use performance metrics to evaluate system usage and effectiveness.
- **Refinement Plans:** Develop plans to refine and enhance the system based on feedback and performance evaluations.

9. Data Security and Compliance

Objectives:

1. Ensure the system complies with data protection laws and best practices.

Key Activities:

- **Security Audits:** Conduct regular security audits to identify vulnerabilities.
- **Compliance Checks:** Ensure the system meets all legal requirements for data handling and privacy.

1.5.2 Unsolved Project

Your part of a team assigned to a new project. Outline the roles and responsibilities typically involved in system development. Propose a team structure tailored to a hypothetical project, including key roles that ensure coverage of all critical areas of development, from initial analysis to deployment.

1.6 Case Study

1.6.1 Solved Case Study

The initiative to enhance local library services involves an integrated approach, adopting the Waterfall System Development Lifecycle (SDLC) to systematically address each component of the system, from conception to deployment. The project team includes a diverse set of roles: the Project Manager, who coordinates the project and ensures adherence to timelines; System Analysts, who gather detailed requirements and design specifications; Developers, who code the system based on these specifications; UI/UX Designers, who focus on creating an accessible and engaging interface; and QA Specialists, who rigorously test the system for both functionality and usability. The project aims to leverage modern technological trends such as real-time data analytics and machine learning to recommend books based on user behavior, but it also faces challenges like maintaining user privacy and managing the technological literacy of library patrons.

Questions:

1. Which SDLC model is adopted in the library enhancement project?

   Answer: The Waterfall System Development Lifecycle (SDLC) model is adopted in the library enhancement project.

2. What is the role of the System Analysts in the project?

   Answer: System Analysts in the project are responsible for gathering detailed requirements and designing system specifications.

3. What technological trend does the project incorporate to improve service?

   Answer: The project incorporates modern technological trends like real-time data analytics and machine learning to recommend books based on user behaviour.

4. What challenge does the project face related to user data?

   Answer: A major challenge faced by the project is maintaining user privacy while implementing advanced technological features.

5. How do QA Specialists contribute to the project?

   Answer: QA Specialists rigorously test the system for both functionality and usability, ensuring the final product meets quality standards.

1.6.2 Unsolved Case Study

To modernize local library services, a comprehensive system development project is initiated, focusing on a deep understanding of integrated library systems. This project adopts the Agile System Development Lifecycle (SDLC) to accommodate rapid adjustments based on user feedback and evolving needs. The project team is structured with clear roles: the Project Manager oversees strategic execution, System Analysts translate user requirements into system specifications, Developers build the software, UI/UX Designers ensure the interface is user-friendly, and QA Specialists enforce quality standards. Contemporary digital trends like cloud storage and advanced search algorithms are integrated to enhance user experience, though the project must navigate challenges such as data security and system integrity in the face of cyber threats.

Questions:

1. What SDLC model is used in the library system development project?
2. Who is responsible for translating user requirements into system specifications?
3. What role do UI/UX Designers play in the project?
4. What is one digital trend incorporated into the library system?
5. What are the major challenges faced by the project?

1.7 Lab Activity

1.7.1 Solved Lab Activity

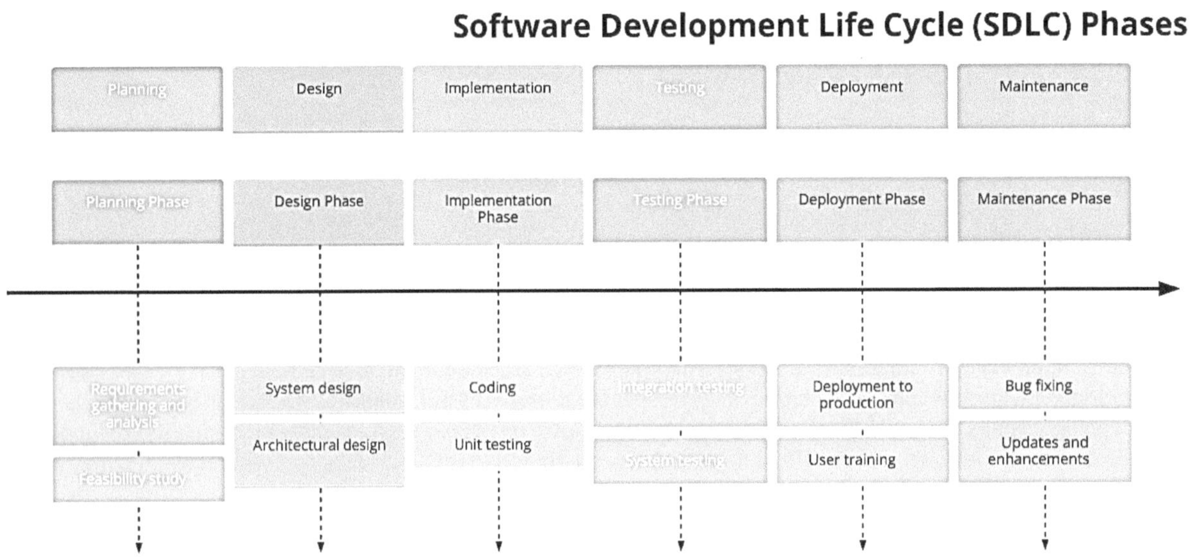

Key Activities Performed in Each Phase

1. Requirements
Objective: Gather and document the functional and non-functional requirements of the system.
Key Activities:
- Conduct stakeholder interviews, surveys, and workshops.
- Analyze business needs and document requirements.
- Create requirement specifications and obtain approval.

2. Design
Objective: Define the architecture and design of the system based on the requirements.
Key Activities:
- Develop system architecture and design models.
-Create detailed design specifications for system components.
- Design user interfaces, databases, and system integrations.
- Review and approve design documents.

3. Implementation
Objective: Convert the design into executable code.
Key Activities:
- Write code for system components and features.
- Follow coding standards and guidelines.
- Perform unit testing to ensure code correctness.
- Integrate individual components into the system.

4. Testing
Objective: Verify that the system meets the specified requirements and is free of defects.

Key Activities:
- Develop test plans and test cases.
- Execute functional, integration, system, and acceptance tests.
- Identify and log defects.
- Perform regression testing to ensure new changes don't affect existing functionality.
- Validate system performance and security.

5. Deployment

Objective: Make the system available for use in the production environment.

Key Activities:
- Prepare the production environment.
- Deploy the system to production.
- Conduct smoke testing to ensure deployment success.
- Train end-users and provide documentation.
- Monitor the system for any post-deployment issues.

6. Maintenance

Objective: Ensure the system remains functional and up to date after deployment.

Key Activities:
- Monitor system performance and reliability.
- Fix bugs and issues reported by users.
- Implement system enhancements and updates.
- Perform regular system backups and updates.
- Provide ongoing user support and training.

1.7.2 Unsolved Lab Activity

Create a chart that maps the roles to their specific responsibilities in a system development project.

Previous Years Solved Questions

Q 1. Describe the role of a Systems Analyst. Also, list various skills that the Systems Analyst should possess. **[IGNOU June 2010]**

Ans 1: A Systems Analyst bridges the gap between business needs and IT solutions. They analyse, design, and implement information systems to improve efficiency and effectiveness. Key responsibilities include gathering and analysing requirements, designing systems, conducting feasibility studies, managing projects, implementing systems, providing user training and support, and maintaining and evaluating systems.

Essential skills for a Systems Analyst include:

1. Technical Skills: Knowledge of programming languages (Java, Python, SQL), system design, database management, and basic networking.

2. Analytical Skills: Strong problem-solving, critical thinking, and attention to detail.

3. Business Skills: Understanding of business processes, requirements gathering, and project management.

4. Interpersonal Skills: Excellent communication, teamwork, and user support.

5. Soft Skills: Adaptability, time management, and leadership.

A Systems Analyst ensures that technology solutions align with business objectives, contributing to organizational efficiency and success.

Previous Years Unsolved Questions

Q 1. With the help of a diagram explain different components of a typical CASE tool. Also cite certain examples of CASE tools, being used at different SDLC levels. **[IGNOU JUNE,2010]**

Q 2. What is structured system analysis and design? Explain the process of SSAD. **[Chaudhary Charan Singh University BCA, May 2019]**

Q 3. Explain the SDLC with diagram. **[Chaudhary Charan Singh University BCA, May 2019]**

Q 4. Define Subsystem. What are the basic types of system? **[Udaipur University, 2018]**

Exercises

Exercise 1 – Multiple Choice Questions

1. What is the primary goal of system analysis in system development?
a. To write code for the system
b. To understand and document the requirements of a system
c. To design the user interface
d. To test the system for bugs

2. Which phase of the System Development Lifecycle (SDLC) involves creating detailed specifications for the system components?
a. Planning
b. Analysis
c. Design
d. Implementation

3. In the context of system development, what is the role of a systems analyst?
a. Writing the system's code
b. Testing the system`
c. Defining the requirements and ensuring they are met in the design
d. Maintaining the system post-deployment

4. Which of the following is a trend in system analysis and design?
a. Decreased reliance on user feedback
b. Adoption of Agile methodologies
c. Elimination of documentation
d. Using the Waterfall model exclusively

5. What is a common challenge faced during system analysis and design?
a. Having too much time for project completion
b. Lack of user involvement
c. Overly detailed requirements from users
d. Excessive budget for the project

Exercise 2 – True/False

1. Understanding systems is not necessary for successful system analysis and design.
2. The System Development Lifecycle (SDLC) includes phases such as planning, analysis, design, implementation, and maintenance.
3. System analysis is solely the responsibility of software developers.
4. One of the roles in system development is the project manager, who oversees the entire project from start to finish.
5. The trend of using Agile methodologies in system analysis and design has decreased in recent years.

Exercise 3 – Fill in the blanks

1. Systems are a set of interrelated components that work together to achieve a __________.
2. The process of understanding and specifying in detail what an information system should do is known as __________.
3. The process of planning, creating, testing, and deploying an information system is referred to as the __________.

Exercise 4- Fill in the blanks with two options

1. System analysis involves understanding ____________, ____________, and constraints.
2. The ____________ phase of SDLC involves gathering and analyzing requirements.
3. ____________ in system design refers to how components are structured and organized.

Exercise 5- Give two answers for the following:

1. Types of Systems
2. Phases in the System Development Lifecycle (SDLC)
3. Roles in System Development
4. Characteristics of Systems
5. Trends in System Analysis and Design

Exercise 6- Rearrange the sentence

1. Analysis /involves /understanding/ requirements/ system.
2. Systems /of/ hardware/ composed/ are/ and /software.
3. Lifecycle/consists/phases/development/of/multiple.

Exercise 7- Choose the Odd One Out

1. Design, Development, Understanding, Challenges.
2. Lifecycle, Roles, Responsibilities, Analysis.
3. Roles, Understanding, Challenges, Development.

Exercise 8- Jumble words

1. mtenoveplde
2. cclfeeyil
3. rsnltiipbiseeoisri

Exercise 9- Match case

Column 1	Column 2
1. Components of systems	a. Planning, analysis
2. Phase that comes after implementation in SDLC	b. Maintenance
3. Involves understanding user needs and business processes	c. Hardware, software
4. Ensures the system remains operational over time	d. Analysis
5. Defined in the planning phase of SDLC	e. Evaluation

Exercise 10- Assertion – Reason

1. Assertion (A): The System Development Lifecycle (SDLC) is critical for successful system development.
Reason (R): The SDLC provides a structured approach for planning, designing, and implementing a system.

Options:

1. Assertion (A) is true and Reason (R) is the correct reason for Assertion (A).
2. Assertion (A) is true, but Reason (R) is not the correct reason for Assertion (A).
3. Assertion (A) is false, but Reason (R) is true.
4. Assertion (A) is true, but Reason (R) is false.

Exercise 11- One- word

1. What is composed of inputs, outputs, and processes?
2. What involves documenting system requirements and specifications?
3. What phase defines user requirements and system specifications?

Exercise 12- Small Answers

1. What are the main components of a system?
2. What is the primary goal of system analysis and design?
3. How do inputs and outputs relate to a system?

Exercise 13- Long Answers

1. Delve into the System Development Lifecycle (SDLC), discussing each key phase in detail and examining the significance of thorough planning and meticulous execution. How does each phase contribute to the overall development process?
2. Analyse the diverse roles and responsibilities within system development teams, highlighting the importance of collaboration and communication among stakeholders. How do these roles intersect, and what are the essential skills required for success in each role?

Answers

Exercise 1- 1) B, 2) C, 3) C, 4) B, 5) B
Exercise 2- 1) False, 2) True, 3) False, 4) True, 5) False
Exercise 3- 1) common goal, 2) system analysis, 3) System Development Lifecycle (SDLC)
Exercise 4- 1) user needs, business processes, 2) analysis, 3) Modularity
Exercise 5- 1) Manual Systems, Automated Systems, 2) Analysis Phase, Design Phase, 3) Systems Analyst, Programmer, 4) Interconnection, Purpose, 5) Agile Methodologies, DevOps Practices
Exercise 6- 1) System analysis involves understanding requirements, 2) Systems are composed of hardware and software, 3) Development lifecycle consists of multiple phases.
Exercise 7- 1) Challenges. 2) Lifecycle, 3) Understanding
Exercise 8- 1) development, 2) lifecycle, 3) responsibilities
Exercise 9- 1) c, 2) e, 3) d, 4) b, 5) a
Exercise 10- a) Assertion (A) is true and Reason (R) is the correct reason for Assertion (A).
Exercise 11- Systems, 2) Documentation, 3) Planning

Online Resources

Online Exam paper
URL https://forms.gle/dnsLz69SnBp8hVHA7
QR Code

YouTube Video
URL https://www.youtube.com/playlist?list=PLzlh_31VWEFo5X5g8rflHjgs6Nbhwq22w
QR Code

More Test Papers Practices

Test Paper-1
URL https://forms.gle/4KdTQCZpQJ2VAVxh7
QR Code

Test Paper-2
URL https://forms.gle/ic7NzFaEZwCdzGXbA
QR Code

System analysis and design Test Paper
Chapter- 1
Introduction to System Analysis and Design

Time Duration: 30 Minutes **Maximum Marks: 25**

General Instructions:
1. The question paper consists of answer any 12 questions out of the given 19 questions and is divided into four sections, A, B, C and D.
2. All questions are compulsory.
3. Section A comprises question numbers 1 to 8. These are MCQs and one liner of one mark each. You are to select one most appropriate response out of the four provided options.
4. Section B comprises question numbers 1 to 5. These are SAQs carrying two marks each.
5. Section C comprises question numbers 1 to 4. These are SAQs carrying four marks each.
6. Section D comprises question numbers 1& 2. These are LAQs carrying five marks each.

SECTION-A

I. <u>Answer any 6 questions out of the given 8 questions</u> **(1*6=6)**

1. What is the primary purpose of system analysis in system development?
a) To write code for the system
b) To understand and document the requirements of a system
c) To design the user interface
d) To test the system for bugs

2. Which phase of the System Development Lifecycle (SDLC) involves creating detailed specifications for the system components?
a) Planning
b) Analysis
c) Design
d) Implementation

3. In the context of system development, what is the role of a systems analyst?
a) Writing the system's code
b) Testing the system
c) Defining the requirements and ensuring they are met in the design
d) Maintaining the system post-deployment

4. Which of the following is a trend in system analysis and design?
a) Decreased reliance on user feedback
b) Adoption of Agile methodologies
c) Elimination of documentation
d) Using Waterfall model exclusively

5. What is a common challenge faced during system analysis and design?
a) Having too much time for project completion
b) Lack of user involvement
c) Overly detailed requirements from users
d) Excessive budget for the project

6. What is the first phase of the SDLC?
7. What methodology emphasizes iterative development and collaboration?
8. Who is responsible for defining system requirements and ensuring they are met?

SECTION-B

II. <u>Answer any 3 questions out of the given 5 questions</u> **(2*3=6)**

1. Define the term 'system' in the context of system analysis.
2. What is the main objective of the analysis phase in the SDLC?
3. List two key responsibilities of a systems analyst.
4. Name one trend in system analysis and design.
5. What is a major challenge in system analysis?

SECTION-C

II. <u>Answer any 2 questions out of the given 4 questions</u> **(4*2=8)**

1. Explain the importance of the design phase in the SDLC.
2. Describe the role of a systems analyst in system development.
3. What are the benefits of using Agile methodologies in system development?
4. Identify and briefly discuss a challenge in system analysis and design.

SECTION-D

III. <u>Answer any 1 question out of the given 2 questions</u> **(5*1=5)**

1. Discuss the trends in system analysis and design that are shaping the future of system development.
2. Describe the System Development Lifecycle (SDLC) and its phases.

Chapter 2: Systems Thinking and Concepts

- Understanding Principles of Systems Thinking
- Comprehending Systems Theory and Concepts
- Applying Systems Thinking to Problem-Solving
- Recognizing the Importance of Interconnectedness
- Utilizing Systems Thinking Tools

2.1 Solving Principles of Systems Thinking

To discuss the principles of systems thinking within the context of system analysis and design, we can start by understanding what systems thinking is and then explore how its principles are applied to analyze and design systems effectively. I will also provide a description for generating some illustrative images to complement the explanation.

Understanding Systems Thinking

Systems thinking is an analytical approach that focuses on understanding how components of a system interact with one another within the whole structure. This methodology is crucial in system analysis and design because it encourages a holistic view rather than concentrating on individual elements in isolation. The goal is to achieve an efficient, sustainable system that addresses all user needs and environmental interactions.

Key Principles of Systems Thinking

1. Interconnectivity and Interdependence

Systems are comprised of interconnected components that depend on each other to function. In system analysis and design, understanding these connections is crucial for predicting how changes in one part of the system might impact others. For instance, modifying a software module could affect the overall performance of the system if not carefully analyzed. This principle encourages designers to consider the cascading effects of their decisions, ensuring that changes enhance the system without causing disruptions.

2. Holism

Holism is the principle that the system should be viewed rather than merely the sum of its parts. This holistic view helps in identifying and understanding the system's purpose, functionality, and performance. In design, this might mean considering how individual software components contribute to the system's goals, such as user satisfaction or operational efficiency. By focusing on the system, analysts can design more robust and coherent systems that align with business objectives and user needs.

3. Feedback Loops

Systems often contain loops where outputs of parts of the system eventually influence their own inputs in future cycles. These feedback loops can be positive (amplifying effects) or negative (dampening effects). In system design, recognizing these loops can help in creating stable and self-regulating systems. For example, a user feedback system in software can help developers understand user needs and adjust the product, accordingly, creating a loop that continually improves the system.

4. Causality

Understanding causality is about recognizing cause-and-effect relationships within the system. In system design, it is important to trace the origins of system behaviours or outcomes back to specific actions or configurations within the system. This understanding can help in pinpointing issues and predicting the impact of changes. For example, if a performance issue is detected, analysts can trace it back to specific changes in the system architecture or codebase.

5. Systems Mapping

Systems mapping involves creating visual representations of system components and their interrelationships. This tool is invaluable in system analysis as it helps stakeholders understand the system's structure and dynamics. Maps can include flowcharts, diagrams, and other tools that depict how data flows through a system, decision points, and interactions between components. These maps are critical in planning system upgrades or diagnosing problems.

6. Change Dynamics

Systems are dynamic; they change and evolve over time. Understanding the dynamics of change within the system ca2 help analysts and designers anticipate future needs and scalability issues. This involves considering how the system might need to adapt to changing external conditions, such as market trends or regulatory changes, and designing flexible systems that can accommodate these changes without extensive rework.

7. Leverage Points

Leverage points are places within a system where a small change can produce a large impact. Identifying and understanding these points can significantly enhance the efficiency of system design and problem-solving. For instance, improving the user interface in a software application can significantly enhance user engagement and satisfaction, more so than other more complex back-end improvements might.

8. Iterative Development

Systems thinking promotes an iterative approach to development, where systems are continuously evaluated and improved upon based on feedback and changing conditions. This approach is aligned with agile development methodologies used in software engineering, where the product is developed, tested, and improved in cycles, allowing for continual refinement and adaptation.

Applying Systems Thinking in System Analysis and Design

In practice, systems thinking aids system analysts and designers in several ways:

1. **Problem Solving**: By focusing on the whole system, analysts can identify real problems rather than just symptoms. This approach leads to more sustainable and effective solutions.
2. **Scalability and Flexibility**: Designing systems with an understanding of interconnections helps ensure that they are scalable and can adapt to future needs without requiring complete redesigns.
3. **Risk Management**: Systems thinking enables better anticipation of potential issues and the design of systems with robust countermeasures.
4. **User-Centric Design**: By understanding how various elements of the system interact with the user, designers can create more intuitive and effective interfaces.
5. **Sustainability**: With a holistic view, systems can be designed to operate efficiently and sustainably, minimizing their environmental impact.

Visual Aids

To further illustrate these concepts, let's create some images:

1. An infographic showing various system components and their interconnections.
2. A diagram illustrating positive and negative feedback loops within a system.
3. A lifecycle graph of a system from inception to retirement.

These visual aids will help in understanding the dynamic and interconnected nature of systems as applied in system analysis and design.

2.2 Systems Theory and Concepts

What is System?

The word System is derived from Greek word Systema, which means an organized relationship between any set of components to achieve some common cause or objective.

A system is "an orderly grouping of interdependent components linked together according to a plan to achieve a specific goal."

Constraints of a System

A system must have three basic constraints –
1. A system must have some **structure and behavior** which is designed to achieve a predefined objective.
2. Interconnectivity and **interdependence** must exist among the system components.
3. The **objectives of the organization** have a **higher priority** than the objectives of its subsystems.
For example, traffic management system, payroll system, automatic library system, human resources information system.

Properties of a System
A system has the following properties –
- Organization

    Organization implies structure and order. It is the arrangement of components that helps to achieve predetermined objectives.

- Interaction
- It is defined by the way the components operate with each other.
- For example, in an organization, purchasing department must interact with production department and payroll with personnel department.
- Interdependence

    Interdependence means how the components of a system depend on one another. For proper functioning, the components are coordinated and linked together according to a specified plan. The output of one subsystem is the required by other subsystem as input.

- Integration

    Integration is concerned with how system components are connected. It means that the parts of the system work together within the system even if each part performs a unique function.

- Central Objective
- The objective of system must be central. It may be real or stated. It is not uncommon for an organization to state an objective and operate to achieve another.
- The users must know the main objective of a computer application early in the analysis for a successful design and conversion.

Elements of a System
The following diagram shows the elements of a system –

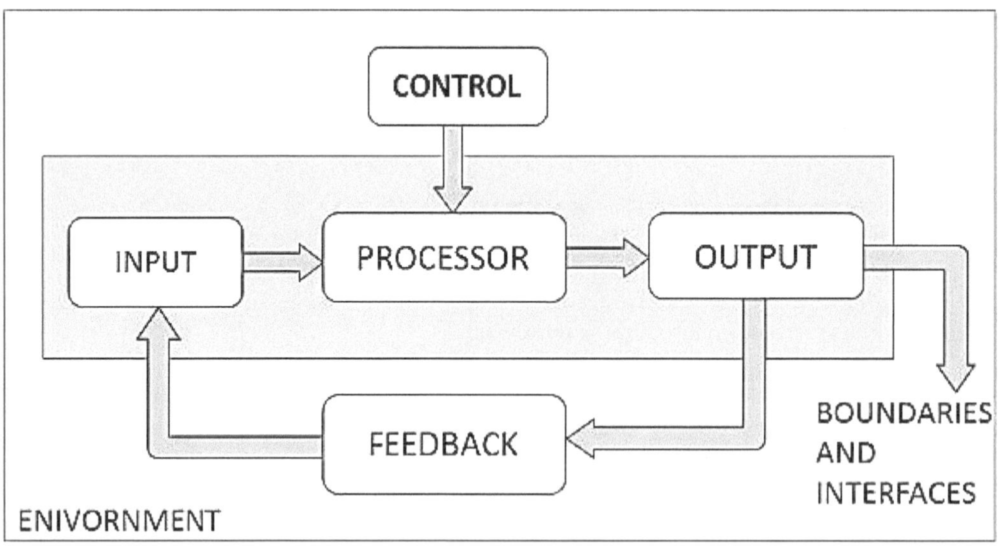

Outputs and Inputs
1. The main aim of a system is to produce an output which is useful for its user.
2. Inputs are the information that enters the system for processing.
3. Output is the outcome of processing.
Processor(s)

1. The processor is the element of a system that involves the actual transformation of input into output.
2. It is the operational component of a system. Processors may modify the input either totally or partially, depending on the output specification.
3. As the output specifications change, so does the processing. In some cases, input is also modified to enable the processor for handling the transformation.

Control

1. The control element guides the system.
2. It is the decision–making subsystem that controls the pattern of activities governing input, processing, and output.
3. The behavior of a computer System is controlled by the Operating System and software. In order to keep system in balance, what and how much input is needed is determined by Output Specifications.

Feedback

1. Feedback provides the control in a dynamic system.
2. Positive feedback is routine in nature that encourages the performance of the system.
3. Negative feedback is informational in nature that provides the controller with information for action.

Environment

1. The environment is the "supersystem" within which an organization operates.
2. It is the source of external elements that strike on the system.
3. It determines how a system must function. For example, vendors and competitors of organization's environment, may provide constraints that affect the actual performance of the business.

Boundaries and Interface

1. A system should be defined by its boundaries. Boundaries are the limits that identify its components, processes, and interrelationship when it interfaces with another system.
2. Each system has boundaries that determine its sphere of influence and control.
3. The knowledge of the boundaries of a given system is crucial in determining the nature of its interface with other systems for successful design.

Types of Systems

The systems can be divided into the following types –

1. Physical or Abstract Systems
2. Physical systems are tangible entities. We can touch and feel them.
3. Physical System may be static or dynamic in nature. For example, desks and chairs are the physical parts of computer center which are static. A programmed computer is a dynamic system in which programs, data, and applications can change according to the user's needs.
4. Abstract systems are non-physical entities or conceptual that may be formulas, representation or model of a real system.
5. Open or Closed Systems
6. An open system must interact with its environment. It receives inputs from and delivers outputs to the outside of the system. For example, an information system which must adapt to the changing environmental conditions.
7. A closed system does not interact with its environment. It is isolated from environmental influences. A completely closed system is rare.
8. Adaptive and Non-Adaptive System
9. Adaptive System responds to the change in the environment in a way to improve their performance and to survive. For example, human beings, animals.
10. Non-Adaptive System is the system which does not respond to the environment. For example, machines.
11. Permanent or Temporary System
12. Permanent System persists for long time. For example, business policies.
13. Temporary System is made for specified time and after that they are demolished. For example, A DJ system is set up for a program and it is dissembled after the program.
14. Natural and Manufactured System
15. Natural systems are created by the nature. For example, Solar system, seasonal system.
16. Manufactured System is the man-made system. For example, Rockets, dams, trains.
17. Deterministic or Probabilistic System
18. Deterministic system operates in a predictable manner and the interaction between system components is known with certainty. For example, two molecules of hydrogen and one molecule of oxygen makes water.
19. Probabilistic System shows uncertain behavior. The exact output is not known. For example, Weather forecasting, mail delivery.

20. Social, Human-Machine, Machine System
21. Social System is made up of people. For example, social clubs, societies.
22. In Human-Machine System, both human and machines are involved to perform a particular task. For example, Computer programming.
23. Machine System is where human interference is neglected. All the tasks are performed by the machine. For example, an autonomous robot.
24. Man–Made Information Systems
25. It is an interconnected set of information resources to manage data for organization, under Direct Management Control (DMC).
26. This system includes hardware, software, communication, data, and application for producing information according to the need of an organization.
27. Man-made information systems are divided into three types –
28. Formal Information System – It is based on the flow of information in the form of memos, instructions, etc., from top level to lower levels of management.
29. Informal Information System – This is employee-based system which solves the day to day work related problems.
30. Computer Based System – This system is directly dependent on the computer for managing business applications. For example, automatic library system, railway reservation system, banking system, etc.

Systems Models

Schematic Models

1. A schematic model is a 2-D chart that shows system elements and their linkages.
2. Different arrows are used to show information flow, material flow, and information feedback.

Flow System Models

1. A flow system model shows the orderly flow of the material, energy, and information that hold the system together.
2. Program Evaluation and Review Technique (PERT), for example, is used to abstract a real-world system in model form.

Static System Models

1. They represent one pair of relationships such as activity–time or cost–quantity.
2. The Gantt chart, for example, gives a static picture of an activity-time relationship.

Dynamic System Models

1. Business organizations are dynamic systems. A dynamic model approximates the type of organization or application that analysts deal with.
2. It shows an ongoing, constantly changing status of the system. It consists of –
3. Inputs that enter the system
4. The processor through which transformation takes place
5. The program(s) required for processing
6. The output(s) that result from processing.

Categories of Information

There are three categories of information related to managerial levels and the decision managers make.

Volume of Information	Type of Information	Information Level	Management Level	System Support
Low Consensed	Unstructured	Strategic Information	Upper	DSS
Medium Moderately Processed	Moderately Structured	Management Control Information	Middle	MIS
Large Detail Reports	Highly Structured	Operational Information	Lower	DPS

Strategic Information

1. This information is required by topmost management for long range planning policies for next few years. For example, trends in revenues, financial investment, and human resources, and population growth.
2. This type of information is achieved with the aid of Decision Support System (DSS).

Managerial Information

1. This type of Information is required by middle management for short and intermediate range planning which is in terms of months. For example, sales analysis, cash flow projection, and annual financial statements.
2. It is achieved with the aid of Management Information Systems (MIS).

Operational information

1. This type of information is required by low management for daily and short-term planning to enforce day-to-day operational activities. For example, keeping employee attendance records, overdue purchase orders, and current stocks available.
2. It is achieved with the aid of Data Processing Systems (DPS).

2.3 Applying Systems Thinking to Problem

Top of Form

Systems thinking is a holistic approach to analysis that focuses on the way that a system's constituent parts interrelate and how systems work overtime and within the context of larger systems. It is particularly beneficial in the field of system analysis and design, where understanding these relationships can lead to more effective solutions and innovative approaches to complex problems.

Understanding Systems Thinking

Systems thinking advocates for viewing problems as part of an overall system, rather than reacting to specific parts, potentially contributing to unintended consequences. This methodology is grounded in the belief that the component parts of a system can best be understood in the context of relationships with each other and with other systems, rather than in isolation.

The fundamental principle of systems thinking is that all aspects of a system are interconnected and that changes to one part of the system can ripple through others, sometimes in unexpected ways. Therefore, when applying systems thinking to system analysis and design, it is crucial to consider not just the software or hardware components, but also the human, procedural, and contextual factors that influence system performance.

The Relevance of Systems Thinking in System Analysis and Design

In the realm of system analysis and design, systems thinking aids in addressing complex and dynamic business problems. For example, when designing an information system, considering how users interact with the system, the data flow between departments, and how these elements connect to the overall business strategy can lead to a more robust and adaptable system.

Systems thinking compels designers to consider broader impacts, such as how the system may evolve over time or how scalable it is if the business grows or shifts direction. It also encourages looking at potential inefficiencies or redundancies in business processes that the new system could address, thereby not just adding technology, but improving processes.

Steps in Applying Systems Thinking to System Analysis and Design

1. Identify the Purpose of the System: Understanding what the system needs to achieve is foundational. This includes the needs it serves, its goals, and its expected performance.

2. Understand the Components of the System: This involves mapping out all components of the system, including software, hardware, users, and data processes. Each component should be understood not just individually but how it interacts with other components.

3. Analyse Relationships and Interactions: After identifying the components, the next step is to study the interactions between these components. This includes data flows, user interactions, and dependencies. Systems thinking especially emphasizes understanding feedback loops where changes in one part of the system might affect another.

4. Consider the System in Its Larger Context: Every system operates within a larger environment. For instance, an e-commerce system might interact with external payment gateways, supply chain software, and customer relationship management systems. Understanding these external interactions is crucial.

5. Simulate and Model System Behaviour: Before fully designing or implementing a new system, simulating how it will operate can provide insights into potential issues or bottlenecks. Systems thinking often involves creating dynamic models that can evolve as more information becomes available.

6. Implement and Monitor the System: After designing the system, it's critical to monitor how it functions within the live environment. This ongoing analysis can help identify areas for improvement and ensure the system continues to meet its intended goals.

7. Iterate Based on Feedback: One of the key components of systems thinking is the use of iterative processes. As feedback is gathered from the system's operation, it should be used to make informed adjustments and enhancements.

Summary

1. Systems Thinking Definition: An analytical approach that views a system holistically, emphasizing the interactions and relationships of components within the whole. This method is essential in system analysis and design, fostering a broad perspective that prioritizes interconnections over isolated elements.

Key Principles:

1. Interconnectivity and Interdependence: Acknowledges that changes in one part of the system can affect others.
2. Holism: Encourages viewing the system as a cohesive whole.
3. Feedback Loops: Identifies cycles within the system that influence future operations and can either amplify or dampen effects.
4. Causality: Focuses on understanding cause-and-effect within the system.
5. Systems Mapping: Involves creating visual representations of system components and their interactions.
6. Change Dynamics: Recognizes the need for systems to adapt over time.
7. Leverage Points: Identifies critical areas where small changes can create significant impacts.
8. Iterative Development: Advocates for continuous refinement of the system based on feedback.
9. Applications in System Analysis and Design:
10. Problem-Solving: Systems thinking addresses the root causes of issues for more effective solutions.
11. Design Flexibility: Helps create scalable systems that are adaptable to future needs without major overhauls.
12. Risk Management: Enhances the anticipation of potential problems and the development of robust systems.
13. User-Centric Design: Aids in developing intuitive and efficient user interfaces.
14. Sustainability: Promotes the design of efficient systems with minimal environmental impact.

Glossary

1. **Systems Thinking**: A holistic approach focusing on interrelationships and interactions within a system.
2. **Interconnectivity and Interdependence**: Understanding how changes in one part of a system affect the whole.
3. **Holism**: Viewing the system as a cohesive whole rather than merely the sum of its parts.
4. **Feedback Loops**: Mechanisms where outputs feed back into the system as inputs, influencing future operations.
5. **Causality**: Analysing cause-and-effect relationships to diagnose issues and predict the impact of changes.
6. **Systems Mapping**: Visualizing system components and their interactions to understand system structure and dynamics.
7. **Change Dynamics**: Recognizing that systems evolve and must be designed to accommodate change.
8. **Leverage Points**: Identifying areas within a system where small changes can have significant impacts.
9. **Iterative Development**: Employing a cyclical approach to system development based on continuous feedback.

2.4 Project

2.4.1 Solved Project

You are part of a community project aiming to use systems thinking to address a local environmental issue. Before implementing your plan, review the principles of systems thinking, provide the community with only essential information to avoid overload, verify the effectiveness of these methods in similar cases, explore alternative problem-solving techniques, and discuss with experts about potential pitfalls in applying systems thinking to environmental issues. This prepares your project for better execution and community engagement.

Approach:
1. Preparation and Planning

Objectives:

1. To understand the local environmental issue fully and prepare the community and project team for a system thinking approach.

Key Activities:

1. Education on Systems Thinking: Host seminars and workshops to educate the project team and community leaders about systems thinking principles. Utilize simple visual aids and examples to explain how systems thinking can be applied to environmental issues.
2. Initial Research: Conduct initial research to understand the scope of the environmental issue, including its causes, impacts, and the stakeholders involved.

2. Gathering and Analysing Information

Objectives:

1. To collect all relevant data and insights necessary to apply systems thinking effectively.

Key Activities:

1. Community Surveys and Interviews: Gather input from residents and businesses to understand their perspectives and how the issue affects them.
2. Case Study Analysis: Research similar environmental projects where systems thinking was applied. Analyse the strategies used, results achieved, and lessons learned.
3. Expert Consultation: Arrange meetings with environmental experts and systems thinkers to discuss the specific challenge and potential pitfalls in applying systems thinking to the local issue.

3. Strategy Development

Objectives:

1. To create a comprehensive, systems-based strategy to address the environmental issue.

Key Activities:

1. Mapping the System: Use the information gathered to map out the system involving the environmental issue, identifying all relevant elements, connections, and feedback loops.
2. Identify Leverage Points: Determine where interventions could be most effective in the system.

3. Developing Alternative Approaches: Brainstorm and develop alternative solutions and mitigation strategies, considering both short-term and long-term impacts.

4. Implementation Planning

Objectives:

1. To prepare for the practical application of the chosen strategies.

Key Activities:

1. Community Workshops: Conduct workshops to present the proposed solutions to the community, gather feedback, and refine the approaches.

2. Pilot Projects: Initiate small-scale pilot projects to test the proposed solutions' effectiveness and feasibility.

3. Adjustments and Optimization: Use feedback and results from the pilot projects to make necessary adjustments before full-scale implementation.

5. Execution and Monitoring

Objectives:

1. To implement the strategies effectively and monitor the results.

Key Activities:

1. Implementation: Roll out the full-scale project, utilizing community volunteers and local resources.

2. Continuous Monitoring: Regularly monitor the project's impact, using predefined metrics to assess both environmental and community engagement outcomes.

3. Feedback Mechanism: Establish a continuous feedback mechanism to allow for ongoing community input and expert advice.

6. Evaluation and Adaptation

Objectives:

1. To evaluate the project's effectiveness and adapt the strategy as needed.

Key Activities:

1. Impact Assessment: Conduct a comprehensive evaluation to determine the project's effectiveness in addressing the environmental issue.

2. Report and Disseminate: Prepare detailed reports on the project outcomes and share them with the community and other stakeholders.

3. Plan for Future Actions: Based on the evaluation, plan any necessary future actions to sustain the positive impacts or address any remaining challenges.

2.4.2 Unsolved Project

Suppose you're a manager at a company looking to implement systems thinking to enhance problem-solving capabilities among your team. Before adopting this approach, study the key principles of systems thinking, provide only relevant details to your team, verify the credibility of the training resources, explore alternative methods for team development, and inquire about the applicability of these principles to various types of business problems. This will ensure you effectively incorporate systems thinking in your management strategy.

2.5 Case Study

2.5.1 Solved Case Study

The integration of systems thinking into the development of smart cities is becoming essential as urban areas continue to expand and evolve. This methodology underlines the importance of seeing the city as a dynamic system where every component is interconnected. For instance, systems thinking helps city planners recognize that enhancing digital infrastructure can streamline city operations, boost economic activities, and elevate the overall quality of urban life. It also involves a broader understanding of how different urban systems influence each other, exemplifying this with the interaction between technology deployment and environmental sustainability. By applying systems thinking, planners can devise multifaceted strategies that address multiple aspects of urban development simultaneously, such as reducing energy consumption while increasing public safety through better lighting and surveillance systems. This holistic approach not only ensures more efficient urban planning but also promotes a sustainable and adaptable urban ecosystem.

Questions:

1. What is the key methodology discussed in the passage for developing smart cities?

Answer: Systems thinking is the key methodology discussed for developing smart cities.

2. How does enhancing digital infrastructure benefit urban areas according to the passage?

   Answer: Enhancing digital infrastructure benefits urban areas by streamlining operations, boosting economic activities, and improving the quality of life.

3. What example is given to illustrate the interaction between different urban systems?

   Answer: The interaction between technology deployment and environmental sustainability is given as an example of how different urban systems influence each other.

4. Name two urban development aspects that systems thinking helps to improve simultaneously.

   Answer: Systems thinking helps to reduce energy consumption and increase public safety through better lighting and surveillance systems simultaneously.

5. What are the main benefits of using a holistic approach in urban planning, as mentioned in the passage?

   Answer: The main benefits of using a holistic approach in urban planning include more efficient planning and the promotion of a sustainable and adaptable urban ecosystem.

2.5.2 Unsolved Case Study

In the realm of urban sustainability, the adoption of systems thinking is pivotal for addressing intricate environmental and societal issues. This approach emphasizes understanding complex interactions within urban environments, such as how enhancements in public transportation can decrease traffic congestion, reduce air pollution, and improve the quality of life for city residents. Systems theory provides a foundational framework for analysing these dynamics, suggesting that modifications in one part of the system can lead to significant impacts in other areas. Applying systems thinking specifically to urban challenges involves strategic planning and integrated solutions. For instance, managing urban sprawl requires not only the promotion of denser housing but also the incorporation of green spaces and improved public transport options, fostering sustainable and liveable communities. This comprehensive method ensures that urban planning is both sustainable and equitable, catering to the diverse needs of all urban dwellers.

Questions:

1. What key concept is emphasized in systems thinking for urban sustainability?
2. How can enhancements in public transportation affect urban environments?
3. What does systems theory suggest about changes within urban systems?
4. What strategic measures are suggested to manage urban sprawl?
5. Why is it important for urban planning solutions to be equitable, according to the passage?

2.6 Lab Activity

2.6.1 Solved Lab Activity

Create a diagram of a simple system and identify its components, boundaries, environment, and feedback loops.

Solution:

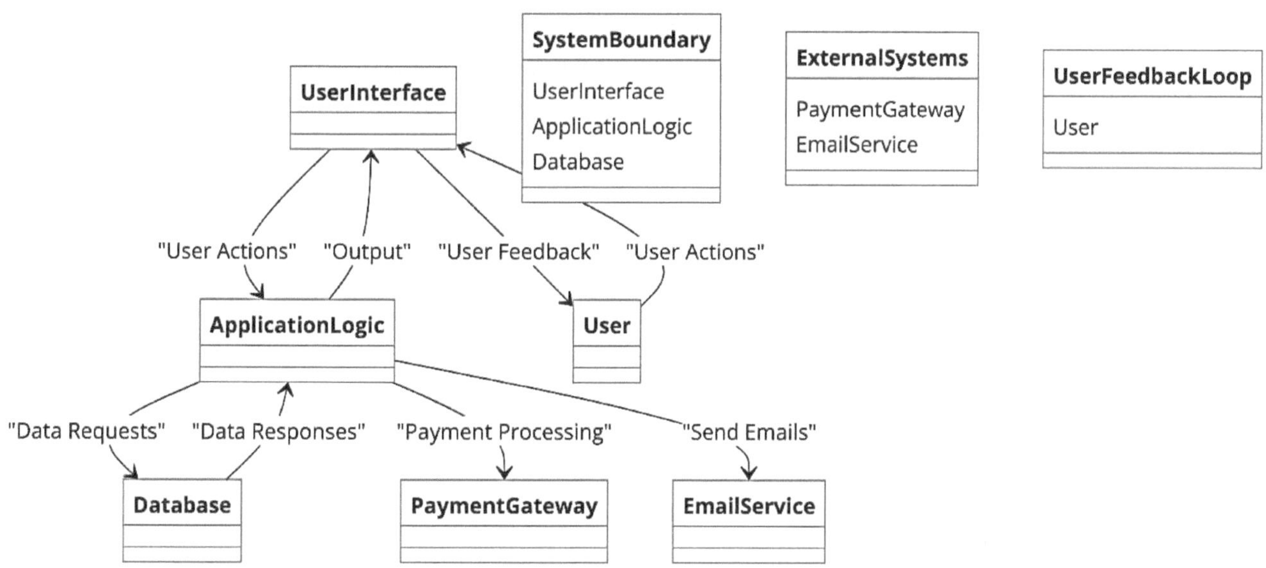

Components:

1. **User Interface**: The interface through which users interact with the system.
2. **Application Logic**: The core logic that processes user actions and manages data interactions.
3. **Database**: The storage system where data is stored and retrieved.
4. **Payment Gateway**: An external system for processing payments.
5. **Email Service**: An external system for sending emails.
6. **User**: Represents the end-user interacting with the system.

Boundaries:

1. **System Boundary**: Encloses the main components of the system, including User Interface, Application Logic, and Database.
2. **External Systems**: Includes systems that are outside the main system boundary but interact with it, such as Payment Gateway and Email Service.
3. **User Feedback Loop**: Indicates the feedback loop from the user back to the system.

Interactions:

1. **User Actions**: Actions performed by the user, such as inputs or requests.
2. **Output**: The system's response to user actions.
3. **User Feedback**: Feedback provided by the user to improve the system.
4. **Data Requests and Data Responses**: Interactions between Application Logic and the Database for storing and retrieving data.
5. **Payment Processing**: Interaction between Application Logic and Payment Gateway for processing payments.
6. **Send Emails**: Interaction between Application Logic and Email Service for sending notifications or confirmations.

Feedback Loops:

User Feedback Loop: Feedback from the user is used to refine and improve the system, indicating an iterative process where the user can influence system development.

2.6.2 Unsolved Lab Activity

Develop a causal loop diagram (CLD) for the chosen problem, showing the relationships between different components of the system.

Previous Years Solved Questions

Q 1. Explain the role of MIS in an organisation. List and explain different kinds of Information Systems. **[IGNOU JUNE, 2010]**

Ans 1. Management Information Systems (MIS) play a crucial role in an organization by providing essential information for decision-making, coordination, control, analysis, and visualization. MIS integrates data from various sources to help management make informed decisions. It enhances efficiency, supports strategic planning, improves internal communication, and aids in problem-solving. Key functions of MIS include:

1. **Data Management**: Collecting, storing, and processing data from various sources.
2. **Information Generation**: Converting raw data into useful information.
3. **Decision Support**: Providing managers with the tools and information needed to make decisions.
4. **Performance Monitoring**: Tracking and evaluating organizational performance.
5. **Strategic Planning**: Supporting long-term planning by analyzing trends and forecasting future conditions.

Different Kinds of Information Systems

Transaction Processing Systems (TPS)
Description: TPS handle routine, day-to-day business transactions.
Examples: Payroll systems, order processing systems, reservation systems.
Function: Ensure accurate and timely processing of transactions, maintaining data integrity.

Management Information Systems (MIS)
Description: MIS provide middle managers with reports and access to the organization's current performance and historical records.
Examples: Sales management systems, inventory control systems.

Function: Summarize and report on basic operations using data from TPS.

Decision Support Systems (DSS)
Description: DSS help managers make decisions by analyzing large amounts of data from various sources.
Examples: Financial planning systems, forecasting systems.
Function: Provide tools for modeling, simulation, and data analysis to support complex decision-making.

Executive Information Systems (EIS)
Description: EIS are designed for top executives to provide easy access to internal and external information relevant to strategic goals.
Examples: Dashboard applications showing key performance indicators.
Function: Offer summarized and high-level information for strategic decision-making.

Enterprise Resource Planning Systems (ERP)
Description: ERP integrate various business processes and functions into a single comprehensive system.
Examples: SAP, Oracle ERP.
Function: Streamline processes and information across the entire organization, improving efficiency and data consistency.

Customer Relationship Management Systems (CRM)
Description: CRM systems manage a company's interactions with current and potential customers.
Examples: Salesforce, HubSpot.
Function: Enhance customer service, improve customer retention, and drive sales growth by managing customer data and interactions.

Knowledge Management Systems (KMS)
Description: KMS capture, store, and disseminate knowledge throughout an organization.
Examples: Document management systems, collaboration tools like SharePoint.
Function: Facilitate the sharing of information and expertise to improve organizational learning and innovation.

Previous Years Unsolved Questions

Q 1. Differentiate between a decision table and a decision tree. Prepare a sample data dictionary for an employee management system. **[IGNOU JUNE, 2011]**
Q 2. Define Decision Table. **[Udaipur University, 2018]**
Q 3. With the help of a neat diagram discuss various components of Decision Support Systems (DSS) **[Jodhpur University, April 2018].**

Exercises

Exercise 1 – Multiple Choice Questions

1. A 'Closed System' is one that:
    A) Interacts frequently with its environment
    B) Does not interact with its environment
    C) Is only found in biological contexts
    D) Cannot change over time
2. Which is an example of a feedback mechanism in a technological system?
    A) A static user manual
    B) A non-interactive website
    C) User reviews influencing product development
    D) A one-time software installation
3. How does 'Systems Thinking' aid in risk management?
    A) By ignoring potential failures
    B) Focusing only on positive outcomes

C) Anticipating potential issues and mitigating them
D) Ensuring systems never fail

4. The concept of 'Adaptation' in systems refers to:
A) Systems maintaining a static operation
B) Systems evolving in response to internal and external changes
C) Systems avoiding any form of feedback
D) Systems operating in a vacuum

5. Which of the following is true about systems thinking in design?
A) It promotes rigidity and inflexibility
B) It discourages consideration of user needs
C) It supports the creation of user-centric interfaces
D) It is only applicable in non-technical fields

Exercise 2 – True/False

1. Systems thinking is only useful for technological systems.
2. In systems thinking, interconnectivity refers to how changes in one part of a system can affect other parts.
3. Feedback loops in systems thinking can only be positive.
4. Holism in systems thinking suggests looking at the system rather than focusing on individual parts.
5. Systems mapping is not necessary in the initial stages of system design.

Exercise 3 – Fill in the blanks

1. Systems thinking often involves viewing problems as part of an overall system rather than in ______.
2. In systems theory, the concept of "feedback loops" helps to understand how systems ______.
3. When applying systems thinking, it is crucial to identify the ______ of the system.

Exercise 4- Fill in the blanks with two options

1. To effectively apply systems thinking, one should consider ____________ and ____________ as interconnected elements of a single entity. Options: a) different departments, their functions **(correct)** b) competing companies, their strategies
2. The resilience of a system in systems theory is often tested through ____________ and ____________.
3. Systems thinking aids in developing strategies that consider ____________ and ____________ to ensure long-term viability.

Exercise 5- Give two answers for the following:

1. Solving Principles of Systems Thinking
2. Elements of Systems Theory
3. Applications of Systems Thinking to Problems
4. Benefits of Applying Systems Thinking
5. Key Concepts in Systems Theory

Exercise 6- Rearrange the sentence

1. Solving involves systems often thinking complexity.
2. Theories relate systems to interconnections.
3. Feedback mechanisms systems are in critical.

Exercise 7- Choose the Odd One Out

1. Integration, Analysis, Collaboration, Isolation
2. Set: Holistic, Fragmented, Comprehensive, Unified
3. Set: Feedback, Linear, Loop, Cyclic

Exercise 8- Jumble words

1. ricpneilps
2. roythe
3. lyapnigp

Exercise 9- Match case

Column 1	Column 2
1. What is the primary focus of systems thinking?	A. Hierarchical organization
2. How does systems theory interpret relationships?	B. System improvement
3. What is a common method used in applying systems thinking to problems?	C. Feedback loops
4. Which concept is key to understanding systems theory?	D. Interconnections and interdependencies
5. What practical application does systems thinking have in system analysis and design?	E. Iterative refinement

Exercise 10- Assertion – Reason

1. Assertion (A): The System Development Lifecycle (SDLC) is critical for successful system development.
Reason (R): The SDLC provides a structured approach for planning, designing, and implementing a system.
Options:
a) Assertion (A) is true and Reason (R) is the correct reason for Assertion (A).
b) Assertion (A) is true, but Reason (R) is not the correct reason for Assertion (A).
c) Assertion (A) is false, but Reason (R) is true.
d) Assertion (A) is true, but Reason (R) is false.

Exercise 11- One- word

1. What type of thinking involves viewing problems as parts of an overall system rather than reacting to specific parts, isolated from the whole?
2. Which concept describes the ongoing interactions and feedback loops among the components of a system?
3. What term is used to describe the application of systems thinking principles to solve complex problems in system design?

Exercise 12- Small Answers

1. Briefly describe one core concept of systems theory that is crucial in system analysis.
2. Provide an example of how systems thinking can be applied to solve a problem in system analysis and design.
3. What is the primary goal of systems thinking in system analysis and design?

Exercise 13- Long Answers

1. Elaborate on how systems thinking can be used to address and solve common challenges in system analysis and design. Provide examples where possible.
2. Examine the role of systems thinking in managing and mitigating risks during the system design phase. How can it help in anticipating and planning for potential system failures?

Answers

Exercise 1- 1) B, 2) C, 3) C, 4) B, 5) C

Exercise 2- 1) False, 2) True, 3) False, 4) True, 5) False
Exercise 3- 1) isolation, 2) function, 3) boundaries
Exercise 4- 1) different departments, their functions, 2) stress scenarios, adaptive responses, 3) environmental impacts, social responsibilities
Exercise 5- 1) Holistic View, Feedback Loops, 2) Interrelated Components, Boundaries, 3) Identifying Root Causes, Developing Sustainable Solutions, 4) Improved Problem-Solving, Enhanced Decision-Making, 5) Open Systems, Closed Systems
Exercise 6- 1) Solving complexity often involves systems thinking, 2) Systems theories relate to interconnections, 3) Feedback mechanisms are critical in systems.
Exercise 7- 1) Isolation, 2) Fragmented, 3) Linear
Exercise 8- 1) Principles, 2) Theory, 3) Applying
Exercise 9- 1) D, 2) C, 3) E, 4) A, 5) B
Exercise 10- a) Assertion (A) is true, and Reason (R) is the correct reason for Assertion (A).
Exercise 11- 1) Holistic, 2) Dynamic, 3) Integration

Online Resources

Online Exam paper
URL: https://forms.gle/sU4v4rwhdwqK5PdP6
QR Code

YouTube Video
URL
https://www.youtube.com/playlist?list=PLzlh_31VWEFryOILzjHNPE757pir-7S8L
QR Code

More Test Papers Practices

Test Paper-1

QR Code

URL: https://forms.gle/c2AHuFEhcQjykh449

QR Code

Test Paper-2

URL: https://forms.gle/7M93952e7cSYBTJGA

QR Code

System analysis and design Test Paper
Chapter- 2
Systems Thinking and Concepts

Time Duration: 30 Minutes **Maximum Marks: 25**

General Instructions:
1. The question paper consists of answer any 12 questions out of the given 19 questions and is divided into four sections, A, B, C and D.
2. All questions are compulsory.
3. Section A comprises question numbers 1 to 8. These are MCQs and one liner of one mark each. You are to select one most appropriate response out of the four provided options.
4. Section B comprises question numbers 1 to 5. These are SAQs carrying two marks each.
5. Section C comprises question numbers 1 to 4. These are SAQs carrying four marks each.
6. Section D comprises question numbers 1& 2. These are LAQs carrying five marks each.

SECTION-A

I. <u>Answer any 6 questions out of the given 8 questions</u> **(1*6=6)**

1. What is the primary goal of systems thinking in problem-solving?
   A) To focus on individual components of a system
   B) To understand the interrelationships between components of a system
   C) To create isolated solutions for each problem
   D) To simplify complex systems by ignoring external factors
2. Which of the following best describes a feedback loop in systems theory?
   A) A linear sequence of events that occur in isolation
   B) A process where the output of a system influences its own input
   C) A random set of changes within a system
   D) A single occurrence of an event within a system
3. In systems theory, what is the term for the boundaries that separate a system from its environment?
   A) Interfaces
   B) Borders
   C) Limits
   D) Constraints
4. What is a key characteristic of a system according to systems theory?
   A) It is always static and unchanging
   B) It has clearly defined boundaries and interacts with its environment
   C) It operates independently without any external influence
   D) It is composed of unrelated components
5. Which of the following is an example of applying systems thinking to a problem?
   A) Focusing solely on increasing the efficiency of a single department
   B) Understanding how changes in one department affect the entire organization
   C) Ignoring external factors to simplify the problem
   D) Solving issues on a case-by-case basis without considering the whole system
6. What term describes the interconnectedness of components within a system?
7. What type of loop in systems theory can either be positive or negative?
8. What concept in systems theory involves seeing the whole rather than just the parts?

SECTION-B

II. <u>Answer any 3 questions out of the given 5 questions</u> **(2*3=6)**

1. Define the term "systems thinking."
2. What is the purpose of identifying feedback loops in a system?
3. Describe a real-world example where systems thinking can be applied.
4. What does it mean to have an open system in systems theory?
5. How does systems thinking differ from traditional analytical thinking?

SECTION-C

II. Answer any 2 questions out of the given 4 questions **(4*2=8)**

1. Explain the principles of systems thinking and their importance in problem-solving.
2. Describe the main concepts of systems theory and provide an example of each.
3. How can systems be thinking help in identifying the root causes of problems?
4. Discuss the role of boundaries in defining a system and its interactions with the environment.

SECTION-D

III. Answer any 1 question out of the given 2 questions **(5*1=5)**

1. Discuss how systems thinking can be applied to address complex problems in healthcare. Provide specific examples to illustrate your points.
2. Explain the concept of feedback loops in systems theory and analyse their significance in understanding system behaviour. Provide examples of positive and negative feedback loops in real-world systems.

Chapter 3: Requirement Analysis and Planning

- Understanding Methods of Gathering User Requirements
- Analyzing and Documenting Requirements
- Managing Requirements Changes
- Ensuring Requirement Clarity and Completeness

3.1 Gathering User Requirements

What are the Requirements of Gathering?

Requirements gathering is a crucial phase in the software development life cycle (SDLC) and project management. It involves collecting, documenting, and managing the requirements that define the features and functionalities of a system or application. The success of a project often depends on the accuracy and completeness of the gathered requirements in software.

Main Requirements Gathering Subprocesses:

Requirements gathering is a critical phase in the software development lifecycle, and it involves several subprocesses to ensure a comprehensive understanding of the project's needs. The main subprocesses include:

Stakeholder Identification:

- **Objective:** Identify all stakeholders who will be affected by the system, directly or indirectly.
- **Process**: Conduct interviews, surveys, or workshops to determine the key individuals or groups involved.

Stakeholder Analysis:

- **Objective:** Understand the needs, expectations, and influence of each stakeholder.
- **Process:** Analyze stakeholder inputs to prioritize requirements and manage conflicting interests.

Problem Definition:

- **Objective:** Clearly define the problems or opportunities that the software system aims to address.
- **Process:** Engage stakeholders in discussions to uncover and articulate the core problems or opportunities.

Requirements Extraction:

- **Objective:** Gather detailed requirements by interacting with stakeholders.
- **Process:** Employ techniques such as interviews, surveys, observations, or brainstorming sessions to extract requirements.

Requirements Documentation:

- **Objective:** Document gathered requirements in a structured format.
- **Process:** Create requirements documents, use cases, user stories, or prototypes to capture and communicate requirements effectively

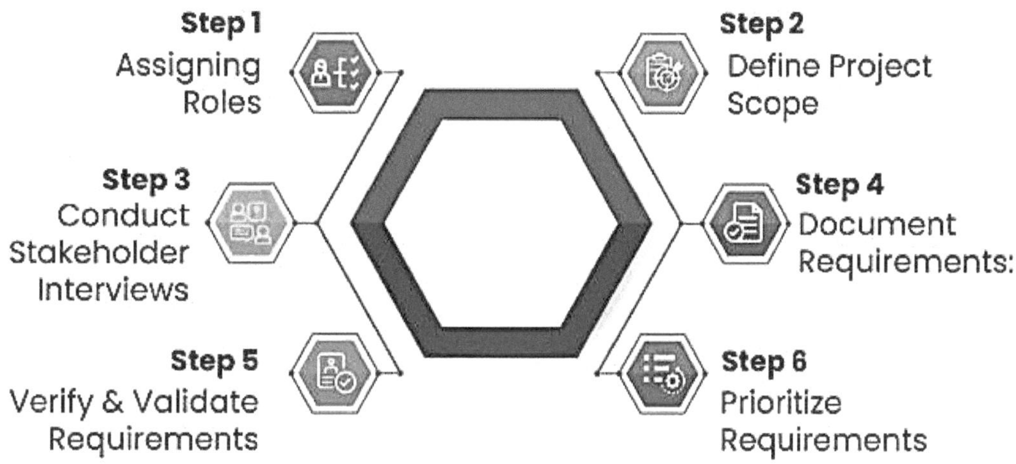

Processes of Requirements Gathering in Software Development

<u>Validation and Verification:</u>

- **Objective:** Ensure that gathered requirements are accurate, complete, and consistent.
- **Process:** Conduct reviews, walkthroughs, or use validation tools to verify that the requirements meet the defined criteria.

Processes of Requirements Gathering in Software Development:

There are 6 steps crucial for requirement gathering processes

<u>Step 1- Assigning roles:</u>

- The first step is to identify and engage with all relevant stakeholders. Stakeholders can include end-users, clients, project managers, subject matter experts, and anyone else who has a vested interest in the software project. Understanding their perspectives is essential for capturing diverse requirements.

<u>Step 2- Define Project Scope:</u>

- Clearly define the scope of the project by outlining its objectives, boundaries, and limitations. This step helps in establishing a common understanding of what the software is expected to achieve and what functionalities it should include.

<u>Step 3- Conduct Stakeholder Interviews:</u>

- Schedule interviews with key stakeholders to gather information about their needs, preferences, and expectations. Through open-ended questions and discussions, I aim to uncover both explicit and implicit requirements. These interviews provide valuable insights that contribute to a more holistic understanding of the project.

<u>Step 4- Document Requirements:</u>

- Systematically document the gathered requirements. This documentation can take various forms, such as user stories, use cases, or formal specifications. Clearly articulate functional requirements (what the system should do) and non-functional requirements (qualities the system should have, such as performance or security).

<u>Step 5- Verify and Validate Requirements:</u>

- Once the requirements are documented, it's crucial to verify and validate them. Verification ensures that the requirements align with the stakeholders' intentions, while validation ensures that the documented requirements will meet the project's goals. This step often involves feedback loops and discussions with stakeholders to refine and clarify requirements.

<u>Step 6- Prioritize Requirements:</u>

- Prioritize the requirements based on their importance to the project goals and constraints. This step helps in creating a roadmap for development, guiding the team on which features to prioritize. Prioritization is essential, especially when resources and time are limited.

Requirement Gathering Techniques:

Effective requirement gathering is essential for the success of a software development project. Various techniques are employed to collect, analyze, and document requirements.

Here are some commonly used requirements gathering techniques:

1. Interviews:
- Conducting one-on-one or group interviews with stakeholders, including end-users, clients, and subject matter experts. This allows for direct interaction to gather detailed information about their needs, expectations, and concerns.
2. Surveys and Questionnaires:
- Distributing surveys and questionnaires to a broad audience to collect information on a larger scale. This technique is useful for gathering feedback from a diverse set of stakeholders and can be particularly effective in large projects.
3. Workshops:
- Organizing facilitated group sessions or workshops where stakeholders come together to discuss and define requirements. Workshops encourage collaboration, idea generation, and the resolution of conflicting viewpoints in a structured environment.
4. Observation:
- Directly observing end-users in their work environment to understand their workflows, pain points, and preferences. Observational techniques help in uncovering implicit requirements that users might not explicitly state.
5. Prototyping:
- Creating mockups or prototypes of the software to provide stakeholders with a tangible representation of the proposed system. Prototyping allows for early visualization and feedback, helping to refine requirements based on stakeholders' reactions.
6. Use Cases and Scenarios:
- Developing use cases and scenarios to describe how the system will be used in different situations. This technique helps in understanding the interactions between users and the system, making it easier to identify and document functional requirements.
7. Document Analysis:
- Reviewing existing documentation, such as business process manuals, reports, and forms, to extract relevant information. This technique provides insights into the current processes and helps identify areas for improvement.

Why is Requirement Gathering important?

Requirement gathering holds immense importance in software development for several critical reasons:

1. Clarity of Project Objectives:
- Requirement gathering sets the stage by defining and clarifying the objectives of the software project. It ensures that all stakeholders, including clients, users, and development teams, have a shared understanding of what needs to be achieved.
2. Customer Satisfaction:
- Understanding and meeting customer needs is paramount for customer satisfaction. Requirement gathering allows developers to comprehend the expectations of end-users and clients, leading to the creation of a product that aligns with their desires and requirements.
3. Scope Definition:
- Clearly defined requirements help in establishing the scope of the project. This delineation is crucial for managing expectations, avoiding scope creep (uncontrolled changes to project scope), and ensuring that the project stays on track.
4. Reduced Misunderstandings:
- Ambiguities and misunderstandings are common sources of project failures. Requirement gathering facilitates clear communication between stakeholders, reducing the risk of misinterpretations and ensuring that everyone involved is on the same page.
5. Risk Mitigation:
- Identifying and addressing potential issues at the requirements stage helps mitigate risks early in the development process. This proactive approach minimizes the chances of costly errors, rework, and delays later in the project life cycle.

Benefits of Requirements Gathering:

The benefits of effective requirements gathering in software development include:
- Cost Reduction: One of the primary benefits of effective requirements gathering is cost reduction. When requirements are well-defined and thoroughly understood at the beginning of a project, it minimizes the likelihood of costly changes and rework later in the development process.
- Customer Satisfaction: Clear and accurate requirements gathering directly contributes to customer satisfaction. When the product aligns closely with the expectations and needs of the stakeholders, it enhances user experience and meets customer demands. This satisfaction is not only vital for the success of the current project but also contributes to positive relationships between the development team and clients, fostering trust and potential future collaborations.
- Improved Communication: Requirements gathering serves as a communication bridge between various stakeholders involved in a project, including developers, clients, users, and project managers. Miscommunication is a common source of project failures and delays. By clearly documenting and understanding requirements, the development team ensures that everyone involved has a shared vision of the project objectives, functionalities, and constraints.
- Efficient Resource Utilization: Thorough requirements gathering enables the efficient allocation and utilization of resources. Resources, including time, manpower, and technology, are finite and valuable. When requirements are well-defined, project teams can allocate resources more accurately, avoiding unnecessary expenditures or overcommitting resources to certain aspects of the project.
- Enhanced Quality: Well-documented requirements serve as the foundation for quality assurance throughout the development process. When the project team has a clear understanding of what needs to be achieved, they can establish quality standards and criteria from the outset. This clarity enables the implementation of effective testing strategies, ensuring that each aspect of the system is thoroughly evaluated against the specified requirements.
- Risk Management: Requirements gathering is a crucial component of effective risk management. By identifying potential risks early in the project, stakeholders can proactively address ambiguities, conflicting requirements, and other challenges that could pose a threat to the project's success.
- Accurate Planning: Accurate project planning is dependent on a clear understanding of project requirements. When requirements are well-documented, project managers can create realistic schedules, milestones, and deliverables. This accurate planning is crucial for setting expectations, managing stakeholder timelines, and ensuring that the project progresses according to the established timeline.

Common Obstacles in Software Requirements Gathering:

Common obstacles in software requirements gathering include:
- Unclear Objectives: Lack of clear project objectives can hinder requirements gathering. When stakeholders are unsure about what they want to achieve, it becomes challenging to define and prioritize requirements effectively. This can lead to confusion, scope creeps, and difficulties in meeting project goals.
- Ambiguous Requirements: Ambiguities in requirements, such as vague language or conflicting statements, can create misunderstandings among stakeholders and the development team. Ambiguous requirements may result in deliverables that do not meet expectations and may require extensive rework.
- Poor Stakeholder Involvement: Insufficient involvement or engagement of key stakeholders can impede the requirements gathering process. When essential stakeholders are not actively participating or providing input, there is a risk of missing critical requirements or making decisions that do not align with the needs of the end-users.
- Changing Requirements: Requirements that undergo frequent changes during the development process, often referred to as "scope creep," can lead to project delays, increased costs, and challenges in maintaining project focus. It is essential to manage and control changes to prevent unnecessary disruptions.
- Communication Barriers: Communication challenges, such as language barriers, misinterpretations, or inadequate channels for information exchange, can hinder effective requirements gathering. It is crucial to establish clear communication channels and ensure that all stakeholders have a shared understanding of the terminology used in the project.
- Overreliance on Documentation: Depending solely on documentation without active collaboration and communication can lead to misunderstandings. Written requirements may not capture the complete context or evolving needs, making it essential to complement documentation with interactive processes like workshops and interviews.
- Lack of User Involvement: Users are often the ultimate beneficiaries of the system, and their input is critical. Lack of user involvement or representation can result in systems that do not effectively meet their needs. It is important to actively involve end-users in the requirements gathering process to ensure the system's usability and acceptance.

How Requirements Gathering helps for Agile in Software Development:

Agile development emphasizes flexibility, collaboration, and continuous improvement. The requirements gathering process in Agile is iterative and adaptive, allowing for changes and adjustments throughout the development lifecycle. Here's a detailed explanation of the requirements gathering process in Agile:

- **User Stories:** In Agile, requirements are often expressed as user stories. A user story is a concise, informal description of a feature told from the end-user's perspective. It typically follows the format: "As a [type of user], I want [an action] so that [benefit/value]." User stories focus on the user and their goals, helping to capture the essence of the required functionality.
- **Backlog Refinement:** The product backlog is a prioritized list of features, enhancements, and fixes. Backlog refinement sessions, often known as backlog grooming, occur regularly to review, clarify, and prioritize the items in the backlog. This process ensures that the most valuable and highest-priority items are at the top of the list and ready for development in upcoming sprints.
- **Iterative Development:** Agile development is iterative, with work organized into time-boxed cycles called sprints. During each sprint, a cross-functional team works on a set of prioritized user stories. The requirements for each user story are refined and clarified as the team progresses, allowing for flexibility and adaptability to changing priorities or emerging insights.
- **Continuous Stakeholder Collaboration:** Agile encourages ongoing collaboration with stakeholders, including product owners, end-users, and business representatives. Regular meetings, such as sprint reviews and sprint planning, provide opportunities for stakeholders to provide feedback on completed work, discuss changes to priorities, and refine requirements for upcoming sprints.
- **Prototyping and Visual Aids:** Agile teams often use prototyping and visual aids to enhance requirements understanding. Prototypes, wireframes, and other visual representations help stakeholders visualize the proposed features and provide early feedback. This iterative approach ensures that the final product closely aligns with stakeholder expectations.
- **Daily Stand-ups:** Daily stand-up meetings, or daily scrums, are a key Agile practice. These brief, focused meetings provide team members with the opportunity to share progress, discuss impediments, and ensure that everyone is aligned on the project's goals. While not specifically for requirements gathering, daily stand-ups facilitate ongoing communication, allowing the team to quickly address any emerging requirements or changes.
- **Acceptance Criteria:** Each user story in Agile is accompanied by acceptance criteria. Acceptance criteria define the conditions that must be met for a user story to be considered complete. They serve as a shared understanding between the development team and stakeholders regarding the expectations for the functionality being delivered. Clear acceptance criteria help prevent misunderstandings and ensure that the developed features meet the desired outcomes.
- **Retrospectives:** Agile teams regularly conduct retrospectives at the end of each sprint to reflect on what went well, what could be improved, and what changes might enhance the development process. This feedback loop includes discussions about the effectiveness of the requirements gathering process, allowing the team to adapt and refine their approach for future sprints.

Challenges and Considerations in Agile Requirements Gathering:

- **Changing Priorities:** Agile embraces changes in requirements, but frequent changes can pose challenges. It's crucial to strike a balance between flexibility and stability, ensuring that changes are well-understood, prioritized, and communicated effectively to the development team.
- **Balancing Detail and Flexibility:** Agile requires enough detail to guide development, but also the flexibility to adapt as requirements evolve. Striking the right balance ensures that the team can respond to changes while maintaining a clear understanding of the project's direction.
- **Effective Communication:** Agile heavily relies on communication and collaboration. Ensuring that all team members, including stakeholders, have open channels for communication is essential to prevent misunderstandings and align everyone with the project's goals.
- **Overemphasis on Documentation:** While Agile values working software over comprehensive documentation, it's important to strike a balance. Minimal but effective documentation, such as user stories and acceptance criteria, should be maintained to ensure a shared understanding among team members and stakeholders.
- **Ensuring Continuous Feedback:** Agile places a strong emphasis on continuous feedback but ensuring active stakeholder involvement can be challenging. Efforts should be made to encourage regular feedback through sprint

reviews, demos, and other collaborative sessions to avoid potential misunderstandings and to keep the development aligned with stakeholder expectations.

By embracing these Agile practices and considering the associated challenges, teams can effectively gather and adapt requirements throughout the development process, delivering value to stakeholders in a dynamic and responsive manner.

Tools for Requirements Gathering in Software Development:

Requirements gathering tools play a crucial role in streamlining the process of collecting, documenting, and managing project requirements. These tools are designed to enhance collaboration, improve communication, and facilitate the organization of complex information. Here are several types of requirements gathering tools and their roles:

- **Collaboration Tools:** Collaboration tools, such as project management platforms (e.g., Jira, Trello, Asana), facilitate teamwork and communication among project stakeholders. These platforms often include features like task assignment, progress tracking, and discussion forums, enabling teams to collaboratively gather, discuss, and manage requirements in real-time.
- **Document Management Tools:** Document management tools (e.g., Confluence, SharePoint) help organize and store project documentation. These tools provide a centralized repository for requirements, ensuring easy access, version control, and collaboration. Document management tools are particularly valuable for maintaining a structured record of evolving project requirements.
- **Survey and Form Builders:** Tools like Google Forms, Type form, or SurveyMonkey enable the creation of online surveys and forms. These are useful for gathering structured data from a large audience, such as feedback, preferences, or specific information required for project requirements. The collected data can be easily analyzed and integrated into the requirements gathering process.
- **Prototyping Tools:** Prototyping tools (e.g., Sketch, Balsamiq, Figma) allow the creation of visual or interactive prototypes. These tools are valuable for translating requirements into tangible representations that stakeholders can interact with, providing a clearer understanding of the proposed features and functionalities.
- **Mind Mapping Tools:** Mind mapping tools (e.g., Mind Meister, XMind) help visualize and organize complex ideas and relationships. During requirements gathering, these tools can be used to create visual representations of interconnected requirements, helping stakeholders and the project team understand the relationships between different features and functionalities.
- **Version Control Systems:** Version control systems (e.g., Git, SVN) are essential for managing changes to project documentation. These tools track revisions, allowing teams to review, revert, or merge changes seamlessly. This is particularly valuable in dynamic projects where requirements may undergo frequent updates or refinements.
- **Requirements Management Software:** Specialized requirements management tools (e.g., IBM Engineering Requirements Management DOORS, Jama Connect) are designed specifically for capturing, tracking, and managing requirements throughout the project lifecycle. These tools often offer features such as traceability, impact analysis, and integration with other project management tools.
- **Visual Collaboration Tools:** Visual collaboration tools (e.g., Miro, Lucidchart) facilitate collaborative diagramming and visual representation of ideas. These tools can be used for creating flowcharts, diagrams, or visual models that help communicate complex requirements in a more intuitive and accessible way.

3.2 Analyzing and Documenting Requirements

1. Introduction

- **Purpose of Requirements Analysis:** Explain the importance of requirements analysis in system design, emphasizing its role in understanding what users need, ensuring the system meets these needs, and establishing the basis for system validation.
- **Overview of Documenting Requirements:** Briefly introduce how documenting requirements ensures clarity, serves as a contractual basis between stakeholders, and guides development teams.

2. Types of Requirements

- **Functional Requirements:** Describe what the system should do, including processes, data handling, and operational capabilities.
- **Non-functional Requirements:** Cover aspects not directly related to specific behaviors, such as performance metrics, usability, reliability, and security.

3. Requirements Gathering Techniques
- **Interviews:** Structured, semi-structured, and unstructured interviews with stakeholders.
- **Surveys and Questionnaires:** Collecting large amounts of data from future users and stakeholders.
- **Observation:** Direct observation of end-users and their interaction with existing systems.
- **Workshops:** Interactive sessions with multiple stakeholders to extract and negotiate requirements.
- **Document Analysis:** Review existing documentation and system artifacts to identify legacy requirements and constraints.

4. Analyzing Requirements
- **Modeling Techniques:** Use of various modeling tools and methods to visualize and analyze requirements.
- **Use Case Diagrams:** Illustrate system functionalities and interactions between actors and the system.
- **Activity Diagrams:** Flowcharts that depict the workflow of processes and business activities.
- **Entity-Relationship Diagrams (ERD):** Show how entities like database tables relate to each other.
- **Prioritization:** Methods to prioritize requirements based on factors such as strategic value, cost, complexity, and urgency.
- **Validation:** Techniques to ensure requirements are feasible, relevant, and based on real needs.

5. Documenting Requirements
- **Requirements Specification Document (RSD):** Structure and elements of an RSD including introduction, purpose, detailed descriptions, glossaries, appendices, and indices.
- **User Stories and Acceptance Criteria:** Agile-focused documentation methods.
- **Traceability:** Implementing a traceability matrix to track requirements throughout the project lifecycle.

6. Managing Requirement Changes
- **Change Control Process:** Steps and controls for managing changes in requirements, including impact analysis and approval workflows.
- **Tools and Systems:** Overview of tools and software that assist in requirement documentation and change management.

7. Best Practices and Common Pitfalls
- **Best Practices:** Recommendations for effectively analyzing and documenting requirements, such as regular stakeholder engagement, continuous feedback cycles, and maintaining clear and concise documentation.
- **Common Pitfalls:** Potential issues such as ambiguous requirements, scope creep, and inadequate stakeholder involvement, with strategies for avoidance.

8. Case Studies
- **Real-world Examples:** Analyzing successful and failed projects to highlight the importance of thorough requirement analysis and proper documentation.

3.3 Managing Requirements Changes

Introduction

In the field of system design, managing requirements changes is a critical aspect that can significantly impact the success or failure of a project. Requirements changes may arise due to evolving client needs, technological advancements, or unforeseen challenges. Effective management of these changes is essential to ensure that the system remains relevant, functional, and within budget. This chapter discusses strategies and best practices for managing requirements changes during the system design process.

Understanding Requirements Changes

Requirements changes refer to any modifications in the predefined needs and expectations that stakeholders have from a system. These changes can range from minor adjustments to major overhauls of the system's scope. It's crucial for system designers and project managers to establish a robust process for identifying, evaluating, and implementing these changes.

1. Establishing a Flexible Requirements Management Process

The first step in managing requirements changes effectively is to establish a flexible and responsive requirements management process. This involves:

- **Documentation:** Clearly document all requirements and their changes. This documentation should be easily accessible and modifiable to reflect new information as it becomes available.
- **Communication:** Maintain open lines of communication with all stakeholders. Regular updates and feedback sessions can help anticipate changes and adjust plans accordingly.
- **Tools and Techniques:** Utilize requirements management tools that allow for tracking changes, maintaining version control, and assessing the impact of these changes.

2. Impact Analysis

Whenever a change is proposed, conducting an impact analysis is crucial to understand its effects on the overall system. Impact analysis helps in:

- **Assessing the scope of change:** Determine how the change will affect the existing requirements and the additional work needed to accommodate the change.
- **Resource adjustment:** Evaluate whether additional resources are needed to implement the change, including time, labor, and costs.
- **Risk assessment:** Identify any new risks introduced by the change and plan mitigation strategies.

3. Prioritization of Changes

Not all changes are created equally. Some might be critical for the functionality of the system, while others could be cosmetic. Prioritizing changes involves:

- **Value assessment:** Determine the added value of implementing the change versus its cost and the risk it introduces.
- **Stakeholder impact:** Consider the impact on different stakeholders, including customers, end-users, and team members.
- **Timeline considerations:** Assess how the change will affect the project timeline and whether it aligns with critical milestones.

4. Change Approval Process

Having a formal change approval process is essential to manage changes systematically. This process usually involves:

- **Change control board (CCB):** A group of key stakeholders responsible for reviewing and approving changes. The CCB evaluates impact analysis and prioritization to make informed decisions.
- **Documentation and tracking:** Once a change is approved, it should be documented and tracked. This ensures that everyone involved is aware of the new requirements and their implementation status.

5. Implementing Changes

The actual implementation of changes needs to be managed carefully to minimize disruption. This includes:

- **Integration with existing systems:** Ensure that the changes are compatible with the existing system components.
- **Testing:** Rigorous testing is necessary to ensure that the new changes do not introduce bugs or degrade the system's performance.
- **Feedback loops:** After implementing changes, gather feedback to assess if the changes meet the stakeholders' needs and make further adjustments as required.

Summary

1. Stakeholder Identification: Identify all relevant stakeholders, including end-users, clients, and project sponsors, through interviews, surveys, or workshops to ensure their needs are considered.

2. Stakeholder Analysis: Analyse stakeholder inputs to understand their expectations, needs, and influence, which helps prioritize and manage requirements effectively.

3. Problem Definition: Clearly define the problems or opportunities the software aims to address by engaging stakeholders in discussions to articulate these issues.

4. Requirements Extraction: Use techniques such as interviews, observations, and brainstorming sessions to gather detailed requirements from stakeholders.

5. Requirements Documentation: Document the gathered requirements in structured formats like use cases, user stories, or prototypes to ensure clarity and communication.

6. Validation and Verification: Ensure that the requirements are accurate, complete, and consistent by conducting reviews and using validation tools.

7. Define Project Scope: Establish a clear project scope to guide the development process and manage stakeholder expectations.

8. Prioritize Requirements: Prioritize requirements based on their importance to the project's goals, which guides the development team on feature prioritization.
9. Change Management: Implement a structured process to manage changes in requirements, including a change control board and impact analysis to assess the effects of changes.
10. Prototyping and Visual Aids: Utilize prototyping and visual aids to provide stakeholders with a tangible understanding of the proposed system, facilitating early feedback and requirement refinement.
11. Agile Requirements Gathering: In Agile methodologies, gather requirements iteratively and adaptively, using user stories and continuous stakeholder collaboration to refine the project scope continuously.
12. Tools for Requirements Gathering: Leverage tools like Jira, Confluence, and prototyping software to enhance collaboration, manage documentation, and streamline the requirements gathering process.

Glossary

1. Stakeholder: Any individual or group who has an interest in the outcome of a project. Stakeholders may include clients, end-users, project managers, and technical teams.
2. User Stories: Informal descriptions of software features from an end-user perspective, commonly used in Agile methodologies to capture functional requirements.
3. Non-functional Requirements: Requirements that describe the quality attributes of a system, such as performance, security, and usability, rather than specific behaviours.
4. Prototyping: The creation of a preliminary model of a system used for testing and evaluation, allowing stakeholders to explore ideas and provide feedback before full-scale development.
5. Change Control Board (CCB): A group responsible for reviewing and approving changes in the project scope, ensuring that modifications meet project goals and are communicated effectively.
6. Impact Analysis: An assessment conducted to understand the potential consequences of a proposed change, focusing on its effects on the project scope, resources, risks, and timelines.
7. Backlog Refinement: A process in Agile development where the team regularly updates and prioritizes the backlog, ensuring that the most important tasks are well-understood and ready for execution.
8. Acceptance Criteria: The conditions under which a user story or other requirement is considered complete, providing a clear definition of the expected outcome for functionality.
9. Version Control Systems: Software tools that manage changes to project documents and code, allowing multiple contributors to track revisions and maintain historical versions.
10. Requirements Specification Document (RSD): A comprehensive document that outlines all requirements for a project, serving as a contractual basis between stakeholders and guiding development efforts.
11. Traceability Matrix: A tool used to track the relationship between requirements throughout the project lifecycle, ensuring that all requirements are addressed during development and testing.

3.4 Project

3.4.1 Solved Project

Imagine you are a business analyst working on an e-commerce platform upgrade. Before proceeding with the analysis, collect detailed requirements from all stakeholders, ensure the documentation captures all necessary details while remaining concise, verify the alignment of documented requirements with business goals, explore alternative documentation tools for better clarity and collaboration, and ask for feedback on the documentation process. This approach guarantees that the requirements are thoroughly understood and accurately represented.

Approach:

1. Initial Planning and Stakeholder Identification

Objectives:
Identify all relevant stakeholders and plan the requirements gathering process.
Key Activities:
- **Stakeholder Identification:** Create a comprehensive list of stakeholders, including customers, sales teams, marketing, IT, and management.
- **Kick-off Meeting:** Organize a kick-off meeting to explain the project goals, scope, and timelines. Ensure all stakeholders understand their roles in the process.
- **Requirement Gathering Plan:** Develop a detailed plan for how and when requirements will be gathered from each stakeholder group.

2. Gathering Detailed Requirements

Objectives:

Collect comprehensive and detailed requirements from all stakeholders.

Key Activities:

- **Interviews and Surveys:** Conduct one-on-one interviews and surveys with key stakeholders to gather detailed insights.
- **Workshops and Focus Groups:** Hold workshops and focus groups to facilitate discussion and gather diverse perspectives on requirements.
- **Observation and Analysis:** Observe current platform usage to identify pain points and areas for improvement.

Outcome:

A comprehensive set of raw requirements from all stakeholders.

3. Documenting Requirements

Objectives:

Ensure all requirements are documented clearly, concisely, and accurately.

Key Activities:

- **Use Cases and User Stories:** Create use cases and user stories to document functional requirements in a user-centric manner.
- **Requirement Templates:** Utilize standardized requirement templates to ensure consistency.
- **Prioritization:** Work with stakeholders to prioritize requirements based on business impact and feasibility.

Outcome:

A well-structured requirements document that captures all necessary details.

4. Verification and Alignment with Business Goals

Objectives:

Ensure the documented requirements align with the overall business goals.

Key Activities:

- **Requirement Reviews:** Conduct review sessions with stakeholders to verify and validate the documented requirements.
- **Alignment Workshops:** Organize workshops to align requirements with business objectives and strategic goals.
- **Gap Analysis:** Perform a gap analysis to identify any discrepancies between current capabilities and desired outcomes.

Outcome:

A refined set of requirements that align with business goals.

5. Exploring Alternative Documentation Tools

Objectives:

Enhance clarity and collaboration through effective documentation tools.

Key Activities:

- **Tool Evaluation:** Research and evaluate different documentation tools (e.g., Confluence, Jira, Trello).
- **Pilot Testing:** Conduct a pilot test of the chosen tools with a subset of the project team.
- **Feedback Collection:** Gather feedback from the team on the effectiveness of the tools in improving clarity and collaboration.

Outcome:

Selection and implementation of the most suitable documentation tool.

6. Feedback and Continuous Improvement

Objectives:

Continuously improve the requirements documentation process based on stakeholder feedback.

Key Activities:

- **Feedback Sessions:** Regularly schedule feedback sessions with stakeholders to discuss the documentation process.
- **Process Refinement:** Make necessary adjustments to the documentation process based on feedback.
- **Training and Support:** Provide training and support to stakeholders on the use of new documentation tools and processes.

Outcome:

An iterative and improved documentation process that ensures ongoing stakeholder satisfaction.

Final Deliverables:

1. **Comprehensive Requirements Document:** A finalized document containing all validated requirements.

2. Use Cases and User Stories: Detailed use cases and user stories that describe the functional aspects of the e-commerce platform.
3. Requirement Traceability Matrix: A matrix to track requirements from identification through to implementation.
4. Tool Implementation Report: A report on the chosen documentation tools and their impact on the project.

3.4.2 Unsolved Project

Your part of a team updating an existing mobile application. Before implementing changes, review the process for managing requirements changes, provide only pertinent information to avoid scope creep, verify the impact of proposed changes on existing functionalities, explore alternative solutions to requirements conflicts, and discuss with the development team about the feasibility of integrating new requirements. This preparation helps in managing changes efficiently and minimizing disruptions to the project timeline.

3.5 Case Study

3.5.1 Solved Case Study

Effective requirement analysis and planning are critical to the success of any software development project. This process begins with gathering user requirements, which involves engaging with stakeholders through interviews, surveys, and observation to understand their needs and expectations. After collecting these requirements, they are meticulously analyzed and documented. Tools such as use cases and user stories help in creating comprehensive and clear documentation that guides the development process. Another vital aspect is managing requirement changes, as project requirements often evolve. A robust change management process ensures that any modifications are assessed for their impact, approved by the relevant stakeholders, and properly incorporated into the project documentation. This systematic approach helps in maintaining alignment with project goals, reducing risks, and enhancing the overall quality of the software.

Questions:

1. What is the initial step in the requirement analysis and planning process?
   Answer: The initial step in the requirement analysis and planning process is gathering user requirements.
2. Mention two methods used to gather user requirements.
   Answer: Two methods used to gather user requirements are interviews and surveys.
3. Why is it necessary to analyse and document requirements?
   Answer: It is necessary to analyse and document requirements to provide a clear guide for the development process.
4. Which tools are used to create comprehensive documentation?
   Answer: Tools used to create comprehensive documentation include use cases and user stories.
5. What is the purpose of a change management process in requirement analysis?
   Answer: The purpose of a change management process in requirement analysis is to ensure that any modifications are properly assessed, approved, and documented to maintain alignment with project goals.

3.5.2 Unsolved Case Study

Requirement analysis and planning are essential components of the software development lifecycle, ensuring that the final product aligns with user needs and business objectives. The process starts with gathering user requirements through various methods such as interviews, surveys, and workshops to collect detailed information about stakeholder expectations. Once gathered, these requirements are analyzed and documented using tools like use cases and user stories to create clear and concise references for the development team. Managing changes to requirements is equally important, as changes are inevitable in any project. A structured change management process allows for the evaluation, approval, and documentation of changes, ensuring that the project remains aligned with its goals. This comprehensive approach ensures a well-organized and transparent development process, leading to successful project outcomes.

Questions:

1. What is the first step in the requirement analysis and planning process?
2. Name one method used to gather user requirements.
3. Why is it important to document requirements?
4. What tool is mentioned for documenting requirements?

5. Why is managing requirements changes crucial in a project?

3.6 Lab Activity

3.6.1 Solved Lab Activity

Create a Requirements Specification Document (RSD) for the analysed requirements. Include functional and non-functional requirements, use cases, and any assumptions made.

Solution:

Requirements Specification Document (RSD)

1. Introduction

1.1 Purpose

This document outlines the requirements for the development of a software system, detailing functional and non-functional requirements, use cases, and assumptions.

1.2 Scope

The system will include a user interface, application logic, database, and interactions with external systems such as a payment gateway and email service.

1.3 Definitions, Acronyms, and Abbreviations

1. **RSD**: Requirements Specification Document
2. **UI**: User Interface
3. **DB**: Database
4. **API**: Application Programming Interface

1.4 References

1. System Design Diagram
2. Stakeholder Interviews
3. Industry Standards

2. System Overview

The system allows users to interact through a user interface, perform actions processed by the application logic, and store/retrieve data from a database. It interacts with external systems for payment processing and email services and includes a feedback loop for user input.

3. Functional Requirements

3.1 User Interface (UI)

1. **FR1**: The system shall provide a browser-based interface.
2. **FR2**: The system shall provide a mobile app interface.
3. **FR3**: The UI shall allow users to submit actions and receive outputs.

3.2 Application Logic

1. **FR4**: The system shall process user actions and generate appropriate responses.
2. **FR5**: The system shall handle data requests and responses to/from the database.
3. **FR6**: The system shall process payments through an external payment gateway.
4. **FR7**: The system shall send emails through an external email service.
5. **FR8**: The system shall log user actions for audit purposes.

3.3 Database

1. **FR9**: The system shall store user data securely.
2. **FR10**: The system shall retrieve data based on user requests.
3. **FR11**: The system shall ensure data integrity and consistency.

3.4 External Systems

1. **FR12**: The system shall integrate with a payment gateway for payment processing.
2. **FR13**: The system shall integrate with an email service for sending notifications.

3.5 User Feedback

1. **FR14**: The system shall capture user feedback and store it for analysis.
2. **FR15**: The system shall allow users to submit feedback through the UI.

4. Non-Functional Requirements

4.1 Performance

1. **NFR1**: The system shall process user requests within 2 seconds.
2. **NFR2**: The system shall handle up to 10,000 concurrent users.

4.2 Security

1. **NFR3**: The system shall enforce user authentication and authorization.
2. **NFR4**: The system shall encrypt sensitive data in transit and at rest.

4.3 Usability

1. **NFR5**: The system shall provide an intuitive and user-friendly interface.
2. **NFR6**: The system shall be accessible to users with disabilities.

4.4 Availability

1. **NFR7**: The system shall have an uptime of 99.9%.

4.5 Maintainability

1. **NFR8**: The system shall be designed for easy maintenance and updates.
2. **NFR9**: The system shall have comprehensive documentation for developers and users.

5. Use Cases

5.1 Use Case 1: User Login

1. **Actors**: User
2. **Preconditions**: User is registered in the system.
3. **Postconditions**: User is authenticated and granted access.
4. Main Flow:
5. User enters credentials.
6. System validates credentials.
7. User is logged in.

5.2 Use Case 2: Submit Payment

1. **Actors**: User, Payment Gateway
2. **Preconditions**: User is authenticated.
3. **Postconditions**: Payment is processed and confirmed.
4. Main Flow:
5. User initiates a payment.
6. System sends payment details to Payment Gateway.
7. Payment Gateway processes the payment.
8. System receives confirmation from Payment Gateway.
9. User receives payment confirmation.

5.3 Use Case 3: Send Feedback

1. **Actors**: User
2. **Preconditions**: User is authenticated.
3. **Postconditions**: Feedback is recorded.
4. Main Flow:
5. User submits feedback through the UI.
6. System records the feedback.
7. User receives acknowledgment of feedback submission.

6. Assumptions

1. The system will have reliable internet connectivity.
2. Users will have basic proficiency in using web and mobile applications.
3. External systems (Payment Gateway, Email Service) will provide stable and documented APIs for integration.

3.6.2 Unsolved Lab Activity

Discuss the role of requirements documentation in ensuring project success. How can well-documented requirements benefit both the development team and the stakeholders?

Exercises

Exercise 1 – Multiple Choice Questions

1. What is the primary purpose of analysing and documenting requirements in system analysis and design?
    A) To increase the project budget
    B) To facilitate stakeholder communication and ensure all system requirements are met
    C) To limit the scope of the project
    D) To finalize the system design immediately
2. Which of the following is NOT typically a technique used in gathering user requirements?
    A) Interviews
    B) Questionnaires
    C) Profit analysis
    D) Observations
3. How are changes to requirements typically managed in system design projects?
    A) By ignoring minor changes to stay on schedule
    B) Through a formal change management process
    C) By making changes as requested by any stakeholder
    D) By postponing all changes to a later project phase
4. Which statement best describes the role of documenting requirements in system analysis and design?
    A) Documentation is unnecessary if the team has experienced members.
    B) It provides a basis for creating system design and validation testing.
    C) It is only useful for complex projects.
    D) It should be avoided as it slows down the development process.
5. What is a common challenge when managing requirement changes during a system design project?
    A) Changes are generally inexpensive and quick to implement.
    B) Keeping the project within original timelines and budgets while accommodating changes.
    C) Decreasing the number of requirements to simplify the project.
    D) Requiring all stakeholders to agree unanimously on all changes.

Exercise 2 – True/False

1. The process of analyzing and documenting requirements does not typically involve the use of models such as use case diagrams or entity-relationship diagrams.
2. Managing requirements changes is an ongoing process that can occur at any stage of the system development lifecycle.
3. Gathering user requirements is primarily concerned with the technical specifications of the new system.
4. Once the requirements are documented, they typically do not change, ensuring the project scope remains fixed.
5. Analyzing requirements involves validating the gathered requirements against business needs and ensuring they are feasible, valuable, and testable.

Exercise 3 – Fill in the blanks

1. In the process of system analysis and design, ____________ is crucial for ensuring that the documented requirements align with the client's needs and expectations.
2. To accommodate evolving project scopes and stakeholder inputs, effective ____________ is essential in maintaining the integrity and relevance of the system requirements.
3. The first step in requirement analysis is ____________, which involves collecting detailed information from end-users and stakeholders to understand their needs for the new system.

Exercise 4- Fill in the blanks with two options

1. In the process of __________, it is crucial to interact with stakeholders to understand their needs and expectations, which can then be translated into functional and non-functional __________ for the system.
2. The __________ of requirements involves a systematic review to ensure that all specifications are actionable, measurable, and testable, while __________ ensures that any amendments or updates to requirements are tracked and integrated seamlessly into the project.
3. Effective management of requirements changes is essential to accommodate __________ during a project's lifecycle, which helps in keeping the system design aligned with __________ and other stakeholder expectations.

Exercise 5- Give two answers for the following:

1. Methods for Gathering User Requirements
2. Techniques for Analyzing Requirements
3. Documents Created During Requirement Analysis
4. Tools for Documenting Requirements
5. Strategies for Managing Requirements Changes

Exercise 6- Rearrange the sentence

1. requirements user from inputs gathers various.
2. requirements documented be must and analyzed clearly.
3. changes Handle carefully requirements to.

Exercise 7- Choose the Odd One Out

1. Specification, Documentation, Gathering, Validation
2. Analyzing, Documenting, Implementing, Categorizing
3. Modifications, Additions, Deletions, Assessments

Exercise 8- Jumble words

1. rgtahigne
2. yninlaasg
3. geahncmsna

Exercise 9- Match case

Column 1	Column 2
1. What is the first step in gathering user requirements?	1. Reviewing the changes and updating the project documentation as necessary.
2. Which technique is NOT typically used for gathering user requirements?	2. Determining how the requirements will be analysed, documented, and managed.
3. What is a key outcome of analysing and documenting requirements?	3. Creating a prototype to confirm user requirements directly.
4. How are changes to requirements typically managed?	4. Establish a clear and structured document that outlines all gathered user requirements.
5. What role does documentation play in requirement analysis?	5. Developing procedures to handle changes in requirements to avoid scope creep and maintain project focus.

Exercise 10- Assertion – Reason

1. Assertion (A): Requirement Analysis and Planning is a vital phase in the System Development Lifecycle (SDLC).

Reason (R): This phase ensures that all user needs are thoroughly understood and documented before the system design begins, which helps in managing requirement changes effectively.

Options:

a) Assertion (A) is true, and Reason (R) is the correct reason for Assertion (A).
b) Assertion (A) is true, but Reason (R) is not the correct reason for Assertion (A).
c) Assertion (A) is false, but Reason (R) is true.
d) Assertion (A) is true, but Reason (R) is false.

Exercise 11- One- word

1. What is the initial step in requirement analysis that involves collecting inputs from stakeholders?
2. What process involves detailing the functional and non-functional needs of a system after they are collected?
3. What is the term for the process of keeping track of and implementing alterations to the initially agreed-upon requirements?

Exercise 12- Small Answers

1. Describe two methods for gathering user requirements in system design.
2. What are the key elements to include in a well-documented system requirement?

Exercise 13- Long Answers

1. Describe in detail various techniques that can be employed for gathering user requirements in system analysis. How do these techniques ensure that all necessary user inputs are captured accurately?
2. Discuss the process of managing changes to system requirements after they have been initially agreed upon. What strategies can be employed to handle changes effectively without disrupting the system development process?

Answers

Exercise 1- 1) To facilitate stakeholder communication and ensure all system requirements are met, 2) Profit analysis, 3) Through a formal change management process, 4) It provides a basis for creating system design and validation testing, 5) Keeping the project within original timelines and budgets while accommodating changes.
Exercise 2- 1) False, 2) True, 3) False, 4) False, 5) True
Exercise 3- 1) Analyzing and Documenting Requirements, 2) Managing Requirements Changes, 3) Gathering User Requirements
Exercise 4- 1) Gathering User Requirements, requirements, 2) Analyzing and Documenting Requirements, Managing Requirements Changes, 3) updates, user needs
Exercise 5- 1) Interviews, Surveys, 2) SWOT Analysis, Use Case Modelling, 3) Requirements Specification Document, Use Case Diagram, 4) Microsoft Word, JIRA, 5) Change Control Board, Impact Analysis
Exercise 6- 1) Gather various inputs from user requirements, 2) Requirements must be analyzed and documented clearly, 3) Handle changes to requirements carefully
Exercise 7- 1) Gathering, 2) Implementing, 3) Assessments
Exercise 8- 1) Gathering, 2) Analysing, 3) Management
Exercise 9- 1 D, 2 C, 3 B, 4 E, 5 A
Exercise 10- a) Assertion (A) is true and Reason (R) is the correct reason for Assertion (A).
Exercise 11- 1) Gathering, 2) Documenting, 3) Managing

Online Resources

Online Exam paper

URL https://forms.gle/Adxdvx3t42iG9wbB8

QR Code

YouTube Video
URL https://www.youtube.com/playlist?list=PLzlh_31VWEFrog74q_3hWqr80zSeU__6V

QR Code

More Test Papers Practices

Test Paper-1

URL https://forms.gle/3G7ig3fbzJ5W24qXA

QR Code

Test Paper-2

URL https://forms.gle/M5zcjckgeCkt5HHN8

QR Code

System analysis and design Test Paper
Chapter- 3
Requirement Analysis and Planning

Time Duration: 30 Minutes **Maximum Marks: 25**

General Instructions:

1. The question paper consists of answer any 12 questions out of the given 19 questions and is divided into four sections, A, B, C and D.
2. All questions are compulsory.
3. Section A comprises question numbers 1 to 8. These are MCQs and one liner of one mark each. You are to select one most appropriate response out of the four provided options.
4. Section B comprises question numbers 1 to 5. These are SAQs carrying two marks each.
5. Section C comprises question numbers 1 to 4. These are SAQs carrying four marks each.
6. Section D comprises question numbers 1& 2. These are LAQs carrying five marks each.

SECTION-A

I. <u>Answer any 6 questions out of the given 8 questions</u> **(1*6=6)**

1. What is the primary objective of gathering user requirements in system development?
   A) To create system architecture
   B) To understand the needs and expectations of users
   C) To test the system for bugs
   D) To write code for the system
2. Which technique is commonly used for gathering user requirements?
   A) Coding
   B) Prototyping
   C) Interviews
   D) Deployment
3. What is the main purpose of analyzing and documenting requirements?
   A) To implement the system
   B) To ensure that the requirements are clear, complete, and feasible
   C) To test the system
   D) To create user manuals
4. Which document is typically created during the requirements analysis phase?
   A) Test Plan
   B) Requirements Specification Document (RSD)
   C) User Manual
   D) Deployment Guide
5. What is a common method for managing requirements changes during a project?
   A) Ignoring changes
   B) Using a change control process
   C) Making changes without documentation
   D) Implementing changes immediately without analysis
6. What document outlines the detailed requirements of a system?
7. What process helps ensure that requirements changes are controlled and documented?
8. What is the term for assessing whether requirements are achievable within constraints?

SECTION-B

II. <u>Answer any 3 questions out of the given 5 questions</u> **(2*3=6)**

1. Define 'user requirements' in the context of system development.

2. What is the purpose of a feasibility study in requirement analysis?
3. List two techniques for gathering user requirements.
4. Why is it important to document requirements clearly and completely?
5. What role does stakeholder feedback play in requirement analysis?

SECTION-C

II. <u>Answer any 2 questions out of the given 4 questions</u> **(4*2=8)**

1. Explain the process of conducting a requirements interview.
2. Describe the main sections typically included in a Requirements Specification Document (RSD).
3. How can prototyping be used to gather user requirements effectively?
4. Discuss the challenges of managing requirements changes and how to address them.

SECTION-D

III. <u>Answer any 1 question out of the given 2 questions</u> **(5*1=5)**

1. Analyze the importance of involving stakeholders during the requirements gathering phase. Provide examples to support your points.
2. Discuss the steps involved in managing requirements changes using a change control process. How does this process help in maintaining project stability and scope?

Chapter 4: System Modelling

- Understanding System Modelling
- Use Case Modelling
- Activity Diagrams
- Entity-Relationship Diagrams
- Data Flow Diagrams
- Process Modelling Concepts
- Business Process Modelling Notation (BPMN)
- Process Improvement Techniques

4.1 Overview of System Modelling

System models are simplified representations of real-world systems that help us to understand, analyze, and design complex systems. These models are important tools used in various fields such as engineering, computer science, economics, and biology to study and predict behavior of the system. System models can be visual, mathematical or conceptual. They provide insights into program design, communication, and development. Here are a few types of system models commonly used: Mathematical, Simulation, Graphical, Physical, Conceptual.

System modeling is the process of developing abstract models of a system, with each model presenting a different view or perspective of that system.

• System modeling may represent a system using graphical notation, e.g. the Unified Modeling Language (UML).
• System modelling helps the analyst to understand the functionality of the system and models are used to communicate with customers.

System Perspectives

• **A context/external perspective** - model the context or environment of the system.
• **An interaction perspective** - model the interactions between a system and its environment, or between the components of a system.
• **A structural perspective** - model the organization of a system or the structure of the data that is processed by the system.
• **A behavioral perspective** - model the dynamic behavior of the system and how it responds to events.

Why Use of Graphical Models?

• As a means of facilitating discussion about an existing or proposed system - Incomplete and incorrect models are OK as their role is to support discussion.
• As a way of documenting an existing system - Models should be an accurate representation of the system but need not be complete.
• As a detailed system description that can be used to generate a system implementation - Models must be both correct and complete.

UML diagram types

• Activity diagrams, which show the activities involved in a process or in data processing.
• Use case diagrams, which show the interactions between a system and its environment.
• Sequence diagrams, which show interactions between actors and the system and between system components.
• Class diagrams, which show the object classes in the system and the associations between these classes.
• State diagrams, which show how the system reacts to internal and external events.

Context models

• Context models are used to illustrate the operational context of a system - they show whatlies outside the system boundaries.
• Social and organizational concerns may affect the decision on where to position system boundaries.
• Architectural models show the system and its relationship with other systems.

The Context of the MHC-PMS

Mental Health Care – Patient Management Systems

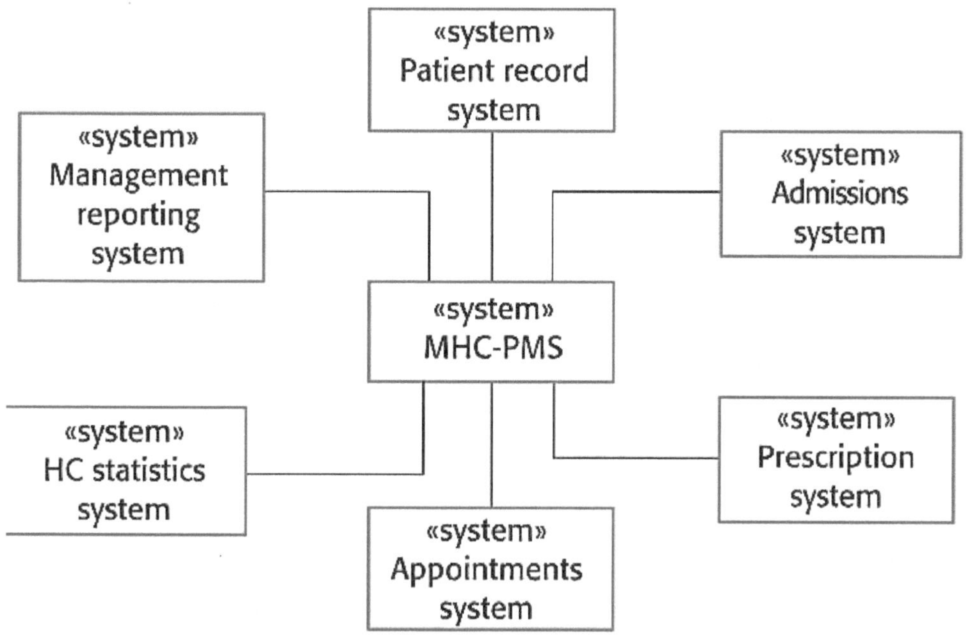

Process perspective

• Context models simply show the other systems in the environment, not how the system being developed is used in that environment. • Process models reveal how the system being developed is used in broader business processes.
• UML activity diagrams may be used to define business process models.

Process model of involuntary detention

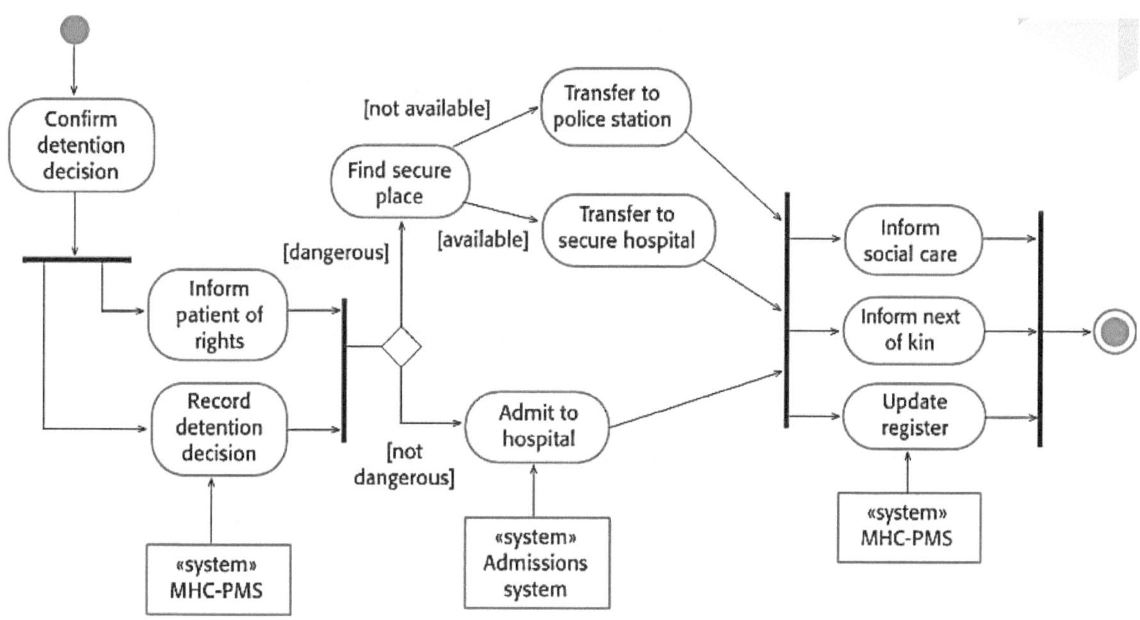

Interaction models

• Modeling user interaction is important as it helps to identify user requirements.

• Modeling system-to-system interaction highlights the communication problems that may arise.
• Modeling component interaction helps us understand if a proposed system structure is likely to deliver the required system performance and dependability.
• Use case diagrams and sequence diagrams may be used for interaction modeling.

Structural models
• Structural models of software display the organization of a system in terms of the components that make up that system and their relationships.
• Structural models may be static models, which show the structure of the system design, or dynamic models, which show the organization of the system when it is executing.
• You create structural models of a system when you are discussing and designing the system architecture.

Behavioral models
• Behavioral models are models of the dynamic behavior of a system as it is executing. They show what happens or what is supposed to happen when a system responds to a stimulus from its environment.
• You can think of these stimuli as being of two types:
▪ Data Some data arrives that must be processed by the system.
▪ Events Some event happens that triggers system processing. Events may have associated data, although this is not always the case.

4.2 Use Case Modelling

A Use Case Diagram is a type of Unified Modeling Language (UML) diagram that represents the interaction between actors (users or external systems) and a system under consideration to accomplish specific goals. It provides a high-level view of the system's functionality by illustrating the various ways users can interact with it.

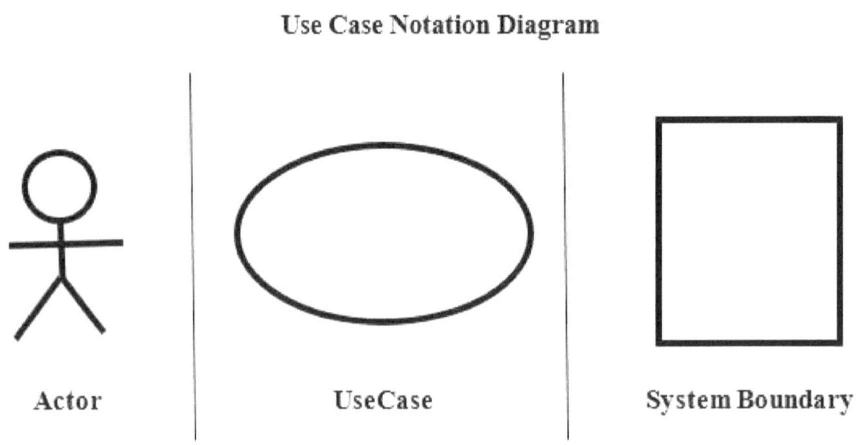

2. Use Case Diagram Notations

UML notations provide a visual language that enables software developers, designers, and other stakeholders to communicate and document system designs, architectures, and behaviors in a consistent and understandable manner.

1.1. Actors

Actors are external entities that interact with the system. These can include users, other systems, or hardware devices. In the context of a Use Case Diagram, actors initiate use cases and receive the outcomes. Proper identification and understanding of actors are crucial for accurately modeling system behavior.

Actor are typically represented by sticks figure

1.2. Use Cases

Use cases are like scenes in the play. They represent specific things your system can do. In the online shopping system, examples of use cases could be "Place Order," "Track Delivery," or "Update Product Information". Use cases are represented by ovals.

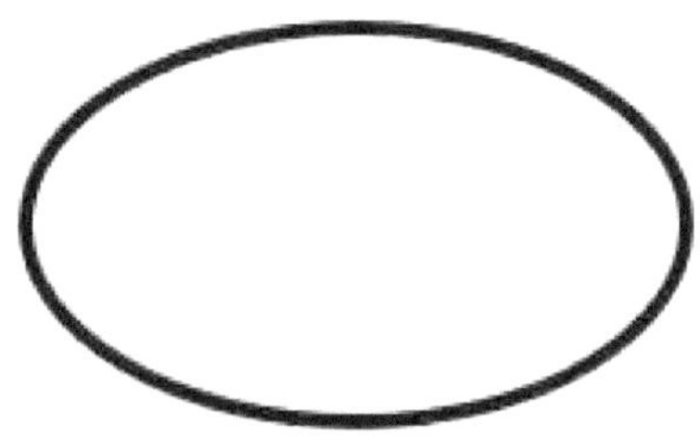

Use Case by represented by ovals

1.3. System Boundary

The system boundary is a visual representation of the scope or limits of the system you are modeling. It defines what is inside the system and what is outside. The boundary helps to establish a clear distinction between the elements that are part of the system and those that are external to it. The system boundary is typically represented by a rectangular box that surrounds all the use cases of the system.

Purpose of System Boundary:

- **Scope Definition:** It clearly outlines the boundaries of the system, indicating which components are internal to the system and which are external actors or entities interacting with the system.
- **Focus on Relevance:** By delineating the system's scope, the diagram can focus on illustrating the essential functionalities provided by the system without unnecessary details about external entities.

System Boundary is represented by rectangular box

3. Use Case Diagram Relationships

In a Use Case Diagram, relationships play a crucial role in depicting the interactions between actors and use cases. These relationships provide a comprehensive view of the system's functionality and its various scenarios. Let's delve into the key types of relationships and explore examples to illustrate their usage.

3.1. Association Relationship

The Association Relationship represents a communication or interaction between an actor and a use case. It is depicted by a line connecting the actor to the use case. This relationship signifies that the actor is involved in the functionality described by the use case.

Example: Online Banking System
- **Actor:** Customer
- **Use Case:** Transfer Funds
- **Association:** A line connecting the "Customer" actor to the "Transfer Funds" use case, indicating the customer's involvement in the funds transfer process.

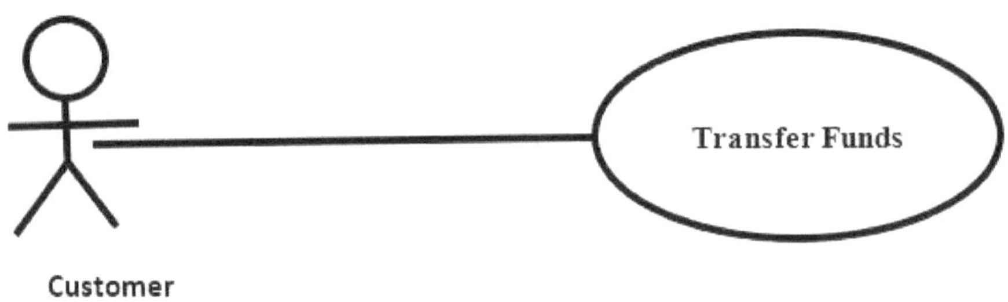

Represents a communication or interaction between an actor (Customer) and a use case (Transfer Funds)

3.2. Include Relationship

The Include Relationship indicates that a use case includes the functionality of another use case. It is denoted by a dashed arrow pointing from the including use case to the included use case. This relationship promotes modular and reusable design.

Example: Social Media Posting
- **Use Cases:** Compose Post, Add Image
- **Include Relationship:** The "Compose Post" use case includes the functionality of "Add Image." Therefore, composing a post includes the action of adding an image.

Include

"Compose Post" includes the functionality of another "Add Image"

3.3. Extend Relationship

The Extend Relationship illustrates that a use case can be extended by another use case under specific conditions. It is represented by a dashed arrow with the keyword "extend." This relationship is useful for handling optional or exceptional behavior.

Example: Flight Booking System
- Use Cases: Book Flight, Select Seat
- Extend Relationship: The "Select Seat" use case may extend the "Book Flight" use case when the user wants to choose a specific seat, but it is an optional step.

Extend

The "Select Seat" use case may extend the "Book Flight" use case when the user wants to choose a specific seat

3.4. Generalization Relationship

The Generalization Relationship establishes an "is-a" connection between two use cases, indicating that one use case is a specialized version of another. It is represented by an arrow pointing from the specialized use case to the general use case.

Example: Vehicle Rental System
- Use Cases: Rent Car, Rent Bike

- **Generalization Relationship:** Both "Rent Car" and "Rent Bike" are specialized versions of the general use case "Rent Vehicle."

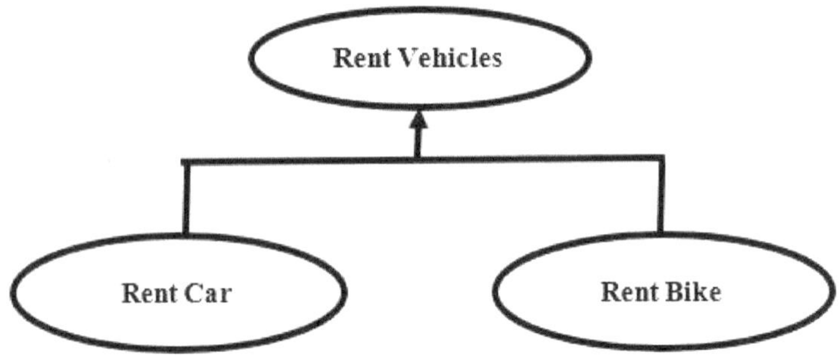

Both "Rent Car" and "Rent Bike" are specialized versions of the general use case "Rent Vehicle."

4. How to draw a Use Case diagram in UML?

Step 1: Identify Actors

Determine who or what interacts with the system. These are your actors. They can be users, other systems, or external entities.

Step 2: Identify Use Cases

Identify the main functionalities or actions the system must perform. These are your use cases. Each use case should represent a specific piece of functionality.

Step 3: Connect Actors and Use Cases

Draw lines (associations) between actors and the use cases they are involved in. This represents the interactions between actors and the system.

Step 4: Add System Boundary

Draw a box around the actors and use cases to represent the system boundary. This defines the scope of your system.

Step 5: Define Relationships

If certain use cases are related or if one use case is an extension of another, you can indicate these relationships with appropriate notations.

Step 6: Review and Refine

Step back and review your diagram. Ensure that it accurately represents the interactions and relationships in your system. Refine as needed.

Step 7: Validate

Share your use case diagram with stakeholders and gather feedback. Ensure that it aligns with their understanding of the system's functionality.

Let's understand how to draw a Use Case diagram with the help of an Online Shopping System:

1. Actors:

- Customer
- Admin

2. Use Cases:

1. Browse Products
2. Add to Cart
3. Checkout
4. Manage Inventory (Admin)

3. Relations:

- The Customer can browse products, add them to the cart, and complete the checkout.
- The admin can manage the inventory.

Below is the usecase diagram of an Online Shopping System:

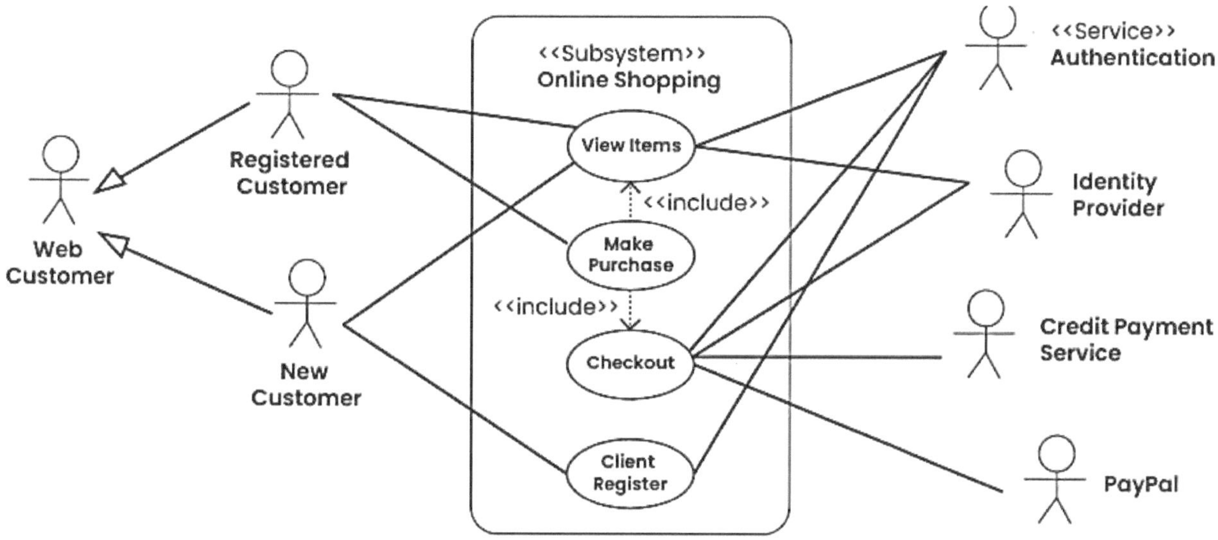

5. What are common Use Case Diagram Tools and Platforms?

Several tools and platforms are available to create and design Use Case Diagrams. These tools offer features that simplify the diagram creation process, facilitate collaboration among team members, and enhance overall efficiency. Here are some popular

6. Use Case Diagram tools and platforms:

6.1. Lucidchart

- Cloud-based collaborative platform.
- Intuitive drag-and-drop interface.
- Real-time collaboration and commenting.
- Templates for various diagram types.
- Integration with other tools like Jira and Confluence.

6.2. draw.io

- Free, open-source diagramming tool.
- Works offline and can be integrated with Google Drive, Dropbox, and others.
- Offers a wide range of diagram types, including Use Case Diagrams.
- Customizable shapes and themes.

6.3. Microsoft Visio

- Part of the Microsoft Office suite.
- Supports various diagram types, including Use Case Diagrams.
- Integration with Microsoft 365 for collaborative editing.
- Extensive shape libraries and templates.

6.4. Smart Draw

- User-friendly diagramming tool.
- Templates for different types of diagrams, including Use Case Diagrams.
- Integration with Microsoft Office and Google Workspace.
- Auto-formatting and alignment features.

6.5. PlantUML

- Open-source tool for creating UML diagrams.
- Text-based syntax for diagram specification.
- Integrates with various text editors and IDEs.
- Supports collaborative work using version control systems.

7. What are Common Mistakes and Pitfalls while making Use Case Diagram?

Avoiding common mistakes ensures the accuracy and effectiveness of the Use Case Diagram. Here are key points for each mistake:

7.1. Overcomplication:

- **Mistake:** Including excessive detail in the diagram.
- **Impact:** Confuses stakeholders and complicates understanding.
- **Prevention:** Focus on essential use cases and maintain an appropriate level of abstraction.

7.2. Ambiguous Relationships:

- **Mistake:** Unclear relationships between actors and use cases.
- **Impact:** Causes misinterpretation of system interactions.
- **Prevention:** Clearly define and label relationships with proper notation.

7.3. Inconsistent Naming Conventions:

- **Mistake:** Inconsistent naming of actors and use cases.
- **Impact:** Causes confusion and hinders communication.
- **Prevention:** Establish and adhere to a consistent naming convention.

7.4. Misuse of Generalization:

- **Mistake:** Incorrect use of generalization relationships.
- **Impact:** Misrepresentation of the "is-a" relationship between use cases or actors.
- **Prevention:** Ensure accurate usage to represent specialization relationships.

7.5. Overlooking System Boundaries:

- **Mistake:** Not clearly defining the system boundary.
- **Impact:** Challenges understanding of the system's scope.
- **Prevention:** Clearly enclose relevant actors and use cases within a system boundary.

7.6. Lack of Iteration:

- **Mistake:** Treating the diagram as a static artifact.
- **Impact:** May become outdated and not reflect the current state of the system.
- **Prevention:** Use an iterative approach, updating the diagram as the system evolves.

8. What are the Purpose and Benefits of Use Case Diagrams?

The Use Case Diagram offers numerous benefits throughout the system development process. Here are some key advantages of using

Use Case Diagrams:

- Visualization of System Functionality:
- Use Case Diagrams provide a visual representation of the system's functionalities and interactions with external entities.
- This visualization helps stakeholders, including non-technical ones, to understand the system's high-level behavior.
- Communication:
- Use Case Diagrams serve as a powerful communication tool, facilitating discussions between stakeholders, developers, and designers.
- They provide a common language for discussing system requirements, ensuring a shared understanding among diverse team members.
- Requirement Analysis:
- During the requirements analysis phase, Use Case Diagrams help in identifying, clarifying, and documenting user requirements.
- They capture the various ways users interact with the system, aiding in a comprehensive understanding of system functionality.
- Focus on User Goals:
- Use Case Diagrams center around user goals and scenarios, emphasizing the perspective of external entities (actors).
- This focus on user interactions ensures that the system is designed to meet user needs and expectations.
- System Design:
- In the system design phase, Use Case Diagrams aid in designing how users (actors) will interact with the system.

- They contribute to the planning of the user interface and help in organizing system functionalities.
- Testing and Validation:
- Use Case Diagrams are valuable for deriving test cases and validating system behavior.
- Testers can use the diagrams to ensure that all possible scenarios, including alternative and exceptional paths, are considered during testing.

4.3 Activity Diagrams

Activity diagram is another important diagram in UML to describe the dynamic aspects of the system.
Activity diagram is basically a flowchart to represent the flow from one activity to another activity. The activity can be described as an operation of the system.
The control flow is drawn from one operation to another. This flow can be sequential, branched, or concurrent. Activity diagrams deal with all types of flow control by using different elements such as fork, join, etc.

Purpose of Activity Diagrams

The basic purposes of activity diagrams are like the other four diagrams. It captures the dynamic behavior of the system. The other four diagrams are used to show the message flow from one object to another, but activity diagram is used to show message flow from one activity to another.
Activity is a particular operation of the system. Activity diagrams are not only used for visualizing the dynamic nature of a system, but they are also used to construct the executable system by using forward and reverse engineering techniques. The only missing thing in the activity diagram is the message part.
It does not show any message flow from one activity to another. Activity diagram is sometimes considered as the flowchart. Although the diagrams look like a flowchart, they are not. It shows different flows such as parallel, branched, concurrent, and single.

The purpose of an activity diagram can be described as −
- Draw the activity flow of a system.
- Describe the sequence from one activity to another.
- Describe the parallel, branched and concurrent flow of the system.

How to Draw an Activity Diagram?

Activity diagrams are mainly used as a flowchart that consists of activities performed by the system. Activity diagrams are not exactly flowcharts as they have some additional capabilities. These additional capabilities include branching, parallel flow, swimlane, etc.
Before drawing an activity diagram, we must have a clear understanding about the elements used in the activity diagram. The main element of an activity diagram is the activity itself. An activity is a function performed by the system. After identifying the activities, we need to understand how they are associated with constraints and conditions.

Before drawing an activity diagram, we should identify the following elements −
- Activities
- Association
- Conditions
- Constraints

Once the above-mentioned parameters are identified, we need to make a mental layout of the entire flow. This mental layout is then transformed into an activity diagram.

Following is an example of an activity diagram for order management system. In the diagram, four activities are identified which are associated with conditions. One important point should be clearly understood that an activity diagram cannot be exactly matched with the code. The activity diagram is made to understand the flow of activities and is mainly used by the business users

Following diagram is drawn with the four main activities −
- Send order by the customer
- Receipt of the order
- Confirm the order
- Dispatch the order

After receiving the order request, condition checks are performed to check if it is normal or special order. After the type of order is identified, dispatch activity is performed and that is marked as the termination of the process.

Activity diagram of an order management system

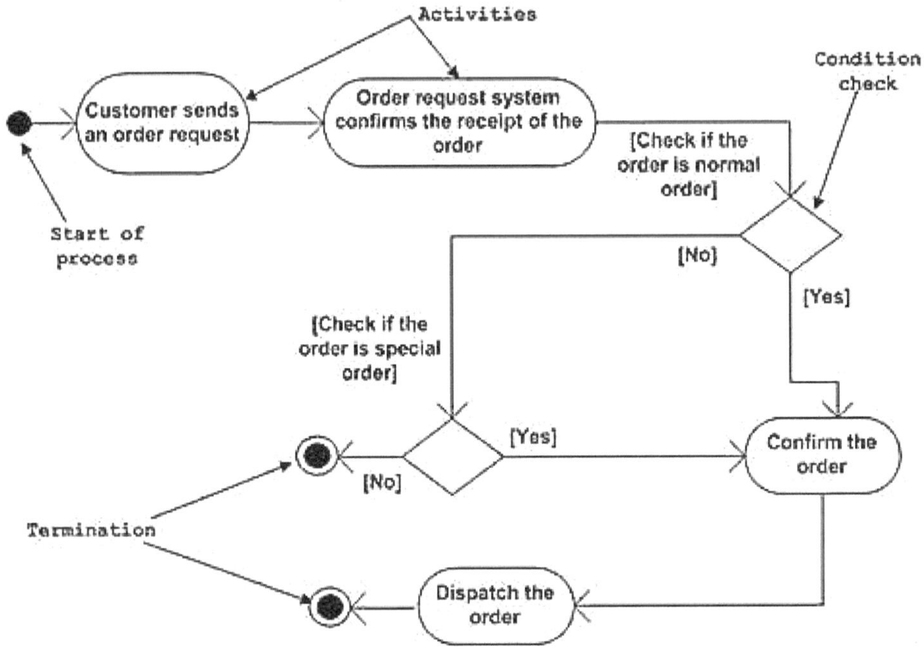

Where to Use Activity Diagrams?

- The basic usage of activity diagram is like the other four UML diagrams. The specific usage is to model the control flow from one activity to another. This control flow does not include messages.
- Activity diagram is suitable for modeling the activity flow of the system. An application can have multiple systems. Activity diagram also captures these systems and describes the flow from one system to another. This specific usage is not available in other diagrams. These systems can be databases, external queues, or any other system.
- We will now investigate the practical applications of the activity diagram. From the above discussion, an activity diagram is drawn from a very high level. So, it gives high level view of a system. This high-level view is mainly for business users or any other person who is not a technical person.

This diagram is used to model the activities which are nothing but business requirements. The diagram has more impact on business understanding rather than on implementation details.

Activity diagram can be used for −

- Modeling workflow by using activities.
- Modeling business requirements.
- High level understanding of the system's functionalities.
- Investigating business requirements at a later stage.

4.4 Entity-Relationship Diagrams

ER-modeling is a data modeling method used in software engineering to produce a conceptual data model of an information system. Diagrams created using this ER-modeling method are called Entity-Relationship Diagrams or ER diagrams or ERDs.

Purpose of ERD

- The database analyst gains a better understanding of the data to be contained in the database through the step of constructing the ERD.
- The ERD serves as a documentation tool.
- Finally, the ERD is used to connect the logical structure of the database to users. In particular, the ERD effectively communicates the logic of the database to users.

Components of an ER Diagrams

1. Entity

An entity can be a real-world object, either animate or inanimate, that can be merely identifiable. An entity is denoted as a rectangle in an ER diagram. For example, in a school database, students, teachers, classes, and courses offered can be treated as entities. All these entities have some attributes or properties that give them their identity.

Entity Set

An entity set is a collection of related types of entities. An entity set may include entities with attributes sharing similar values. For example, a student set may contain all the students at a school; likewise, a teacher set may include all the teachers at a school from all faculties. Entity set need not be disjoint.

2. Attributes

Entities are denoted utilizing their properties, known as attributes. All attributes have values. For example, a student entity may have name, class, and age as attributes.
There exists a domain or range of values that can be assigned to attributes. For example, a student's name cannot have a numeric value. It must be alphabetic. A student's age cannot be negative, etc.

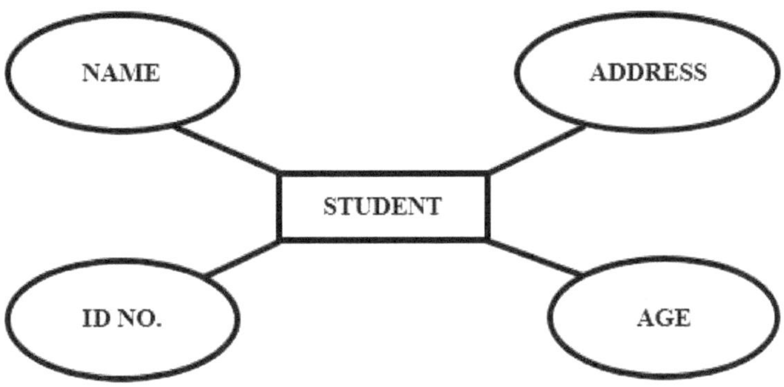

There are four types of Attributes:
1. Key attribute
2. Composite attribute
3. Single-valued attribute
4. Multi-valued attribute
5. Derived attribute

1. Key attribute: Key is an attribute or collection of attributes that uniquely identifies an entity among the entity set. For example, the roll number of a student makes him identifiable among students.

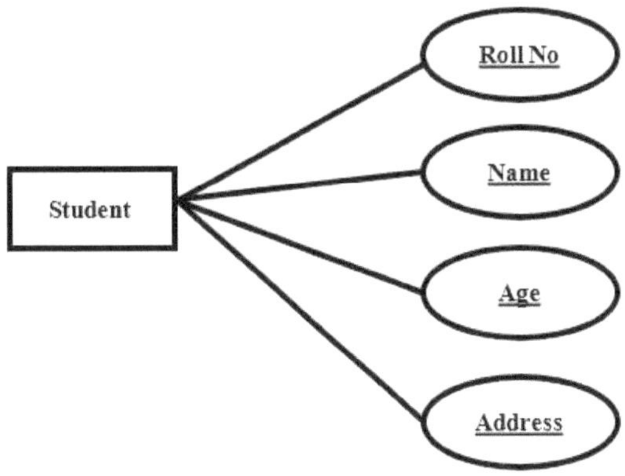

There are mainly three types of keys:
Super key: A set of attributes that collectively identifies an entity in the entity set.
Candidate key: A minimal super key is known as a candidate key. An entity set may have more than one candidate key.
Primary key: A primary key is one of the candidate keys chosen by the database designer to uniquely identify the entity set.

2. Composite attribute: An attribute that is a combination of other attributes is called a composite attribute. For example, in student entity, the student address is a composite attribute as an address is composed of other characteristics such as pin code, state, country.

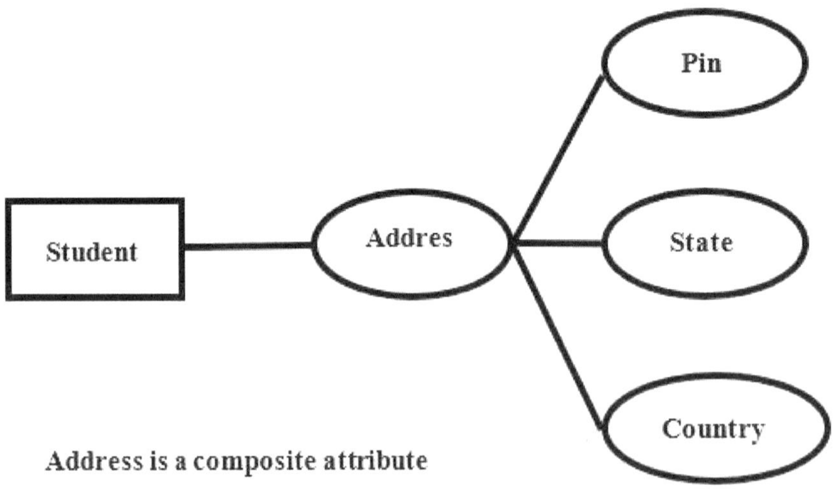

Address is a composite attribute

3. Single-valued attribute: Single-valued attribute contains a single value. For example, Social_Security_Number.

4. Multi-valued Attribute: If an attribute can have more than one value, it is known as a multi-valued attribute. Multi-valued attributes are depicted by the double ellipse. For example, a person can have more than one phone number, email address, etc.

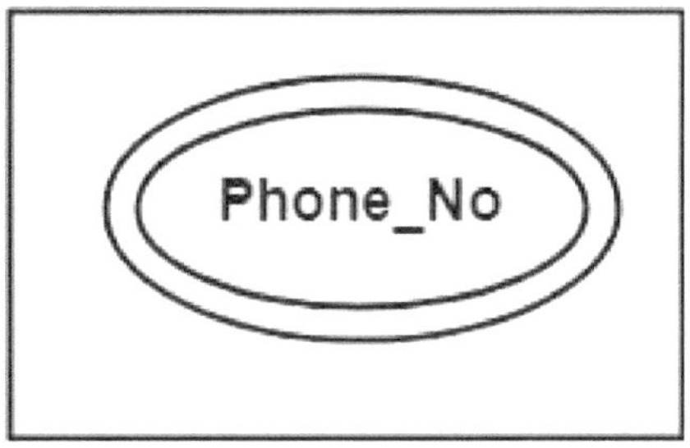

5. Derived attribute: Derived attributes are the attributes that do not exist in the physical database, but their values are derived from other attributes present in the database. For example, age can be derived from date_of_birth. In the ER diagram, Derived attributes are depicted by the dashed ellipse.

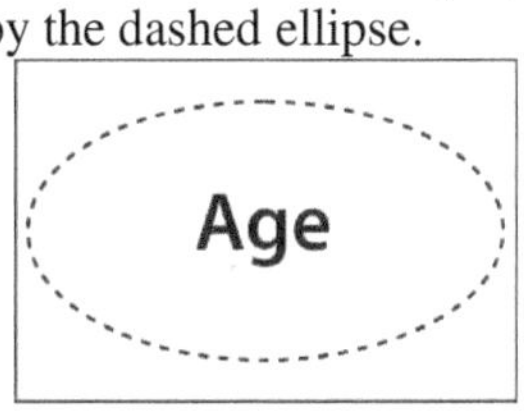

The Complete entity type Student with its attributes can be represented as:

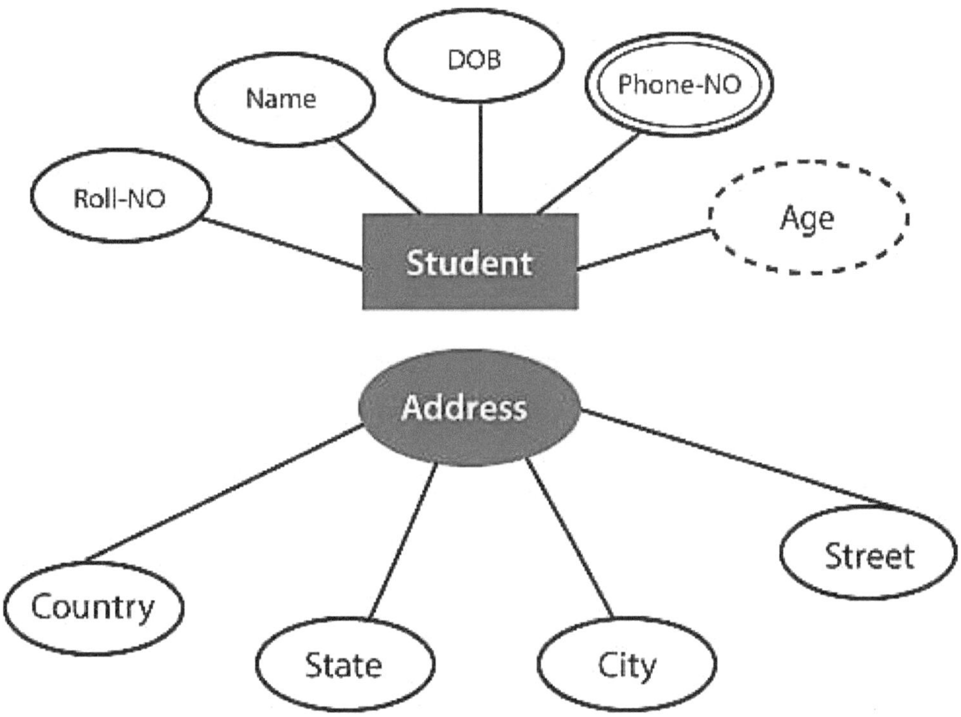

3. Relationships

The association among entities is known as a relationship. Relationships are represented by the diamond-shaped box. For example, an employee works at a department, a student enrolls in a course. Here, Works at and Enrolls are called relationships.

Fig: Relationships in ERD

Relationship set

- A set of relationships of a similar type is known as a relationship set. Like entities, a relationship too can have attributes. These attributes are called descriptive attributes.
- Degree of a relationship set

The number of participating entities in a relationship describes the degree of the relationship. The three most common relationships in E-R models are:
1. Unary (degree1)
2. Binary (degree2)
3. Ternary (degree3)

1. Unary relationship: This is also called recursive relationships. It is a relationship between the instances of one entity type. For example, one person is married to only one person.

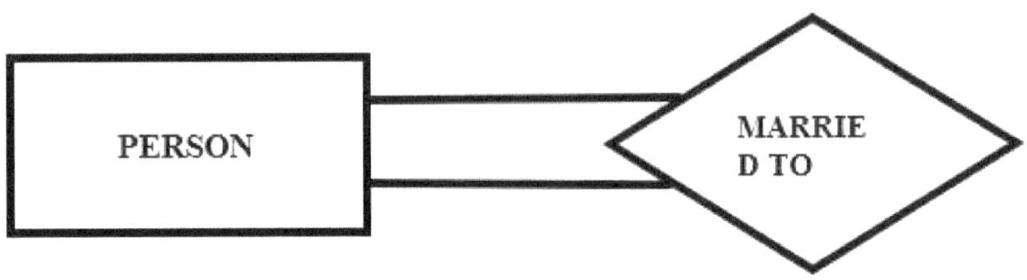

Fig: Unary Relationship

2. Binary relationship: It is a relationship between the instances of two entity types. For example, the Teacher teaches the subject.

Fig: Binary Relationship

3. Ternary relationship:

It is a relationship amongst instances of three entity types. In fig, the relationships "**may have**" provide the association of three entities, i.e., TEACHER, STUDENT, and SUBJECT. All three entities are many-to-many participants. There may be one or many participants in a ternary relationship.
In general, "**n**" entities can be related by the same relationship and is known as **n-ary** relationship.

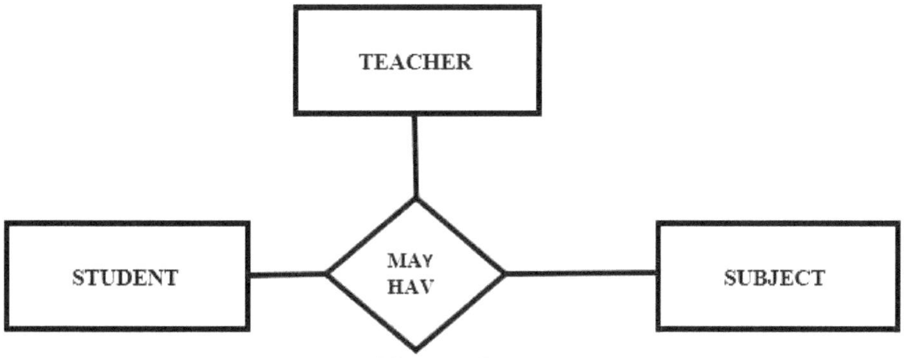

(Many to Many)

Fig: Ternary relationship

Cardinality

Cardinality describes the number of entities in one entity set, which can be associated with the number of entities of other sets via relationship set.

Types of Cardinalities

1. One to One: One entity from entity set A can be contained with at most one entity of entity set B and vice versa. Let us assume that each student has only one student ID, and each student ID is assigned to only one person. So, the relationship will be one to one.

Using Sets, it can be represented as:

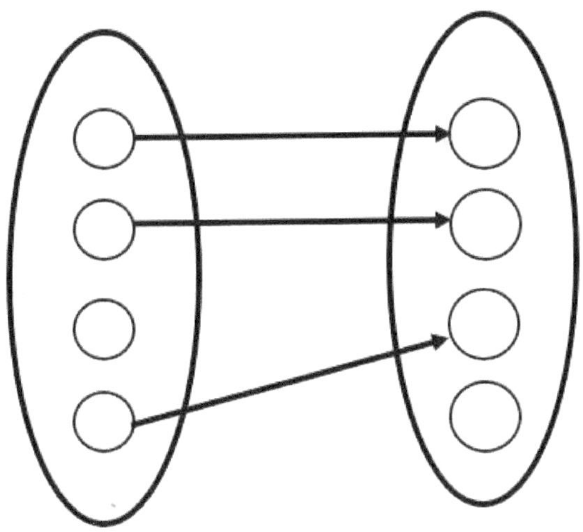

2. One-to-many: When a single instance of an entity is associated with more than one instance of another entity then it is called one-to-many relationships. For example, a client can place many orders; an order cannot be placed by many customers.

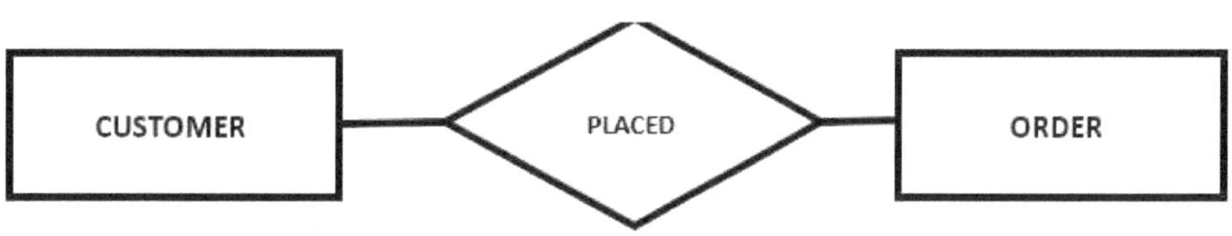

Using Sets, it can be represented as:

3. Many to One: More than one entity from entity set A can be associated with at most one entity of entity set B, however an entity from entity set B can be associated with more than one entity from entity set A. For example - many students can study in a single college, but a student cannot study in many colleges at the same time.

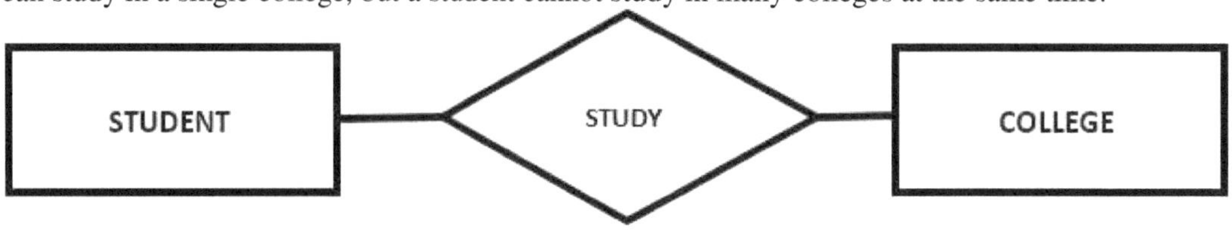

Using Sets, it can be represented as:

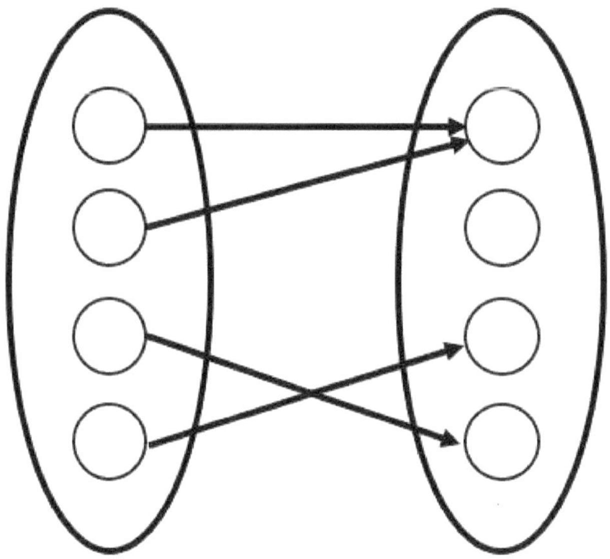

4. Many to Many: One entity from A can be associated with more than one entity from B and vice versa. For example, the student can be assigned to many projects, and a project can be assigned to many students.

Using Sets, it can be represented as:

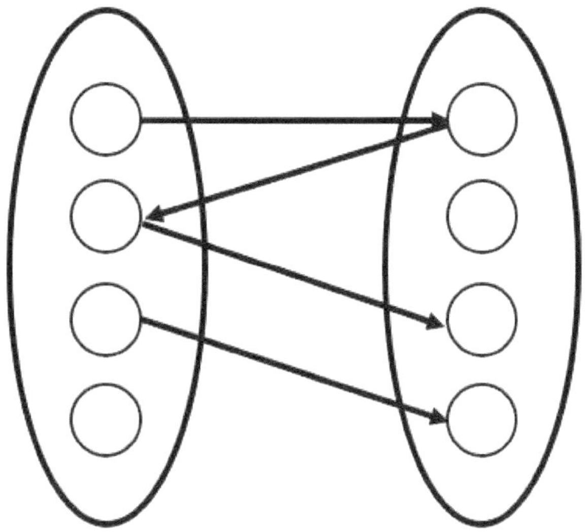

4.5 Data Flow Diagrams

A Data Flow Diagram (DFD) is a traditional visual representation of the information flows within a system. A neat and clear DFD can depict the right amount of the system requirement graphically. It can be manual, automated, or a combination of both.

It shows how data enters and leaves the system, what changes the information, and where data is stored.

The objective of a DFD is to show the scope and boundaries of a system. It may be used as a communication tool between a system analyst and any person who plays a part in the order that acts as a starting point for redesigning a system. The DFD is also called a data flow graph or bubble chart.

The following observations about DFDs are essential:

1. All names should be unique. This makes it easier to refer to elements in the DFD.
2. Remember that DFD is not a flow chart. Arrows is a flow chart that represents the order of events; arrows in DFD represent flowing data. A DFD does not involve any order of events.
3. Suppress logical decisions. If we ever have the urge to draw a diamond-shaped box in a DFD, suppress that urge! A diamond-shaped box is used in flow charts to represent decision points with multiple exists paths of which the only one is taken. This implies an ordering of events, which makes no sense in a DFD.
4. Do not become bogged down with details. Defer error conditions and error handling until the end of the analysis.

Standard symbols for DFDs are derived from the electric circuit diagram analysis and are shown in fig:

Symbol	Name	Function
	Data flow	Used to Connect Processes to each , other , to sources or Sinks; te arrow head indicates direction of data flow.
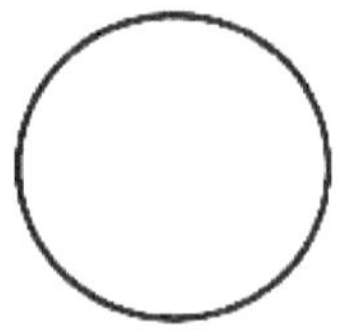	Process	Perfroms Some transformation of Input data to yield output data.
	Source of Sink (External Entity)	A Source of System inputs or Sink of System outputs.
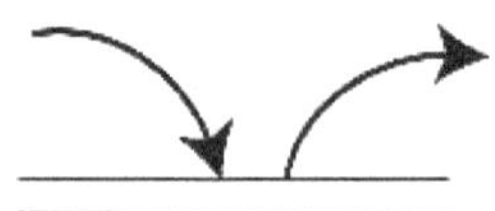	Data Store	A repository of data; the arrow heads indicate net inputs and net outputs to store.

Symbols for Data Flow Diagrams

- **Circle:** A circle (bubble) shows a process that transforms data inputs into data outputs.
- **Data Flow:** A curved line shows the flow of data into or out of a process or data store.
- **Data Store:** A set of parallel lines shows a place for the collection of data items. A data store indicates that the data is stored which can be used at a later stage or by the other processes in a different order. The data store can have an element or group of elements.
- **Source or Sink:** Source or Sink is an external entity and acts as a source of system inputs or sink of system outputs.

Levels in Data Flow Diagrams (DFD)

The DFD may be used to perform a system or software at any level of abstraction. Infact, DFDs may be partitioned into levels that represent increasing information flow and functional detail. Levels in DFD are numbered 0, 1, 2 or beyond. Here, we will see primarily three levels in the data flow diagram, which are: 0-level DFD, 1-level DFD, and 2-level DFD.

- 0-level DFDM

It is also known as fundamental system model, or context diagram represents the entire software requirement as a single bubble with input and output data denoted by incoming and outgoing arrows. Then the system is decomposed and described as a DFD with multiple bubbles. Parts of the system represented by each of these bubbles are then decomposed and documented as more and more detailed DFDs. This process may be repeated at as many levels as necessary until the program at hand is well understood. It is essential to preserve the number of inputs and outputs between levels, this concept is called leveling by DeMacro. Thus, if bubble "A" has two inputs x_1 and x_2 and one output y, then the expanded DFD, that represents "A" should have exactly two external inputs and one external output as shown in fig:

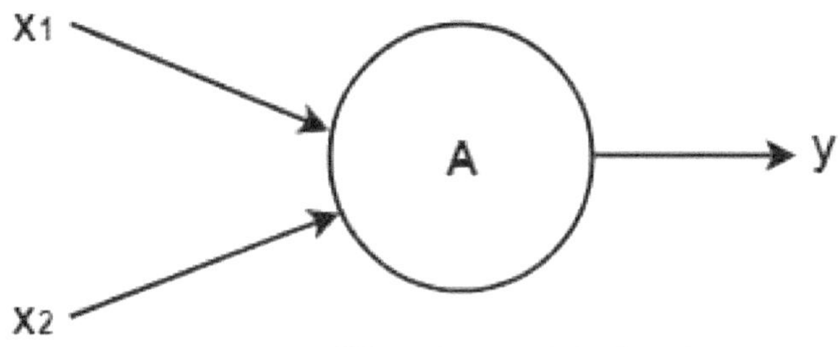

Fig: Level-0 DFD.

The Level-0 DFD, also called context diagram of the result management system is shown in fig. As the bubbles are decomposed into less and less abstract bubbles, the corresponding data flow may also be needed to be decomposed.

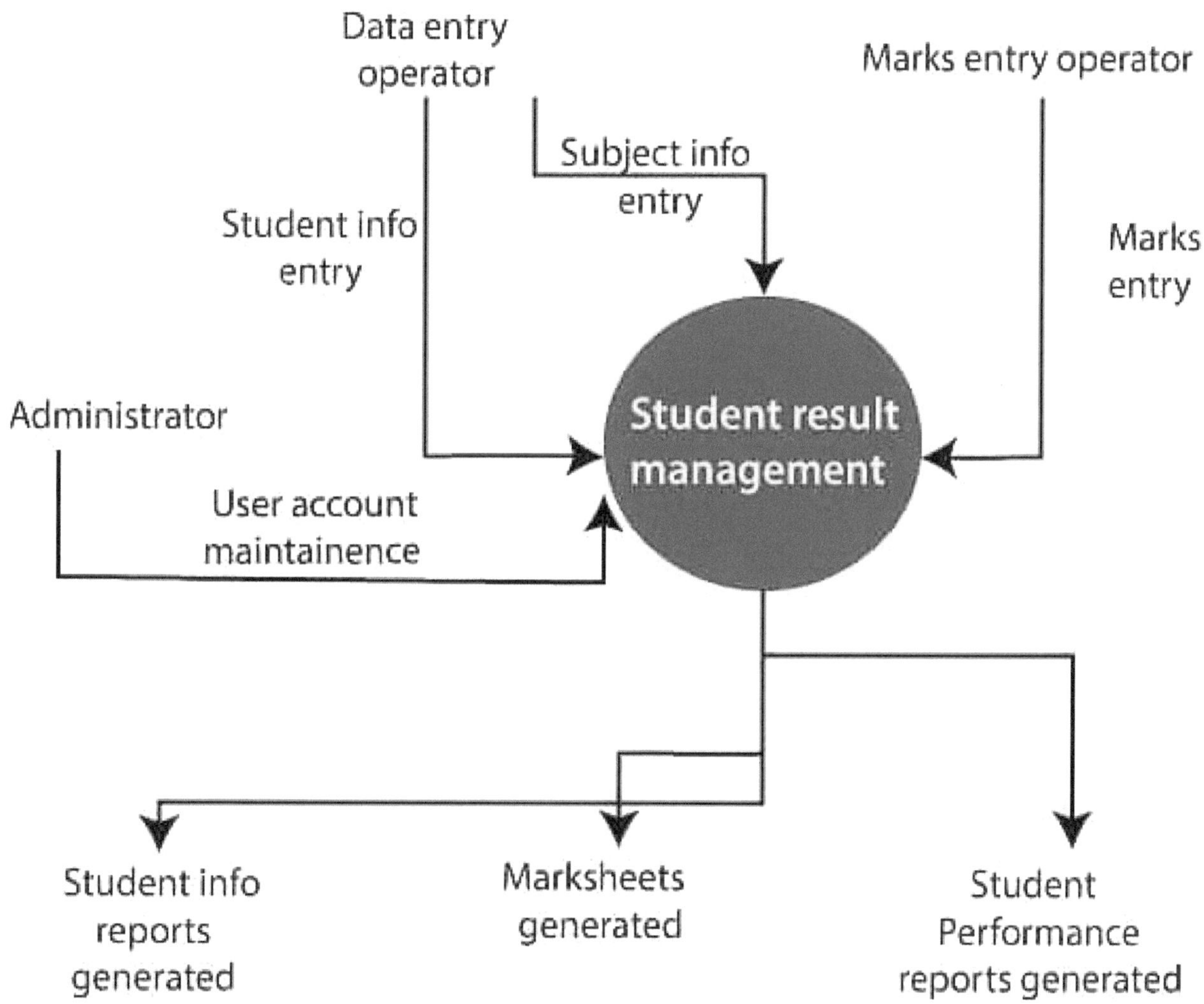

Fig: Level-0 DFD of result management system

- 1-level DFD

In 1-level DFD, a context diagram is decomposed into multiple bubbles/processes. In this level, we highlight the main objectives of the system and breakdown the high-level process of 0-level DFD into subprocesses.

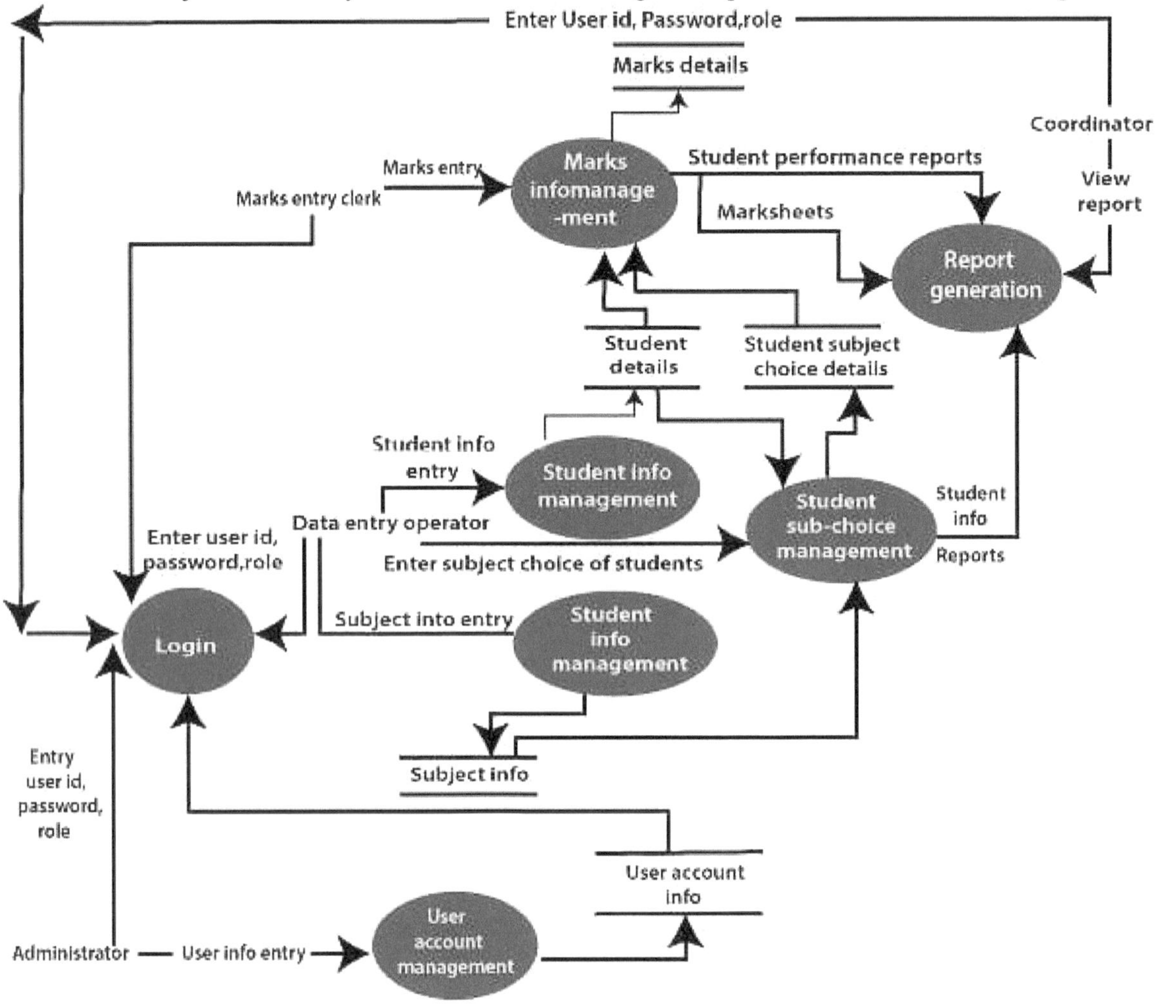

Fig: Level-1 DFD of result management system

- 2-Level DFD

2-level DFD goes one process deeper into parts of 1-level DFD. It can be used to project or record the specific/necessary detail about the system's functioning.

1.User Account Maintenance

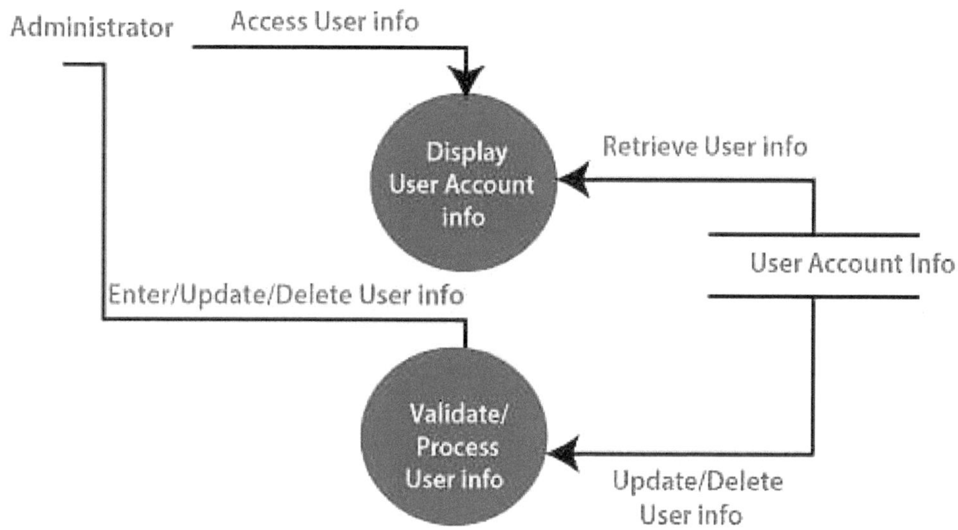

2. Login

The level 2 DFD of this process is given below:

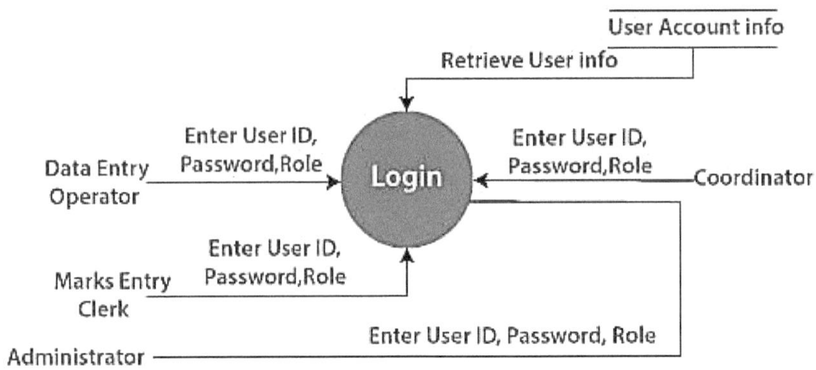

3. Student Information Management

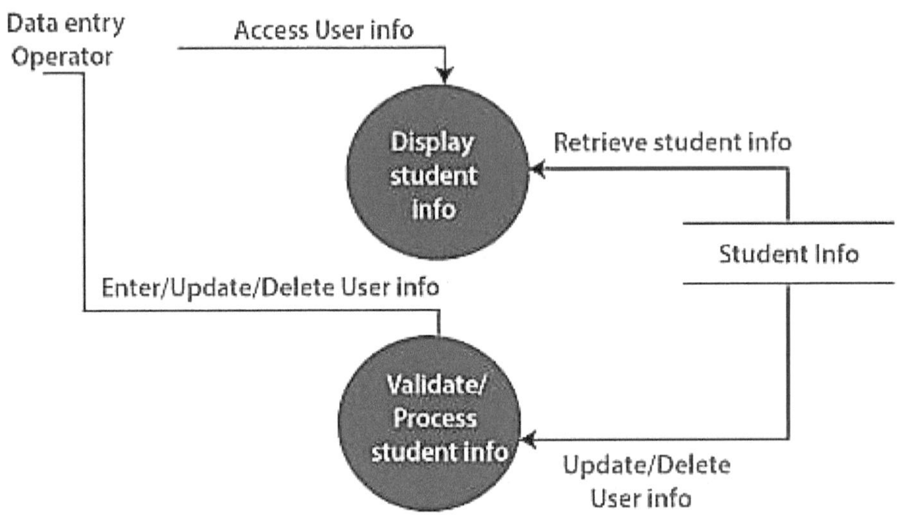

4. Subject Information Management

The level 2 DFD of this process is given below:

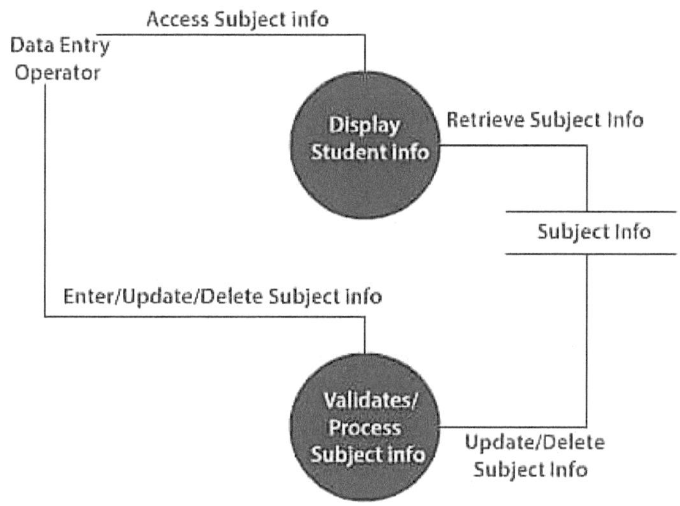

5. Student's Subject Choice Management

The Level 2 DFD of this Process is given below:

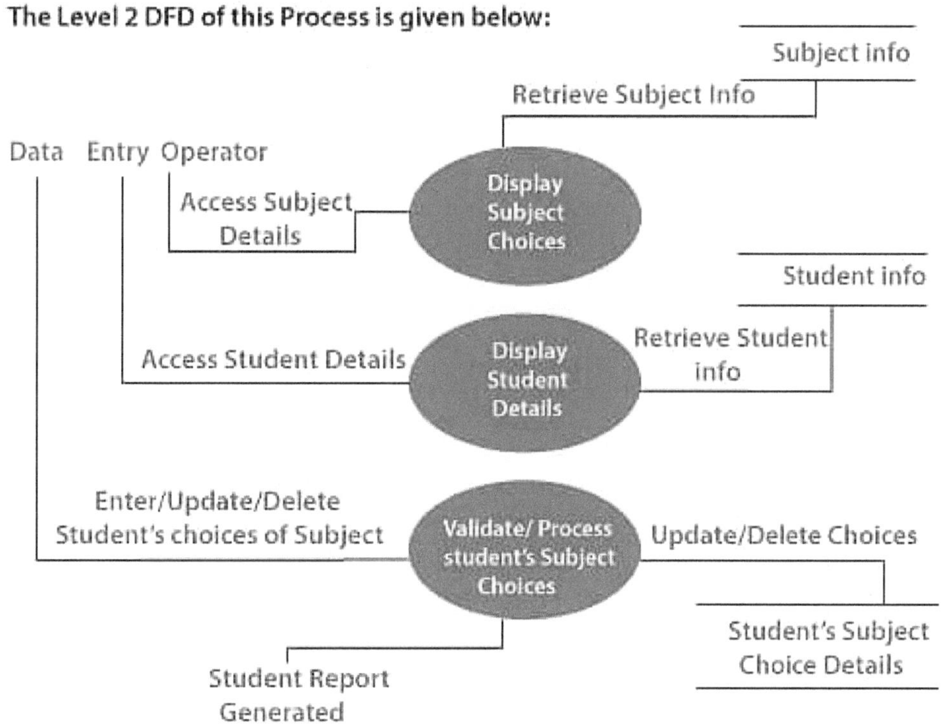

6. Marks Information Managment

The Level 2 DFD of this Process is given below:

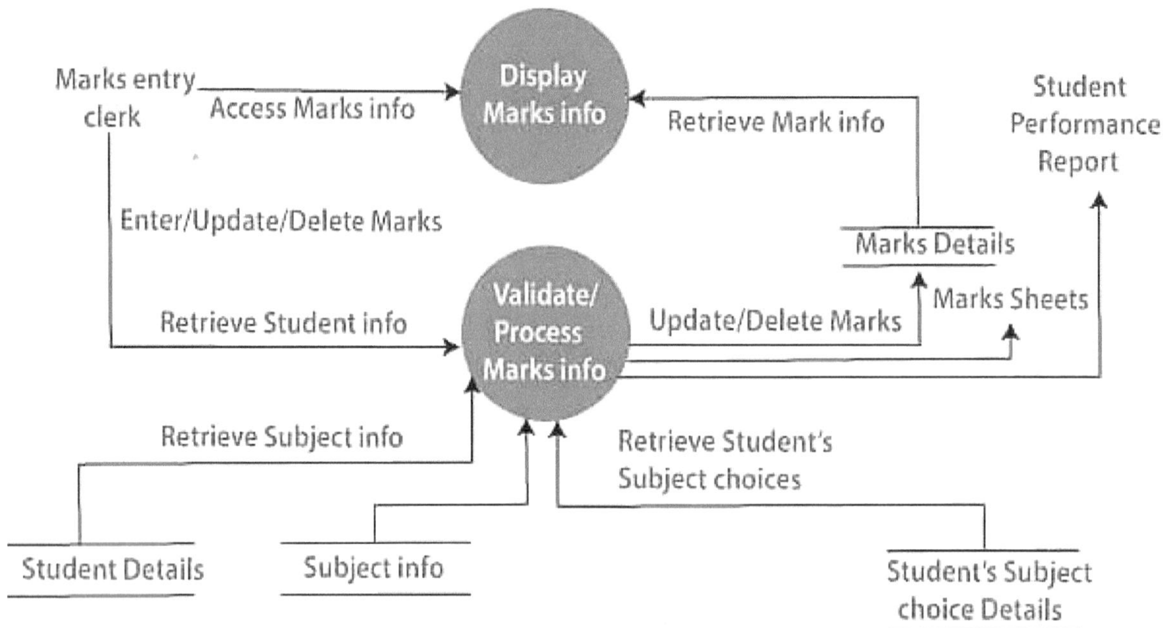

4.6 Process Modelling Concepts

Process modeling is a critical component in system design, serving as the conceptualization phase where the **processes** that operate within a system are visualized, analyzed, and optimized. This chapter delves into the fundamental concepts of process modeling, explores different modeling techniques, and discusses their application in designing complex systems. Understanding these concepts is essential for system designers to create efficient, scalable, and adaptable systems.

1. Definition and Purpose of Process Modeling

Process modeling is the graphical representation of a system's processes and their interactions. The main purpose of process modeling is to provide clear documentation and understanding of complex processes. It aids in visualizing how system processes operate, interact with one another, and how they can be improved. It is also indispensable in identifying bottlenecks and inefficiencies within a system.

2. Components of Process Models

A process model generally includes the following components:

- **Activities:** These are tasks or operations performed within the system, often represented as boxes or nodes in the model.
- **Flows:** These denote the direction of process steps, usually shown as arrows that connect activities.
- **Decisions:** Points within the process where choices are made, typically represented by diamond-shaped symbols.
- **Actors:** Entities that perform the activities. These can be people, external systems, or automated systems.
- **Data:** Information used or generated during the process, often illustrated as documents or databases.

3. Types of Process Models

Several types of process models are utilized in system design, each serving different purposes:

- **Flowcharts:** Simple diagrams that represent a sequence of steps in a process. They are useful for basic processes and are easy to understand.
- **Data Flow Diagrams (DFDs):** Focus on the movement of data through the system. They are crucial for understanding which data is input, processed, and output in different parts of the system.

- **Business Process Model and Notation (BPMN):** A more comprehensive approach that includes detailed aspects of process modeling like events, messages, and the interaction between different business entities.
- **Petri Nets:** Used for modeling concurrent processes and their synchronization and interaction. They are particularly useful in systems where multiple processes occur simultaneously.

4. Principles of Effective Process Modeling

Effective process modeling is guided by several principles:

- **Clarity:** The model should be easy to understand, with clear labels, legends, and a logical flow.
- **Accuracy:** All aspects of the model must accurately reflect the real processes.
- **Relevance:** The model should only include information that is relevant to the problem being solved.
- **Simplicity:** While maintaining accuracy, the model should be as simple as possible to avoid unnecessary complexity.

5. Process Modeling Tools and Software

Various tools and software are available to assist in the creation of process models. These tools provide functionalities ranging from simple drawing tools to complex simulation capabilities. Popular process modeling tools include Microsoft Visio, Lucidchart, and more specialized software like ARIS or Bizagi, which support specific modeling methodologies like BPMN.

6. Applying Process Modeling in System Design

- Process modeling is not just about creating diagrams; it's about understanding and improving systems. In system design, process models are used to:
- Analyze existing systems to identify inefficiencies or redundancies.
- Design new systems by specifying in detail how processes should operate.
- Communicate ideas about system changes or proposals among stakeholders.
- Support system implementation by providing clear, detailed guidelines for developers and engineers.

7. Challenges in Process Modeling

- While process modeling is highly beneficial, it also comes with challenges:
- Complexity in large systems: Larger systems may have incredibly complex processes that are difficult to model comprehensively.
- Dynamic environments: Processes might need to be updated frequently to reflect changes in the system or its environment, requiring ongoing maintenance of the models.
- Stakeholder agreement: Different stakeholders may have different views on how processes should be modeled or implemented.

4.7 Business Process Modelling Notation (BPMN)

Business Process Modeling Notation (BPMN) is a standardized graphical notation that helps stakeholders, including business analysts, software developers, and managers, visualize business processes. BPMN was developed by the Business Process Management Initiative (BPMI) and is now maintained by the Object Management Group (OMG). It serves as a common language, bridging the understanding gap between business process design and process implementation.

Purpose and Scope of BPMN

The primary goal of BPMN is to provide a notation that is readily understandable by all business users, ranging from the business analysts who create the initial drafts of processes to the technical developers responsible for implementing the technology that will perform those processes. BPMN is also aimed at the operational managers who monitor and manage these processes.

Core Elements of BPMN

BPMN's strength lies in its comprehensive set of standard symbols divided into four main categories:

1. Flow Objects

- **Events**: Circles that denote something that happens (automatically or manually) impacting the flow.
- **Activities**: Rectangles with rounded corners that represent work that needs to be done.
- **Gateways**: Diamond shapes that control the divergence and convergence of paths, depending on conditions expressed.

2. Connecting Objects
- **Sequence Flow**: Arrows that show the order in which activities occur and connect flow objects.
- **Message Flow**: Dashed arrows that show the flow of messages between two participants that are not in the same process.
- **Association**: Dotted lines used to link artifacts and data with flow objects.
3. Swimlanes
- **Pools and Lanes**: Rectangular boxes that represent participants in a process. A pool contains lanes, and each lane is a sub-participant within the pool.
4. Artifacts
- **Data Objects**: Show how data is required or produced by activities.
- **Group**: A rectangle that groups different activities but does not affect the flow.
- **Annotation**: A way of adding descriptive text.

Using BPMN in System Design

The application of BPMN in system design is integral for several reasons:
- **Clarity and Communication**: BPMN diagrams provide a clear visual representation of business processes, which improves communication among various stakeholders. This clarity helps in identifying and rectifying bottlenecks, redundancies, or inefficiencies.
- **Standardization**: BPMN's standardized approach ensures consistency in process modeling across diverse business units and technology teams.
- **Implementation and Automation**: Detailed BPMN diagrams serve as blueprints that facilitate easier and more accurate implementation of processes in BPM systems. They help in automating complex business processes into manageable tasks.

BPMN Tools

Several tools support BPMN modeling, ranging from simple diagramming tools to complex enterprise process design solutions. Popular tools include Bizagi Modeler, Visual Paradigm, and Lucidchart. These tools often provide drag-and-drop functionalities to create and edit detailed process diagrams.

Challenges and Considerations

Implementing BPMN requires careful consideration of the following:
- **Complexity Management**: While BPMN is designed to handle complexity, the creation of very complex models can sometimes defeat the purpose of using the notation, which is to clarify and streamline processes.
- **Training and Expertise**: Effective use of BPMN necessitates adequate training and understanding of its elements and best practices.
- **Integration with Existing Systems**: BPMN models need to be aligned with the existing systems and business operations to ensure they are practical and implementable.

4.8 Process Improvement Techniques

Process improvement is a critical component in the design and development of systems, emphasizing the optimization of efficiency, quality, and effectiveness. This section explores various techniques that can be utilized to enhance system design, ensuring that systems are not only robust and functional but also adaptable and scalable.

1. Lean Methodology

Lean methodology focuses on minimizing waste without sacrificing productivity. In system design, it encourages the identification and elimination of non-value-adding activities. Key principles include:
- **Value Definition:** Understanding what the customer truly needs, ensuring that the system design aligns with these expectations.
- **Value Stream Mapping:** Analyzing the flow of information and materials through the system design process to identify and eliminate inefficiencies.
- **Continuous Improvement (Kaizen):** Regularly seeking ways to reduce waste and enhance quality.

2. Six Sigma

Six Sigma is a data-driven approach aimed at improving quality by removing the causes of defects and minimizing variability in processes. It uses a structured methodology known as DMAIC (Define, Measure, Analyze, Improve, Control) to tackle problems systematically:
- **Define:** Clearly articulate the problem and the project goals.
- **Measure:** Collect data to establish baselines and understand the impact of variability.
- **Analyze:** Investigate to determine the root causes of the problem.

- **Improve:** Develop and implement solutions to address these root causes.
- **Control:** Put mechanisms in place to ensure the new process is sustainable.

3. Agile Development

Originally derived from software development, Agile practices can be applied to system design to enhance adaptability and responsiveness. It promotes iterative development, where requirements and solutions evolve through collaboration between self-organizing cross-functional teams. Key aspects include:

- **Iterative Design:** Break down the system design into manageable units and complete these in short cycles or sprints.
- **Customer Collaboration:** Regular feedback sessions with stakeholders to ensure the system meets their needs and adjust the course as needed.
- **Adaptive Planning:** Being responsive to changes in requirements, technology, and market conditions.

4. Total Quality Management (TQM)

TQM is a holistic approach to long-term success through customer satisfaction. In a TQM effort, all members of an organization participate in improving processes, products, services, and the culture in which they work. Key components in system design include:

- **Customer-Focused:** The customer ultimately determines the level of quality, so all activities focus on meeting or exceeding customer expectations.
- **Employee Involvement:** Everyone in the organization is encouraged to take part in identifying areas for improvement.
- **Process-Centric:** A fundamental part of TQM is focusing on process thinking.

5. Benchmarking

Benchmarking involves comparing the current project or process with best practices from other industries or companies. By understanding how others achieve high performance, system designers can incorporate these insights into their processes. The steps typically involve:

- **Identifying Benchmarking Partners:** Finding companies or industries that excel in areas relevant to the system design.
- **Data Collection:** Gathering data on how these entities perform and manage their systems.
- **Analysis and Implementation:** Analyzing the data to determine best practices that can be adopted and adapted.

6. Root Cause Analysis (RCA)

RCA is used to diagnose the underlying reasons for deficiencies or problems so that you can prevent them in future iterations of system design. Techniques such as the "Five Whys" help peel away layers of symptoms to reach the core of the problem.

7. Business Process Reengineering (BPR)

BPR involves radically redesigning core business processes to achieve dramatic improvements in productivity, cycle times, and quality. In system design, this might mean starting over from scratch, which can be particularly useful when existing processes are fundamentally flawed or outdated.

8. Failure Modes and Effects Analysis (FMEA)

FMEA is a systematic, proactive method for evaluating a process to identify where and how it might fail and to assess the relative impact of different failures. Implementing FMEA can help ensure that failures are minimized by the time the system design is implemented.

Summary

1. System Model Types: Includes mathematical, simulation, graphical, physical, and conceptual models, aiding in understanding, analysing, and predicting system behaviour across various fields.
2. System Modelling Techniques: Utilizes graphical notations like Unified Modelling Language (UML) to represent different system perspectives such as external, interaction, structural, and behavioural views.
3. Graphical Models: Serve multiple purposes including facilitating discussions, documenting existing systems, and describing detailed system implementations for development.
4. UML Diagrams: Essential types include activity, use case, sequence, class, and state diagrams, each providing unique insights into system operations and structure.
5. Use Case Diagrams: Show interactions between actors (users or external systems) and the system, illustrating functionalities and relationships through association, include, extend, and generalization links.

6. Activity Diagrams: Depict the dynamic aspects of the system, highlighting the flow from one activity to another with capabilities such as branching and parallel flows.
7. Entity-Relationship Diagrams (ERD): Visualize entities, attributes, and relationships within a system, crucial for database design and understanding data interactions.
8. Data Flow Diagrams (DFD): Focus on the flow of data within a system, important for analysing information movements and interactions without fixed sequence.
9. Process Modelling: Involves creating visual representations of system processes to identify inefficiencies and optimize operations, using tools like flowcharts, DFDs, and BPMN.
10. Business Process Modelling Notation (BPMN): A standardized method for detailing business processes in a visual format, helping bridge the gap between process design and implementation.
11. Process Improvement Techniques: Includes methodologies like Lean, Six Sigma, Agile, TQM, and FMEA, each aiming to enhance system design and effectiveness through specific strategies.
12. Tools and Platforms: Various tools like Lucidchart, draw.io, Microsoft Visio, and PlantUML facilitate the creation of system diagrams, supporting better collaboration and precision in design.

Glossary

1. System Models: Abstract representations that simplify and mimic real-world systems to facilitate understanding and analysis.
2. Unified Modelling Language (UML): A standardized modelling language used to visualize the design and structure of system components.
3. Mathematical Models: Use mathematical equations and formulas to simulate the behaviour and performance of systems.
4. Simulation Models: Employ software and algorithms to replicate the actions of a system to predict its behaviour in real-world scenarios.
5. Graphical Models: Visual diagrams that represent the components and workflows within a system to aid in discussion and documentation.
6. Physical Models: Tangible, often scaled-down versions of a system used for demonstrations, planning, and further study.
7. Conceptual Models: Focus on the high-level design and ideas of a system without delving into the specifics of its operations.
8. Activity Diagram: A UML diagram type that represents workflows and dynamic activities within a system.
9. Use Case Diagram: A form of UML diagram that shows how users (actors) interact with a system to achieve specific goals.
10. Entity-Relationship Diagram (ERD): Illustrates entities within a system and their interrelationships, particularly useful in database design.
11. Data Flow Diagram (DFD): Focuses on the movement and exchange of data within a system, emphasizing sources, destinations, and storage points.
12. Business Process Modelling Notation (BPMN): Provides a graphical representation of business processes in a workflow to facilitate analysis and improvement.

4.9 Project

4.9.1 Solved Project

The goal of this project is to develop an integrated Hospital Management System (HMS) to streamline operations, improve patient care, and enhance data management across various departments of a hospital. The project will encompass all aspects of system modelling, including use case modelling, activity diagrams, entity-relationship diagrams, data flow diagrams, process modelling concepts, business process modelling notation (BPMN), and process improvement techniques.

Step-by-Step Approach:

Phase 1: Overview of System Modelling

Objectives:

To gain a comprehensive understanding of system modelling principles and apply them to the HMS project.

Key Activities:

1. Literature Review: Study key concepts and best practices in system modelling.

2. Component Identification: Identify primary components of the HMS that need to be modelled, such as patient management, scheduling, billing, and medical records.
3. Expert Consultation: Engage with industry experts to gain insights and best practices in system modelling.
Outcome:
A solid understanding of system modelling principles and a clear plan for the modelling approach.

Phase 2: Use Case Modelling
Objectives:
To develop use case models that describe interactions between users and the HMS.
Key Activities:
1.Stakeholder Interviews: Conduct interviews with hospital staff (doctors, nurses, administrative personnel) to gather requirements.
2. Develop Use Cases: Create use case diagrams that capture various interactions with the HMS.
3. Verification and Validation: Review use cases with stakeholders to ensure accuracy and completeness.
Outcome:
Comprehensive use case diagrams that accurately reflect user interactions with the HMS.

Phase 3: Activity Diagrams
Objectives:
To detail the workflow of different processes within the hospital using activity diagrams.
Key Activities:
1. Process Identification: Identify key processes such as patient admission, discharge, and treatment.
2. Create Activity Diagrams: Develop activity diagrams for each identified process.
3. Stakeholder Review: Verify the accuracy and completeness of the diagrams with end-users.
Outcome:
Detailed activity diagrams that represent the workflow of hospital processes effectively.

Phase 4: Entity-Relationship Diagrams (ERDs)
Objectives:
1. To design ERDs that model the data structure for the hospital's database.
Key Activities:
1. Identify Entities and Relationships: Determine entities (e.g., patients, doctors, treatments) and their relationships.
2. Develop ERDs: Create entity-relationship diagrams.
3. Validation: Review the ERDs with database administrators to ensure accuracy and optimization.
Outcome:
Well-structured ERDs that represent the hospital's data structure accurately.

Phase 5: Data Flow Diagrams (DFDs)
Objectives:
To illustrate how data moves through the HMS using data flow diagrams.
Key Activities:
1. Map Data Flows: Identify key data flows within the system.
2. Create DFDs: Develop data flow diagrams at various levels of detail.
3. Expert Feedback: Review and refine DFDs with system analysts.
Outcome:
1. Detailed DFDs that provide a clear view of data movements within the HMS.

Phase 6: Process Modelling Concepts and BPMN
Objectives:
To apply process modelling concepts and BPMN to visualize and improve business processes.
Key Activities:
1. Select Processes: Choose critical processes for modelling, such as patient care workflows, billing, and inventory management.
2. Develop BPMN Diagrams: Create BPMN diagrams to represent these processes.

3. Optimize Processes: Identify and implement improvements based on the BPMN diagrams.
Outcome:
Optimized and well-documented business processes using BPMN.

Phase 7: Process Improvement Techniques
Objectives:
To implement techniques to enhance existing hospital processes.
Key Activities:
1. Analyse Current Processes: Evaluate existing processes for inefficiencies.
2. Apply Improvement Techniques: Implement techniques such as Lean, Six Sigma, or Kaizen to enhance processes.
3. Monitor and Adjust: Continuously monitor the impact of improvements and make necessary adjustments.
Outcome:
Enhanced and efficient hospital processes resulting in improved operations.

Deliverables:

1. System Modelling Overview Document: A comprehensive document detailing the system modelling approach.
2. Use Case Diagrams: Visual representations of user interactions with the HMS.
3. Activity Diagrams: Detailed workflow diagrams for hospital processes.
4. Entity-Relationship Diagrams: Structured data models for the hospital database.
5. Data Flow Diagrams: Clear illustrations of data movements within the system.
6. BPMN Diagrams: Visualizations of business processes and identified improvements.
7. Process Improvement Report: Documentation of implemented improvements and their impact.

4.9.2 Unsolved Project

Imagine you are developing a new application for online booking. To understand the system's functionality better, create use case models that describe the interactions between users and the system. Before proceeding, review examples of use case modelling, ensure each use case captures all essential details, verify the accuracy with stakeholders, explore alternative scenarios, and seek feedback from experienced modelers. This provides a clear picture of system requirements and user interactions.

4.10 Case Study

4.10.1 Solved Case Study

System modelling plays a crucial role in the design and implementation of complex systems by providing a structured approach to understanding various components and their interactions. It begins with an overview to identify and outline the primary elements of the system and their relationships. Use case modelling is then employed to capture the functional requirements, showcasing how different users will interact with the system in various scenarios. Activity diagrams are used to map out the workflow and sequence of operations within the system, helping to identify potential inefficiencies and areas for optimization. Entity-relationship diagrams (ERDs) are essential for detailing the data structure, defining entities, and their relationships, which is vital for effective database design. Data flow diagrams (DFDs) depict how data moves through the system, highlighting inputs, outputs, and data processing steps. Business Process Modelling Notation (BPMN) offers a standardized way to create detailed diagrams of business processes, facilitating clear communication and understanding among stakeholders. Finally, process improvement techniques are applied to refine and enhance existing processes, ensuring that the system operates efficiently and meets organizational goals.

Questions:

1. What is the initial step in system modelling?

   Answer: The initial step in system modelling is providing an overview to identify and outline the primary elements of the system and their relationships.

1. How does use case modelling contribute to system design?

Answer: Use case modelling contributes to system design by capturing functional requirements and showcasing how different users will interact with the system in various scenarios.

2. What is the role of activity diagrams in system modelling?

   Answer: Activity diagrams map out the workflow and sequence of operations within the system, helping to identify potential inefficiencies and areas for optimization.

3. Why are entity-relationship diagrams (ERDs) crucial?

   Answer: Entity-relationship diagrams (ERDs) are crucial for detailing the data structure, defining entities, and their relationships, which is vital for effective database design.

4. How does Business Process Modelling Notation (BPMN) benefit communication among stakeholders?

   Answer: Business Process Modelling Notation (BPMN) benefits communication among stakeholders by offering a standardized way to create detailed diagrams of business processes, facilitating clear understanding and communication.

4.10.2 Unsolved Case Study

System modelling is essential for developing complex projects, starting with an overview to identify key components and interactions. Use case modelling captures functional requirements by illustrating user interactions with the system. Activity diagrams represent workflows, showing the sequence of activities and decisions, which aids in optimizing process flows. Entity-relationship diagrams (ERDs) model the data structure, crucial for designing databases. Data flow diagrams (DFDs) illustrate how data moves through the system, highlighting sources, destinations, and processes involved in data handling. Business Process Modelling Notation (BPMN) provides a standardized method to create detailed diagrams of business processes, enhancing communication among stakeholders. Finally, process improvement techniques analyse and optimize existing processes to improve overall system performance.

Questions:

1. What is the purpose of use case modelling in system development?
2. How do activity diagrams help in system modelling?
3. Why are entity-relationship diagrams (ERDs) important for database design?
4. What do data flow diagrams (DFDs) illustrate in a system?
5. How does Business Process Modelling Notation (BPMN) benefit stakeholders?

4.11 Lab Activity

4.11.1 Solved Lab Activity

Create a use case diagram for an online shopping system. Include at least five use cases and three actors.

Solution:

Use Cases

1. Browse Products
2. Add to Cart
3. Checkout
4. Make Payment
5. View Order History

Actors

1. Customer
2. Payment Gateway
3. Administrator

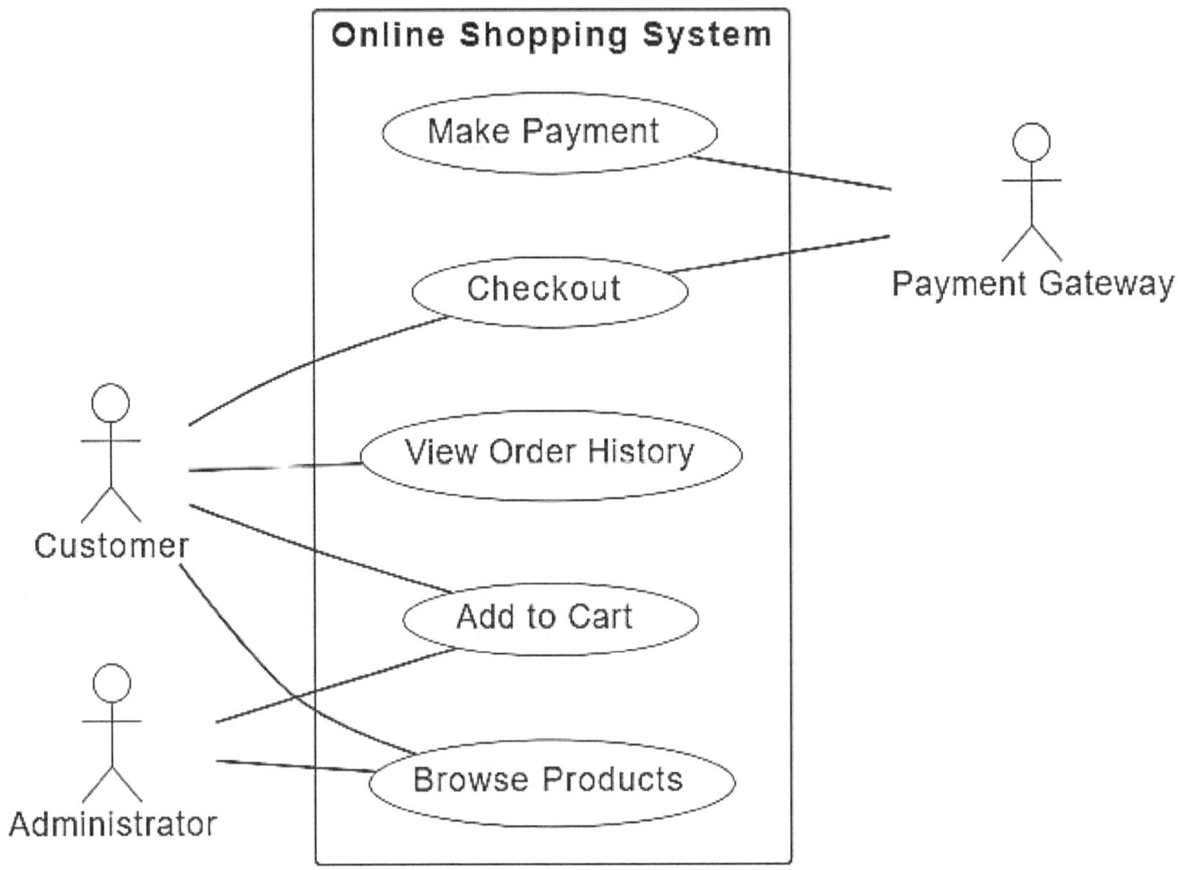

Explanation

Actors:

1. Customer: The user who interacts with the system to browse products, add items to the cart, checkout, make payments, and view order history.
2. Payment Gateway: An external system that processes payments during checkout.
3. Administrator: Manages the product listings and oversees the system operations.

Use Cases:

1. Browse Products: Customers and Administrators can browse through the list of products available in the system.
2. Add to Cart: Customers can add selected products to their shopping cart.
3. Checkout: Customers can proceed to check out the items in their cart, which interacts with the Payment Gateway.
4. Make Payment: The process where customers make payments through the Payment Gateway.
5. View Order History: Customers can view their past orders.

4.11.2 Unsolved Lab Activity

Create an activity diagram for the process of booking a flight online, from searching for flights to receiving the booking confirmation.

Previous Years Solved Questions

Q 1. Construct an Entity Relationship Diagram for employee management system. Also construct a relational database schema for it. **[IGNOU December, 2010]**

Ans 1. Entity Relationship Diagram (ERD)

Entities and Relationships:

1. Employee

2. Attributes: EmployeeID (Primary Key), FirstName, LastName, DateOfBirth, Email, Phone, HireDate, JobID (Foreign Key), DepartmentID (Foreign Key)
3. Department
4. Attributes: DepartmentID (Primary Key), DepartmentName, ManagerID (Foreign Key)
5. Job
6. Attributes: JobID (Primary Key), JobTitle, Salary
7. Project
8. Attributes: ProjectID (Primary Key), ProjectName, StartDate, EndDate
9. EmployeeProject
10. Attributes: EmployeeID (Composite Key, Foreign Key), ProjectID (Composite Key, Foreign Key), Role

Relationships:

1. Each employee works in one department, but a department can have many employees.
2. Each employee has one job, but a job can be held by many employees.
3. Each department has one manager (who is also an employee), but a manager can manage multiple departments.
4. Employees can work on multiple projects, and each project can have multiple employees working on it.
5. The role of an employee in a project is tracked.

Relational Database Schema

Employee Table

```
CREATE TABLE Employee (
   EmployeeID INT PRIMARY KEY,
   FirstName VARCHAR(50),
   LastName VARCHAR(50),
   DateOfBirth DATE,
   Email VARCHAR(100),
   Phone VARCHAR(20),
   HireDate DATE,
   JobID INT,
   DepartmentID INT,
   FOREIGN KEY (JobID) REFERENCES Job(JobID),
   FOREIGN KEY (DepartmentID) REFERENCES Department(DepartmentID)
);
```

Department Table

```
CREATE TABLE Department (
   DepartmentID INT PRIMARY KEY,
   DepartmentName VARCHAR(100),
   ManagerID INT,
   FOREIGN KEY (ManagerID) REFERENCES Employee(EmployeeID)
);
```

Job Table

```
CREATE TABLE Job (
   JobID INT PRIMARY KEY,
   JobTitle VARCHAR(100),
   Salary FLOAT
);
```

Project Table

```
CREATE TABLE Project (
   ProjectID INT PRIMARY KEY,
   ProjectName VARCHAR(100),
   StartDate DATE,
   EndDate DATE
);
```

EmployeeProject Table

```
CREATE TABLE EmployeeProject (
    EmployeeID INT,
    ProjectID INT,
    Role VARCHAR(50),
    PRIMARY KEY (EmployeeID, ProjectID),
    FOREIGN KEY (EmployeeID) REFERENCES Employee(EmployeeID),
    FOREIGN KEY (ProjectID) REFERENCES Project(ProjectID)
);
```

Previous Years Unsolved Questions

Q 1. A system analyst is a change agent, motivator, an organizer, an architect and an intelligent sales person. Elucidate. [Udaipur University, 2018]
Q 2. Draw a detailed DFD for Hospital Management. [Udaipur University, 2018]
Q 3. What are DFDs? What are the considerations involved in developing DFD? Illustrate through a suitable example of your choice. [Jodhpur University, April 2018]
Q 4. Draw a data flow diagrams (DFDs) fill 2-levels depicting the various processes, data flow and data repositories for a "Computer-Institute Management System". Follow the appropriate conventions/ symbols as given in your study material. **[IGNOU JUNE, 2010]**

Exercises

Exercise 1 – Multiple Choice Questions

1. Which diagram is primarily used to illustrate the flow of data through a system?
   A) Entity-Relationship Diagram
   B) Data Flow Diagram
   C) Activity Diagram
   D) Use Case Diagram
2. Which of the following is NOT a component of an Entity-Relationship Diagram?
   A) Actor
   B) Entity
   C) Relationship
   D) Attribute
3. Activity diagrams are used to:
   A) Show the logical flow of data within the system.
   B) Represent the dynamic aspects of a system.
   C) Illustrate the system's database structure.
   D) Model the system's higher-level business process.
5. Business Process Modelling Notation (BPMN) is used for:
   A) Designing user interfaces.
   B) Structuring system databases.
   C) Modelling business processes.
   D) Creating data flow diagrams.
6. Which modelling concept is specifically designed to represent system processes and their interactions?
   A) Data Flow Diagram
   B) Use Case Diagram
   C) Activity Diagram
   D) Process Modelling

Exercise 2 – True/False

1. Data Flow Diagrams (DFDs) are used to represent the timing of processes within a system.
2. Process modeling concepts only apply to the manufacturing sector.
3. Business Process Modelling Notation (BPMN) is a graphical representation that describes the steps in a business process.

Exercise 3 – Fill in the blanks

1. A __________ provides a graphical overview of the functional requirements of a system.
2. __________ diagrams are used to represent the flow of control or data within a system and help in specifying the interactions between different parts.
3. In system modelling, __________ Modelling Concepts focus on the systematic representation of the system processes.

Exercise 4- Fill in the blanks with two options

1. __________ is a graphical representation that uses symbols to convey the steps and sequence of activities within a process, commonly used in __________.
2. To visualize the relationships and dependencies between entities in a system, one would use an __________ diagram, which is crucial in __________.
3. A __________ is a behavioral diagram that illustrates the actors and their interaction with a system, widely employed in __________.

Exercise 5- Give two answers for the following:

1. Techniques for System Modeling's
2. Components of Use Case Modelling
3. Types of Diagrams in System Modelling
4. Elements of an Entity-Relationship Diagram
5. Elements in Data Flow Diagrams

Exercise 6- Rearrange the sentence

1. modelling system use case involves user interactions.
2. diagrams represent entities relationship entity and there.
3. flow data of diagrams movement data represent.

Exercise 7- Choose the Odd One Out

1. Use Case Modelling, Activity Diagrams, Entity-Relationship Diagrams, Process Improvement
2. Data Flow Diagrams, Process Modelling Concepts, Business Process Modelling Notation, Use Case Modelling
3. Entity-Relationship Diagrams, Activity Diagrams, Data Flow Diagrams, Overview of System Modelling

Exercise 8- Jumble words

1. asceu
2. tatadiag
3. londesihta

Exercise 9- Match case

Column 1	Column 2
1. What modelling tool is primarily used for capturing the dynamic aspects and the flow of activities within a system?	a. Entity-Relationship Diagrams
2. Which diagram is used to model the data aspects of systems, showing how entities are related to each other?	b. Data Flow Diagrams
3. What is the focus of Business Process Modelling Notation (BPMN)?	c. Process Improvement Techniques
4. What diagram provides a visual outline of the data movement throughout an organization?	d. Activity Diagrams
5. What modelling concept is critical for documenting the steps in business processes to analyse and improve them?	e. Use Case Modelling

Exercise 10- Assertion – Reason

1. Assertion (A): Entity-Relationship Diagrams (ERDs) are essential for effectively modeling the relationships between data entities in a system.

Reason (R): ERDs provide a visual representation of data entities, which helps in understanding how different parts of the system interact and manage data.

Options:

1. Assertion (A) is true, and Reason (R) is the correct reason for Assertion (A).
2. Assertion (A) is true, but Reason (R) is not the correct reason for Assertion (A).
3. Assertion (A) is false, but Reason (R) is true.
4. Assertion (A) is false, and Reason (R) is also false.

Exercise 11- One- word

1. What diagram is used to show how entities relate to each other within a system?
2. Which diagram focuses on the flow of data within a system and does not show control logic?
3. What general term is used for representing the steps in a system process?

Exercise 12- Small Answers

1. Describe the main components of a use case diagram.
2. What is an activity diagram and how does it differ from a process flow diagram?
3. Identify the three primary components of an entity-relationship diagram.

Exercise 13- Long Answers

1. Discuss the significance of activity diagrams in modelling business processes. How do they differ from flowcharts, and in what scenarios are activity diagrams particularly useful? Illustrate your answer with an example involving a customer service process.
2. What is an entity-relationship diagram, and how does it help in designing databases? Provide a detailed example of an ERD for a library management system, including entities, relationships, and cardinalities.

Answers

Exercise 1- 1) Data Flow Diagram, 2) Actor, 3) Represent the dynamic aspects of a system, 4) Modelling business processes, 5) Process Modelling
Exercise 2- 1) False, 2) False, 3) True
Exercise 3- Use Case Diagram 1) Use Case, 2) Activity, 3) Process
Exercise 4- 1) Activity Diagrams, system design, 2) Entity-Relationship, database design, 3 Use Case Modelling, requirements gathering
Exercise 5- 1) Use-Case Modelling, Activity Diagrams, 2) Actors, Use Cases, 3) Entity-Relationship Diagrams, Data Flow Diagrams Entity-Relationship Diagrams, Data Flow Diagrams, 4) Entities, Relationships, 5) Processes, Data Stores
Exercise 6- 1) Use case modelling involves user interactions, 2) Entity-relationship diagrams represent entities and their relationship, 3) Data flow diagrams represent movement of data
Exercise 7- 1) Process Improvement, 2) Use Case Modelling, 3) Overview of System Modelling
Exercise 8- 1) Case, 2) Diagram, 3) Relationship
Exercise 9- 1 d, 2 a, 3 b, 4 b, 5 e
Exercise 10- a) Assertion (A) is true and Reason (R) is the correct reason for Assertion (A).
Exercise 11- 1) Entity-Relationship, 2) Data Flow, 3) Process Modelling

Online Resources

Online Exam paper

URL https://forms.gle/jd4vjQvaH4LywJbv5

QR Code

YouTube Video
URL https://www.youtube.com/playlist?list=PLzlh_31VWEFpa7PV3GpfX2YOKVcRdoDSR
QR Code

More Test Papers Practices

Test Paper-1
URL: https://forms.gle/BGKWKPgtTFcmsQ229
QR Code

Test Paper-2
URLhttps://forms.gle/VQUnyUA1JUxQjTub7
QR Code

System analysis and design Test Paper
Chapter- 4
System Modelling

Time Duration: 30 Minutes **Maximum Marks: 25**

General Instructions:

1. The question paper consists of answer any 12 questions out of the given 19 questions and is divided into four sections, A, B, C and D.
2. All questions are compulsory.
3. Section A comprises question numbers 1 to 8. These are MCQs and one liner of one mark each. You are to select one most appropriate response out of the four provided options.
4. Section B comprises question numbers 1 to 5. These are SAQs carrying two marks each.
5. Section C comprises question numbers 1 to 4. These are SAQs carrying four marks each.
6. Section D comprises question numbers 1& 2. These are LAQs carrying five marks each.

SECTION-A

I. <u>Answer any 6 questions out of the given 8 questions</u> **(1*6=6)**

1. What is the primary purpose of system modelling in system development?
   A) To write code for the system
   B) To create a blueprint for system design and implementation
   C) To test the system for bugs
   D) To deploy the system
2. Which diagram is primarily used to represent the functional requirements of a system through user interactions?
   A) Activity Diagram
   B) Entity-Relationship Diagram
   C) Use Case Diagram
   D) Data Flow Diagram
3. What does an Entity-Relationship Diagram (ERD) mainly depict?
   A) Workflow processes
   B) System functionalities
   C) Data and the relationships between data entities
   D) User interfaces
4. Which diagram is used to show the flow of data within a system, including the sources, processes, and destinations?
   A) Use Case Diagram
   B) Activity Diagram
   C) Entity-Relationship Diagram
   D) Data Flow Diagram
5. What does BPMN stand for in the context of system modelling?
   A) Business Process Modelling Network
   B) Business Process Model and Notation
   C) Business Process Management Notation
   D) Business Process Mapping Network
6. What type of diagram is used to represent the dynamic aspects of a system's workflow?
7. What diagram type is used to model the logical structure of databases?
8. What term describes the iterative enhancement of processes within an organization?

SECTION-B

II. <u>Answer any 3 questions out of the given 5 questions</u> **(2*3=6)**

1. Define 'use case modelling' in system development.
2. What is the primary purpose of an activity diagram?
3. List two components typically found in an Entity-Relationship Diagram (ERD).
4. What is a data flow diagram used for in system analysis?
5. How does BPMN help in process modelling?

SECTION-C

II. <u>Answer any 2 questions out of the given 4 questions</u> **(4*2=8)**

1. Explain the significance of system modelling in the context of software development.
2. Describe the key elements of a use case diagram and their roles.
3. What are the main differences between an activity diagram and a data flow diagram?
4. Discuss the benefits of using Entity-Relationship Diagrams (ERDs) in database design.

SECTION-D

III. <u>Answer any 1 question out of the given 2 questions</u> **(5*1=5)**

1. Analyse the role of Business Process Modelling Notation (BPMN) in improving organizational workflows. Provide examples of how BPMN can be applied in a real-world business scenario.
2. Discuss the importance of process improvement techniques in system development. How do these techniques contribute to the efficiency and effectiveness of organizational processes?

Chapter 5: Database Fundamentals

- Understanding Database Fundamentals
- Entity-Relationship Modelling (ERD)
- Normalization Techniques
- Designing Efficient Databases

5.1 Database Fundamentals

A database is a structured collection of data that supports the storage, manipulation, and retrieval of information. Databases are integral to modern software systems, enabling data persistence across various applications and platforms.

Types of Databases

1. Relational Databases (RDBMS): The most common type of database in system design is the Relational Database Management System (RDBMS). These databases store data in tables, which are linked by relationships (foreign keys). This structure supports a wide range of data types and complex querying through SQL (Structured Query Language). Popular examples include MySQL, PostgreSQL, and Oracle.
2. NoSQL Databases: As system requirements have evolved, NoSQL databases have gained popularity for scenarios where relational databases might not be the best fit. These databases are designed for specific data models and have flexible schemas for handling large volumes of distributed data. Types of NoSQL databases include key-value stores, document databases, wide-column stores, and graph databases. Examples are MongoDB (document), Redis (key-value), Cassandra (wide-column), and Neo4j (graph).

Database Design Principles

1. Normalization: Normalization is a fundamental concept in database design, especially for RDBMS. It involves organizing columns (attributes) and tables (relations) to minimize data redundancy and improve data integrity. Normalization is typically implemented through several normal forms, each addressing different types of anomalies.
2. Denormalization: In contrast, denormalization involves adding redundant data to one or more tables to improve read performance. This technique is often used in read-heavy applications and can be beneficial in NoSQL database systems, where join operations are not as efficient as in relational systems.
3. Data Integrity: Ensuring data integrity involves maintaining the accuracy, consistency, and reliability of data throughout its lifecycle. This is achieved through constraints (such as primary keys and foreign keys), which enforce rules on the data entered the database.

SQL and Transactions

1. SQL: SQL is the standard language used to interact with relational databases. It provides powerful tools to create, modify, manage, and query data. SQL commands are divided into several types, including DDL (Data Definition Language), DML (Data Manipulation Language), and DCL (Data Control Language).
2. Transactions: A transaction in a database system is a sequence of operations that are executed as a single logical unit of work. Transactions must adhere to the ACID properties (Atomicity, Consistency, Isolation, Durability) to ensure that the database remains in a consistent state even in case of system failures.

Database Performance and Optimization

1. Indexing: Indexes are critical for improving database query performance. An index creates a data structure that allows for fast searching, which can significantly speed up the retrieval of data.
2. Query Optimization: Query optimization involves rewriting queries in ways that maximize their efficiency. Database systems often include a query optimizer, which automatically attempts to determine the most efficient way to execute a given query.
3. Caching: Caching is another vital aspect of enhancing database performance. It involves temporarily storing copies of frequently accessed data in a faster storage system, which reduces the load on the database server.

Applying Databases in System Design

1. Scalability: Designing databases for scalability involves considering how the database will handle increased loads. This can be achieved through techniques such as sharding, partitioning, and replication.

2. Security: Security in databases involves implementing measures to protect data from unauthorized access and breaches. This includes encryption, secure access controls, and regular audits.
3. Data Warehousing and Business Intelligence: For analytical processing, data warehousing provides a system for reporting and analyzing data. This is crucial in business intelligence applications where decision-makers need to query large amounts of historical data for insights.

5.2 Entity-Relationship Modelling

Entity-Relationship (ER) Modeling is a fundamental aspect of systems design, providing a visual representation of the data requirements of a system. This conceptual modeling technique helps in designing a database at the conceptual level, serving as a bridge between system requirements and the eventual database design. In this chapter, we explore the components, methodologies, and practical applications of ER modeling in system design.

1. Introduction to ER Modeling

Entity-Relationship modeling was developed by Peter Chen in 1976 to address the need for a standardized approach to database design. This method uses a graphical approach to create data models that represent the informational needs of a system. ER models are pivotal in the systems design phase because they facilitate understanding and communication among stakeholders such as database designers, developers, and business analysts.

2. Components of an ER Diagram

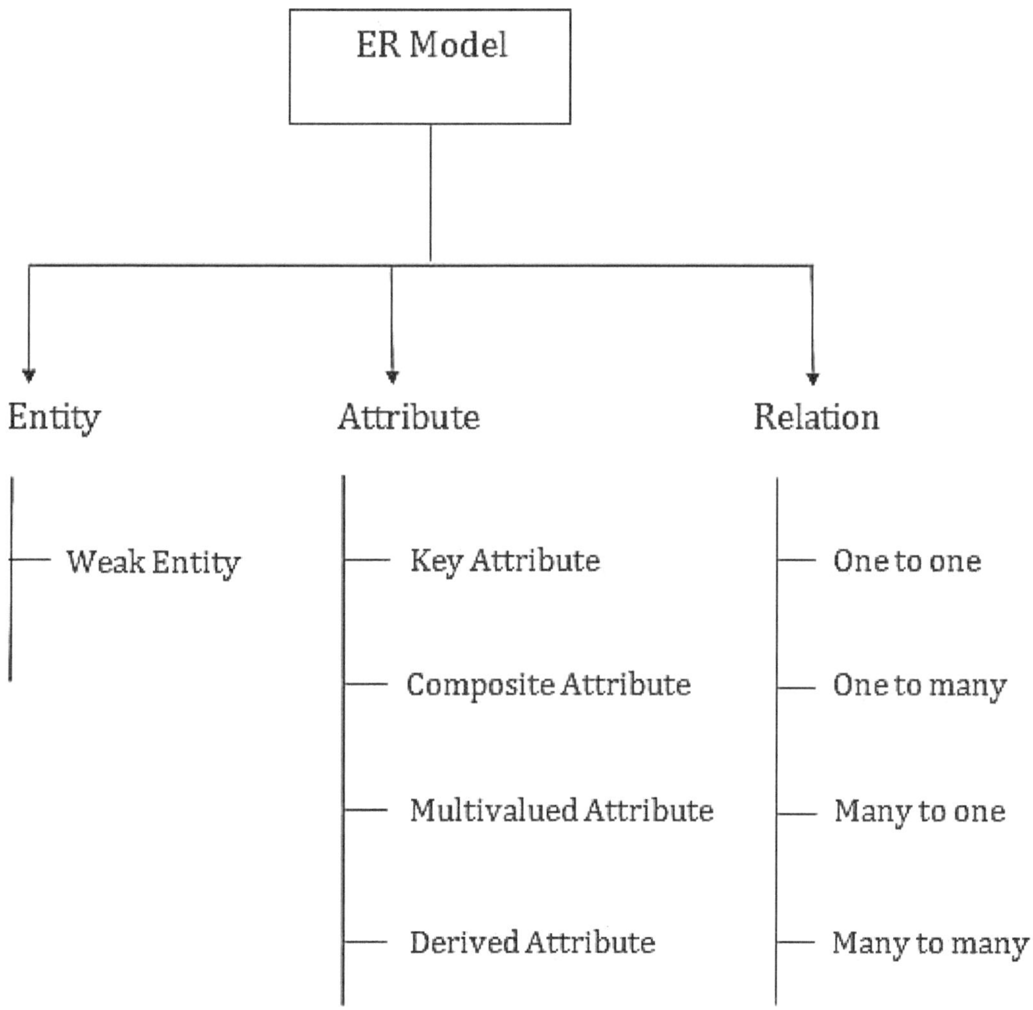

1. Entity:

An entity may be any object, class, person or place. In the ER diagram, an entity can be represented as rectangles.

Consider an organization as an example- manager, product, employee, department etc. can be taken as an entity.

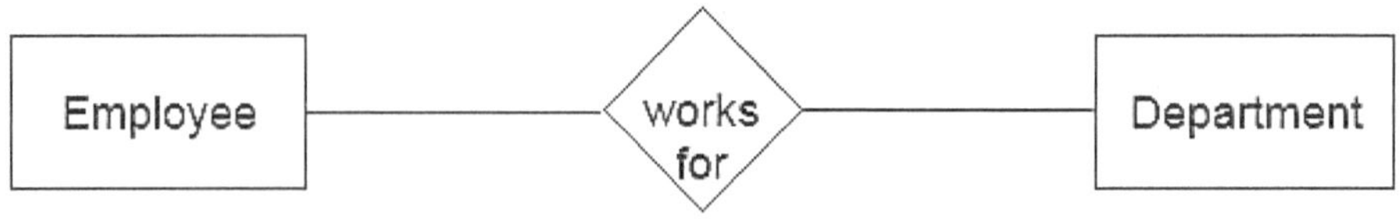

a. Weak Entity

An entity that depends on another entity is called a weak entity. The weak entity doesn't contain any key attribute of its own. The weak entity is represented by a double rectangle.

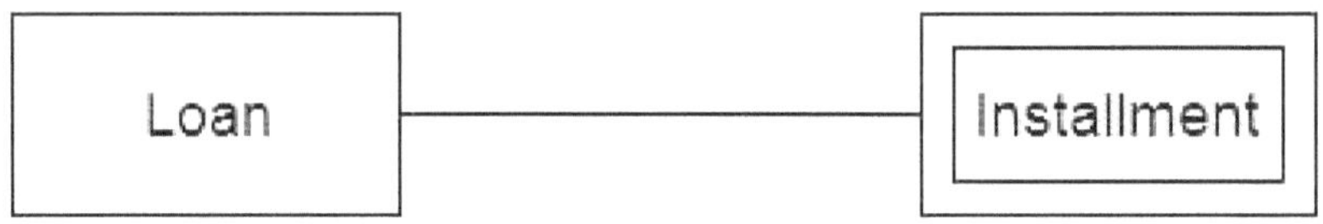

2. Attribute

The attribute is used to describe the property of an entity. Eclipse is used to represent an attribute.
For example, id, age, contact number, name, etc. can be attributes of a student.

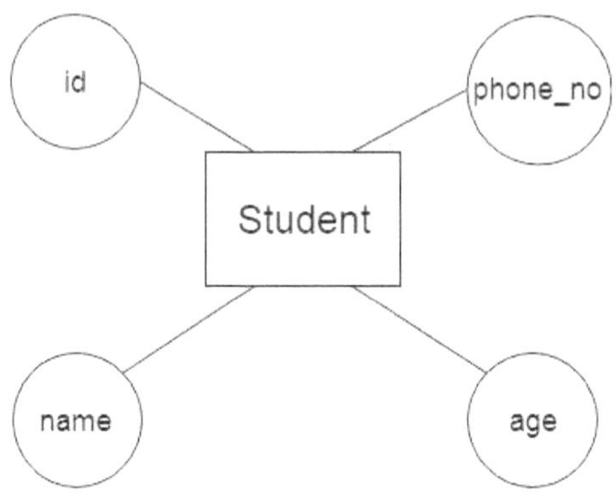

a. Key Attribute

The key attribute is used to represent the main characteristics of an entity. It represents a primary key. The key attribute is represented by an ellipse with the text underlined.

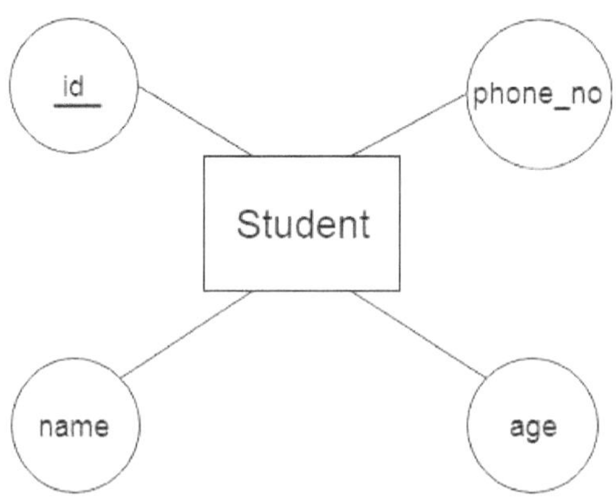

b. Composite Attribute

An attribute that is composed of many other attributes is known as a composite attribute. The composite attribute is represented by an ellipse, and those ellipses relate to an ellipse.

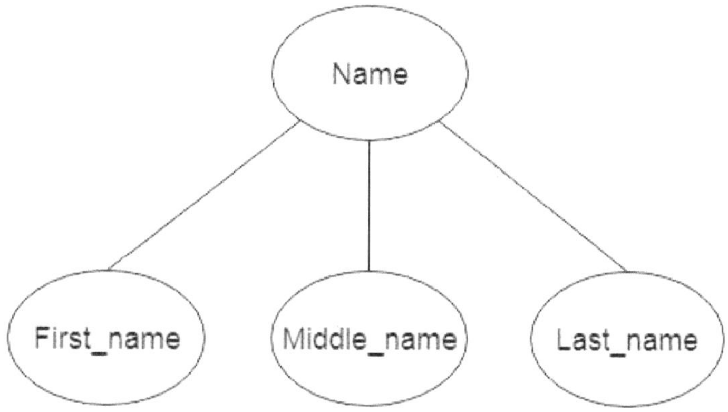

c. Multivalued Attribute

An attribute can have more than one value. These attributes are known as multivalued attributes. The double oval is used to represent multivalued attributes.

For example, a student can have more than one phone number.

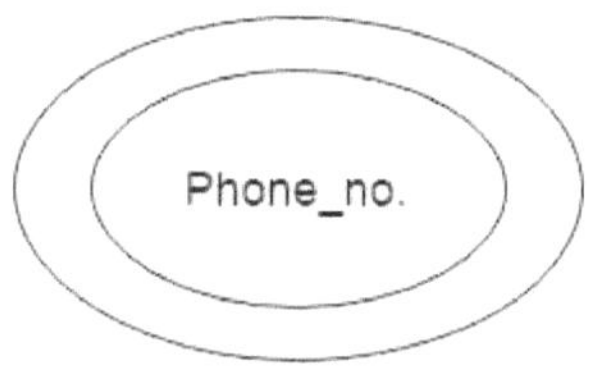

d. Derived Attribute

An attribute that can be derived from another attribute is known as a derived attribute. It can be represented by a dashed ellipse.

For example, A person's age changes over time and can be derived from another attribute like Date of birth.

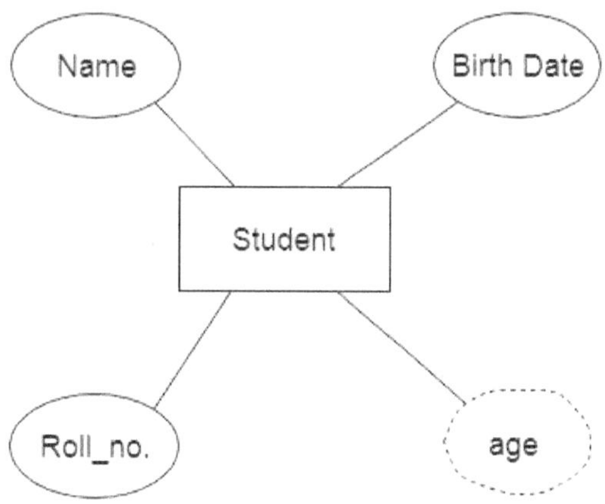

3. Relationship

A relationship is used to describe the relation between entities. Diamond or rhombus is used to represent the relationship.

Types of relationship are as follows:
a. One-to-One Relationship
When only one instance of an entity is associated with the relationship, then it is known as one-to-one relationship.
For example, A female can marry to one male, and a male can marry to one female.

b. One-to-many relationship
When only one instance of the entity on the left, and more than one instance of an entity on the right associates with the relationship then this is known as a one-to-many relationship.
For example, Scientist can invent many inventions, but the invention is done by the only specific scientist.

c. Many-to-one relationship
When more than one instance of the entity on the left, and only one instance of an entity on the right associates with the relationship then it is known as a many-to-one relationship.
For example, Student enrolls for only one course, but a course can have many students.

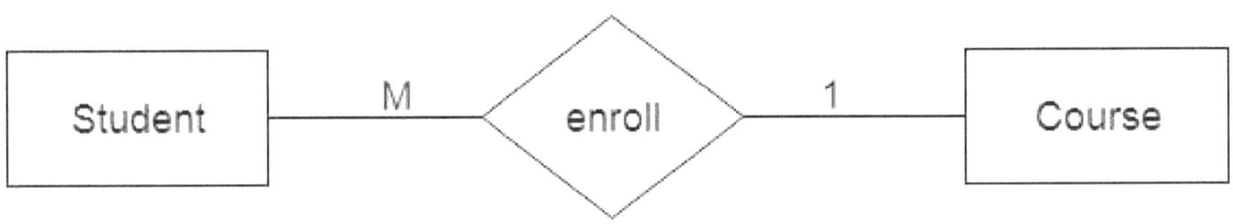

d. Many-to-many relationship
When more than one instance of the entity on the left, and more than one instance of an entity on the right associates with the relationship then it is known as a many-to-many relationship.
For example, Employee can assign by many projects and projects can have many employees.

4. Developing an ER Diagram
The process of developing an ER diagram involves several steps:

- **Requirement Gathering:** Understanding the informational needs of the system through discussions with stakeholders.
- **Identifying Entities:** Recognizing the key elements that should be represented in the database.
- **Defining Relationships:** Determining how entities are associated with each other.
- **Determining Cardinalities:** Defining the numerical aspects of relationships between entities.

This structured approach ensures that the ER diagram fully represents all data requirements of the system.

5. Enhanced ER (EER) Models

Enhanced ER Models extend basic ER diagrams by introducing concepts like specialization, generalization, and categorization, which are useful for more complex databases. These concepts allow for a more nuanced representation of relationships and entity hierarchies, providing a deeper level of detail in the modeling process.

6. Practical Applications of ER Diagrams

ER diagrams are widely used in database design, particularly in:
- **Database Development:** They serve as a blueprint for creating the database structure.
- **Database Normalization:** ER diagrams help identify redundant data and thereby support the normalization process.
- **System Documentation:** They provide a clear and concise way to document database designs in system manuals and technical papers.

7. Tools for ER Diagramming

Various tools and software applications, such as Microsoft Visio, Lucidchart, and ER/Studio, facilitate the creation of ER diagrams. These tools offer drag-and-drop interfaces, making it easy to visualize and modify aspects of the database structure.

8. Challenges in ER Modeling

While ER diagrams are powerful, they come with challenges such as handling complex relationships and the potential for over-normalization, which can lead to inefficient database designs. Additionally, the initial learning curve can be steep for new system designers.

5.3 Normalization

A large database defined as a single relation may result in data duplication. This repetition of data may result in:
- Making relations very large.
- It isn't easy to maintain and update data as it would involve searching many records in relation.
- Wastage and poor utilization of disk space and resources.
- The likelihood of errors and inconsistencies increases.

So, to handle these problems, we should analyze and decompose the relations with redundant data into smaller, simpler, and well-structured relations that satisfy desirable properties. Normalization is a process of decomposing the relations into relations with fewer attributes.

What is Normalization?

- Normalization is the process of organizing the data in the database.
- Normalization is used to minimize the redundancy from a relation or set of relations. It is also used to eliminate undesirable characteristics like Insertion, Update, and Deletion Anomalies.
- Normalization divides the larger table into smaller and links them using relationships.
- The normal form is used to reduce redundancy from the database table.

Why do we need Normalization?

The main reason for normalizing the relations is removing these anomalies. Failure to eliminate anomalies leads to data redundancy and can cause data integrity and other problems as the database grows. Normalization consists of a series of guidelines that helps to guide you in creating a good database structure.

Data modification anomalies can be categorized into three types:

- Insertion Anomaly: Insertion Anomaly refers to when one cannot insert a new tuple into a relationship due to lack of data.
- Deletion Anomaly: The delete anomaly refers to the situation where the deletion of data results in the unintended loss of some other important data.
- Updatation Anomaly: The update anomaly is when an update of a single data value requires multiple rows of data to be updated.

Types of Normal Forms:

Normalization works through a series of stages called Normal forms. The normal forms apply to individual relations. The relation is said to be in a particular normal form if it satisfies constraints.
Following are the various types of Normal forms:

Normal Form	Description
1NF	A relation is in 1NF if it contains an atomic value.
2NF	A relation will be in 2NF if it is in 1NF, and all non-key attributes are fully functional dependent on the primary key.
3NF	A relation will be in 3NF if it is in 2NF, and no transition dependency exists.
BCNF	A stronger definition of 3NF is known as Boyce Codd's normal form.
4NF	A relation will be in 4NF if it is in Boyce Codd's normal form and has no multi-valued dependency.
5NF	A relation is in 5NF. If it is in 4NF and does not contain any join dependency, joining should be lossless.

Advantages of Normalization

- Normalization helps to minimize data redundancy.
- Greater overall database organization.
- Data consistency within the database.
- Much more flexible database design.
- Enforces the concept of relational integrity.

Disadvantages of Normalization

- You cannot start building the database before knowing what the user needs.
- The performance degrades when normalizing the relations to higher normal forms, i.e., 4NF, 5NF.
- It is very time-consuming and difficult to normalize relations to a higher degree.
- Careless decomposition may lead to a bad database design, leading to serious problems.

Summary

- **Database Types**: Distinguishes between Relational Databases (RDBMS), which use tables and SQL for complex querying, and NoSQL databases, which accommodate large volumes of distributed data with flexible schemas across various types such as document, key-value, wide-column, and graph stores.
- **Database Design Principles**: Emphasizes the importance of normalization to minimize redundancy and improve integrity in RDBMS, and denormalization to enhance read performance, particularly in NoSQL systems.
- **Data Integrity**: Stresses the implementation of constraints like primary keys and foreign keys to maintain data accuracy and consistency throughout its lifecycle.
- **SQL and Transactions**: Highlights SQL as the standard language for relational database interactions, and the role of transactions in ensuring database consistency with ACID properties (Atomicity, Consistency, Isolation, Durability).
- **Performance and Optimization**: Discusses the critical roles of indexing, query optimization, and caching in enhancing database query performance and overall efficiency.
- **Scalability and Security**: Outlines techniques like sharding, partitioning, and replication for scaling databases, and stresses the importance of security measures including encryption and access controls.
- **Entity-Relationship (ER) Modelling**: Introduces ER modelling as a crucial tool for visualizing data requirements and relationships in system design, using entities, attributes, and relationships to conceptualize database structures.

- **Components of an ER Diagram**: Describes entities, attributes (including key, composite, and multivalued), and relationships (including types like one-to-one and many-to-many), illustrated using graphical symbols.
- **Developing an ER Diagram**: Involves steps such as requirement gathering, identifying entities, defining relationships, and determining cardinalities to ensure comprehensive representation of data requirements.
- **Enhanced ER Models**: Explores more complex modelling features such as specialization, generalization, and categorization to address intricate database scenarios.
- **Practical Applications of ER Diagrams**: Covers their use in database development, normalization processes, and system documentation, serving as blueprints for database construction and maintenance.
- **Normalization Process**: Details the objectives of normalization in reducing data redundancy and avoiding anomalies during data modification, with various stages from 1NF through 5NF to ensure data integrity and optimal database design.

Glossary

1. **Relational Database Management System (RDBMS)**: A type of database that stores data in a structured format, using rows and tables interconnected by relationships.
2. **NoSQL Database**: Databases designed for high scalability and flexibility, supporting varied data models such as key-value, document, wide-column, and graph structures.
3. **Normalization**: A process in database design used to reduce redundancy and dependency by organizing fields and table of a database.
4. **Denormalization**: A technique used to improve the read performance of a database by adding redundant data or grouping data.
5. **SQL (Structured Query Language)**: A programming language used to manage and manipulate relational databases.
6. **ACID Properties**: Set of properties (Atomicity, Consistency, Isolation, Durability) that guarantee database transactions are processed reliably.
7. **Indexing**: A database optimization technique that uses a data structure to speed up data retrieval operations.
8. **Caching**: Storing parts of data in faster storage systems to improve performance and reduce database load.
9. **Entity**: A real-world object or concept, represented as a rectangle in ER diagrams, which has attributes and participates in relationships.
10. **Attribute**: A property or characteristic of an entity, depicted as an ellipse in ER diagrams.
11. **Relationship**: A logical connection between two or more entities that defines interaction among them, represented by a diamond shape in ER diagrams.
12. **Cardinality**: Describes the attributes of the relationship in terms of the number of entities involved (one-to-one, one-to-many, many-to-many).

5.4 Project

5.4.1 Solved Project

Suppose you are tasked with designing a new database for a retail store. Before starting, review the fundamentals of database design, ensure you understand the types of databases and their uses, verify the store's specific requirements, explore different database management systems (DBMS) to find the best fit, and ask about data security and backup solutions. This ensures a robust and efficient database design that meets the store's needs.

Approach:

Phase 1: Review Database Fundamentals

Objectives:

To build a solid foundation in database design principles.

Key Activities:

1. **Study Database Concepts:** Review key concepts such as relational databases, NoSQL databases, and hierarchical databases.
2. **Understand Uses:** Learn about different database types and their specific use cases (e.g., relational for transaction processing, NoSQL for large-scale data storage).
3. **Database Design Principles:** Study normalization, indexing, keys, and constraints to ensure efficient database design.

Outcome:
A comprehensive understanding of database design fundamentals.

Phase 2: Verify Retail Store's Specific Requirements

Objectives:
To gather and verify the specific requirements of the retail store to ensure the database meets their operational needs.

Key Activities:

1. Stakeholder Interviews: Conduct interviews with store management, sales staff, inventory managers, and IT personnel to gather detailed requirements.

2. Document Requirements: Create a detailed requirements document outlining the data to be stored, types of transactions, reporting needs, and any specific business rules.

3. Validation: Review the requirements document with stakeholders to ensure completeness and accuracy.

Outcome:
1. A validated requirements document that accurately reflects the store's needs.

Phase 3: Explore Different Database Management Systems (DBMS)

Objectives:
To evaluate and select the most suitable DBMS for the retail store's needs.

Key Activities:

1. Research DBMS Options: Explore different DBMS options such as MySQL, PostgreSQL, Oracle, Microsoft SQL Server, MongoDB, and Firebase.

2. Comparison Criteria: Compare DBMS options based on criteria such as scalability, performance, cost, ease of use, and support for required features.

3. Pilot Testing: Set up pilot databases using top DBMS candidates to test performance with sample data and typical transactions.

Outcome:
Selection of the best-fit DBMS for the retail store's requirements.

Phase 4: Design the Database

Objectives:
To design a robust and efficient database schema.

Key Activities:

1. Schema Design: Create an initial database schema based on the requirements, including tables, fields, relationships, and constraints.

2. Normalization: Apply normalization techniques to eliminate redundancy and ensure data integrity.

3. Indexing: Design indexes to optimize query performance.

4. Documentation: Document the schema design, including ER diagrams and data dictionaries.

Outcome:
A detailed and optimized database schema.

Phase 5: Implement Data Security and Backup Solutions

Objectives:
To ensure data security and establish reliable backup procedures.

Key Activities:

1. Security Measures: Implement security measures such as user authentication, role-based access control, encryption, and secure connections.

2. Backup Strategies: Develop and implement backup strategies, including full backups, incremental backups, and off-site storage.

3. Disaster Recovery Plan: Create a disaster recovery plan detailing steps to restore data and operations in case of data loss.

Outcome:
A secure database with robust backup and recovery procedures.

5.4.2 Unsolved Project

Imagine you are working on a project to create a database for a university. To accurately model the data, use entity-relationship diagrams (ERDs). Before you begin, review the principles of ER modelling, ensure you identify all relevant entities and their relationships, verify the model with university staff for accuracy, explore alternative ways to optimize the data structure, and ask for feedback from experienced database designers. This will help you create an effective and comprehensive database model.

5.5 Case Study

5.5.1 Solved Case Study

Understanding database fundamentals is crucial for designing effective data management systems. Databases can be categorized into several types, including relational databases, which use tables to store data, NoSQL databases suited for large-scale and flexible data storage needs, and hierarchical databases that arrange data in a tree-like structure. Entity-relationship (ER) modelling is a key method used to map out the data and its interrelations through entities, attributes, and relationships. Another essential component of database design is normalization, a process that organizes data to eliminate redundancy and enhance data integrity. This involves applying various normal forms (1NF, 2NF, 3NF, etc.), each with specific guidelines to streamline the database, making it more efficient, easier to manage, and scalable.

Questions:

1. What are the three types of databases mentioned in the passage?

   Answer: The three types of databases mentioned in the passage are relational databases, NoSQL databases, and hierarchical databases.

2. How do relational databases store data?

   Answer: Relational databases store data using tables.

3. What is the purpose of entity-relationship (ER) modelling?

   Answer: The purpose of entity-relationship (ER) modelling is to map out the data and its interrelations through entities, attributes, and relationships.

4. What does normalization aim to achieve in a database?

   Answer: Normalization aims to eliminate redundancy and enhance data integrity in a database.

5. What are the stages of normalization referred to as?

   Answer: The stages of normalization are referred to as normal forms (1NF, 2NF, 3NF, etc.).

5.5.2 Unsolved Case Study

Database design is fundamental for efficient data management and begins with understanding various types of databases such as relational, NoSQL, and hierarchical databases. Relational databases, the most common type, use tables to store data, whereas NoSQL databases are often used for large-scale data storage with flexible schemas, and hierarchical databases organize data in a tree-like structure. Entity-relationship (ER) modelling is a critical technique in this process, visually representing the data and its relationships through entities, attributes, and relationships. Normalization is another vital aspect, involving organizing data to reduce redundancy and improve integrity. This process, carried out in stages known as normal forms, ensures the database is efficient, scalable, and easier to maintain by eliminating duplicated data and ensuring logical data dependencies.

Questions:

1. What is the first fundamental step in database design?
2. Name the most common type of database mentioned in the passage.
3. What does entity-relationship (ER) modelling visually represent?
4. What is the purpose of normalization in database design?
5. How does normalization benefit a database?

5.6 Lab Activity

5.6.1 Solved Lab Activity

Create an Entity-Relationship Diagram (ERD) for an online bookstore, including entities such as Books, Authors, Customers, and Orders. Identify primary keys and relationships.

Solution:

Entities and Relationships:

1. Books:
2. Attributes: BookID (Primary Key), Title, Genre, Price, AuthorID (Foreign Key)
3. Authors:
4. Attributes: AuthorID (Primary Key), Name, Bio
5. Customers:
6. Attributes: CustomerID (Primary Key), Name, Email, Address
7. Orders:
8. Attributes: OrderID (Primary Key), OrderDate, CustomerID (Foreign Key)
9. OrderDetails:
10. Attributes: OrderID (Composite Key, Foreign Key), BookID (Composite Key, Foreign Key), Quantity

Relationships:

1. Each book has one author, but an author can write multiple books.
2. A customer can place multiple orders, but each order is placed by one customer.
3. Each order can contain multiple books, and a book can appear in multiple orders.

Here is the entity-relationship diagram illustrating an online bookstore:

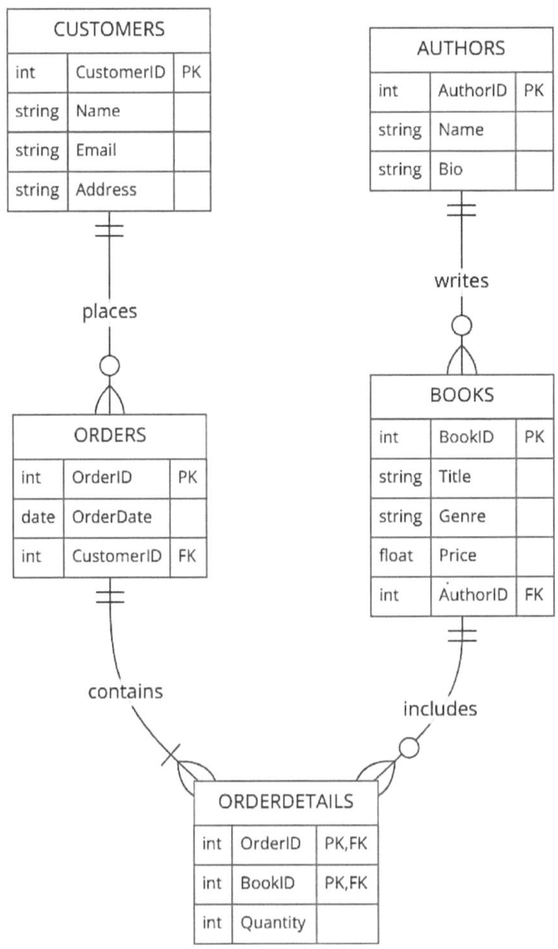

Explanation:

Entities:

1. Books
2. Attributes: BookID (Primary Key), Title, Genre, Price, AuthorID (Foreign Key)

3. Authors
4. Attributes: AuthorID (Primary Key), Name, Bio
5. Customers
6. Attributes: CustomerID (Primary Key), Name, Email, Address
7. Orders
8. Attributes: OrderID (Primary Key), OrderDate, CustomerID (Foreign Key)
9. Order Details
10. Attributes: OrderID (Composite Key, Foreign Key), BookID (Composite Key, Foreign Key), Quantity

Relationships:
1. Authors write multiple **Books**, but each **Book** has one **Author**.
2. Customers place multiple **Orders**, but each **Order** is placed by one **Customer**.
3. Each **Order** contains multiple **Books** through **OrderDetails**, and each **Book** can appear in multiple **Orders**.
4. OrderDetails links **Books** and **Orders**, capturing the quantity of each book in an order.

5.6.2 Unsolved Lab Activity

Given a sample database table with repeating groups and redundancy, normalize the table to 3NF. Document the steps and rationale for each transformation.

Previous Years Solved Questions

Q 1. What is denormalization? Give a suitable example to explain it. Also explain the process of denormalization of tables. **[IGNOU JUNE, 2011]**
Ans 1. Denormalization is the process of introducing redundancy into a database by merging tables or adding redundant data. This is done to improve the read performance of a database by reducing the number of joins needed to retrieve data. While normalization is aimed at minimizing redundancy to improve data integrity, denormalization trades off some data integrity and storage efficiency for faster query performance.

Example of Denormalization
Consider a normalized database with the following two tables:

Customer Table:

CustomerID	CustomerName
1	Alice
2	Bob

Order Table:

OrderID	CustomerID	OrderDate
101	1	2023-01-10
102	2	2023-01-12

In a normalized form, to get the customer's name along with their order details, we need to perform a join operation:

```
SELECT OrderID, CustomerName, OrderDate
FROM Order
JOIN Customer ON Order.CustomerID = Customer.CustomerID;
```

Denormalized Table: To denormalize, we combine the Customer and Order tables into one:
OrderDetails Table:

OrderID	CustomerID	CustomerName	OrderDate
101	1	Alice	2023-01-10
102	2	Bob	2023-01-12

Now, we can retrieve the order details with the customer name without needing a join:

```
SELECT OrderID, CustomerName, OrderDate
FROM OrderDetails;
```

Process of Denormalization

1. Identify Performance Bottlenecks:
2. Determine which queries are slow due to multiple joins or complex relationships between tables.
3. Analyse the Data Access Patterns:
4. Understand the common queries and access patterns to identify where denormalization might be beneficial.
5. Decide on Denormalization Strategy:
6. Choose the tables or fields to denormalize based on the analysis. This could involve combining tables, adding redundant fields, or creating summary tables.
7. Modify the Database Schema:
8. Alter the database schema to include the redundant data. This might involve creating new tables or modifying existing ones.
9. Update the Application Logic:
10. Ensure that the application logic is updated to handle the denormalized schema. This might involve changes in the data insertion, update, and deletion processes to maintain data consistency.
11. Monitor and Optimize:
12. Continuously monitor the performance of the denormalized database. Further optimizations might be required based on the performance metrics.

Previous Years Unsolved Questions

Q 1. Differentiate between various types of databases and differentiate between a DBMS and a file-system. **[IGNOU JUNE, 2011]**
Q 2. What is transaction audit? Explain four advantages of transaction audit. **[IGNOU JUNE, 2012]**
Q 3. What are the various duties performed by DBA? **[Udaipur University, 2019]**

Exercises

Exercise 1 – Multiple Choice Questions

1. What is a database?
   A) A collection of programs that manages hardware operations.
   B) A collection of related data organized for convenient access.
   C) A set of isolated data.
   D) A tool for organizing data in a spreadsheet.
2. Which of the following best defines an entity in database design?
   A) A relationship between tables.
   B) A tangible or intangible object that can be identified.
   C) The description of a role played by a user.
   D) A type of database management system.
3. What is the purpose of normalization in databases?
   A) To increase data redundancy.
   B) To reduce data integrity.
   C) To minimize data redundancy.
   D) To complicate database structure.
4. Which normal form is primarily concerned with the removal of partial dependencies?
   A) First Normal Form (1NF)
   B) Second Normal Form (2NF)
   C) Third Normal Form (3NF)
   D) Boyce-Codd Normal Form (BCNF)
5. In an entity-relationship diagram, what does a diamond symbol represent?
   A) Entity
   B) Attribute
   C) Relationship
   D) Weak Entity

Exercise 2 – True/False

1. A database management system (DBMS) is software designed to store, retrieve, and manage data in a database.
2. Normalization is a process used to minimize redundancy and dependency by organizing fields and table relationships.
3. A foreign key is a key used to link two tables together.

Exercise 3 – Fill in the blanks

1. A _______ is a collection of related data organized in a way that allows for data management and retrieval.
2. An entity-relationship (ER) diagram is used to visually represent the _______ between entities in a database.
3. The process of organizing data into tables and establishing relationships between these tables is known as _______ modeling.

Exercise 4- Fill in the blanks with two options

1. In database design, __________ is the process of organizing data attributes (or fields) to reduce redundancy and improve data integrity. The primary goal of this process is to separate data into multiple related tables to achieve __________.
2. A __________ diagram is used in database design to illustrate the logical structure of databases. It visually represents entities, attributes, and the relationships between them, which is essential in __________.
3. __________ refers to the core concepts and architectures, including data structures, data types, and data relationships, which are crucial for the design and implementation of __________.

Exercise 5- Give two answers for the following:

1. Database Management Systems
2. Components of an Entity-Relationship Diagram
3. Levels of Database Normalization
4. Types of Attributes in Entity-Relationship Modelling
5. Goals of Normalization

Exercise 6- Rearrange the sentence

1. Entities strong relationships have with other each.
2. Data is stored database in a.
3. Normalization data organizes efficiently.

Exercise 7- Choose the Odd One Out

1. Attribute, Entity, Relationship, Index
2. Primary Key, Foreign Key, Composite Key, Schema
3. First Normal Form, Second Normal Form, Third Normal Form, Data Mining

Exercise 8- Jumble words

1. atebdasa
2. iytnetliatr
3. nooaritzlmani

Exercise 9- Match case

Column 1	Column 2
1. What is the purpose of normalization?	A. Reduces data redundancy and improves data integrity
2. What does an entity in ER modelling represent?	B. Illustrates relationships between entities
3. What is a primary function of a database?	C. A collection of related data entries
4. What does the ER diagram help with?	D. An object or component within the database
5. What is a database?	E. Organizing data into structured tables to prevent anomalies

Exercise 10- Assertion – Reason

1. Assertion (A): Entity-Relationship (ER) modeling is essential for creating a well-structured database.

Reason (R): ER modeling helps in defining the data and their relationships clearly, which facilitates the process of database normalization.

Options:

1. Assertion (A) is true, and Reason (R) is the correct reason for Assertion (A).
2. Assertion (A) is true, but Reason (R) is not the correct reason for Assertion (A).
3. Assertion (A) is false, but Reason (R) is true.
4. Assertion (A) is false, and Reason (R) is also false.

Exercise 11- One- word

1. What type of diagram is used to visually represent entities and their relationships in a database?
2. What is the term for the process of organizing data to minimize redundancy?
3. In an ER diagram, what term describes a line that connects two related entities?

Exercise 12- Small Answers

1. Describe the main advantage of using a database management system (DBMS) over traditional file processing systems.
2. What are the two basic components of an entity-relationship (ER) diagram? Briefly define each component.
3. Explain the concept of the first normal form (1NF) in database normalization. What requirement must a table satisfy to be considered in 1NF?

Exercise 13- Long Answers

1. Describe the core components of a database management system (DBMS) and explain how they interact to manage data.
2. Discuss the different types of relationships in an ER diagram. Provide examples of one-to-one, one-to-many, and many-to-many relationships and explain how they are represented in the model.

Answers

Exercise 1- 1) A collection of related data organized for convenient access, 2) A tangible or intangible object that can be identified, 3) To minimize data redundancy, 4) Second Normal Form (2NF), 5) C) Relationship
Exercise 2- 1) True, 2) True, 3) True
Exercise 3- 1) database, 2) relationships, 3) entity-relationship
Exercise 4- 1) Normalization, optimal database structure, 2) Entity-Relationship, conceptual design, 3) Database Fundamentals, effective databases
Exercise 5- 1) MySQL, PostgreSQL, 2) Entities, Attributes, 3) First Normal Form (1NF), Second Normal Form (2NF), 4) Simple Attribute, Composite Attribute, 5) Eliminate Redundancy, Ensure Data Integrity
Exercise 6- 1) Entities have strong relationships with each other, 2) Data is stored in a database, 3) Normalization organizes data efficiently.
Exercise 7- 1) Index, 2) Schema, 3) Data Mining
Exercise 8- 1) Database, 2) Entity, 3) Normalization
Exercise 9- 1 A, 2 D, 3 C, 4 B, 5 E
Exercise 10- a) Assertion (A) is true, and Reason (R) is the correct reason for Assertion (A).

Exercise 11- 1) ERD (Entity-Relationship Diagram), 2) Normalization, 3) Relationship

Online Resources

Online Exam paper
URL https://forms.gle/LCEF2JTZimLa89ge7

QR Code

YouTube Video
URL https://www.youtube.com/playlist?list=PLzlh_31VWEFqy0Sa33JI5TpTakUDAario

QR Code

More Test Papers Practices

Test Paper-1
URL https://forms.gle/kZBdo5ALrfEXY2uy8
QR Code

Test Paper-2
URL https://forms.gle/y4qscyDSPYkJ7ba36
QR Code

System analysis and design Test Paper
Chapter- 5
Database Fundamentals

Time Duration: 30 Minutes **Maximum Marks: 25**

General Instructions:
1. The question paper consists of answer any 12 questions out of the given 19 questions and is divided into four sections, A, B, C and D.
2. All questions are compulsory.
3. Section A comprises question numbers 1 to 8. These are MCQs and one liner of one mark each. You are to select one most appropriate response out of the four provided options.
4. Section B comprises question numbers 1 to 5. These are SAQs carrying two marks each.
5. Section C comprises question numbers 1 to 4. These are SAQs carrying four marks each.
6. Section D comprises question numbers 1& 2. These are LAQs carrying five marks each.

SECTION-A

I. <u>Answer any 6 questions out of the given 8 questions</u> **(1*6=6)**

1. What is the primary purpose of a database in information systems?
   A) To perform calculations
   B) To store and manage data efficiently
   C) To design user interfaces
   D) To develop software applications
2. Which of the following best describes an Entity-Relationship Diagram (ERD)?
   A) A diagram that shows the flow of data within a system
   B) A diagram that represents the relationships between entities in a database
   C) A diagram that models the business processes
   D) A diagram that illustrates the user interface design
3. What is the main goal of database normalization?
   A) To improve the user interface
   B) To minimize data redundancy and improve data integrity
   C) To increase database size
   D) To speed up database development
4. Which normal form eliminates repeating groups in a table?
   A) First Normal Form (1NF)
   B) Second Normal Form (2NF)
   C) Third Normal Form (3NF)
   D) Boyce-Codd Normal Form (BCNF)
5. In an ERD, what does a diamond shape typically represent?
   A) An entity
   B) An attribute
   C) A relationship
   D) A data flow
6. What does ERD stand for in database design?
7. What term describes the process of organizing data to minimize redundancy?
8. What shape represents an entity in an ERD?

SECTION-B

II. <u>Answer any 3 questions out of the given 5 questions</u> **(2*3=6)**

1. Define 'database' in the context of information systems.
2. What is the purpose of an Entity-Relationship Diagram (ERD)?

3. List two benefits of database normalization.
4. What is the First Normal Form (1NF) in database normalization?
5. Describe the relationship between entities and attributes in an ERD.

SECTION-C

II. <u>Answer any 2 questions out of the given 4 questions</u> **(4*2=8)**

1. Explain the concept of database normalization and its importance.
2. How does an Entity-Relationship Diagram (ERD) help in database design?
3. Describe the process of converting a table to First Normal Form (1NF).
4. Discuss the differences between First Normal Form (1NF) and Third Normal Form (3NF).

SECTION-D

III. <u>Answer any 1 question out of the given 2 questions</u> **(5*1=5)**

1. Discuss the three main normal forms in database normalization (1NF, 2NF, 3NF) and provide examples of each. Explain how these forms help in reducing data redundancy and improving data integrity.
2. Analyse the role of Entity-Relationship Diagrams (ERDs) in the database design process. Provide examples to illustrate how ERDs contribute to understanding and organizing data requirements for a system.

Chapter 6: Advanced Database Design

-Database Design
- Architectural Design
- Interface Design
- Design Patterns

6.1 Database Design

Database design can be generally defined as a collection of tasks or processes that enhance the designing, development, implementation, and maintenance of enterprise data management system. Designing a proper database reduces the maintenance cost thereby improving data consistency and the cost-effective measures are greatly influenced in terms of disk storage space. Therefore, there must be a brilliant concept of designing a database. The designer should follow the constraints and decide how the elements correlate and what kind of data must be stored.
The main objectives behind database designing are to produce physical and logical design models of the proposed database system. To elaborate this, the logical model is primarily concentrated on the requirements of data and the considerations must be made in terms of monolithic considerations and hence the stored physical data must be stored independent of the physical conditions. On the other hand, the physical database design model includes a translation of the logical design model of the database by keeping control of physical media using hardware resources and software systems such as Database Management System (DBMS).

Why is Database Design important?

The important considerations that can be considered while emphasizing the importance of database design can be explained in terms of the following points given below.
1. Database designs provide the blueprints of how the data is going to be stored in a system. The proper design of a database highly affects the overall performance of any application.
2. The designing principles defined for a database give a clear idea of the behavior of any application and how the requests are processed.
3. Another instance to emphasize database design is that a proper database design meets all the requirements of users.
4. Lastly, the processing time of an application is greatly reduced if the constraints of designing a highly efficient database are properly implemented.

Life Cycle

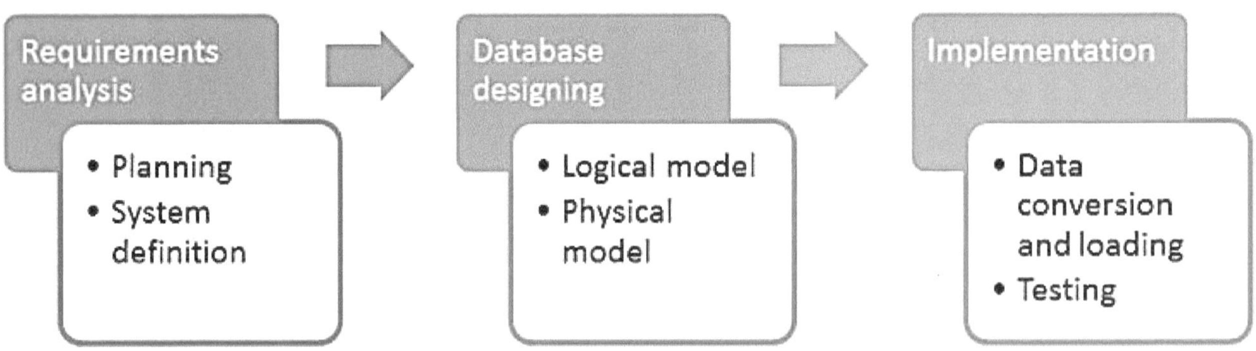

Although, the life cycle of a database is not an important discussion that has to be taken forward in this article because we are focused on the database design. But before jumping directly on the designing models constituting database design it is important to understand the overall workflow and life cycle of the database.

Requirement Analysis

First, the planning must be done regarding what are the basic requirements of the project under which the design of the database must be taken forward. Thus, they can be defined as: -

- **Planning** - This stage is concerned with planning the entire DDLC (Database Development Life Cycle). The strategic considerations are considered before proceeding.
- **System definition** - This stage covers the boundaries and scopes of the proper database after planning.

Database Designing

The next step involves designing the database considering the user-based requirements and splitting them out into various models so that load or heavy dependencies on a single aspect are not imposed. Therefore, there has been some model-centric approach and that's where logical and physical models play a crucial role.
- **Physical Model** - The physical model is concerned with the practices and implementations of the logical model.
- **Logical Model** - This stage is primarily concerned with developing a model based on the proposed requirements. The entire model is designed on paper without any implementation or adopting DBMS considerations.

Implementation

The last step covers the implementation methods and checking out the behavior that matches our requirements. It is ensured with continuous integration testing of the database with different data sets and conversion of data into machine understandable language. The manipulation of data is primarily focused on these steps where queries are made to run and check if the application is designed satisfactorily or not.
- **Data conversion and loading** - This section is used to import and convert data from the old to the new system.
- **Testing** - This stage is concerned with error identification in the newly implemented system. Testing is a crucial step because it checks the database directly and compares the requirement specifications.

Database Design Process

The process of designing a database carries various conceptual approaches that need to be kept in mind. An ideal and well-structured database design must be able to:
1. Save disk space by eliminating redundant data.
2. Maintains data integrity and accuracy.
3. Provides data access in useful ways.
4. Comparing Logical and Physical data models.

Logical

A logical data model generally describes the data in as many details as possible, without having to be concerned about the physical implementations in the database. Features of logical data model might include:
1. All the entities and relationships amongst them.
2. Each entity has well-specified attributes.
3. The primary key for each entity is specified.
4. Foreign keys which are used to identify a relationship between different entities are specified.
5. Normalization occurs at this level.

A logical model can be designed using the following approach:
1. Specify all the entities with primary keys.
2. Specify concurrent relationships between different entities.
3. Figure out each entity attributes
4. Resolve many-to-many relationships.
5. Carry out the process of normalization.

Also, one important factor after following the above approach is to critically examine the design based on requirement gathering. If the above steps are strictly followed, there are chances of creating a highly efficient database design that follows the native approach.
To understand these points, see the image below to get a clear picture.

Logical Data Model

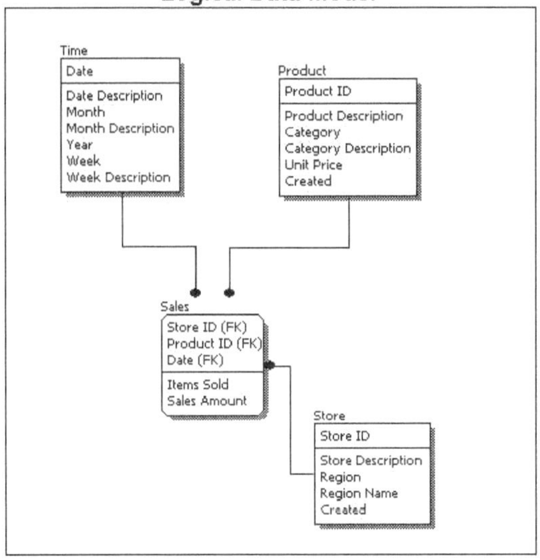

If we compare the logical data model as shown in the figure above with some sample data in the diagram, we can come up with facts that in a conceptual data model there are no presence of a primary key whereas a logical data model has primary keys for all its attributes. Also, logical data models the cover relationship between different entities and carries room for foreign keys to establish relationships among them.

Physical

A Physical data mode generally represents the approach or concept of designing the database. The main purpose of the physical data model is to show all the **structures** of the table including the **column name, column data type, constraints, keys (primary and foreign)**, and the relationship among tables. The following are the features of a physical data model:

1. Specifies all the columns and tables.
2. Specifies foreign keys that usually define the relationship between tables.
3. Based on user requirements, de-normalization might occur.
4. Since the physical consideration is considered so there will be straightforward reasons for difference than a logical model.
5. Physical models might be different for different RDBMS. For example, the data type column may be different in MySQL and SQL Server.

While designing a physical data model, the following points should be taken into consideration:

1. Convert the entities into tables.
2. Convert the defined relationships into foreign keys.
3. Convert the data attributes into columns.
4. Modify the data model constraints based on physical requirements.

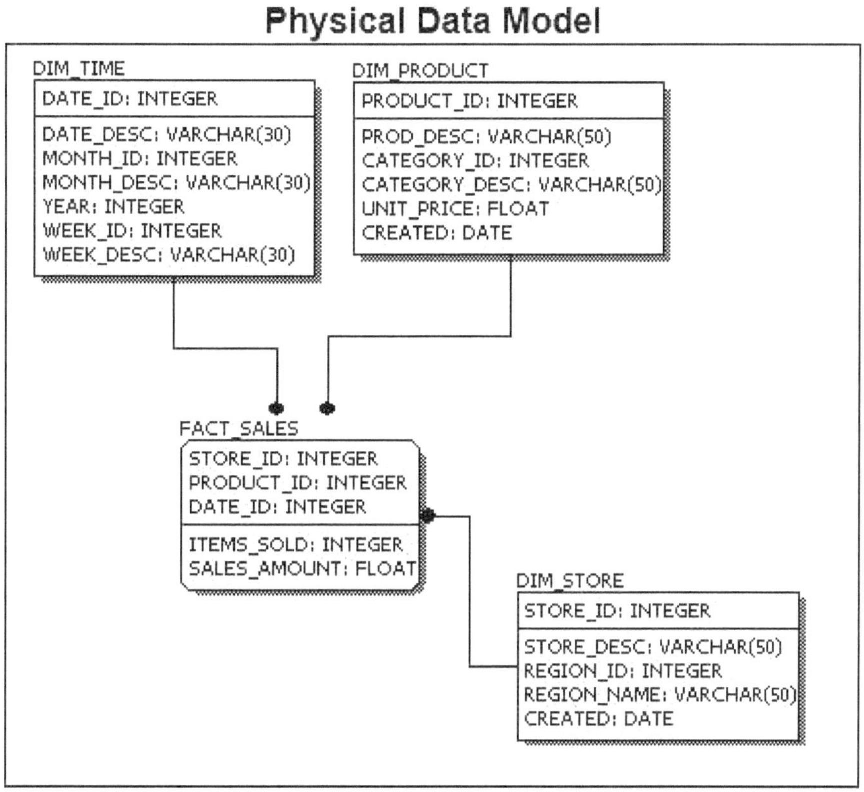

Comparing this physical data model with the logical with the previous logical model, we might conclude the differences that in physical database entity names are considered table names and attributes are considered column names. Also, the data type of each column is defined in the physical model depending on the actual database used.

6.2 Architectural Design

The architecture of a system describes its major components, their relationships (structures), and how they interact with each other. Software architecture and design includes several contributory factors such as Business strategy, quality attributes, human dynamics, design, and IT environment.

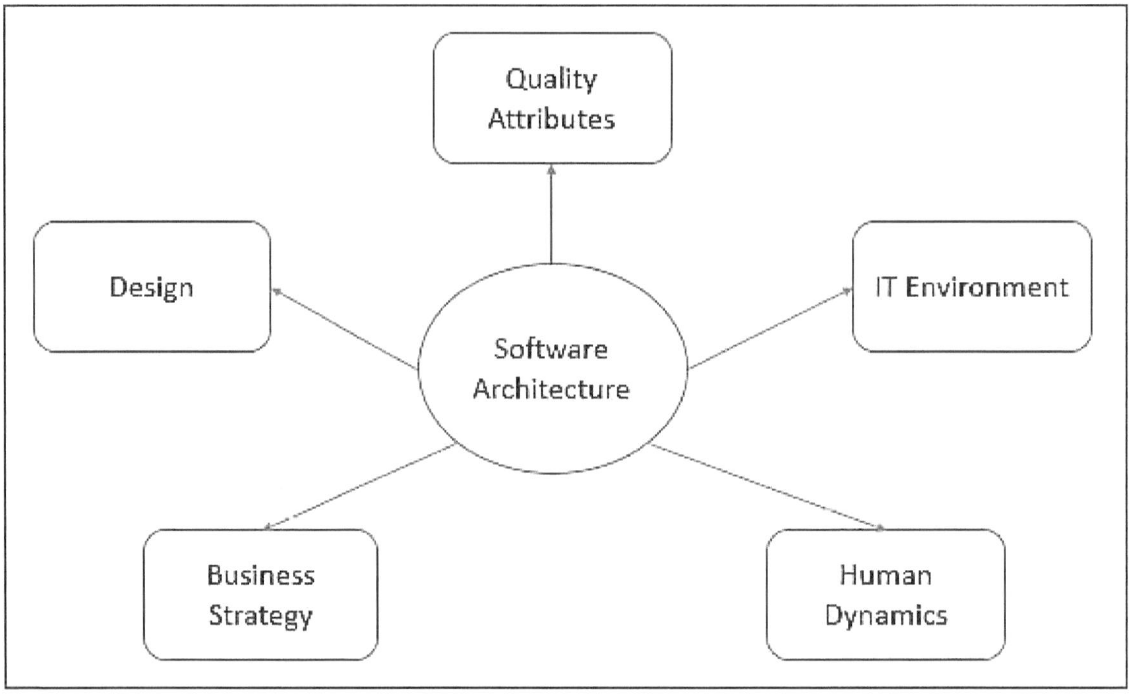

We can segregate Software Architecture and Design into two distinct phases: Software Architecture and Software Design.
In **Architecture**, nonfunctional decisions are cast and separated by the functional requirements. In Design, functional requirements are accomplished.

Software Architecture

Architecture serves as a **blueprint for a system**. It provides an abstraction to manage the system complexity and establish a communication and coordination mechanism among components.

It defines a **structured solution** to meet all the technical and operational requirements, while optimizing the common quality attributes like performance and security.

Further, it involves a set of significant decisions about the organization related to software development and each of these decisions can have a considerable impact on quality, maintainability, performance, and the overall success of the final product. These decisions comprise of –
- Selection of structural elements and their interfaces by which the system is composed.
- Behavior as specified in collaborations among those elements.
- Composition of these structural and behavioral elements into large subsystem.
- Architectural decisions align with business objectives.
- Architectural styles guide the organization.

Software Design

Software design provides a **design plan** that describes the elements of a system, how they fit, and work together to fulfill the requirement of the system. The objectives of having a design plan are as follows –
- To negotiate system requirements, and to set expectations with customers, marketing, and management personnel.
- Act as a blueprint during the development process.
- Guide the implementation tasks, including detailed design, coding, integration, and testing.
- It comes before the detailed design, coding, integration, and testing and after the domain analysis, requirements analysis, and risk analysis.

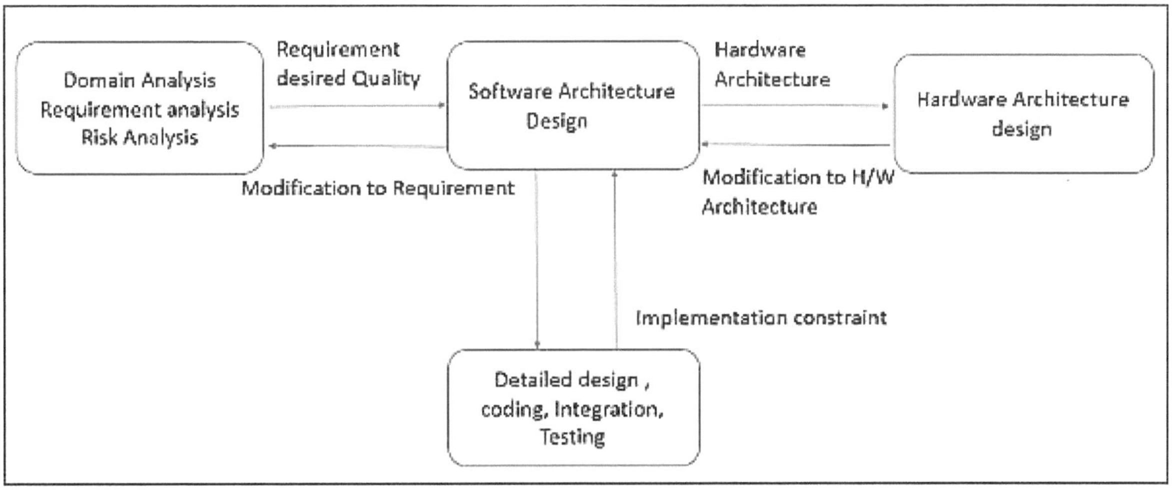

Goals of Architecture

The primary goal of the architecture is to identify requirements that affect the structure of the application. A well-laid architecture reduces the business risks associated with building a technical solution and builds a bridge between business and technical requirements.

Some of the other goals are as follows –

- Expose the structure of the system but hide its implementation details.
- Realize all the use-cases and scenarios.
- Try to address the requirements of various stakeholders.
- Handle both functional and quality requirements.
- Reduce the goal of ownership and improve the organization's market position.
- Improve the quality and functionality offered by the system.
- Improve external confidence in either the organization or system.

Limitations

Software architecture is still an emerging discipline within software engineering. It has the following limitations –

- Lack of tools and standardized ways to represent architecture.
- Lack of analysis methods to predict whether architecture will result in an implementation that meets the requirements.
- Lack of awareness of the importance of architectural design to software development.
- Lack of understanding of the role of software architect and poor communication among stakeholders.
- Lack of understanding of the design process, design experience and evaluation of design.

Role of Software Architect

A Software Architect provides a solution that the technical team can create and design for the entire application. A software architect should have expertise in the following areas –

1. Design Expertise
- Expert in software design, including diverse methods and approaches such as object-oriented design, event-driven design, etc.
- Lead the development team and coordinate the development efforts for the integrity of the design.
- Should be able to review design proposals and tradeoff among themselves.

2. Domain Expertise
- Expert on the system being developed and plan for software evolution.
- Assist in the requirement investigation process, assuring completeness and consistency.
- Coordinate the definition of domain model for the system being developed.

3. Technology Expertise
- Expert on available technologies that help in the implementation of the system.

- Coordinate the selection of programming language, framework, platforms, databases, etc.
4. Methodological Expertise
- Expert on software development methodologies that may be adopted during SDLC (Software Development Life Cycle).
- Choose the appropriate approaches for development that helps the entire team.
5. Hidden Role of Software Architect
- Facilitates the technical work among team members and reinforcing the trust relationship in the team.
- Information specialist who shares knowledge and has vast experience.
- Protect the team members from external forces that would distract them and bring less value to the project.
6. Deliverables of the Architect
- A clear, complete, consistent, and achievable set of functional goals
- A functional description of the system, with at least two layers of decomposition
- A concept for the system
- A design in the form of the system, with at least two layers of decomposition
- A notion of the timing, operator attributes, and the implementation and operation plans
- A document or process which ensures functional decomposition is followed, and the form of interfaces is controlled

Quality Attributes

Quality is a measure of excellence or the state of being free from deficiencies or defects. Quality attributes are the system properties that are separate from the functionality of the system.

Implementing quality attributes makes it easier to differentiate a good system from a bad one. Attributes are overall factors that affect runtime behavior, system design, and user experience.

They can be classified as –

1. Static Quality Attributes

Reflect the structure of a system and organization, directly related to architecture, design, and source code. They are invisible to the end-user, but affect the development and maintenance cost, e.g.: modularity, testability, maintainability, etc.

1. Dynamic Quality Attributes
- Reflect the behavior of the system during its execution. They are directly related to system's architecture, design, source code, configuration, deployment parameters, environment, and platform.
- They are visible to the end-user and exist at runtime, e.g. throughput, robustness, scalability, etc.

Quality Scenarios

Quality scenarios specify how to prevent a fault from becoming a failure. They can be divided into six parts based on their attribute specifications –

- **Source** – An internal or external entity such as people, hardware, software, or physical infrastructure that generates the stimulus.
- **Stimulus** – A condition that needs to be considered when it arrives on a system.
- **Environment** – The stimulus occurs within certain conditions.
- **Artifact** – A whole system or some part of it such as processors, communication channels, persistent storage, processes etc.
- **Response** – An activity undertaken after the arrival of stimulus such as detecting faults, recovering from fault, disable event source etc.
- **Response measure** – Should measure the occurred responses so that the requirements can be tested.

Common Quality Attributes

The following table lists the common quality attributes a software architecture must have –

Category	Quality Attribute	Description
Design Qualities	**Conceptual Integrity**	Defines the consistency and coherence of the overall design. This includes the way components or modules are designed.
	Maintainability	Ability of the system to undergo changes with a degree of ease.
	Reusability	Defines the capability for components and subsystems to be suitable for use in other applications.
Run-time Qualities	**Interoperability**	Ability of a system or different systems to operate successfully by communicating and exchanging information with other external systems written and run by external parties.
	Manageability	Defines how easy it is for system administrators to manage the application.
	Reliability	Ability of a system to remain operational over time.
	Scalability	Ability of a system to either handle the load increase without impacting the performance of the system or the ability to be readily enlarged.
	Security	Capability of a system to prevent malicious or accidental actions outside of the designed usages.
	Performance	Indication of the responsiveness of a system to execute any action within a given time interval.
	Availability	Defines the proportion of time that the system is functional and working. It can be measured as a percentage of the total system downtime over a predefined period.
System Qualities	**Supportability**	Ability of the system to provide information helpful for identifying and resolving issues when it fails to work correctly.
	Testability	Measure how easy it is to create test criteria for the system and its components.
User Qualities	**Usability**	Defines how well the application meets the requirements of the user and consumer by being intuitive.
Architecture Quality	**Correctness**	Accountability for satisfying all the requirements of the system.
Non-runtime Quality	**Portability**	Ability of the system to run under different computing environments.
	Integrality	Ability to make separately developed components of the system work correctly together.
	Modifiability	Ease with which each software system can accommodate changes to its software.
Business quality attributes	**Cost and schedule**	Cost of the system with respect to time to market, expected project lifetime & utilization of legacy.
	Marketability	Use of system with respect to market competition.

6.3 Interface Design

- User interface is the front-end application view to which user interacts to use the software. Users can manipulate and control the software as well as hardware by means of user interface. Today, user interface is found at almost every place where digital technology exists, right from computers, mobile phones, cars, music players, airplanes, ships etc.
- User interface is part of software and is designed in such a way that it is expected to provide the user insight of the software. UI provides a fundamental platform for human-computer interaction.
- UI can be graphical, text-based, audio-video based, depending upon the underlying hardware and software combination. UI can be hardware or software or a combination of both.

The software becomes more popular if its user interface is:

- Attractive

- Simple to use
- Responsive in short time
- Clear to understand
- Consistent on all interfacing screens

UI is broadly divided into two categories:

1. Command Line Interface
2. Graphical User Interface

Command Line Interface (CLI)

- CLI has been a great tool of interaction with computers until the video display monitors came into existence. CLI is the first choice of many technical users and programmers. CLI is the minimum interface a software can provide to its users.
- CLI provides a command prompt, the place where the user types the command and feeds to the system. The user needs to remember the syntax of command and its use. Earlier CLI were not programmed to handle the user errors effectively.
- A command is a text-based reference to a set of instructions, which are expected to be executed by the system. There are methods like macros and scripts that make it easy for the user to operate.
- CLI uses less computer resources as compared to GUI.

CLI Elements

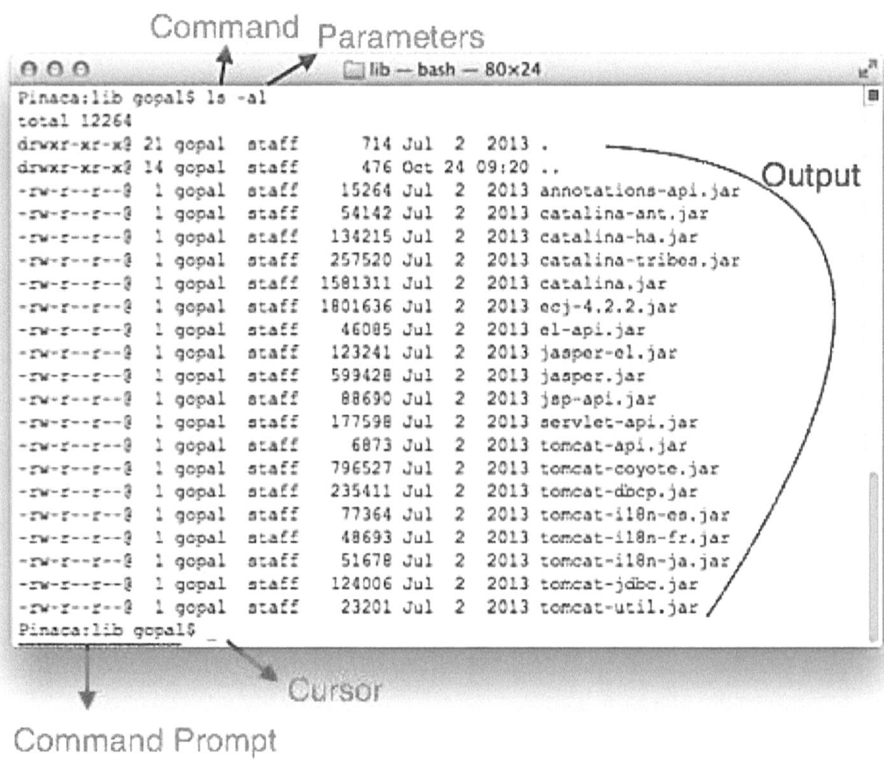

A text-based command line interface can have the following elements:

- **Command Prompt** - It is text-based notifier that mostly shows the context in which the user is working. It is generated by the software system.
- **Cursor** - It is a small horizontal line or a vertical bar of the height of line, to represent position of character while typing. Cursors are mostly found in blinking state. It moves as the user writes or deletes something.
- **Command** - A command is an executable instruction. It may have one or more parameters. Output on command execution is shown inline on the screen. When output is produced, command prompt is displayed on the next line.

Graphical User Interface

- Graphical User Interface provides the user graphical means to interact with the system. GUI can be a combination of both hardware and software. Using GUI, the user interprets the software.
- Typically, GUI is more resource consuming than CLI. With advancing technology, programmers and designers create complex GUI designs that work with more efficiency, accuracy and speed.

GUI Elements

GUI provides a set of components to interact with software or hardware.
Every graphical component provides a way to work with the system. A GUI system has following elements such as:

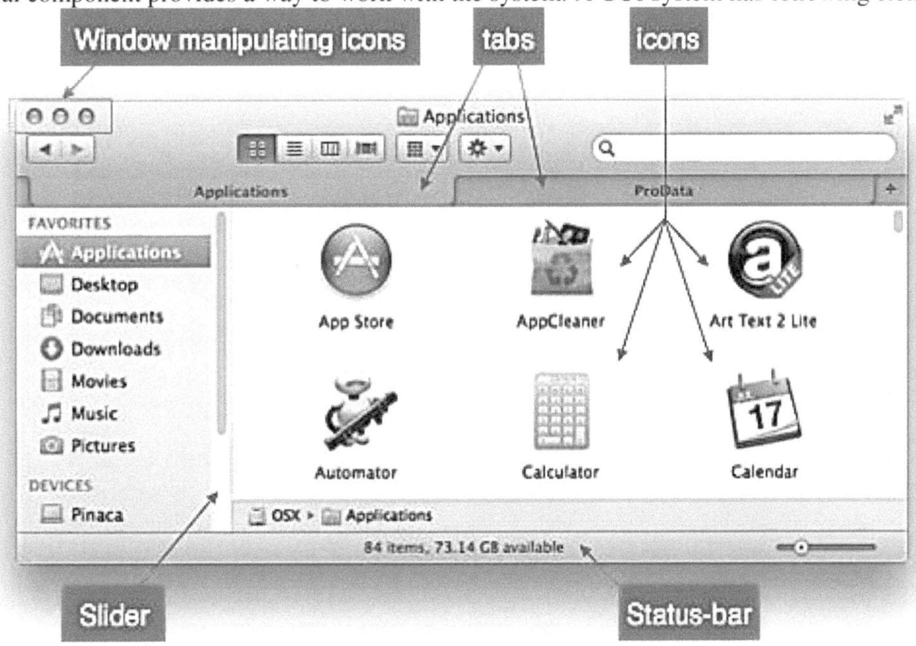

1. Window - An area where contents of application are displayed. Contents in a window can be displayed in the form of icons or lists, if the window represents file structure. It is easier for a user to navigate in the file system in an exploring window. Windows can be minimized, resized or maximized to the size of screen. They can be moved anywhere on the screen. A window may contain another window of the same application, called child window.
2. Tabs - If an application allows executing multiple instances of itself, they appear on the screen as separate windows. **Tabbed Document Interface** has come up to open multiple documents in the same window. This interface also helps in viewing preference panel in application. All modern web-browsers use this feature.
3. Menu - Menu is an array of standard commands, grouped together and placed at a visible place (usually top) inside the application window. The menu can be programmed to appear or hide on mouse clicks.
4. Icon - An icon is a small picture representing an associated application. When these icons are clicked or double clicked, the application window is opened. Icon displays applications and programs installed on a system in the form of small pictures.
5. Cursor - Interacting devices such as mouse, touch pad, digital pen are represented in GUI as cursors. On screen cursor follows the instructions from hardware in almost real-time. Cursors are also named pointers in GUI systems. They are used to select menus, windows and other application features.

Application specific GUI components

A GUI of an application contains one or more of the listed GUI elements:

- Application Window - Most application windows use the constructs supplied by operating systems, but many use their own customer created windows to contain the contents of application.
- Dialogue Box - It is a child window that contains messages for the user and requests for some action to be taken. For Example: Application generates a dialogue to get confirmation from user to delete a file.

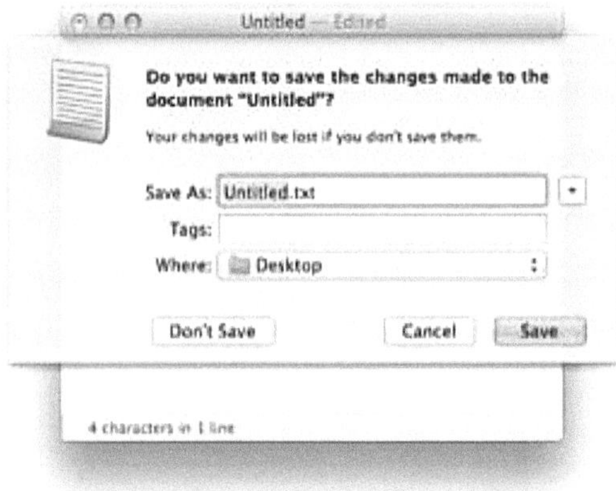

- Text-Box - Provides an area for users to type and enter text-based data.
- Buttons - They imitate real life buttons and are used to submit inputs to the software.

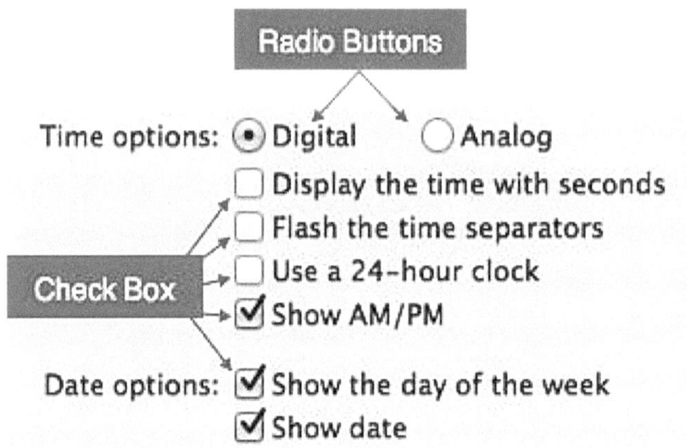

- Radio-button - Displays available options for selection. Only one can be selected from all offered.
- Checkbox - Functions like list-box. When an option is selected, the box is marked as checked. Multiple options represented by check boxes can be selected.
- List-box - Provides a list of available items for selection. More than one item can be selected.

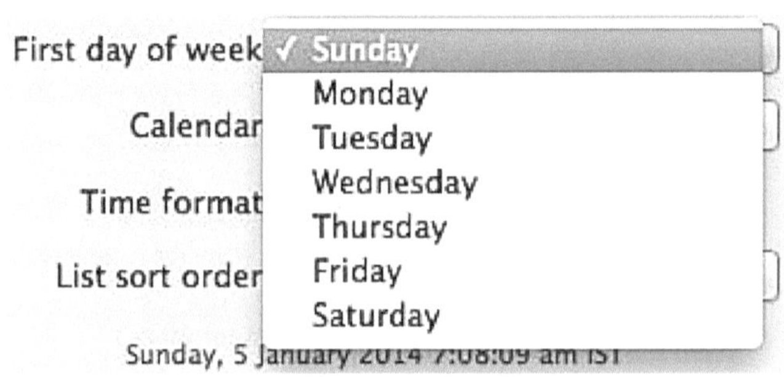

Other impressive GUI components are:
- Sliders
- Combo-box
- Data-grid
- Drop-down list

User Interface Design Activities

There are several activities performed for designing user interface. The process of GUI design and implementation is like SDLC. Any model can be used for GUI implementation among Waterfall, Iterative or Spiral Model.
A model used for GUI design and development should fulfill these GUI specific steps.

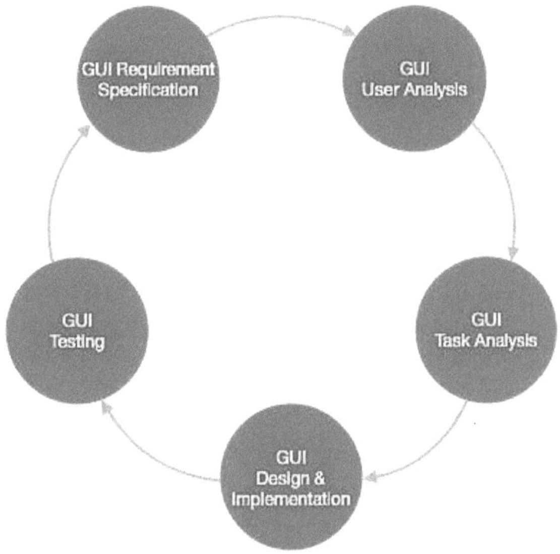

- GUI Requirement Gathering - The designers may like to have a list of all functional and non-functional requirements of GUI. This can be taken from the user and their existing software solution.
- User Analysis - The designer who is going to use the software GUI. The target audience matters as the design details change according to the knowledge and competency level of the user. If the user is technical savvy, advanced and complex GUI can be incorporated. For a novice user, more information is included on how-to of software.
- Task Analysis - Designers have to analyze what task is to be done by the software solution. Here in GUI, it does not matter how it will be done. Tasks can be represented in a hierarchical manner by taking one major task and dividing it further into smaller sub-tasks. Tasks provide goals for GUI presentation. Flow of information among sub-tasks determines the flow of GUI contents in the software.
- GUI Design & implementation - Designers, after having information about requirements, tasks and user environment, design the GUI and implement it into code and embed the GUI with working or dummy software in the background. It is then self-tested by the developers.
- Testing - GUI testing can be done in various ways. Organizations can have in-house inspection; direct involvement of users and release of beta version are few of them. Testing may include usability, compatibility, user acceptance etc.

GUI Implementation Tools

- There are several tools available using which the designers can create entire GUI with a mouse click. Some tools can be embedded into the software environment (IDE).
- GUI implementation tools provide a powerful array of GUI controls. For software customization, designers can change the code accordingly.
- There are different segments of GUI tools according to their different use and platform.

Example

Mobile GUI, Computer GUI, Touch-Screen GUI etc. Here is a list of few tools which come handy to build GUI:
- FLUID
- App Inventor (Android)
- LucidChart
- Wavemaker

- Visual Studio

User Interface Golden rules

The following rules are mentioned to be the golden rules for GUI design, described by Schneiderman and Plaisant in their book (Designing the User Interface).

- Strive for consistency - Consistent sequences of actions should be required in similar situations. Identical terminology should be used in prompts, menus, and help screens. Consistent commands should be employed throughout.

- Enable frequent users to use short-cuts - The user's desire to reduce the number of interactions increases with the frequency of use. Abbreviations, function keys, hidden commands, and macro facilities are very helpful to an expert user.

- Offer informative feedback - For every operator's action, there should be some system feedback. For frequent and minor actions, the response must be modest, while for infrequent and major actions, the response must be more substantial.

- Design dialog to yield closure - Sequences of actions should be organized into groups with a beginning, middle, and end. The informative feedback at the completion of a group of actions gives the operators the satisfaction of accomplishment, a sense of relief, the signal to drop contingency plans and options from their minds, and this indicates that the way ahead is clear to prepare for the next group of actions.

- Offer simple error handling - As much as possible, design the system so the user will not make a serious error. If an error is made, the system should be able to detect it and offer simple, comprehensible mechanisms for handling the error.

- Permit easy reversal of actions - This feature relieves anxiety, since the user knows that errors can be undone. Easy reversal of actions encourages exploration of unfamiliar options. The units of reversibility may be a single action, a data entry, or a complete group of actions.

- Support internal locus of control - Experienced operators strongly desire the sense that they oversee the system and that the system responds to their actions. Design the system to make users the initiators of actions rather than the responders.

- Reduce short-term memory load - The limitation of human information processing in short-term memory requires the displays to be kept simple, multiple page displays be consolidated, window-motion frequency be reduced, and sufficient training time be allotted for codes, mnemonics, and sequences of actions.

6.4 Design Patterns

Design patterns in system design provide a structured approach to solving design problems in software engineering by offering reusable solutions that have been proven effective over time. These patterns help to streamline the development process, reduce errors, and improve the maintainability and scalability of systems. This section outlines key design patterns that are commonly used in system architecture, highlighting their importance, applications, and benefits.

What is Gang of Four (GOF)?

In 1994, four authors Erich Gamma, Richard Helm, Ralph Johnson and John Vlissides published a book titled **Design Patterns - Elements of Reusable Object-Oriented Software** which initiated the concept of Design Pattern in Software development.

These authors are collectively known as **Gang of Four (GOF)**. According to these authors design patterns are primarily based on the following principles of object orientated design.

- Program to an interface not an implementation
- Favor object composition over inheritance

Usage of Design Pattern

Design Patterns have two main usages in software development.

Common platform for developers

Design patterns provide a standard terminology and are specific to scenarios. For example, a singleton design pattern signifies use of single object so all developers familiar with single design pattern will make use of single object and they can tell each other that the program is following a singleton pattern.

Best Practices

Design patterns have evolved over a long period of time, and they provide the best solutions to certain problems faced during software development. Learning these patterns helps unexperienced developers to learn software design in an easy and faster way.

Types of Design Patterns

1. Structural Patterns
Structural patterns are concerned with how classes and objects are composed to form larger structures. These patterns simplify the design by identifying a simple way to realize relationships among entities.
- **Adapter Pattern**: This pattern allows interfaces of different classes to work together despite incompatible interfaces. It acts as a bridge between two incompatible interfaces by encapsulating one object and presenting a different interface to the other object. For instance, when integrating new software components that cannot be altered to match an existing system interface, an adapter can be used to bridge the gap.
- **Facade Pattern**: Provides a simplified interface to a complex subsystem. It encapsulates a complicated system, offering a higher-level interface that makes the subsystem easier to use. For example, an operating system can provide a simple API for file operations, hiding the complex underlying interactions with the storage devices.
- **Composite Pattern**: This pattern is designed to treat individual objects and compositions of objects uniformly. It allows clients to interact with individual objects and compositions of objects the same way. This can be particularly useful in graphics drawing applications where both individual shapes and groups of shapes must be treated as complex objects.

2. Creational Patterns
Creational patterns abstract the instantiation process. They help make a system independent of how its objects are created, composed, and represented.
- **Singleton Pattern**: Ensures that a class has only one instance and provides a global point of access to it. This pattern is often used in scenarios where a single instance of a class must control action throughout the execution, like in the management of a database connection.
- **Factory Method Pattern**: Defines an interface for creating an object but let's subclasses decide which class to instantiate. This pattern is particularly useful when a system needs to enhance the capabilities of class instantiation by allowing for flexibility under dynamic loading conditions.
- **Prototype Pattern**: Specifies the kinds of objects to create using a prototypical instance and creates new objects by copying this prototype. It is used when creating an instance of a given class that is either expensive or complicated.

3. Behavioral Patterns
Behavioral patterns are concerned with algorithms and the assignment of responsibilities between objects. They help in providing solutions concerning the interactions between objects and help in reducing intricate flow controls by associating behaviors to the objects.
- **Observer Pattern**: Defines a one-to-many dependency between objects so that when one object changes state, all its dependents are notified and updated automatically. This pattern is widely used in implementing distributed event-handling systems, where the action of one component needs to automatically trigger a response in other systems.
- **Strategy Pattern**: Allows a method to be swapped out at runtime by encapsulating the algorithm inside a class. This pattern defines a family of algorithms, encapsulates each one, and makes them interchangeable. Strategy lets the algorithm vary independently from clients that use it. For example, a text rendering engine could use different algorithms to format text depending on the context of use.
- **Command Pattern**: Encapsulates a command request as an object, thereby letting you parameterize clients with different requests, queue or log requests, and support undoable operations. This is often used in designing complete undo functionalities in applications like word processors or graphic design tools.

6.5 Security Design Considerations

When designing a system, security is a critical consideration that cannot be an afterthought. Effective security measures ensure the protection of data, safeguard system operations, and maintain user trust. This section explores key security design considerations that should be integrated into the system design process from the very beginning.

1. Principle of Least Privilege

The Principle of Least Privilege (PoLP) is foundational in security architecture. It dictates that a user, program, or system should have no more privilege than necessary to perform its task. This minimizes the potential damage from accidental, intentional, or unauthorized actions. In practice, this means that user accounts and processes are given the minimum levels of access needed to perform their duties. For instance, a database management system might restrict access to certain tables such that only finance officers can modify financial records, while other employees can only view them.

2. Secure Default Settings

Systems should be deployed with secure default settings. Many security breaches occur due to unchanged defaults, such as passwords or open ports, which are easily exploited by attackers. Designers should ensure that defaults are secure if not configured further by the end users. This includes disabling unnecessary services, closing unused ports, and requiring users to change passwords during their first login.

3. Defense in Depth

Defense in Depth is a strategy that involves layering multiple security measures to protect the integrity of the information and the systems. If one mechanism fails, another will still provide protection. For example, a network might use firewalls, intrusion detection systems, and multi-factor authentication collectively to secure its data. This approach is critical because it considers the possibility of failure in one or more security measures.

4. Encryption

Encryption should be used to protect data both at rest and in transit. By encrypting databases and network traffic, you ensure that data confidentiality and integrity are maintained, even if unauthorized access occurs. For instance, using Transport Layer Security (TLS) for data in transit and robust encryption standards like AES for data at rest can significantly enhance security.

5. Regular Security Audits

Regular security audits are crucial to ensure that the system remains secure over time. These audits help identify vulnerabilities that could be exploited by attackers and ensure compliance with security policies and standards. Auditing can involve both automated scanning tools and manual expert review. The findings from these audits should lead to refinements in the system's security measures.

6. Fail-Securely

Systems should be designed to handle failures securely. In the event of a system failure, security should not be compromised. Designing for fail-security involves ensuring that defaults are safe, and that backup systems or modes do not inadvertently bypass security mechanisms. For example, if an authentication system fails, it should deny all access rather than permitting unchecked entries.

7. User Authentication and Authorization

Robust mechanisms for user authentication and authorization are essential. This involves not only ensuring that users are who they claim to be (authentication) but also that they are permitted to do what they are trying to do (authorization). Techniques such as multi-factor authentication (MFA), biometrics, and role-based access controls (RBAC) are effective ways to enhance security in these areas.

8. Secure Software Development Lifecycle (SDLC)

Incorporating security into every phase of the software development lifecycle is critical to producing secure systems. This means integrating security considerations into planning, development, testing, and deployment. Secure SDLC processes help to identify and mitigate vulnerabilities early, reducing the risk of security issues in the production environment.

9. Incident Response Plan

A well-prepared incident response plan is vital. This plan outlines how to respond to security breaches and helps minimize damage by restoring services and processes as quickly as possible. The plan should include identification of roles and responsibilities, steps to contain and mitigate breaches, and communication strategies both internally and externally.

10. Privacy by Design

Privacy by Design is an approach that calls for privacy to be considered throughout the whole engineering process. The concept is to implement strong privacy policies and ensure they are strictly adhered to from the start. For systems that handle personal data, incorporating features like data anonymization and minimal data retention can help meet these goals.

Conclusion

Security design is an integral part of the system design process. By integrating these considerations into the initial design and throughout the system's lifecycle, developers can create systems that are not only functional but also secure. This proactive approach to security helps prevent breaches and reduces potential damage, thereby maintaining the trust and reliability of the system for its users.

Summary

1. Database Design Importance: Proper database design reduces maintenance costs, improves data consistency, and optimizes disk storage space, significantly affecting application performance and user requirements fulfilment.
2. Database Design Process: Includes requirement analysis, logical and physical design models, implementation, and testing. Logical models focus on data requirements, while physical models translate these into hardware and DBMS considerations.
3. Normalization and Denormalization: Normalization organizes data to minimize redundancy and maintain integrity, while denormalization improves read performance by adding redundant data for specific use cases.
4. Logical vs. Physical Data Models: Logical models detail data entities and relationships without physical constraints, while physical models specify table structures, column data types, and database-specific considerations.
5. Architectural Design Goals: Involves creating a blueprint that addresses technical and operational requirements, focusing on performance, security, maintainability, and scalability to reduce business risks.
6. Software Design Objectives: Aims to provide a plan that guides development, ensuring system requirements are met, improving quality, and facilitating communication among stakeholders.
7. Quality Attributes in Architecture: Includes design qualities (e.g., maintainability, reusability), run-time qualities (e.g., reliability, scalability), and user qualities (e.g., usability) that impact system performance and user satisfaction.
8. User Interface Design: Critical for user interaction, comprising command-line interfaces (CLI) and graphical user interfaces (GUI). Effective UI design enhances usability, clarity, and responsiveness.
9. Design Patterns: Reusable solutions to common design problems. Structural patterns (e.g., Adapter, Facade), Creational patterns (e.g., Singleton, Factory Method), and Behavioural patterns (e.g., Observer, Strategy) streamline development and improve system design.
10. Security Design Considerations: Emphasize principles like least privilege, secure defaults, defines in depth, encryption, regular audits, fail-secure design, robust authentication/authorization, secure SDLC, incident response plans, and privacy by design.
11. Défense in Depth: A multi-layered security approach to ensure redundancy in protection mechanisms, making systems more resilient to attacks by using various security measures concurrently.
12. Fail-Secure Design: Ensures that systems handle failures without compromising security, maintaining safe defaults and preventing unauthorized access during system disruptions.

Glossary

1. Database Development Life Cycle (DDLC): A series of stages in database design, including planning, system definition, designing, implementation, and testing, ensuring comprehensive development and maintenance.
2. Logical Data Model: A detailed representation of data requirements and relationships, independent of physical implementation, specifying entities, attributes, primary keys, and foreign keys.
3. Physical Data Model: A design that translates the logical model into actual database structures, including tables, columns, data types, and constraints, tailored to specific DBMS requirements.
4. Normalization: The process of organizing database tables to reduce redundancy and improve data integrity, achieved through various normal forms like 1NF, 2NF, 3NF, and beyond.
5. Denormalization: A technique that adds redundant data to improve read performance, often used in scenarios where database reads are frequent and need to be optimized.
6. ACID Properties: Set of principles (Atomicity, Consistency, Isolation, Durability) ensuring reliable transaction processing in databases, maintaining data integrity even during failures.
7. Principle of Least Privilege (PoLP): A security principle that restricts user and system access rights to the minimum necessary to perform their functions, reducing potential damage from misuse or attacks.
8. Defence in Depth: A layered security strategy that uses multiple security measures to protect systems, ensuring that if one layer fails, additional layers provide continued protection.
9. Encryption: The process of converting data into a secure format to prevent unauthorized access, used for protecting data at rest and in transit.
10. User Interface (UI): The part of a software system that users interact with, including graphical user interfaces (GUI) and command-line interfaces (CLI), designed for ease of use and accessibility.

11. Design Patterns: Reusable solutions to common software design problems, categorized into structural, creational, and behavioural patterns to streamline development and enhance system architecture.
12. Quality Attributes: Characteristics that determine the performance and behaviour of a system, including attributes like scalability, reliability, usability, and maintainability, which affect both development and user experience.

6.6 Project

6.6.1 Solved Project

Suppose you are tasked with designing a new advanced database for a healthcare application. Before starting, review the principles of database design, ensure you understand how to structure data effectively, verify the application's specific data requirements, explore different database design methodologies, and ask for expert advice on best practices. This ensures a robust and efficient database design that meets the application's needs.

Approach:

1. Requirements Analysis

- **Understand Stakeholders:** Identify all stakeholders, including healthcare providers, administrative staff, patients, and IT personnel.
- **Gather Requirements:** Conduct interviews, surveys, and workshops to gather detailed requirements. This includes understanding the types of data to be stored, data workflows, reporting needs, and compliance requirements (e.g., HIPAA in the US).
- **Define Use Cases:** Document various use cases to understand how different users will interact with the database.

2. Data Modelling

- Conceptual Design:
- **Entity-Relationship Diagram (ERD):** Create an ERD to identify entities (e.g., patients, appointments, medical records) and their relationships.
- **Attributes:** Define attributes for each entity, ensuring you capture all necessary data fields.
- Logical Design:
- **Normalization:** Apply normalization techniques to reduce data redundancy and improve data integrity. Typically, normalize to at least the third normal form (3NF).
- **Data Integrity:** Define primary keys, foreign keys, and constraints to maintain data integrity and relationships between tables.
- Physical Design:
- **Database Schema:** Create a detailed schema including tables, columns, data types, indexes, and relationships.
- **Storage Requirements:** Consider the storage requirements for the database, including data volume, growth projections, and performance considerations.

3. Database Design Methodologies

- **Top-Down Approach:** Start with a broad overview and break it down into smaller components. Useful for understanding the overall system and ensuring all high-level requirements are captured.
- **Bottom-Up Approach:** Start with detailed specifications and integrate them into a larger system. This approach can be useful for incorporating existing systems or components.
- **Inside-Out Approach:** Focus on the most critical components first and build outwards. This ensures that the core functionality is robust and reliable.

4. Database Technology Selection

- **Relational Databases (RDBMS):** Consider traditional relational databases like MySQL, PostgreSQL, or Oracle for structured data and complex queries.
- **NoSQL Databases:** Evaluate NoSQL options like MongoDB or Cassandra for unstructured data, flexibility, and scalability.
- **Hybrid Solutions:** In some cases, a combination of relational and NoSQL databases might be suitable.

5. Best Practices and Expert Advice

- **Data Security:** Implement robust security measures, including encryption, access controls, and regular audits to protect sensitive healthcare data.

- **Backup and Recovery:** Design a comprehensive backup and recovery strategy to ensure data availability and integrity.
- **Performance Optimization:** Optimize queries, use indexing judiciously, and monitor performance regularly to maintain high efficiency.
- **Compliance:** Ensure the database design adheres to relevant healthcare regulations and standards, such as HIPAA, GDPR, or other regional requirements.
- **Scalability:** Design for scalability to handle increasing data volumes and user load without compromising performance.
- **Documentation:** Maintain thorough documentation of the database design, schema, and any custom procedures or functions.

6. Implementation and Testing

- **Prototyping:** Develop a prototype to validate the design and gather feedback from stakeholders.
- **Testing:** Conduct rigorous testing, including unit tests, integration tests, and user acceptance tests (UAT) to ensure the database meets all requirements.
- **Deployment:** Plan and execute a deployment strategy, including data migration, if necessary, and ensure minimal disruption to existing operations.

7. Maintenance and Iteration

- **Monitoring:** Continuously monitor the database for performance, security, and integrity issues.
- **Regular Updates:** Apply regular updates and patches to the database software.
- **Feedback Loop:** Establish a feedback loop with users to gather insights and make iterative improvements to the database design.

6.6.2 Unsolved Project

You are part of a team developing a user-friendly interface for a mobile banking application. Before designing the interface, review key interface design principles, ensure you understand the needs and preferences of the target users, verify the application's specific interface requirements, explore different interface design tools and methodologies, and ask for user feedback on prototype designs. This results in an intuitive and effective user interface.

6.7 Case Study

6.7.1 Solved Case Study

Advanced database design is essential for the effective functioning of complex software systems. It starts with a detailed database design that structures data and defines entity relationships to enhance performance and scalability. Architectural design follows, ensuring the database's seamless integration with other system components and accommodating future growth and modifications. Interface design is crucial for creating user-friendly and accessible interactions with the database. Design patterns offer standardized solutions to recurring problems in database management and integration. Lastly, security design considerations are vital, involving the implementation of robust security measures such as encryption, access controls, and regular security audits to safeguard sensitive data and maintain the system's integrity.

Questions:

1. What is the purpose of structuring data and defining entity relationships in database design?

   Answer: The purpose of structuring data and defining entity relationships in database design is to enhance performance and scalability.

2. How does architectural design benefit a database system?

   Answer: Architectural design benefits a database system by ensuring seamless integration with other system components and accommodating future growth and modifications.

3. What is the focus of interface design in database systems?

   Answer: The focus of interface design in database systems is on creating user-friendly and accessible interactions with the database.

4. Why are design patterns used in advanced database design?

   Answer: Design patterns are used in advanced database design to offer standardized solutions to recurring problems in database management and integration.

5. Name two security measures mentioned in the passage that help protect sensitive data.

Answer: Two security measures mentioned in the passage that help protect sensitive data are encryption and access controls.

6.7.2 Unsolved Case Study

Advanced database design is a crucial aspect of developing complex software systems. It begins with the structuring of data and defining relationships between data entities to ensure optimal performance and scalability. Architectural design then ensures the database integrates seamlessly with other system components and supports future growth. Interface design focuses on user interaction with the database, emphasizing user-friendliness and accessibility. Design patterns provide proven solutions to common problems in database management and system integration. Security design considerations are essential for protecting sensitive data, involving measures such as encryption, access controls, and regular security audits to maintain data integrity and security.

Questions:

1. What is the first step in advanced database design?
2. Why is architectural design important for a database?
3. What does interface design emphasize in database systems?
4. How do design patterns help in advanced database design?
5. What are two key security design considerations mentioned in the passage?

6.8 Lab Activity

6.8.1 Solved Lab Activity

Solution:

1. Header
- Logo
- Navigation Menu (Home, Search, My Account, Help)
- User Profile (Login/Logout)
2. Search Section
- Search Bar
- Filter Options (Genre, Author, Availability, etc.)
3. Book List/Results
- Book Title
- Author
- Availability Status
- Action Buttons (View Details, Reserve, Borrow)
4. Book Details Section
- Book Cover Image
- Book Title
- Author
- Description
- Availability
- Action Buttons (Reserve, Borrow)
5. Account Management Section
- User Information
- Borrowed Books List
- Reserved Books List
- Account Settings (Change Password, Contact Info)

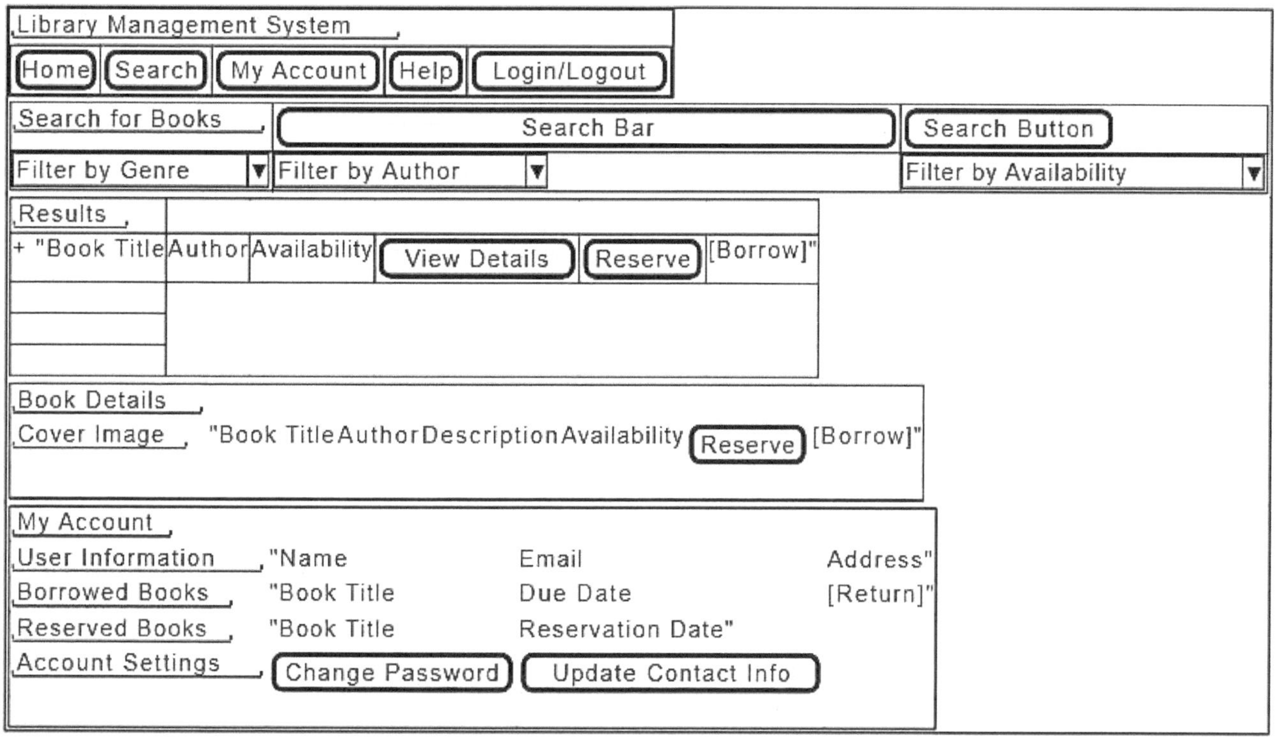

Explanation

Header:

1. Logo and Navigation Menu: Includes links to Home, Search, My Account, Help, and Login/Logout options.

Search Section:

1. Search Bar: Allows users to enter search queries for books.

2. Filter Options: Provides filters for genre, author, and availability to refine search results.

Book List/Results:

1. Results Table: Displays the search results with columns for book title, author, availability, and action buttons (View Details, Reserve, Borrow).

Book Details Section:

1. Book Information: Shows detailed information about the selected book, including cover image, title, author, description, availability, and action buttons (Reserve, Borrow).

Account Management Section:

1. User Information: Displays the user's personal information (name, email, address).

2. Borrowed Books List: Lists the books currently borrowed by the user with due dates and return options.

3. Reserved Books List: Shows the books reserved by the user with reservation dates.

4. Account Settings: Allows users to change their password and update contact information.

6.8.2 Unsolved Lab Activity

Provide a practical example of how the Repository design pattern can be implemented in a database application. Include code snippets or pseudo-code.

Previous Years Solved Questions

Q 1. Describe all the steps involved in database design for the system discussed. **[IGNOU MCA, June, 2013]**

Ans 1. Steps Involved in Database Design for a System

Designing a database involves a systematic process to ensure that the data is well-organized, easily accessible, and maintained with integrity. Below are the steps typically involved in database design:
1. Requirements Analysis:
- **Gather Requirements:** Collect detailed information on the data requirements from stakeholders. This includes understanding what data needs to be stored, how it will be used, and any constraints or rules.
- **Analyze Requirements:** Document and analyze the gathered requirements to identify the scope and objectives of the database.
2. Conceptual Design:
- **Create an Entity-Relationship Diagram (ERD):** Identify the main entities (e.g., Customer, Order, Product) and their relationships. Define attributes for each entity.
- **Define Relationships:** Establish how entities relate to each other (one-to-one, one-to-many, many-to-many).
3. Logical Design:
- **Normalize the Database:** Apply normalization rules to eliminate redundancy and ensure data integrity. Typically, normalize up to the Third Normal Form (3NF).
- **Define Primary and Foreign Keys:** Identify primary keys for each entity and establish foreign keys to define relationships between tables.
- **Create Detailed ERD:** Update the ERD to reflect the normalized tables and relationships.
4. Physical Design:
- **Choose Database Management System (DBMS):** Select an appropriate DBMS based on requirements, budget, and scalability needs.
- **Define Table Structures:** Create the actual tables, specifying data types, constraints, indexes, and default values.
- **Denormalization (if necessary):** Consider denormalization for performance optimization, such as adding redundant data or combining tables.
5. Implementation:
- **Create the Database Schema:** Use the DBMS to create the database schema, including tables, indexes, views, and stored procedures.
- **Insert Initial Data:** Populate the tables with initial data, if necessary, to validate the design and test queries.
6. Data Loading and Migration:
- **Develop ETL Processes:** If migrating from another system, develop Extract, Transform, Load (ETL) processes to migrate data to the new database.
- **Data Validation:** Ensure data integrity and consistency during the migration process.
7. Testing:
- **Unit Testing:** Test individual components (tables, views, procedures) to ensure they work as expected.
- **Integration Testing:** Test the database as a whole, ensuring all components work together seamlessly.
- **Performance Testing:** Conduct performance tests to ensure the database meets the required performance standards.
8. Security Design:
- **Define Access Controls:** Implement security measures such as user roles, permissions, and encryption to protect sensitive data.
- **Backup and Recovery Plans:** Establish backup and recovery procedures to protect data against loss or corruption.
9. Documentation:
- **Create Documentation:** Document the database design, including schema diagrams, data dictionaries, and procedures for future maintenance and development.
10. Maintenance:
- **Monitor Performance:** Continuously monitor the database performance and optimize as needed.
- **Update Database:** Apply patches, updates, and changes to the database schema as the system evolves.

Example: Library Management System
1. Requirements Analysis
- **Entities:** Books, Members, Loans, Authors, Categories
- **Data Requirements:** Book title, author, publication year, member details, loan dates, etc.
- **Constraints:** A book can be loaned to one member at a time, each loan has a due date.

2. Conceptual Design
- ERD:
- **Entities:** Book, Member, Loan, Author, Category

- **Relationships:** A Book can have multiple Authors, a Member can have multiple Loans.

3. Logical Design
- Normalization:
- **1NF:** Ensure atomic values.
- **2NF:** Remove partial dependencies.
- **3NF:** Remove transitive dependencies.
- Keys:
- **Primary Keys:** BookID, MemberID, LoanID
- **Foreign Keys:** AuthorID in Book table, MemberID in Loan table.

4. Physical Design
- Table Structures:
- **Book:** BookID, Title, CategoryID, PublicationYear
- **Member:** MemberID, Name, Address, Phone
- **Loan:** LoanID, BookID, MemberID, LoanDate, DueDate
- **Author:** AuthorID, Name
- **BookAuthor:** BookID, AuthorID (for many-to-many relationship)

5. Implementation
- **Schema Creation:** Use SQL scripts to create tables.
- **Initial Data:** Populate tables with sample data.

6. Data Loading and Migration
ETL Processes: Define processes to load data from existing systems.

7. Testing
- **Unit Testing:** Test individual tables and queries.
- **Integration Testing:** Test the system as a whole, including relationships and constraints.
- **Performance Testing:** Ensure the system handles expected loads.

8. Security Design
- **Access Controls:** Define user roles (e.g., librarian, member) and permissions.
- **Backup Plans:** Set up regular backups and test recovery procedures.

9. Documentation
Schema Documentation: Provide detailed ERDs and data dictionaries.

10. Maintenance
- **Monitor:** Regularly monitor performance and make necessary optimizations.
- **Updates:** Apply updates as new requirements arise.

Exercises

Exercise 1 – Multiple Choice Questions

1. What is the focus of architectural design in databases?
   A. Determining how users interact with the system
   B. Ensuring that the database is protected from unauthorized access
   C. Defining the overall structure of the database system
   D. Applying reusable templates to solve common problems
2. Which of the following best describes interface design in the context of database systems?
   A. Structuring the database to reduce redundancy
   B. Designing how users interact with the database system
   C. Securing the database from potential threats
   D. Creating an outline of the database's architecture

3. What is a primary consideration in security design for databases?
   A. How components fit together within the system
   B. The aesthetics of the user interface
   C. Protection of data from unauthorized access and vulnerabilities
   D. How the database handles large volumes of data
4. What role do design patterns play in database design?
   A. They prescribe how to minimize data duplication
   B. They provide reusable solutions to commonly encountered problems
   C. They define how to visually represent the database structure
   D. They are primarily concerned with optimizing query performance
5. In the context of database design, what does the term 'Database Design' specifically focus on?
   A. The physical layout of the hardware on which the database runs
   B. The visual elements used in the creation of the database
   C. The design of secure access systems to protect data
   D. The structure of the database including tables, fields, and relationships

Exercise 2 – True/False

1. Database design involves defining detailed database structures that meet the requirements of the intended business functions.
2. Architectural design in databases is primarily concerned with the aesthetics of the user interface rather than the structural framework that supports the database system.
3. Design patterns in database design are reusable solutions to commonly occurring problems within a given context.

Exercise 3 – Fill in the blanks

1. In ______ design, the overall structure and data flow of the database are determined, focusing on how data is stored, accessed, and managed.
2. ________ design involves creating a framework that supports the functional requirements, including the model for interaction between different components of the database system.
3. The _______ design in databases involves developing the part of the system that users interact with, ensuring usability and accessibility.

Exercise 4- Fill in the blanks with two options

1. In database design, ensuring data is correctly partitioned to support __________ and maintain __________ is crucial.
2. A __________ is a standard solution to a common problem in a given context in software design, particularly useful in __________.
3. When considering __________ in a database system, one must prioritize data encryption and __________ to protect data integrity and access.

Exercise 5- Give two answers for the following:

1. Database Design Tools
2. Architectural Design Patterns
3. Interface Design Principles
4. Commonly Used Design Patterns
5. Methods to Secure Databases

Exercise 6- Rearrange the sentence

1. Design /data/ensuring/security/focuses/on.
2. architectural/are/considerations/important/design/in.
3. patterns/be/designed/systems/should/using/design.

Exercise 7- Choose the Odd One Out

1. Schema, Blueprint, User Interface, Template
2. SQL Injection, Data Encryption, Load Balancing, Access Control
3. MVC, Singleton, Observer, Scalability

Exercise 8- Jumble words

1. teryneiti
2. slamarhcetiut
3. reiuscty

Exercise 9- Match case

Column 1	Column 2
1. What is the focus of architectural design in databases?	A. Enhancing user interaction with the database
2. What are security design considerations?	B. Creating templates for database structures
3. What is the role of interface design in databases?	C. Protecting data from unauthorized access
4. What do design patterns provide in database design?	D. Framework for building robust database architectures
5. What involves defining the structure of the database?	E. Strategies for ensuring data integrity and security

Exercise 10- Assertion – Reason

1. Assertion (A): A comprehensive security design is essential for robust database systems.

Reason (R): Security design considerations help prevent unauthorized access and ensure data integrity.

Options:

1. Assertion (A) is true and Reason (R) is the correct reason for Assertion (A).
2. Assertion (A) is true, but Reason (R) is not the correct reason for Assertion (A).
3. Assertion (A) is false, but Reason (R) is true.
4. Assertion (A) is false and Reason (R) is also false.

Exercise 11- One- word

1. What type of design focuses on the overall structure and relationships among system components in a database system?
2. Which aspect of database design involves defining how users interact with the database system?
3. What is essential to ensure data confidentiality and prevent unauthorized access within a database design?

Exercise 12- Small Answers

1. What are the key principles to consider when designing a database schema to ensure it supports both performance and scalability?
2. What are some critical security measures that should be implemented in database design to protect against data breaches and unauthorized access?

Exercise 13- Long Answers

1. Discuss various design patterns that can be applied in database design. How do patterns like MVC (Model-View-Controller) or Repository enhance database applications?
2. Security is a critical consideration in database design. What are the essential security design considerations that need to be addressed during the database design process? Detail the strategies to mitigate common security vulnerabilities.

Answers

Exercise 1- 1) C, 2) B, 3) C 4) B, 5) D
Exercise 2- 1) True, 2) False, 3) True
Exercise 3- 1) Database, 2) Architectural, 3) Interface
Exercise 4- 1) scalability, performance optimization, 2) design patterns, architectural design, 3) Security design consideration, role-based access controls
Exercise 5- 1) ER/Studio, dbForge Studio, 2) Layered Architecture, Microservices Architecture, 3) Consistency, Feedback, 4) Singleton, Observer, 5) Use of Firewalls, Regular Audits
Exercise 6- 1) Design focuses on ensuring data security, 2) Architectural considerations are important in design, 3) Systems should be designed using design patterns.
Exercise 7- 1) User Interface, 2) Load Balancing, 3) Scalability
Exercise 8- 1) Integrity, 2) Architectural, 3) Security
Exercise 9- 1 D, 2 E, 3 A, 4 B, 5 C
Exercise 10- a) Assertion (A) is true and Reason (R) is the correct reason for Assertion (A).
Exercise 11- 1) Architectural, 2) Interface, 3) Security

Online Resources

Online Exam paper
URL https://forms.gle/U7qtHWPBeKRyZxLj6
QR Code

YouTube Video
URL
https://www.youtube.com/playlist?list=PLzlh_31VWEFpeMWLB8G-vjDj96lUvxwh-
QR Code

More Test Papers Practices

Test Paper-1
URL https://forms.gle/mC66vRsEfW3qFgxH8
QR Code

Test Paper-2

URL https://forms.gle/ZpdyzLewvj7cJVZW9

QR Code

System analysis and design Test Paper
Chapter- 6
Advanced Database Design

Time Duration: 30 Minutes **Maximum Marks: 25**

General Instructions:

1. The question paper consists of answer any 12 questions out of the given 19 questions and is divided into four sections, A, B, C and D.
2. All questions are compulsory.
3. Section A comprises question numbers 1 to 8. These are MCQs and one liner of one mark each. You are to select one most appropriate response out of the four provided options.
4. Section B comprises question numbers 1 to 5. These are SAQs carrying two marks each.
5. Section C comprises question numbers 1 to 4. These are SAQs carrying four marks each.
6. Section D comprises question numbers 1& 2. These are LAQs carrying five marks each.

SECTION-A

I. Answer any 6 questions out of the given 8 questions **(1*6=6)**

1. What is the primary goal of database design?
   A) To create user interfaces
   B) To structure data in a way that supports efficient storage, retrieval, and management
   C) To test system performance
   D) To develop security protocols
2. Which architectural design model separates the database layer from the application and presentation layers?
   A) Monolithic architecture
   B) Client-server architecture
   C) Three-tier architecture
   D) Peer-to-peer architecture
3. In interface design, what is a key principle to enhance user experience?
   A) Complexity
   B) Consistency
   C) Randomness
   D) Redundancy
4. Which design pattern is commonly used to encapsulate database access logic in an application?
   A) Singleton pattern
   B) Observer pattern
   C) Factory pattern
   D) Repository pattern
5. What is a primary consideration in security design for databases?
   A) Performance optimization
   B) User interface design
   C) Data encryption and access control
   D) Database normalization
6. What design pattern encapsulates database access logic?
7. What type of architecture separates database, application, and presentation layers?
8. What principle in interface design enhances user experience through uniformity?

SECTION-B

II. Answer any 3 questions out of the given 5 questions **(2*3=6)**

1. Define 'database design' in the context of advanced database systems.

2. What is the primary goal of architectural design in database systems?
3. List two key principles of effective interface design.
4. What is the role of design patterns in software development?
5. Why is security a critical consideration in database design?

SECTION-C

II. Answer any 2 questions out of the given 4 questions **(4*2=8)**

1. Explain the importance of three-tier architecture in database design.
2. Describe the key components of effective interface design.
3. How do design patterns improve software development efficiency and maintenance?
4. Discuss the major security threats to databases and how they can be mitigated.

SECTION-D

III. Answer any 1 question out of the given 2 questions **(5*1=5)**

1. Analyse the impact of architectural design on the scalability and performance of database systems. Provide examples to illustrate your points.
2. Discuss the role of security design considerations in protecting sensitive data within databases. Explain the importance of encryption, access control, and regular security audits.

Chapter 7: Development Methodologies

- Understand the Waterfall Model
- Explore Agile Methodologies
- Discover DevOps Practices
- Choosing the Right Methodology

7.1 Waterfall Model

The Waterfall Model was the first Process Model to be introduced. It is also referred to as a **linear-sequential life cycle model**. It is very simple to understand and use. In a waterfall model, each phase must be completed before the next phase can begin and there is no overlapping in the phases.
The Waterfall model is the earliest SDLC approach that was used for software development.
The waterfall Model illustrates the software development process in a linear sequential flow. This means that any phase in the development process begins only if the previous phase is complete. In this waterfall model, the phases do not overlap.

Waterfall Model - Design

Waterfall approach was first SDLC Model to be used widely in Software Engineering to ensure success of the project. In "The Waterfall" approach, the whole process of software development is divided into separate phases. In this Waterfall model, typically, the outcome of one phase acts as the input for the next phase sequentially.
The following illustration is a representation of the different phases of the Waterfall Model.

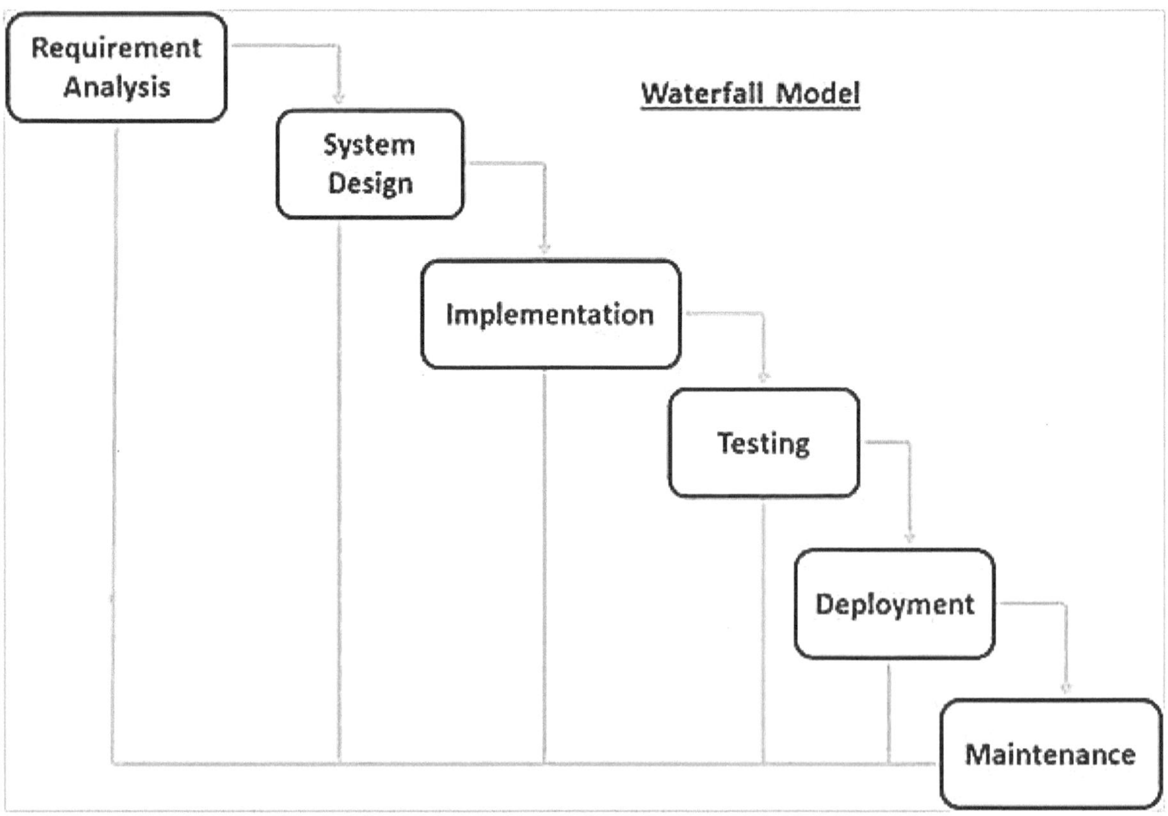

The sequential phases in Waterfall model are –
- **Requirement Gathering and analysis** – All possible requirements of the system to be developed are captured in this phase and documented in a requirement specification document.

- System Design – The requirement specifications from the first phase are studied in this phase and the system design is prepared. This system design helps in specifying hardware and system requirements and helps in defining the overall system architecture.
- Implementation – With inputs from the system design, the system is first developed in small programs called units, which are integrated in the next phase. Each unit is developed and tested for its functionality, which is referred to as Unit Testing.
- Integration and Testing – All the units developed in the implementation phase are integrated into a system after testing of each unit. Post integration, the entire system is tested for any faults and failures.
- Deployment of system – Once the functional and non-functional testing is done, the product is deployed in the customer environment or released into the market.
- Maintenance – There are some issues which come up in the client environment. To fix those issues, patches are released. Also to enhance the product some better versions have been released. Maintenance is done to deliver these changes in the customer environment.
All these phases are cascaded to each other in which progress is seen as flowing steadily downwards (like a waterfall) through the phases. The next phase is started only after the defined set of goals are achieved for previous phase and it is signed off, so the name "Waterfall Model". In this model, phases do not overlap.

Waterfall Model - Application

Every software developed is different and requires a suitable SDLC approach to be followed based on internal and external factors. Some situations where the use of Waterfall model is most appropriate are –
- Requirements are very well documented, clear and fixed.
- Product definition is stable.
- Technology is understood and is not dynamic.
- There are no ambiguous requirements.
- Ample resources with required expertise are available to support the product.
- The project is short.

Waterfall Model - Advantages

The advantages of waterfall development are that it allows for departmentalization and control. A schedule can be set with deadlines for each stage of development and a product can proceed through the development process model phases one by one.
Development moves from concept, through design, implementation, testing, installation, troubleshooting, and ends up at operation and maintenance. Each phase of development proceeds in strict order.
Some of the major advantages of the Waterfall Model are as follows –
- Simple and easy to understand and use
- Easy to manage due to the rigidity of the model. Each phase has specific deliverables and a review process.
- Phases are processed and completed one at a time.
- Works well for smaller projects where requirements are very well understood.
- Clearly defined stages.
- Well understood milestones.
- Easy to arrange tasks.
- Process and results are well documented.

Waterfall Model - Disadvantages

The disadvantage of waterfall development is that it does not allow much reflection or revision. Once an application is in the testing stage, it is very difficult to go back and change something that was not well-documented or thought upon in the concept stage.
The major disadvantages of the Waterfall Model are as follows –
- No working software is produced until late during the life cycle.
- High amounts of risk and uncertainty.
- Not a good model for complex and object-oriented projects.
- Poor model for long and ongoing projects.
- Not suitable for projects where requirements are at a moderate to high risk of changing. So, risk and uncertainty are high with this process model.
- It is difficult to measure progress within stages.

- Cannot accommodate changing requirements.
- Adjusting scope during the life cycle can end a project.
- Integration is done as a "big bang". at the very end, which doesn't allow identifying any technological or business bottleneck or challenges early.

7.2 Agile Methodologies

Agile methodology is an project management approach that allows successful and efficient execution of the project while emphasizing the improvement of a project and team collaboration. The approach is applicable in software development for flexibility, customer satisfaction, and collaboration. It refers to the application of a set of principles that functions through an interactive and incremental approach. The Agile methodology in software development emphasizes the importance of team collaboration and delivering a working product quickly to meet customer needs and expectations.

How does the Agile Software Development Process Work?

The Agile software development process is a set of steps to be performed in order. The importance of sequence is as follows:

- **Requirements:** The companies here gather information on customers' requirements and prioritize them based on different factors. It is an initial factor to understand the direction of thc project and progress.
- **Planning:** Developing a plan is an essential part of delivering the complete software comprising all the features. The plan includes time for the development and delivery of each iteration.
- **Development:** The software development is carried out by the development team while using frequent and rapid iterations.
- **Testing:** It involves software testing to make sure it meets the quality delivered by the organization and expected by the customer
- **Deployment:** Here, the organization serves the aim, which is to allow usage of the software.
- **Maintenance:** The software is regularly maintained to ensure customers' needs and expectations are met.

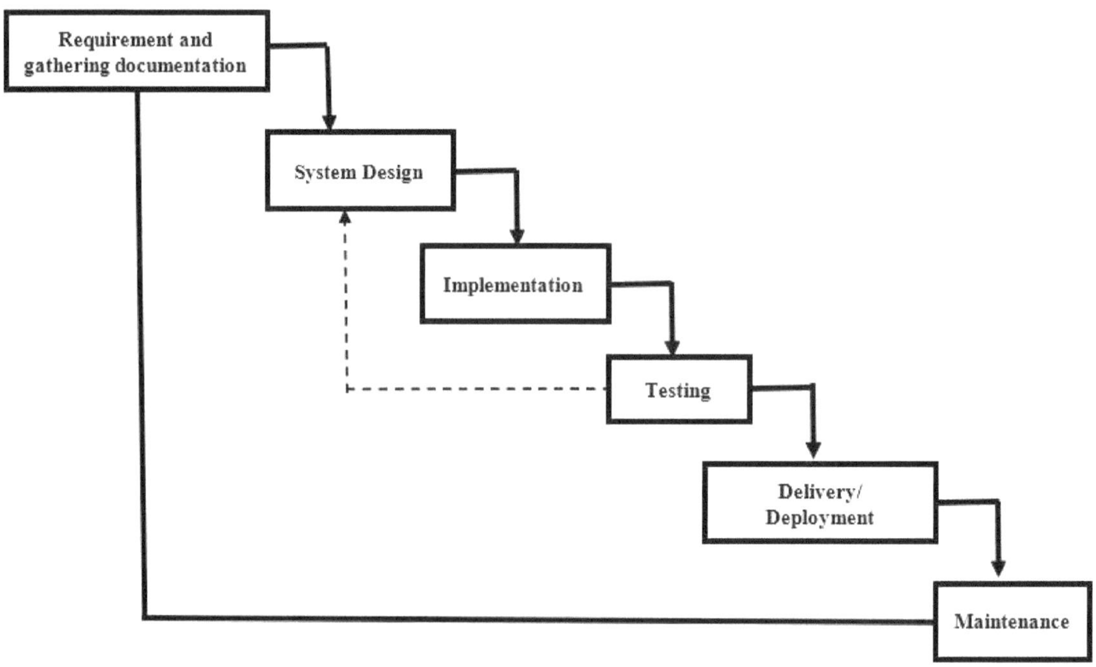

Core Principles of Agile Software Development Methodology

- Achieving customer satisfaction by timely and regular delivery fitting the customer requirements
- Delivering working software with minimal or no errors
- Earning a competitive edge by adapting to the changes in the market
- Sticking to the shortest time delivery with quality
- Including motivated and passionate individuals in building and developing the project

- Accepting change in requirements and deliveries despite nearness to delivery date
- Choosing the face-to-face communication method for efficient and effective information disbursal
- Embracing excellence while estimating and improving the progress

Key Agile Development Concepts

The key concepts of Agile development and Agile software development are:

- Adaptability

  The changing demands and development process require adaptability in the project. It helps the team and project get back on track, increases the team's confidence, saves time, and decreases productivity due to mess. It also allows changing the path of development and deployment to deliver the results timely.

- Disruption

  Agile methodology encourages changes to deliver quality results and improve customer satisfaction. It includes changing priorities, culture, and goals. Though the changes are hard and unacceptable, management on collective agreement becomes easier while providing better results.

- Collaboration

  It is another valued key Agile concept that contributes to building trust and accountability. It helps bring different ideas and collective discussion to improve poor but potentially holding ideas.

- Iterative Developments

  Rework for improvements is a common thing in software development. The iterative process here follows a continuous and close feedback loop for improvement. It is the core concept in Agile development.

- Incremental Development

  It involves creating a basic version of software with all the required features. Further improvements are made as decided during the meetups or calls. The changes to the software are made to the modules, along with the addition of user-friendly features.

- Milestone Checks

  It is aimed at client and team improvement and development. Here, the teams analyze the previous developments after reaching a specific and significant part of the project.

Popular Tools in Agile Software Development

- Jira

  The tool eases the planning of software projects such as Agile and sprint planning. It also contributes to responsive and transparent collaboration. Project managers and developers generally use Jira for task distribution, story tracking, and development tasks. Additionally, Jira also provides real-time updates on release details and improves the team performance.

- Docker

  The docker platform is widely used to set up and manage the containers required to meet the need for flexibility and application deployment on a certain host. The platform delivers the containers through virtualization at the Operating System. The containers comprise different components such as configuration files, software, and libraries, thus meeting the needs. Docker also helps to communicate between containers. Moreover, it holds more benefits than traditional virtual machines.

- Kubernetes

  The tool is used to effortlessly solve the problem of handling multiple containers. It is an open-source platform that supports scaling and automated application deployment. It also manages container applications, containerized workloads, and automation of container deployments, and it supports declarative configuration. Kubernetes is used for its ability to automate the deployment and scaling processes of complex containerized applications.

- Jenkins

  It is another open-source automation that is free to use for Continuous Integration (CI) and Continuous Delivery (CD) tasks. The software development teams use it to build, test, deployment of CI/CD tasks. It offers effective integration options and automates the CI/CD environment.

- Slack

  Slack is a popular tool in Agile software development, most used in business communications, and it is effective for collaboration. It is considered better than emails for team members as it provides an opportunity for natural collaboration. Here, two types of communication are possible: direct messaging and conventional IRC or Internet Relay Chat. The IRC includes functionalities such as private groups and topic-specific chat rooms or channels. Moreover, the conversations are also divided into public and private channels along with direct messages. It eliminates the one-to-one or group chats and introduces thread-based chats, which are easier to follow.

Advantages of Agile Software Development

The incorporation of Agile development in software engineering has the following advantages:
- People and interactions are preferred over tools and processes in the usage of Agile software development methodology.
- It leads to a regular focus on improved design and technical excellence.
- The Agile development process assists in improvement by allowing immediate feedback.
- Fastens the software development process, thus increasing customer trust.
- Allows quick adaptability to meet the change in requirements.
- Incorporates flexibility and adaptability.
- Enhances quality and reliability through a focus on quality assurance and continuous improvement.
- Increase team confidence and allow the setup of a collaborative, positive, and supportive workplace culture.

Disadvantages of Agile Software Development Life Cycle

The disadvantages of the Agile software development process are listed as follows:
- Agile development is linked with lesser documentation and a higher focus on codes.
- Agile software development depends on continuous iteration and feedback from customers, leading to difficult estimation of timelines, outcomes, and budgets of projects.
- Understanding the quantity and intensity of effort required for project completion is challenging at an early stage of the Agile software development lifecycle.
- Dependency on the customer leads to wrong progress in the project if the team encounters ambiguity.
- It is difficult for new programmers to adapt to the workplace environment as the senior programmers make most decisions.
- Higher flexibility and adaptability can also lead to scope creep and lack of control over project scope.
- The swiftness of Agile development with high intensity, a greater number of sprints, and close deadlines lead to mental exhaustion and increased pressure on team members, further leading to burnout.
- Agile development lack's structure compared to other methodologies, which results in oversight and poor governance.

Roles and Responsibilities in Agile Development

In the Agile software development life cycle, each team member plays a significant role in the development. Let us explore each member's role and responsibilities from the following:

Product Owner:
- They work as facilitators in review sessions and sprint planning.
- Product owners assume the role of a liaison between investors and team members.
- They help to determine the sprint goals and lead the development of user stories and tasks.
- They check if the tasks are complete and accurate to meet the client's expectations.
- Product owners give feedback and suggestions to enhance the quality of the processes.

Scrum Master or Team Lead:
- They eliminate obstacles to ensure team progress.
- They understand the foundations of Scrum and Agile.
- They assist in the development of tasks and user stories.
- Scrum masters monitor tasks and sprints.
- They focus on productivity and high-quality deliverables.

Development Team Members:
- They must have a strong understanding of the scrum framework.
- They are responsible for product implementation.
- They collaborate with other team members to ensure effective and efficient product development.
- They ensure that products or processes meet the client's or customer's expectations.
- They work on prioritized work by the product owner in the sprint.

Stakeholders:

- They take the lead in sprint planning.
- They provide feedback and suggestions to stakeholders and team members.
- Stakeholders guide product owners to ensure user stories and productivity meet expectations.
- They provide training to team members in Scrum and Agile processes
- Stakeholders aid in determining sprint goals and objectives

How to Implement Agile Software Development?

To implement the Agile methodology successfully for software development, you need to review the following points:

Step 1: Define and Plan the Project Scope and Vision

Communicate with the team and use the Elevator Pitch method. Find the target customer, statement of need, specific product name and category, its benefits, primary competitive alternative, and final statement of primary differentiation.

Step 2: Develop the Path to Reaching the Product

The product owner must use the strategy to develop the path to the product or software. It will include goals and how to achieve them. Every goal will have features, metrics, and other key information.

Step 3: Schedule Deadlines

It includes prioritizing the software features to be launched first, followed by subsequent losses. It will include 3 to 5 sprints.

Step 4: Plan the Sprint

The steps shift from macro-level workings to micro-level working, which involves focusing on specific tasks. Now, the sprints must also be planned to take place with the project managers, product owners, and scrum masters. The sprint will involve creating a list of backlog items, such as undeveloped features or other components of software, to be completed in the timeframe.

Step 5: Conduct Daily Meetings

It is essential to get daily updates through a small meeting to be concluded in 10 to 15 minutes. Team members here will inform us of their previous day's accomplishments, present-day works, and challenges being faced, if any.

Step 6: Sprint Reviews

Accomplishment of milestones, such as delivery of specific software updates, bug removal or introduction of new software functionality, must be linked with the analysis of previous tasks. It includes checking the alignment of plans with deliveries. Here, product owners also reflect on inaccuracies and inefficiencies by finding the associated reasons.

Step 7: Sprint Retrospective

It includes learning from the previous processes and finding the shortcomings. Here, all the involved members must identify the learnings and scope of improvement by avoiding negative actions in their next task.

7.3 DevOps Practices

DevOps, an amalgamation of 'Development' and 'Operations', emphasizes collaboration and communication between software developers and IT professionals while automating the process of software delivery and infrastructure changes. In system design, DevOps practices can lead to significant improvements in the creation, deployment, and operation of software systems. This chapter explores the core DevOps practices that are integral to modern system design.

1. Continuous Integration and Continuous Deployment (CI/CD)

Continuous Integration (CI) is a DevOps practice where developers frequently merge their code changes into a central repository, after which automated builds and tests are run. The key goals of CI are to find and address bugs quicker, improve software quality, and reduce the time it takes to validate and release new software updates.

Continuous Deployment (CD) extends CI by automatically deploying all code changes to a testing or production environment after the build stage. This practice aims to reduce the time elapsed between writing a line of code and making that code available to users in a production environment.

Implementing CI/CD

- **Automated Testing:** Develop comprehensive automated tests to ensure each integration meets functional and performance standards.
- **Build Servers:** Use tools like Jenkins, Travis CI, or GitLab CI to automate the execution of your build scripts.

- **Deployment Automation:** Utilize configuration management tools such as Puppet, Chef, or Ansible to automate the deployment process.

2. Infrastructure as Code (IaC)

Infrastructure as Code is a key DevOps practice that involves managing and provisioning computer data centers through machine-readable definition files, rather than physical hardware configuration or interactive configuration tools. This approach allows developers and system administrators to automatically manage, monitor, and provision resources, reducing manual processes and leading to more consistent environments.

Tools and Practices for IaC

- **Configuration Management Tools:** Puppet, Chef, Ansible, and SaltStack automate the provisioning and management of infrastructure.
- **Provisioning Tools:** Terraform and AWS CloudFormation allow for the creation of scripts for deploying infrastructure, enabling the quick setup and replication of environments.

3. Monitoring and Logging

In DevOps, monitoring and logging are crucial for understanding the performance of the system and quickly addressing issues as they occur. Effective monitoring means that performance bottlenecks, system anomalies, and other potential issues are detected and resolved quickly.

Strategies for Effective Monitoring and Logging

- **Real-time Monitoring:** Tools like Nagios, Prometheus, and New Relic can provide real-time insights into the system's health.
- **Log Management:** Use tools like ELK Stack or Splunk to collect, analyze, and visualize logs from all parts of the system in one centralized location.

4. Communication and Collaboration

Effective communication and collaboration are the cornerstones of the DevOps philosophy. Integrating operations and development teams encourages a culture of transparency, where knowledge and skills are shared across the teams to innovate and solve problems more efficiently.

Tools to Enhance Communication

- **Version Control Systems:** Tools like Git encourage collaboration by allowing multiple developers to work on the same codebase.
- **Instant Messaging and Collaboration Tools:** Slack, Microsoft Teams, and similar tools facilitate ongoing communication and integration between teams.

5. Microservices Architecture

Adopting a microservices architecture is a common approach in DevOps practices. This involves designing a single application as a suite of small services, each running in its own process and communicating with lightweight mechanisms, usually an HTTP resource API. Microservices allow for small, focused teams that can build, test, and deploy services independently of other services in the application.

Benefits of Microservices

- **Scalability:** Each component can be scaled independently, improving the system's responsiveness and efficiency.
- **Flexibility:** Teams can deploy updates more frequently and with fewer dependencies.

Conclusion

Incorporating DevOps practices in system design not only streamlines the software development and deployment process but also fosters a culture of continuous improvement. Practices such as CI/CD, Infrastructure as Code, effective monitoring, and microservices architecture contribute significantly to building resilient, scalable, and efficient software systems. By embracing these methodologies, organizations can enhance collaboration between teams, optimize product quality, and accelerate time to market. This strategic integration of development and operations paves the way for a more dynamic, responsive, and interconnected digital infrastructure.

7.4 Choosing the Right Methodology

Choosing the right methodology in system design is crucial for the success of any project. System design involves the process of defining the architecture, modules, interfaces, and data for a system to satisfy specified requirements. The methodology selected influences the efficiency, effectiveness, and overall success of the project. This chapter aims to guide system designers in selecting the most appropriate methodology based on various project needs and constraints.

Understanding System Design Methodologies

Before choosing a methodology, it's essential to understand the different approaches available. System design methodologies can broadly be classified into structured methodologies, agile methodologies, and hybrid methodologies.

1. **Structured Methodologies**: These methodologies, such as the Waterfall model and the V-Model, emphasize a sequential design process. Each phase must be completed before the next begins, and there is little backtracking or iteration. These are best suited for projects with very clear requirements and where changes are unlikely or very costly.
2. **Agile Methodologies**: Agile approaches, including Scrum, Kanban, and Extreme Programming (XP), focus on iterative and incremental development. Requirements and solutions evolve through collaboration between self-organizing cross-functional teams. Agile methodologies are well-suited to projects where requirements are expected to change or are not fully understood at the outset.
3. **Hybrid Methodologies**: These methodologies combine elements of both structured and agile approaches. They aim to provide the flexibility of agile with the controlled aspects of a structured methodology. Hybrid approaches can be tailored to fit specific project needs and are useful when dealing with both stable and dynamic system requirements.

Factors Influencing Methodology Choice

Several factors must be considered when choosing a methodology for system design. These include:

- **Project Size and Complexity**: Larger projects with many interconnected parts might benefit from a structured approach, whereas smaller, more adaptive projects could leverage agile methodologies.
- **Stakeholder and Team Dynamics**: The experience and skills of the team, along with the involvement and expectations of stakeholders, play a critical role in selecting a methodology. Agile methodologies require a high level of collaboration and self-management from the team.
- **Risk and Uncertainty**: Projects with high levels of uncertainty might benefit from an agile approach, which allows for more flexibility and responsiveness to change.
- **Budget and Time Constraints**: Tight deadlines and limited budgets may influence the choice towards more iterative approaches that can produce working systems rapidly.

Evaluating Methodologies for Specific Needs

To select the most suitable methodology, system designers should evaluate how well each methodology aligns with the project's specific requirements and constraints.

1. **Alignment with Business Goals**: The methodology should align with the business's strategic goals. For instance, if time-to-market is a critical factor, agile methodologies might be more appropriate.
2. **Regulatory and Compliance Needs**: Projects in highly regulated industries (like healthcare or finance) may require more documentation and formal phases, as seen in structured methodologies.
3. **Integration with Existing Processes**: The chosen methodology should integrate smoothly with existing business processes and systems. This integration is crucial for ensuring that system design processes do not disrupt ongoing operations.
4. **Feedback and Adaptation**: Methodologies that incorporate regular feedback loops allow for continual improvement and adaptation, which can be crucial in dynamic business environments.

Implementing the Chosen Methodology

Once the methodology is selected, implementing it effectively involves several key steps:

1. **Training and Education**: Ensure that all stakeholders and team members are adequately trained in the chosen methodology.
2. **Tool Support**: Utilize tools that support the methodology's practices, such as project management software for agile methodologies or design and documentation tools for structured approaches.
3. **Monitoring and Adjustment**: Continuously monitor the effectiveness of the methodology and be prepared to adjust as the project progresses and as lessons are learned.

Conclusion

Choosing the right methodology in system design is not a one-size-fits-all solution. It requires a thorough understanding of both the project requirements and the strengths and weaknesses of each methodology. By carefully considering the factors discussed and evaluating how different methodologies meet these needs, system designers can select an approach that maximizes the likelihood of project success. This strategic choice is vital in navigating the complexities of modern system development and ensuring that the final system meets both its functional and business objectives effectively.

Summary

1. Waterfall Model: A linear-sequential life cycle model where each phase must be completed before the next begins, suitable for projects with well-documented, clear, and fixed requirements.
2. Waterfall Model Advantages: Simple to understand and use, easy to manage, well-defined stages and milestones, effective for smaller projects with stable requirements.
3. Waterfall Model Disadvantages: High risk and uncertainty, inflexible to changes, no working software until late in the cycle, and difficulty in measuring progress within stages.
4. Agile Methodology: Emphasizes flexibility, customer satisfaction, and collaboration through iterative and incremental development. Suitable for projects with changing requirements.
5. Agile Core Principles: Focuses on customer satisfaction, delivering working software quickly, adapting to changes, face-to-face communication, and maintaining a motivated and collaborative team.
6. Agile Key Concepts: Includes adaptability, disruption, collaboration, iterative and incremental development, and milestone checks to ensure continuous improvement.
7. Agile Tools: Common tools include Jira for project management, Docker and Kubernetes for container management, Jenkins for CI/CD, and Slack for team communication.
8. Agile Advantages: Enhances quality and reliability, allows quick adaptability, promotes continuous improvement, and fosters a collaborative and supportive workplace culture.
9. Agile Disadvantages: Can lead to scope creep, difficult to estimate timelines and budgets, depends heavily on customer feedback, and can cause burnout due to intense sprints and deadlines.
10. DevOps Practices: Integrates development and operations to automate software delivery and infrastructure changes, improving collaboration and efficiency.
11. DevOps Core Practices: Includes Continuous Integration and Continuous Deployment (CI/CD), Infrastructure as Code (IaC), effective monitoring and logging, and adopting a microservices architecture.
12. Choosing the Right Methodology: Involves considering project size, complexity, stakeholder dynamics, risk and uncertainty, budget and time constraints, and alignment with business goals to select the most suitable approach for system design.

Glossary

1. Waterfall Model: A sequential design process in which progress flows in one direction downwards like a waterfall through phases such as requirement gathering, design, implementation, testing, deployment, and maintenance.
2. Sequential Phases: In the Waterfall model, each phase must be completed before the next begins, with no overlap between phases, ensuring a linear progression through the development lifecycle.
3. Requirement Gathering: The first phase in the Waterfall model, where all possible system requirements are captured and documented to guide the entire development process.
4. System Design: The phase in the Waterfall model where the requirements are translated into a detailed system design, specifying hardware, software, and system architecture.
5. Agile Methodology: An iterative and incremental approach to software development emphasizing flexibility, customer satisfaction, and team collaboration, allowing for rapid and continuous delivery of working software.
6. Sprint: A time-boxed iteration in Agile development during which a specific set of features or tasks are developed and tested, typically lasting two to four weeks.
7. Product Owner: In Agile, the role responsible for defining project vision, prioritizing tasks, and ensuring that the development team delivers value to the business.
8. Scrum Master: A facilitator in Agile who ensures the team follows Agile principles, removes impediments, and helps the team achieve its goals through effective collaboration and communication.
9. Continuous Integration (CI): A DevOps practice where developers frequently merge code changes into a central repository, with automated builds and tests to identify and fix bugs early in the development cycle.
10. Continuous Deployment (CD): Extends CI by automatically deploying code changes to production environments after passing the build stage, aiming to deliver software updates to users quickly and reliably.
11. Infrastructure as Code (IaC): A DevOps practice that manages and provisions infrastructure through machine-readable scripts, ensuring consistent and reproducible environments across different stages of the development lifecycle.

12. Microservices Architecture: A design approach in DevOps where a single application is composed of small, independent services that communicate through APIs, allowing for scalable and flexible system development.

7.5 Project

7.5.1 Solved Project

Imagine you are working on a dynamic and fast-paced software project that requires flexibility and quick iterations. Before proceeding, review Agile Methodologies, ensure your team understands the principles and practices, verify the project's scope for Agile suitability, explore different Agile frameworks like Scrum or Kanban, and ask for feedback from experienced Agile practitioners. This helps in fostering a collaborative and adaptive project environment.

Approach:

1. Review Agile Methodologies:
2. Understand key Agile principles: customer collaboration, responding to change, delivering frequently.
3. Emphasize iterative development and incremental delivery.
4. Ensure Team Understanding:
5. Conduct Agile training sessions.
6. Clarify roles: Product Owner, Scrum Master, Development Team.
7. Verify Project Scope:
8. Ensure flexibility for iterative development.
9. Confirm stakeholder engagement for regular feedback.
10. Assess project complexity for Agile suitability.
11. Explore Agile Frameworks:
12. **Scrum**: Sprints, daily stand-ups, sprint reviews, and retrospectives.
13. **Kanban**: Visualize workflow, limit WIP, focus on continuous delivery.
14. Gather Feedback:
15. Consult Agile coaches or experienced practitioners.
16. Participate in Agile communities for shared insights.
17. Foster Collaboration:
18. Encourage open communication and empowerment.
19. Hold regular retrospectives for continuous improvement.
20. Use Agile tools (e.g., Jira, Trello) for workflow management.

Implementation Steps

- **Setup**: Kick-off meeting, select framework, set up tools.
- **Training**: Conduct sessions, assign roles.
- **Planning**: Start with sprint/iteration planning, prioritize backlog.
- **Execution**: Daily stand-ups (Scrum), track progress (Kanban), regular reviews and retrospectives.
- **Feedback**: Engage practitioners, adapt processes based on feedback.

7.5.2 Unsolved Project

Suppose you are leading a software development project that needs a clear and structured approach. Before starting, review the principles of the Waterfall Model, ensure each phase is well-defined, verify the project's requirements, explore how this model can be applied to your project, and ask for advice on managing each phase effectively. This ensures a systematic and predictable development process.

7.6 Case Study

7.6.1 Solved Case Study

In software engineering, selecting the right development methodology is critical for project success. The Waterfall Model is a traditional, linear, and sequential approach, progressing through distinct phases like requirements analysis, design, implementation, testing, and maintenance. It is straightforward but inflexible, making changes difficult once the project is underway. In contrast, Agile Methodologies emphasize flexibility, collaboration, and iterative development, allowing teams to adapt quickly to changes and continuously improve the product based on user feedback. DevOps Practices combine software development and IT operations to shorten the development lifecycle and ensure continuous delivery of high-quality software. This approach promotes collaboration between developers and operations teams through practices such as continuous integration and automated testing. Choosing the right methodology depends on factors like project size, complexity, requirements, and team dynamics, ensuring that the selected approach aligns with the project's specific needs and goals.

Questions:

1. What is a key characteristic of the Waterfall Model?
   Answer: A key characteristic of the Waterfall Model is that it is linear and sequential.
2. How do Agile Methodologies handle product development?
   Answer: Agile Methodologies handle product development by emphasizing flexibility, collaboration, and iterative development.
3. What is the main goal of DevOps Practices?
   Answer: The main goal of DevOps Practices is to shorten the development lifecycle and ensure continuous delivery of high-quality software.
4. Which methodology is known for being straightforward but inflexible?
   Answer: The methodology known for being straightforward but inflexible is the Waterfall Model.
5. What factors should be considered when choosing a development methodology?
   Answer: Factors to consider when choosing a development methodology include project size, complexity, requirements, and team dynamics.

7.6.2 Unsolved Case Study

Choosing the right development methodology is crucial for the success of any software project. The Waterfall Model, a traditional approach, follows a linear sequence of phases: requirements analysis, design, implementation, testing, and maintenance. This model is simple and structured but lacks flexibility, making it difficult to incorporate changes once the project has progressed. Agile Methodologies, on the other hand, promote adaptability and iterative development. Teams work in short, incremental cycles called sprints, allowing for continuous feedback and adjustments based on user needs. DevOps Practices further enhance software development by integrating development and operations teams. This collaboration fosters continuous integration and continuous delivery (CI/CD), leading to more efficient and reliable software releases. The choice of methodology depends on several factors, including the nature of the project, the need for flexibility, and the importance of rapid deployment. Evaluating these aspects ensures that the selected approach aligns with the project's objectives and constraints.

Questions:

1. What are the sequential phases followed by the Waterfall Model?
2. How do Agile Methodologies handle development cycles?
3. What is the purpose of DevOps Practices in software development?
4. Why is the Waterfall Model considered inflexible?
5. What factors influence the choice of a development methodology?

7.7 Lab Activity

7.7.1 Solved Lab Activity

Create a flow diagram that shows the DevOps pipeline for a project, including stages such as code commit, build, test, and deploy.

Solution:

Stages in the DevOps Pipeline:

1. **Code Commit**: Developers commit code to a version control system (e.g., Git).
2. **Build**: The code is built into an executable application.
3. **Test**: The application is tested to ensure it works as expected.
4. **Deploy**: The application is deployed to a production environment.

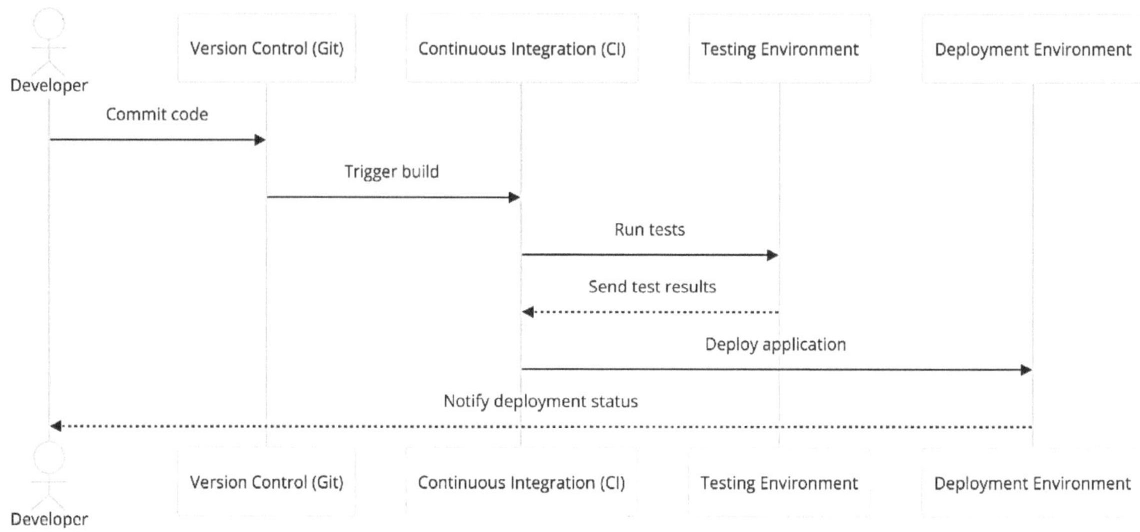

Explanation:

Actors and Participants:
1. **Developer**: The person who writes and commits code.
2. **Version Control (Git)**: The system where the code is stored and managed.
3. **Continuous Integration (CI)**: The system that builds the code and runs initial tests.
4. **Testing Environment**: The system where comprehensive tests are executed.
5. **Deployment Environment**: The system where the application is deployed.

Flow of Activities:
1. **Code Commit**: Developer commits the code to the Version Control system (Git).
2. **Build**: The Version Control system triggers the Continuous Integration system to build the code.
3. **Test**: The Continuous Integration system runs tests in the Testing Environment.
4. **Test Results**: The Testing Environment sends test results back to the Continuous Integration system.
5. **Deploy**: The Continuous Integration system deploys the application to the Deployment Environment.
6. **Notify Deployment Status**: The Deployment Environment notifies the Developer about the deployment status.

7.7.2 Unsolved Lab Activity
Create a Scrum board for a project to develop a new website. Include user stories, tasks, and sprints.

Previous Years Solved Questions

Q 1. Explain what kind of fact-finding techniques would you use for deciding on the design of a new application/system for some "Assignments Management System" at a study centre. **[IGNOU MCA, December, 2012]**
Ans 1. Designing a new "Assignments Management System" for a study centre involves thorough fact-finding to ensure the system meets the needs of all stakeholders. Here are some effective fact-finding techniques:
1. Interviews
1. **Purpose**: To gather detailed, qualitative information from stakeholders.
- Stakeholders to Interview:
- Teachers and instructors who assign and grade assignments.
- Students who will submit assignments.
- Administrators who manage records and oversee the process.
- Questions to Ask:
- What are the current methods for assignment submission and grading?
- What challenges do you face with the current system?
- What features would you like to see in the new system?
2. Surveys and Questionnaires

- **Purpose**: To collect quantitative data from a large number of stakeholders.
- Focus Areas:
- Ease of use of the current system.
- Desired features in the new system.
- Frequency and types of assignments.
- Sample Questions:
- How satisfied are you with the current assignment management process?
- What features do you find most useful in an assignment management system?
- How often do you encounter issues with assignment submissions?

3. Focus Groups

- **Purpose**: To facilitate discussions among small groups of stakeholders to gain insights into their needs and preferences.
- Key Activities:
- Brainstorming sessions to identify pain points and desired features.
- Discussions on user interface and user experience preferences.
- Feedback on preliminary design ideas.

4. Observation

- **Purpose**: To understand the real-world usage of the current system and identify implicit requirements.
- Activities:
- Observe students submitting assignments and teachers grading them.
- Note the time taken, steps involved, and any issues encountered.
- Identify any workarounds or additional tools used by stakeholders.

5. Document Analysis

- **Purpose**: To review existing documentation related to assignment management.
- Documents to Analyze:
- Current system manuals and user guides.
- Policies and procedures for assignment submission and grading.
- Feedback and issue logs related to the current system.

6. Prototyping

- **Purpose**: To create a preliminary model of the new system to gather feedback.
- Steps:
- Develop wireframes or mockups of the new system.
- Share prototypes with stakeholders and gather their feedback.
- Iterate on the design based on feedback received.

7. Competitive Analysis

- **Purpose**: To understand what similar systems offer and identify best practices.
- Activities:
- Research and analyze other assignment management systems in the market.
- Identify features and functionalities that are well-received.
- Evaluate the pros and cons of these systems.

8. Use Case Analysis

- **Purpose**: To define and analyze the specific ways stakeholders will interact with the system.
- Steps:
- Identify different use cases (e.g., submitting an assignment, grading an assignment, generating reports).
- Define the steps involved in each use case.
- Identify potential issues or improvements for each use case.

Previous Years Unsolved Questions

Q 1. What are the various advantages and disadvantages of waterfall model? **[Chaudhary Charan Singh University BCA, May]**

Exercises

Exercise 1 – Multiple Choice Questions

1. Which methodology emphasizes continuous feedback and iterative development?
    A) Waterfall Model
    B) Agile Methodologies
    C) DevOps Practices
    D) None of the above
2. What is the primary focus of DevOps practices?
    A) Sequential project phases
    B) Integrating development and operations teams
    C) Complete documentation before development
    D) Single deployment per project
3. Which model is traditionally known for its strict sequential phase structure?
    A) Agile Methodologies
    B) DevOps Practices
    C) Waterfall Model
    D) Spiral Model
4. When choosing a development methodology, what is a crucial factor to consider?
    A) The size of the development team only
    B) The complexity of the project and adaptability requirements
    C) The preferred programming language
    D) The geographic location of stakeholders
5. Which development practice is least likely to accommodate changes once a project phase has begun?
    A) Agile Methodologies
    B) DevOps Practices
    C) Waterfall Model
    D) Kanban

Exercise 2 – True/False

1. The Waterfall model is highly flexible and allows for easy changes throughout the development process.
2. Agile methodologies encourage frequent inspection and adaptation of processes.
3. DevOps practices eliminate the need for traditional software testing.

Exercise 3 – Fill in the blanks

1. The __________ model is a linear sequential software development process where each phase must be completed before the next begins.
2. __________ methodologies are characterized by iterative and incremental development, where requirements and solutions evolve through collaboration between self-organizing cross-functional teams.
3. __________ is a set of practices that combines software development (Dev) and IT operations (Ops) aimed at shortening the systems development life cycle and providing continuous delivery with high software quality.

Exercise 4- Fill in the blanks with two options

1. The __________ model is a linear and sequential approach to software development, often resulting in longer project timelines but thorough documentation and clear project phases, commonly used in __________.
2. __________ methodologies focus on iterative development, collaboration, and flexibility, making them suitable for __________ environments where requirements can change rapidly.
3. __________ practices combine software development and IT operations to improve collaboration, increase deployment frequency, and ensure more reliable releases, often applied in __________ organizations aiming for continuous delivery and integration.

Exercise 5- Give two answers for the following:

1. Development Methodologies
2. Key Principles of Agile Methodologies

3. DevOps Practices
4. Phases of the Waterfall Model
5. Common Tools Used in DevOps

Exercise 6- Rearrange the sentence

1. Sequential/a/process/Waterfall/is/model
2. stages/fixed/includes/Waterfall/the/model
3. increments/developed/small/in/Agile/is

Exercise 7- Choose the Odd One Out

1. Waterfall Model, Agile Methodologies, Scrum Practices, DevOps Practices
2. Waterfall Model, Agile Methodologies, Continuous Integration, DevOps Practices
3. Waterfall Model, Agile Methodologies, DevOps Practices, Software Testing

Exercise 8- Jumble words

1. erfallWat
2. igleA
3. OpsDev

Exercise 9- Match case

Column 1	Column 2
1. A linear and sequential approach to software development.	A. Agile Methodologies
2. A flexible and iterative approach focusing on collaboration.	B. Waterfall Model
3. Practices that combine software development and IT operations.	C. DevOps Practices
4. Factors to consider when selecting a development approach.	D. Choosing the Right Methodology

Exercise 10- Assertion – Reason

1. Assertion (A): The Waterfall model is a suitable development methodology for projects with well-defined requirements.

Reason (R): The Waterfall model follows a linear and sequential approach, which ensures each phase is completed before moving to the next, making it ideal for projects where requirements are clear and unchanging.

Options:
1. Assertion (A) is true, and Reason (R) is the correct reason for Assertion (A).
2. Assertion (A) is true, but Reason (R) is not the correct reason for Assertion (A).
3. Assertion (A) is false, but Reason (R) is true.
4. Assertion (A) is false, and Reason (R) is also false.

Exercise 11- One- word

1. Which development methodology follows a linear and sequential approach?
2. Which development methodology emphasizes flexibility and iterative progress?
3. What practice integrates software development and IT operations?

Exercise 12- Small Answers

1. What are the key characteristics of the Waterfall Model in software development?
2. How do Agile Methodologies differ from traditional Waterfall Model approaches in terms of project flexibility and adaptability?
3. Explain the main objectives of DevOps practices and how they benefit the software development lifecycle.

Exercise 13- Long Answers

1. Describe the iterative and incremental nature of Agile methodologies, contrasting it with the sequential phases of the Waterfall Model. How does this difference impact project adaptability and response to change?
2. Discuss the core concepts of DevOps practices and how they contribute to the integration and collaboration between development and operations teams throughout the software development lifecycle.

Answers

Exercise 1- 1) B, 2) B, 3) C, 4) B, 5) C
Exercise 2- 1) False, 2) True, 3) False
Exercise 3- 1) Waterfall, 2) Agile, 3) DevOps
Exercise 4- 1) Waterfall, traditional software development, 2) Agile, dynamic, 3) DevOps, modern
Exercise 5- 1) Waterfall Model, Agile Methodologies, 2) Iterative Development, Continuous Feedback, 3) Continuous Integration (CI), Continuous Deployment (CD), 4) Requirements Analysis, System Design, 5) Jenkins, Docker
Exercise 6- 1) Waterfall model is a sequential process, 2) Waterfall model includes fixed stages, 3) Agile is developed in small increments
Exercise 7- 1) Scrum Practices, 2) Continuous Integration, 3) Software Testing
Exercise 8- 1) Waterfall, 2) Agile, 3) DevOps
Exercise 9- 1 B, 2 A, 3 C, 4 D
Exercise 10- a) Assertion (A) is true and Reason (R) is the correct reason for Assertion (A).
Exercise 11- 1) Waterfall, 2) Agile, 3) DevOps

Online Resources

Online Exam paper
URL https://forms.gle/9RiKHyxe87owsc7Y9

QR Code

YouTube Video

URL https://www.youtube.com/playlist?list=PLzlh_31VWEFomrD2VyjpfRPx5Ye6Z3fT9

QR Code

More Test Papers Practices

Test Paper-1
URL https://forms.gle/3RUXADarE6858BT17
QR Code

Test Paper-2
URL https://forms.gle/sEy7QUVQmf2cr4NQ7

QR Code

System analysis and design Test Paper
Chapter- 7
Development Methodologies

Time Duration: 30 Minutes **Maximum Marks: 25**

General Instructions:

1. The question paper consists of answer any 12 questions out of the given 19 questions and is divided into four sections, A, B, C and D.
2. All questions are compulsory.
3. Section A comprises question numbers 1 to 8. These are MCQs and one liner of one mark each. You are to select one most appropriate response out of the four provided options.
4. Section B comprises question numbers 1 to 5. These are SAQs carrying two marks each.
5. Section C comprises question numbers 1 to 4. These are SAQs carrying four marks each.
6. Section D comprises question numbers 1& 2. These are LAQs carrying five marks each.

SECTION-A

I. <u>Answer any 6 questions out of the given 8 questions</u> **(1*6=6)**

1. What is a primary characteristic of the Waterfall Model?
   A) Iterative development
   B) Flexibility in changing requirements
   C) Linear and sequential phases
   D) Continuous integration
2. Which of the following is a key principle of Agile Methodologies?
   A) Rigid structure
   B) Comprehensive documentation
   C) Customer collaboration over contract negotiation
   D) Following a strict plan
3. What is a primary goal of DevOps practices?
   A) Isolating development and operations teams
   B) Slowing down the release process
   C) Increasing the frequency and reliability of software releases
   D) Reducing communication between teams
4. Which methodology emphasizes responding to change over following a fixed plan?
   A) Waterfall Model
   B) Agile Methodologies
   C) DevOps Practices
   D) Spiral Model
5. When choosing the right development methodology, what should be considered most important?
   A) The current trends in the industry
   B) The specific needs and constraints of the project
   C) The popularity of the methodology
   D) The size of the development team
6. What is the term for a development model with linear and sequential phases?
7. Which methodology focuses on continuous integration and delivery?
8. What key principle does Agile prioritize over contract negotiation?

SECTION-B

II. <u>Answer any 3 questions out of the given 5 questions</u> **(2*3=6)**

1. Define the Waterfall Model in software development.
2. What is a key advantage of Agile Methodologies?
3. List two main practices of DevOps.
4. Why is flexibility important in Agile Methodologies?
5. What factors should be considered when choosing a development methodology for a project?

SECTION-C

II. <u>Answer any 2 questions out of the given 4 questions</u> **(4*2=8)**

1. Explain the primary phases of the Waterfall Model and their sequence.
2. Describe the key principles of Agile Methodologies and how they differ from traditional models.
3. Discuss the main benefits of implementing DevOps practices in software development.
4. What are the main criteria to consider when choosing a development methodology for a new project?

SECTION-D

III. <u>Answer any 1 question out of the given 2 questions</u> **(5*1=5)**

1. Analyse the advantages and disadvantages of the Waterfall Model and Agile Methodologies. Provide examples to illustrate when each model is most appropriate.
2. Explain the role of DevOps in modern software development. Discuss how DevOps practices can improve the efficiency and reliability of software delivery.

Chapter 8: Implementation and Testing

- Understand the process of Coding and Unit Testing
- Gain insights into Integration Testing
- Explore Deployment Strategies
- Comprehend User Training and Acceptance Testing
- Familiarize with Software Maintenance Activities

8.1 Coding and Unit Testing

Introduction to Coding in System Design

In the realm of system design, coding is the process where system specifications are transformed into executable code. This process is not merely about writing code but involves the implementation of design decisions made during the system design phase. Effective coding requires adherence to coding standards, guidelines, and best practices to ensure the code is reliable, maintainable, and scalable.

1. Coding Standards and Practices

Coding standards are essential in system design to ensure consistency, readability, and maintainability of code. These standards cover various aspects, including naming conventions, code layout, and commenting. For example, variable names should be meaningful and self-explanatory, enhancing understanding and maintainability. Comments should be used judiciously to explain "why" something is done, rather than "what" is done, which should be evident from the code itself.

Implementing best practices such as DRY (Don't Repeat Yourself) and KISS (Keep It Simple, Stupid) principles also play a crucial role. The DRY principle avoids redundancy and helps in reducing the possibility of discrepancies during updates, whereas the KISS principle keeps the complexity of the system at a manageable level, making the system easier to maintain and extend.

2. Code Quality and Security

Quality and security are paramount in coding. Developers must write secure code that protects the system from vulnerabilities like SQL injections and cross-site scripting (XSS). Utilizing secure coding practices and regularly reviewing and testing the security of the code can mitigate potential risks.

Quality can be ensured through various static and dynamic code analysis tools which help in identifying potential bugs and security threats before the code goes into production. Regular code reviews, both peer and automated, also ensure that the code meets the set quality standards.

What is Unit Testing?

Unit testing of the software is conducted by the developers. It is done at the early stages of the software development process when each of the software units are not yet integrated. This is the first stage of functional testing of the software. The unit test cases may be executed manually or through automation.

The correctness of each isolated unit developed - function, method etc are verified. The unit testing is done to identify defects at the early stages of software development life cycle (SDLC) to improve the software quality and have a quicker fix for the defects. Each unit of software is tested independently by the developers.

What are the Prerequisites for Unit Testing?

In unit testing, individual software units consisting of methods, functions, procedures etc. are tested to check if they are working as expected. An individual unit is validated independently by the developer himself while he is working on it. A separate software component can be a specific method, function, procedure, block of code etc.

Once the unit testing has been completed, it moves to the integration testing phase. Bypassing unit testing leads to a higher number of defects detected at the integration, system, acceptance, and beta testing. Thus, unit testing clarifies software code, and fixes loopholes. The unit test cases consist of the below steps –

- Design Test Cases
- Review Test Cases
- Baseline Test Cases
- Run Test Cases

Why is Unit Testing Performed?
Th unit testing is performed because of the reasons listed below –
- It is performed to segregate a piece of code.
- It is performed to validate the accuracy of the developed code.
- Unit testing is done to test every function, method, procedure etc in the code.
- It detects bugs in the early phases of SDLC.
- It helps the developers to comprehend their code better and find loopholes there.
- Unit testing enables better reusability of the code.

Types of Unit Testing
The unit testing types are listed below –
1. Black Box Testing
    In black box testing technique, testers are unaware of the internal logic of software, and are only concerned with data input to software and its output.
1. White Box Testing
    In the white box testing technique, testers verify all the software functionalities along with the internal code.
1. Gray Box Testing
    The gray box testing is a combination of both black and white box testing.

Different Unit Testing Tools
The different unit testing tools are listed below –
- **JUnit** – JUnit is a unit testing framework for Java programming language. JUnit has been important in the development of test-driven development and is one of a family of unit testing frameworks collectively known as xUnit, that originated with JUnit.
- **NUnit** – It is a unit testing framework for .NET.
- **PHPUnit** – It is a unit testing framework for PHP.
- **EMMA** - It is a free and open-source framework working with Java.

Advantages of Unit Testing
The advantages of unit testing are listed below –
- Unit testing helps the developers to improve the code and make each software component work properly.
- It allows testing of independent clusters of the software without depending on other clusters.
- It allows early detection of defects in the initial stages of SDLC, and to fix them quickly.
- It helps the developers to build confidence on the code they developed by enhancing its quality.
- Unit testing helps to resolve the defects faster without requiring us to wait for the development of all the modules of the software.
- It assists the developers to refactor the code safely without breaking the existing functionalities.
- Unit testing saves a lot of time and resources as fixing defects at the early stages of SDLC is easier and faster than at the later stages.

Disadvantages of Unit Testing
The disadvantages of unit testing are listed below –
- It requires time to develop and maintain test cases for unit testing and modify them as the requirements change.
- It only identifies defects in individual units of the software and not in the integration of the units.
- It cannot detect errors in the user interface of the software.
- Unit testing does not include non-functional requirements of the software such as scalability, security, reliability, responsiveness, usability etc.
- The quality of the unit testing depends solely on how well the unit test cases are written by the developers.
- The developers face problems performing unit testing on complex applications as it is difficult to segregate their individual components and verify them.
- Unit testing does not involve testing of all the execution paths within the tested module.

8.2 Integration Testing
Integration testing is a critical phase in the system design process where individual software modules are combined and tested as a group. The primary objective of integration testing is to expose faults in the interaction between

integrated units. This chapter explores the fundamentals of integration testing, its importance in system design, methodologies, tools, and best practices.

1. Understanding Integration Testing

Integration testing is performed after unit testing and before system testing. In unit testing, individual components are tested in isolation. Once these units function correctly individually, integration testing ensures that their combination also works as expected.

The goal is to identify issues related to data flow, interfaces, and interactions between modules. Problems like data type mismatches, interface contract violations, and timing issues are common in this stage. By catching such issues early, developers can avoid complex problems in later stages of development, such as system testing or even after deployment.

2. Approaches to Integration Testing

Several approaches can be used for integration testing, each with its own advantages:

1. Big Bang Approach: This involves integrating all the modules at once and testing the entire application. While simple, it often makes it difficult to isolate errors.

2. Incremental Approach: This is more systematic and involves integrating modules step by step. It can be further divided into:

- **Top-down Integration:** Integration begins with top-level modules and progressively integrates lower-level modules. Stubs may be used to simulate lower-level modules until they are ready for integration.
- **Bottom-up Integration:** Starts with lower-level modules and progressively integrates upwards. Drivers are used to simulating higher-level modules until they are ready.
- **Sandwich/Hybrid Integration:** A combination of both top-down and bottom-up approaches.

3. Test Cases and Scenarios

Developing test cases for integration testing involves defining input data and determining the expected output. These test cases should focus on the interaction between modules. Scenarios include:

- Interface Testing: Ensuring that all interaction points between modules perform as expected.
- Regression Testing: Verifying that new code changes have not adversely affected existing integrated components.
- Performance Testing: Testing the performance and behavior of the system when multiple integrated units work together.

4. Tools for Integration Testing

There are several tools available that help in automating and managing integration tests:

- Jenkins: Used for continuous integration, it can automatically run integration tests every time changes are made.
- JUnit and NUnit: Frameworks that help in creating and running tests, particularly useful for automated unit and integration testing.
- Selenium: Primarily used for testing web applications, it is effective in integration testing for GUI components.

5. Best Practices in Integration Testing

To maximize the effectiveness of integration testing, certain best practices should be adopted:

- Plan Early: Start planning tests during the design phase to ensure comprehensive coverage.
- Continuous Integration: Integrate continuously to identify and fix issues early, reducing the cost and effort of fixing them later.
- Mock and Simulate: Use mocks and simulations to isolate areas under test, particularly when certain components are unavailable or incomplete.
- Prioritize Critical Modules: Focus on critical paths and modules that have the most dependencies or are most crucial to the application's functionality.
- Documentation and Reporting: Maintain thorough documentation of test cases, results, and anomalies. Regular reporting helps in tracking the progress and effectiveness of testing.

Conclusion

Integration testing is a vital part of the system design that ensures different components of a software system work together as expected. By using systematic approaches and appropriate tools, teams can ensure that integration issues are identified and resolved early in the development cycle, leading to a more reliable and robust final product. This testing not only helps in verifying the functionality but also enhances the quality and performance of the software system. As technology evolves, integration testing continues to adapt, making use of advanced tools and methodologies to tackle new challenges in system integration.

8.3 Deployment Strategies

Deployment strategies are a critical aspect of system design that can significantly impact the reliability, availability, scalability, and manageability of software applications. In this section, we will explore various deployment strategies that can be employed in the design of systems, ensuring that they meet business requirements and user expectations effectively.

Introduction to Deployment Strategies

In system design, deployment refers to the process of delivering a software application to a production environment where it can be accessed by end-users. A well-planned deployment strategy not only ensures smooth rollout of new features but also minimizes downtime and risks associated with changes. The choice of deployment strategy depends on various factors, including the nature of the application, business objectives, risk tolerance, and infrastructure considerations.

1. Big Bang Deployment

Big Bang deployment is the simplest form of deployment, where all components of the system are deployed simultaneously. This strategy is straightforward but risky, as it involves replacing the entire application at once. It is suitable for small, less complex systems or when introducing a brand-new application.

Pros:

- Simplicity in planning and execution.
- Immediate availability of the entire application.

Cons:

- High risk of failure and system downtime if issues arise.
- Difficult to rollback changes if needed.

2. Phased Deployment

Phased deployment involves rolling out the application in stages according to different parameters such as features, user groups, or geographical locations. This method allows for gradual exposure and minimizes risk by limiting the impact of potential issues to a subset of users.

Pros:

- Reduced risk compared to Big Bang deployment.
- Easier to identify and address issues when they affect a smaller segment of the user base.

Cons:

- More complex planning and coordination.
- Longer overall deployment time.

3. Blue-Green Deployment

Blue-green deployment is a technique where two identical environments, Blue and Green, are maintained. At any time, one environment is live (handling all production traffic), while the other serves as a staging area. After testing in the green environment, traffic is switched (typically via routing rules) so that Green becomes live, and Blue is turned to staging.

Pros:

- Zero-downtime deployments and instant rollback capabilities.
- Allows thorough testing of the new version in a production-like environment.

Cons:

- Requires double the resources since two full environments are maintained.
- Can be complex to manage.

4. Canary Deployment

Canary deployments involve deploying a new version of the application to a small subset of users initially. Based on the performance and the feedback, the deployment is gradually rolled out to more users. This strategy is named after the 'canary in a coal mine' concept.

Pros:

- Minimizes impact of potential issues on the user base.

- Allows fine-tuning of the application based on real user feedback.

Cons:

- More complex to implement, requiring sophisticated traffic routing and monitoring.
- Longer rollout periods can delay full availability.

5. A/B Testing Deployment

A/B testing, or split testing, is a method where two or more versions of an application are run simultaneously with different groups of users. This strategy is often used not only for deployment but also for testing different features or designs to determine which performs better.

Pros:

- Provides concrete data on user preference and system performance.
- Allows optimization of features based on user feedback.

Cons:

- Requires complex setup for segmenting users and analyzing results.
- Potentially long testing periods before full deployment.

Conclusion

Choosing the right deployment strategy is crucial in system design. It affects how smoothly and successfully a software application is rolled out to end-users. Each strategy has its strengths and weaknesses, and the best choice depends on the specific requirements of the project and the operational dynamics of the organization.

8.4 User Training and Acceptance Testing

User training is an essential phase in the implementation of any system. It ensures that end-users can utilize the software to its full potential, thereby maximizing the efficiency and effectiveness of the organization. Training strategies should be designed to accommodate diverse learning styles and proficiencies.

Objectives of User Training

1. Enhance User Competence: Equip users with the necessary skills to operate the new system efficiently.

2. Reduce Resistance: Familiarize users with the system to mitigate resistance stemming from unfamiliarity and fear of change.

3. Promote Efficient Use: Ensure that users are proficient in using the system and can leverage its features fully to improve their daily tasks.

Training Methods

- **Workshops:** Interactive sessions that allow hands-on experience with the system.
- **E-Learning Modules:** Online training resources that users can access at their convenience.
- **Simulation and Role-playing:** Realistic scenarios that help users understand system navigation and functionality.
- **On-the-Job Training:** Supplementing training with real-time guidance as users begin to use the system in their work environment.
- **Support Desks:** Ongoing support for troubleshooting and queries post-training.

Content Development

Training content should be clear, concise, and tailored to the user's job role. It should include:

- Step-by-step tutorials for common tasks.
- Troubleshooting guides for common issues.
- Frequently asked questions and their answers.
- Contact information for technical support.

Assessment and Feedback

Assessing user competency post-training through quizzes and practical tests is crucial. Feedback should also be collected to improve future training sessions.

What is Acceptance Testing?

Acceptance testing, a testing technique performed to determine whether the software system has met the requirement specifications. The main purpose of this test is to evaluate the system's compliance with the business requirements and verify if it has met the required criteria for delivery to end users.

There are various forms of acceptance testing:
- User acceptance Testing
- Business acceptance Testing
- Alpha Testing
- Beta Testing

Acceptance Testing - In SDLC
The following diagram explains the fitment of acceptance testing in the software development life cycle.

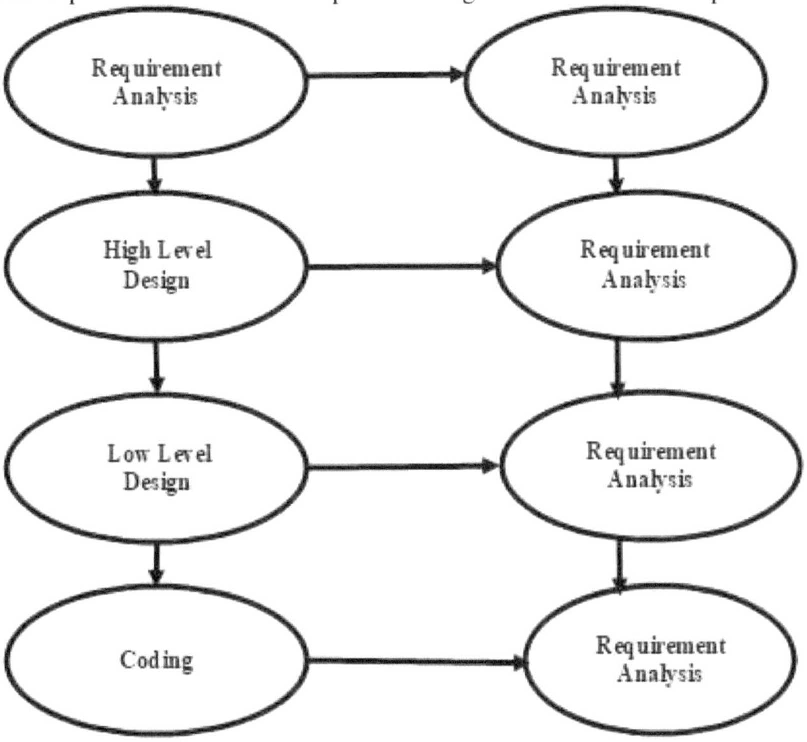

The acceptance test cases are executed against the test data or using an acceptance test script and then the results are compared with the expected ones.

Acceptance Criteria
Acceptance criteria are defined based on the following attributes
- Functional Correctness and Completeness
- Data Integrity
- Data Conversion
- Usability
- Performance
- Timeliness
- Confidentiality and Availability
- Installability and Upgradability
- Scalability
- Documentation

Acceptance Test Plan - Attributes
The acceptance test activities are carried out in phases. Firstly, the basic tests are executed, and if the test results are satisfactory then the execution of more complex scenarios are carried out.
The Acceptance test plan has the following attributes:
- Introduction
- Acceptance Test Category

- operation Environment
- Test case ID
- Test Title
- Test Objective
- Test Procedure
- Test Schedule
- Resources

The acceptance test activities are designed to reach at one of the conclusions:
- Accept the system as delivered
- Accept the system after the requested modifications have been made
- Do not accept the system

Acceptance Test Report - Attributes
The Acceptance test Report has the following attributes:
- Report Identifier
- Summary of Results
- Variations
- Recommendations
- Summary of To-Do List
- Approval Decision

8.5 Software Maintenance Activities

In the realm of software engineering, the completion of a software product's initial development marks the beginning of an equally crucial phase—software maintenance. This chapter delves into the core activities involved in software maintenance within the context of system design. We aim to elucidate how maintenance activities are integral not just for the correction of defects but also for the system's evolution in response to changing requirements and technologies.

1. Understanding Software Maintenance
Software maintenance in system design refers to the modifications made to a software product after it has been delivered to correct faults, improve performance, or adapt the product to a changed environment. Maintenance is a continuous requirement and consumes a significant portion of the total lifecycle costs of a system. This activity ensures that the software continues to operate in the new or changed conditions of its environment.

2. Types of Software Maintenance
Maintenance activities can be broadly classified into four categories:
- **Corrective Maintenance**: This involves the correction of identified defects in the software. It is usually performed after the software is released and is often triggered by error reports from users.
- **Adaptive Maintenance**: This includes modifications to the software to keep it usable in a changed or changing environment. It may involve making the software operable in a new operating system, hardware, or with different data formats.
- **Perfective Maintenance**: This encompasses enhancements to improve performance or maintainability. It includes refining the code to make it cleaner and easier to understand, which can reduce future maintenance costs.
- **Preventive Maintenance**: Often referred to as "software re-engineering," this aims to anticipate future problems and address them before they manifest. It involves updating documentation and restructuring the code to adapt more easily to future changes or enhancements.

3. Maintenance Processes
Effective software maintenance requires a structured approach to manage the complexity and ensure consistency in the treatment of the software. The maintenance process generally involves the following steps:
- **Problem Identification and Classification**: This step involves recognizing a defect or improvement area, classifying it under one of the maintenance types, and prioritizing it.
- **Analysis**: The impact of the required change is analyzed in terms of system functionality and integration with other system components. This step determines the feasibility of the maintenance request.
- **Design**: Once the change is deemed necessary and feasible, the next step is to design the modification. This involves updating the existing design documents to reflect the change.

- **Implementation**: The design changes are implemented in the code. This might involve editing small sections of the code or a significant part of the system in the case of major enhancements or corrections.
- **Testing**: After implementation, the new or modified software is tested to ensure that the change has been implemented correctly and that it has not adversely affected existing functionalities.
- **Deployment**: Once testing is completed, the software is deployed. This could be a patch for a small change or a new version of the software for major revisions.
- **Documentation**: Throughout the maintenance process, all changes made to the software and their impacts are documented thoroughly. This documentation is crucial for future maintenance activities.

4. Challenges in Software Maintenance

Maintaining software systems presents several challenges, including:
- **Understanding Legacy Code**: In many cases, the original developers of the software may no longer be available, and the documentation might be incomplete or outdated.
- **Dealing with Increasing Complexity**: As software is modified and extended, its structure can degrade, making it more difficult to understand and maintain.
- **Limited Understanding of Impact**: Changes in one part of the software can have unexpected effects on other parts, which may not be anticipated by the developers making the changes.

5. Best Practices in Software Maintenance

To effectively manage these challenges, the following best practices are recommended:
- **Maintain Robust Documentation**: Keeping documentation up to date is critical for effective maintenance.
- **Use Standardized Processes**: Standard processes and guidelines help maintain consistency and quality in maintenance activities.
- **Invest in Automated Testing**: Automated tests can significantly reduce the time and cost of the testing phases.
- **Continuous Training**: Keeping the maintenance team well-trained in the latest development technologies and best practices can prevent many common issues in software maintenance.

Conclusion

Software maintenance is an indispensable aspect of system design that requires attention to detail, careful planning, and adherence to best practices. It extends the life of the software, ensures its relevance in changing environments, and enhances user satisfaction. By understanding and implementing robust maintenance practices, organizations can significantly improve the longevity and performance of their software systems.

8.6 Enhancements and Upgrades

In the ever-evolving landscape of technology and organizational needs, system design cannot remain static. Enhancements and upgrades are critical components that ensure a system remains efficient, effective, and aligned with business goals. This chapter explores the strategic approach to system enhancements and upgrades, focusing on methodologies, best practices, and real-world applications to optimize system performance and sustainability.

The Need for Enhancements and Upgrades

Systems are designed to meet specific objectives at a point in time. However, as technology advances, business goals change, and external conditions evolve, the initial system may no longer be optimal. Enhancements (incremental improvements to existing features) and upgrades (substantial changes or additions) ensure systems continue to provide value, meet new standards, and leverage technological advancements.

Planning and Assessing Upgrades

- **Assessment of Current Systems**: Before planning enhancements, it's crucial to thoroughly assess the current system's performance. This involves reviewing system metrics against performance goals, gathering user feedback, and identifying pain points and bottlenecks.
- **Identifying Opportunities**: Enhancement opportunities can often be identified through SWOT analysis (Strengths, Weaknesses, Opportunities, Threats), focusing on leveraging strengths and opportunities while mitigating weaknesses and threats.
- **Feasibility Studies**: Each potential upgrade should undergo a feasibility study, considering technical, economic, and operational aspects to ensure that the enhancement is practical and beneficial.

Designing System Enhancements

- **Incremental vs. Radical Changes**: Deciding between incremental improvements and comprehensive upgrades involves balancing risk, cost, and impact. Incremental changes typically involve less risk and cost but might lead to slower overall improvement.
- **User-Centric Design**: Enhancements should focus on user experience, aiming to simplify interfaces, reduce workload, and improve interaction. This approach helps in achieving higher user satisfaction and productivity.
- **Scalability and Flexibility**: Upgrades should be designed with scalability in mind, anticipating future needs and potential expansions. This foresight reduces the need for future redesigns and increases the system's longevity.

Implementation Strategies
- **Prototyping and Testing**: Before full-scale implementation, prototyping and testing are essential. These phases help identify unforeseen issues and gather user feedback, which can be used to refine the system.
- **Change Management**: Successful upgrades require effective change management strategies to ensure smooth transition and adoption. This includes training for users, support during the transition period, and clear communication about the benefits and changes.
- **Monitoring and Evaluation**: After implementation, continuous monitoring is crucial to assess the impact of the enhancements. Evaluation against pre-set goals helps determine if the upgrade has achieved its intended outcomes.

Case Studies
- **E-commerce Platform Upgrade**: An e-commerce company upgraded its platform to handle increased traffic and incorporate AI for better customer recommendations. This case study discusses the planning, implementation, and outcomes of this upgrade.
- **Healthcare System Integration**: A healthcare provider integrated its various information systems to create a unified platform that improved patient care and data accessibility. The project highlights the challenges of integrating existing systems and the strategies used to overcome them.

Challenges in System Enhancements
- **Resource Allocation**: Ensuring adequate resources, including time, budget, and skilled personnel, is a common challenge. Resource constraints can delay or reduce the effectiveness of upgrades.
- **Technological Compatibility**: With rapid technological changes, ensuring compatibility between new upgrades and existing systems can be difficult. This requires careful selection of technology and sometimes intermediate steps to bridge technology gaps.
- **Security Concerns**: Upgrades must also address security, as new functionalities can introduce vulnerabilities. A proactive approach to security is essential, considering both current threats and future potential.

8.7 Bug Fixes and Patch Management

In the field of software development, maintaining the integrity and functionality of a system over time is crucial. Bug fixes and patch management are central practices in ensuring that software systems remain robust, secure, and efficient. These activities not only address immediate functional issues but also contribute to the long-term health of the software. This section of the system design concept book delves into the processes, strategies, and best practices involved in effective bug fixing and patch management.

Understanding Bugs and Patches
Bugs are flaws or errors in a software system that can cause it to behave unexpectedly or to cease functioning. They can arise from a multitude of sources, including coding errors, system misconfigurations, or unforeseen interactions between different parts of the software.

A **patch** is a piece of software designed to update a computer program or its supporting data, to fix or improve it. This includes fixing security vulnerabilities and other bugs and improving the usability or performance.

The Bug Fixing Process
The bug fixing process typically follows these steps:
1. Identification: Bugs are often reported by users or identified by internal testing teams. Automated error reporting tools can also detect bugs by monitoring software operations.
2. Classification and Prioritization: Once a bug is identified, it is important to classify its severity and prioritize its resolution based on the impact on the users and the system.

3. Analysis and Reproduction: Developers analyze the bug and attempt to reproduce it in a controlled environment to understand its cause.
4. Resolution: After identifying the cause, developers make code changes, test the solution to ensure it resolves the bug without introducing new issues.
5. Verification: Once a bug fix is applied, it must be verified. This involves testing the fixed version to ensure the problem is fully resolved and that no new problems have been introduced.
6. Deployment: The final step is to deploy the fix, often in the form of a patch, to the user environment, ensuring that all systems are updated.

Patch Management Strategies
Effective patch management is a systematic approach to manage updates of software that includes bug fixes, security patches, and other updates. The patch management process involves:
1. Patch Testing: Before deployment, patches should be tested in a staging environment. This helps to mitigate any potential impact on the system's performance and functionality.
2. Scheduling and Rollout: Depending on the severity of the issues addressed by the patch, the rollout might be immediate or scheduled for a less disruptive time. Critical security patches are usually deployed immediately.
3. Automation: Automating the patch management process can help in the timely deployment of patches and reduce the workload on IT staff. Tools like WSUS (Windows Server Update Services) or SCCM (System Center Configuration Manager) can be used.
4. Compliance and Documentation: Ensuring that all systems are compliant with the latest patches is crucial for security. Detailed documentation of the patch levels of all systems helps in audits and troubleshooting.

Best Practices for Bug Fixes and Patch Management
1. Regular Updates: Maintain regular updates of all software, not just the operating system but all applications in use.
2. Comprehensive Testing: Extensive testing of both bugs and patches ensures fewer issues in the production environment.
3. Clear Communication: Communicate clearly with all stakeholders about the nature of the bugs and the necessary patches, including potential impacts and downtimes.
4. Feedback Loops: Establish a feedback loop with users and testers to continuously improve the process.
5. Security First: Always prioritize patches that fix security vulnerabilities to protect data and users from breaches.

Conclusion
Effective bug fixes and patch management are fundamental to maintaining the reliability, security, and efficiency of software systems. By understanding and implementing rigorous processes and best practices, developers and system administrators can ensure that software continues to serve its purpose and meet user needs safely and effectively. This proactive approach to system maintenance not only improves performance but also significantly reduces the risk associated with software vulnerabilities.

8.8 Help Desk and User Support

In the context of system design, the Help Desk and User Support functions are critical components that provide end users with necessary assistance, guidance, and troubleshooting services. A well-designed help desk not only enhances user satisfaction but also ensures the longevity and scalability of a system. This section outlines the best practices, strategic implementations, and essential considerations for integrating an effective help desk and user support framework into system design.

1. Objectives of Help Desk and User Support
The primary objective of help desk and user support is to facilitate effective interaction between the users and the technology. This support should aim to resolve problems, provide information, and ensure continuous improvement in user experience. The specific goals include:
1. Resolving Technical Issues: Quickly and efficiently solving problems that users encounter.
2. Educating Users: Providing necessary training and documentation to help users understand and effectively use the system.
3. Gathering Feedback: Collecting user feedback to guide future updates and improvements.
4. Ensuring System Availability: Maintaining and monitoring system performance to avoid downtimes.

2. Structure of Help Desk Support
The structure of a help desk can vary based on the size of the organization and the complexity of the system. Generally, it includes:
1. Tier 1 Support: This is the first line of support dealing with basic user issues and FAQs. Issues not resolved at this level are escalated to higher tiers.
2. Tier 2 Support: Handles more complex issues that require technical expertise.
3. Tier 3 Support: Deals with advanced technical challenges, often involving system developers or engineers.

3. Integration with System Design
Integrating help desk and user support into system design involves several strategic elements:
1. User Interface Design: Design interfaces that are intuitive and user-friendly. Incorporate help features, such as tooltips, inline help texts, and accessible user manuals.
2. Feedback Mechanisms: Embed systems to collect user feedback directly through the interface, which can inform support services and system improvements.
3. Automation: Use automated tools like chatbots or AI-driven helpdesk software to provide instant responses to common queries.

4. Technology and Tools
Leveraging the right technology is key to an effective help desk. Tools commonly used include:
1. Ticketing Systems: Software like Zendesk or JIRA to manage, track, and resolve user issues.
2. Remote Support Software: Tools that allow support personnel to take control of a user's system remotely to diagnose and fix issues.
3. Knowledge Bases and FAQs: Online resources that users can access anytime to find solutions to common problems.
4. Communication Tools: Email, live chat, and phone systems that facilitate easy communication between users and support staff.

5. Training and Development
Training is crucial for help desk staff to ensure they are equipped with the necessary skills and knowledge. Training programs should cover:
1. Technical Skills: Understanding the system's architecture, functionality, and potential issues.
2. Soft Skills: Communication, empathy, and problem-solving skills to effectively interact with users.
3. Continuous Learning: Keeping up with new technologies, system updates, and best practices in customer support.

6. Measuring Success
To evaluate the effectiveness of the help desk, several metrics should be monitored:
1. Response Time: The speed with which support requests are acknowledged and resolved.
2. User Satisfaction: Feedback and surveys to gauge the user's experience with the support they receive.
3. Resolution Rate: The percentage of issues resolved without escalation to higher tiers.
4. System Uptime: The operational availability of the system, which can indicate the success of support activities in maintaining system health.

Conclusion
The Help Desk and User Support functions are vital to the success of any system design. They not only solve user problems but also contribute to the system's continuous improvement by providing insights into user experiences and system performance. Effective integration of help desk and user support into system design enhances user satisfaction, promotes system efficiency, and supports business objectives through improved technological interaction.
This framework provides a comprehensive approach to building and maintaining robust help desk and user support services as an integral part of system design.

Summary

1. Coding Standards and Practices: Essential for ensuring code consistency, readability, and maintainability, including meaningful variable names and judicious comments.
2. Code Quality and Security: Emphasizes the importance of secure coding practices and regular code reviews to mitigate potential vulnerabilities and ensure high-quality code.

3. Unit Testing: Conducted by developers to verify the functionality of individual units (functions, methods) early in the development process, improving software quality and detecting defects early.
4. Integration Testing: Combines and tests individual software modules as a group to identify issues related to data flow and interaction between modules, using approaches like Big Bang, Incremental, Top-down, and Bottom-up.
5. Deployment Strategies: Various strategies include Big Bang (simultaneous deployment), Phased (staged rollout), Blue Green (dual environment), and Canary (gradual deployment to a subset of users), each with its pros and cons.
6. User Training: Ensures users can effectively utilize the system through workshops, e-learning modules, on-the-job training, and support desks, aiming to enhance user competence and reduce resistance.
7. Acceptance Testing: Validates the system against business requirements before delivery, including user acceptance testing, business acceptance testing, alpha testing, and beta testing.
8. Software Maintenance: Involves corrective, adaptive, perfective, and preventive maintenance to ensure ongoing system functionality and adaptation to changing environments and requirements.
9. Enhancements and Upgrades: Ensure systems remain efficient and aligned with business goals, involving assessment of current systems, user-centric design, scalability considerations, and effective implementation strategies.
10. Bug Fixes and Patch Management: Critical for maintaining software integrity, involving identification, classification, analysis, resolution, verification, and deployment of bug fixes, along with strategic patch management.
11. Help Desk and User Support: Provides essential assistance, guidance, and troubleshooting to users, structured into tiers of support, integrated with system design, utilizing technology and tools like ticketing systems and remote support software.
12. Measuring Support Effectiveness: Evaluates the success of help desk and support services through metrics like response time, user satisfaction, resolution rate, and system uptime.

Glossary

1. Coding Standards: Guidelines and best practices for writing code to ensure consistency, readability, and maintainability across a software project.
2. DRY Principle: "Don't Repeat Yourself," a principle aimed at reducing code duplication to improve maintainability and reduce errors.
3. Unit Testing: A type of software testing where individual units or components of a software are tested independently to ensure they function correctly.
4. Integration Testing: Testing combined parts of an application to determine if they function together correctly, often following unit testing.
5. Big Bang Integration: An integration testing approach where all components are combined at once, making it difficult to isolate errors.
6. Incremental Integration: An approach to integration testing where components are integrated and tested step-by-step, often categorized as top-down or bottom-up.
7. Blue-Green Deployment: A deployment strategy using two identical environments (blue and green) to enable zero-downtime releases by switching between them.
8. Canary Deployment: A deployment strategy that involves releasing changes to a small subset of users before rolling out to the entire user base to minimize risk.
9. User Acceptance Testing (UAT): The process of verifying that a system meets the agreed-upon requirements and is ready for deployment, often involving end users.
10. Corrective Maintenance: Software maintenance performed to fix identified defects in the system.
11. Adaptive Maintenance: Changes made to software to keep it functional in a changed or changing environment, such as updates for new operating systems.
12. Preventive Maintenance: Updates and changes made to a software system to prevent potential future problems and improve long-term functionality.
13. Patch Management: The process of managing a network of computers by regularly performing system updates and patches to address vulnerabilities and bugs.
14. Help Desk Support: A service providing end users with technical assistance, troubleshooting, and guidance for system usage and problem resolution.
15. Knowledge Base: A centralized repository of information, FAQs, and troubleshooting guides that users can access for self-help and issue resolution.
16. SWOT Analysis: A strategic planning tool used to identify strengths, weaknesses, opportunities, and threats related to system enhancements and upgrades.

17. Sandbox Environment: A testing environment that isolates untested changes and experiments from the production environment, used to safely test new features or changes.
18. Continuous Integration (CI): A DevOps practice where developers frequently integrate code changes into a shared repository, with each change being automatically tested.

8.9 Project

8.9.1 Solved Project

You are leading a project to develop, deploy, and maintain an e-commerce platform. The project covers all phases of implementation and testing, including coding and unit testing, integration testing, deployment strategies, user training and acceptance testing, software maintenance activities, enhancements and upgrades, bug fixes and patch management, and help desk and user support.

Approach:
Phase 1: Coding and Unit Testing
1. Objectives:
2. Key Activities:
3. Coding Standards
4. Development
5. Unit Testing
6. Testing Frameworks
7. Outcome:

Phase 2: Integration Testing
Objectives:
Key Activities:
- Integration Points
- Integration Tests
- Automated Testing Tools
- Feedback Loop

Outcome:

Phase 3: Deployment Strategies
Objectives:
Key Activities:
- Deployment Plan
- Environment Setup
- Automated Deployment Tools
- Risk Mitigation

Outcome:

Phase 4: User Training and Acceptance Testing
Objectives:
Key Activities:
- Training Materials
- Training Sessions
- Acceptance Testing
- Pilot Feedback

Outcome:

Phase 5: Software Maintenance Activities
Objectives:
Key Activities:
- Issue Tracking
- Maintenance Schedule

- Documentation
- Maintenance Tools

Outcome:

Phase 6: Enhancements and Upgrades

Objectives:

Key Activities:

- Performance Review
- Enhancement Plan
- Compatibility Testing
- Rollout Strategy
- Outcome:

Phase 7: Bug Fixes and Patch Management

Objectives:

Key Activities:

- Bug Tracking
- Criticality Assessment
- Patch Development
- Automated Deployment

Outcome:

Phase 8: Help Desk and User Support

Objectives:

Key Activities:

- Help Desk Setup
- Support Documentation
- Ticketing System
- User Feedback

Outcome:

Deliverables:

1. Coding Standards Document
2. Unit Test Reports
3. Integration Test Reports
4. Deployment Plan
5. Training Materials
6. UAT Feedback Reports
7. Maintenance Schedule
8. Enhancement and Upgrade Plan
9. Bug Tracking Reports
10. Help Desk Documentation

8.9.2 Unsolved Project

Suppose you need to manage bug fixes and patch releases for a software application. Before starting, review best practices for bug tracking and patch management, ensure all reported bugs are documented, verify the criticality of each bug, explore automated tools for patch deployment, and ask for expert advice on minimizing downtime during patch releases. This ensures that bugs are efficiently resolved, and patches are effectively managed.

8.10 Case Study

8.10.1 Solved Case Study

The implementation and testing phase of software development is essential for creating a reliable and efficient application. It begins with coding and unit testing, where developers write and validate the code for individual components using frameworks like JUnit or pytest. Next is integration testing, ensuring all modules work together seamlessly with tools like Jenkins and CircleCI automating the process. Deployment strategies are carefully planned, including environment setup, detailed deployment plans, and automated deployment tools such as Ansible or Chef, along with risk mitigation strategies. User training and acceptance testing ensure the system meets user needs, with comprehensive training materials and user acceptance testing sessions. Software maintenance activities keep the application up to date, involving issue tracking, maintenance schedules, and documentation. Enhancements and upgrades are based on user feedback and technological advancements. Bug fixes and patch management involve tracking bugs, developing patches, and deploying them efficiently. Finally, a help desk and user support system is established to manage inquiries and improve support services continuously.

Questions:

1. What is the purpose of coding and unit testing in software development?

   Answer: The purpose of coding and unit testing is to write and validate the code for individual components.
2. Which tools are used to automate integration testing?

   Answer: Tools used to automate integration testing include Jenkins and CircleCI.
3. What are some key activities involved in deployment strategies?

   Answer: Key activities involved in deployment strategies include environment setup, developing detailed deployment plans, using automated deployment tools, and risk mitigation.
4. Why are user training and acceptance testing important?

   Answer: User training and acceptance testing are important to ensure the system meets user needs and to validate the system's functionality.
5. What does bug fixes and patch management involve?

   Answer: Bug fixes and patch management involve tracking bugs, developing patches, and deploying them efficiently.

8.10.2 Unsolved Case Study

Effective software development involves meticulous steps to ensure the final product is robust and user-friendly. Coding involves writing the software's source code, followed by unit testing to verify individual components work as intended. Integration testing combines these units to identify issues in their interactions. Deployment strategies, like phased rollouts and continuous deployment, outline how software is distributed to users, minimizing downtime. User training ensures end-users understand the software, while acceptance testing verifies it meets user needs. Software maintenance includes updates and performance tuning to ensure continued functionality. Enhancements and upgrades add or improve features based on user feedback and technological advancements. Bug fixes and patch management correct errors and vulnerabilities, improving stability and security. A robust help desk and user support system addresses user issues, providing essential assistance and guidance.

Questions:

1. What is the purpose of unit testing?
2. What does integration testing aim to identify?
3. Name one deployment strategy mentioned in the passage.
4. Why is user training important in the software deployment process?
5. What is the goal of bug fixes and patch management?

8.11 Lab Activity

8.11.1 Solved Lab Activity

1. Create a test plan for integrating two modules of a library management system: one for user management and another for book inventory. Include test cases and expected results.

Solution:

Test Plan for Integration

1. Introduction

This test plan covers the integration testing of the User Management and Book Inventory modules of the library management system. The objective is to ensure that the modules interact correctly and meet the functional requirements.

2. Scope

The test plan includes the following key integration points:

1. User account creation and book borrowing

2. User account deletion and book return
3. Updating user details and reflecting changes in borrowed books

3. Test Environment

The integration tests will be conducted in a staging environment with the following setup:
1. Database: MySQL
2. Application Server: Tomcat
3. Frontend: React.js
4. Backend: Spring Boot

4. Test Cases

Test Case 1: User Account Creation and Book Borrowing

Test Case ID	**TC_001**
Description	Verify that a new user can borrow a book after account creation
Precondition	The user management module and book inventory module are deployed
Steps	1. Create a new user account 2. Log in with the new account 3. Search for a book in the inventory 4. Borrow the book
Expected Result	The user should be able to borrow the book, and the book inventory should update to show the book as borrowed

Test Case 2: User Account Deletion and Book Return

Test Case ID	**TC_002**
Description	Verify that when a user account is deleted, all borrowed books are returned to the inventory
Precondition	The user has borrowed at least one book
Steps	1. Delete the user account 2. Verify the borrowed books are returned to the inventory
Expected Result	The books previously borrowed by the deleted user should be marked as available in the inventory

Test Case 3: Updating User Details and Reflecting Changes in Borrowed Books

Test Case ID	**TC_003**
Description	Verify that updating user details (e.g., email, address) is reflected correctly in the user management module and associated borrowed books information
Precondition	The user has borrowed books
Steps	1. Update the user details 2. Verify the updated details are reflected in the user profile 3. Check the borrowed books information to ensure consistency
Expected Result	The updated user details should be accurately reflected in the user profile and borrowed books information

5. Test Execution

1. Each test case will be executed according to the steps defined.
2. Results will be recorded and compared with the expected outcomes.
3. Any discrepancies will be logged as defects and reported to the development team for resolution.

Explanation

The test plan outlines the strategy and specific test cases for verifying the integration between the User Management and Book Inventory modules. Each test case includes a unique identifier, description, preconditions, steps, and expected results to ensure comprehensive coverage of integration points.

Diagram:

Here is the sequence diagram illustrating the integration test cases for the User Management and Book Inventory modules:

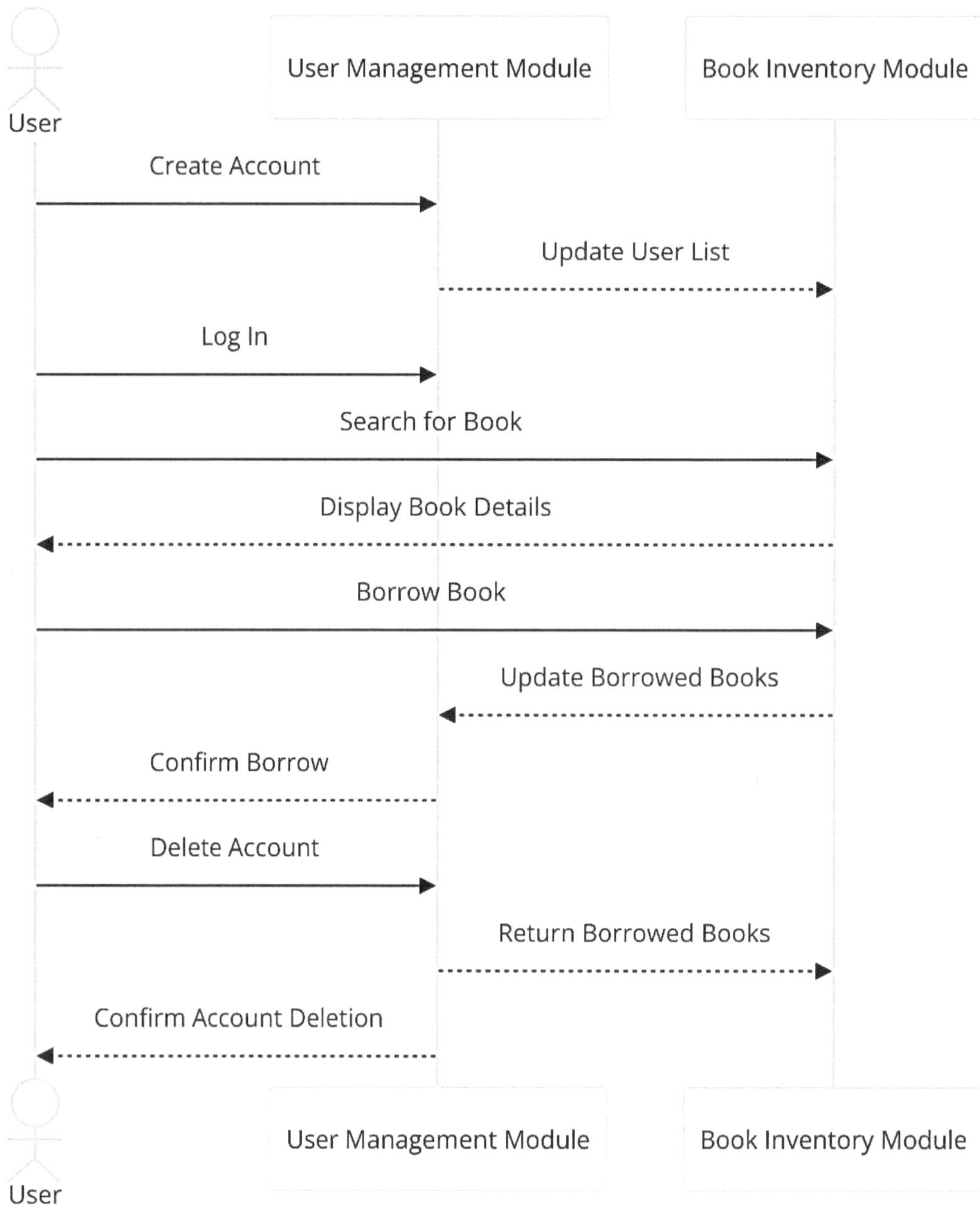

Explanation

Actors and Participants:

1. User: The person interacting with the system.
2. User Management Module: Manages user accounts and their details.
3. Book Inventory Module: Manages the inventory of books, including borrowing and returning of books.

Flow of Activities:

1. Create Account: The user creates an account in the User Management Module, which then updates the user list in the Book Inventory Module.
2. Log In: The user logs into the system.
3. Search for Book: The user searches for a book in the Book Inventory Module, which displays the book details.
4. Borrow Book: The user borrows a book. The Book Inventory Module updates the borrowed books list in the User Management Module, and the user receives a confirmation.

5. Delete Account: The user deletes their account. The User Management Module ensures that all borrowed books are returned to the Book Inventory Module and then confirms the account deletion to the user.

Test Cases

1. Test Case 1: User Account Creation and Book Borrowing verifies the process from account creation to borrowing a book.
2. Test Case 2: User Account Deletion and Book Return ensures borrowed books are returned when an account is deleted.
3. Test Case 3: Updating User Details and Reflecting Changes in Borrowed Books confirms user details updates and their reflection in the borrowed books information.

1. Develop a deployment plan for a new version of an e-commerce website. Include steps for pre-deployment, deployment, and post-deployment activities.

Solution:
Deployment Plan for E-commerce Website

1. **Pre-Deployment Activities**

1. Code Review and Testing: Ensure all new code has been reviewed and tested in a staging environment.
2. Backup Data: Take a full backup of the current production database.
3. Notify Stakeholders: Inform all relevant stakeholders (e.g., support team, marketing team) about the upcoming deployment.
4. Prepare Rollback Plan: Develop a rollback plan in case the deployment fails.
5. Update Documentation: Ensure all documentation (e.g., deployment scripts, user manuals) is up to date.
6. Verify Server Requirements: Ensure that all server requirements (e.g., disk space, software versions) are met.

2. **Deployment Activities**

1. Deploy to Staging Environment: First, deploy the new version to the staging environment to ensure it works as expected.
2. Final Testing in Staging: Perform final testing in the staging environment.
3. Deploy to Production: Deploy the new version to the production environment.
4. Steps:
5. Put Website in Maintenance Mode: Display a maintenance message to users.
6. Deploy Code: Deploy the new code to the production servers.
7. Update Database Schema: Apply any database schema changes.
8. Run Migrations: Run any necessary database migrations.
9. Clear Cache: Clear the application cache to ensure the latest changes are reflected.
10. Restart Services: Restart any necessary services (e.g., web server, database).

3. **Post-Deployment Activities**

1. Smoke Testing: Perform smoke testing to ensure the basic functionality of the website is working.
2. Monitor System: Monitor the system for any issues (e.g., performance, errors).
3. User Acceptance Testing (UAT): Allow a small group of users to test the new version.
4. Full System Testing: Conduct full system testing to ensure all functionalities are working.
5. Collect Feedback: Collect feedback from users and stakeholders.
6. Resolve Issues: Address any issues that arise during post-deployment.
7. Notify Users: Inform users that the website is live with the new version.

Diagram

We will now create a flow diagram to illustrate the deployment plan activities.

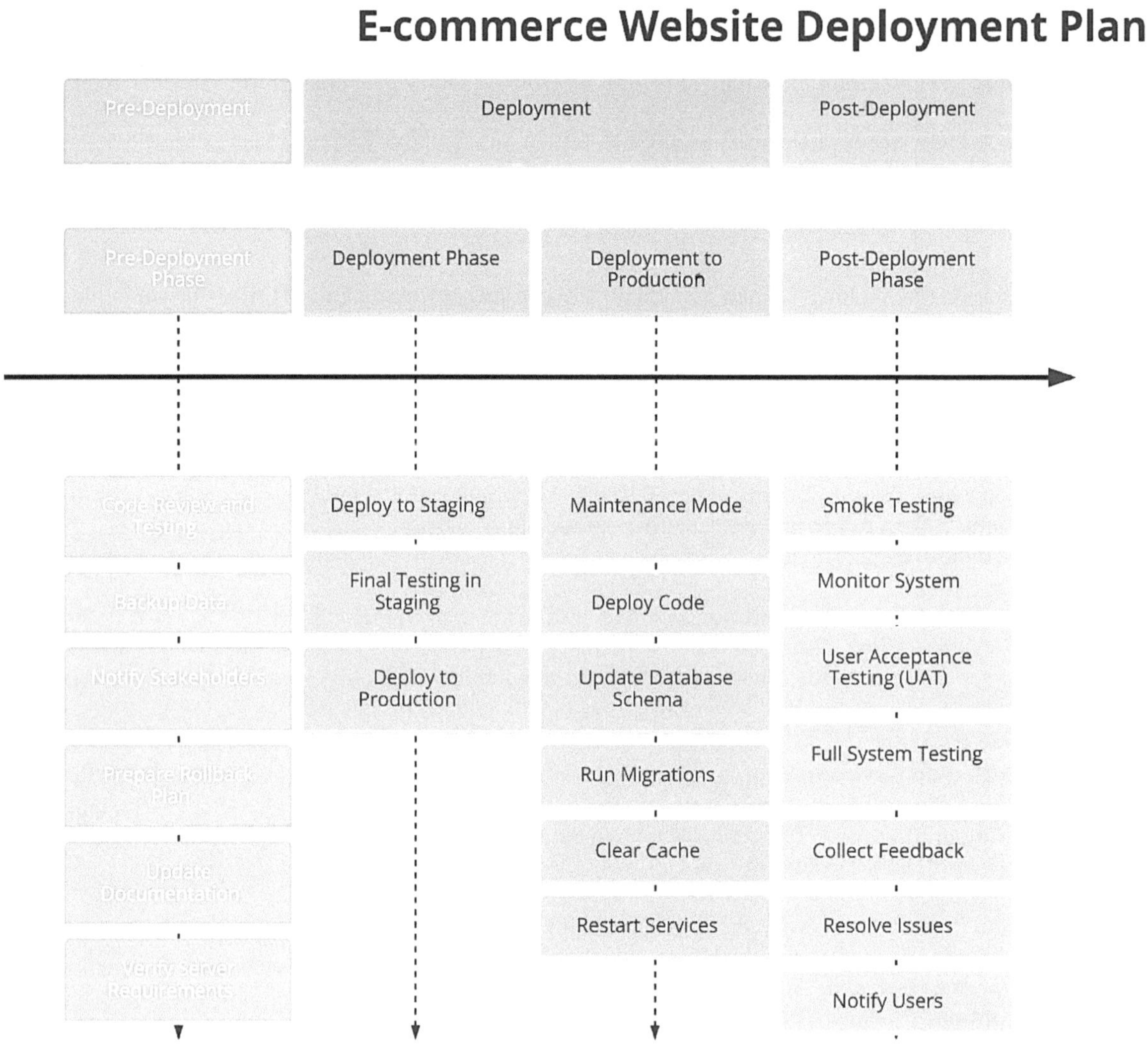

Explanation

Pre-Deployment Activities:

1. **Code Review and Testing**: Ensure all code changes are reviewed and tested.
2. **Backup Data**: Take a full backup of the current database.
3. **Notify Stakeholders**: Inform all relevant stakeholders about the deployment schedule.
4. **Prepare Rollback Plan**: Develop a plan to revert changes if the deployment fails.
5. **Update Documentation**: Ensure all relevant documentation is updated.
6. **Verify Server Requirements**: Check that all server requirements are met.

Deployment Activities:

1. **Deploy to Staging**: Deploy the new version to a staging environment for testing.
2. **Final Testing in Staging**: Conduct final testing in the staging environment.
3. **Deploy to Production**: Perform the actual deployment to the production environment.
4. Steps:
5. **Maintenance Mode**: Enable maintenance mode to inform users.
6. **Deploy Code**: Deploy the new code.

7. Update Database Schema: Apply necessary database schema changes.
8. Run Migrations: Run database migrations.
9. Clear Cache: Clear the application cache.
10. Restart Services: Restart necessary services.

Post-Deployment Activities:
1. Smoke Testing: Conduct smoke tests to verify basic functionality.
2. Monitor System: Monitor the system for any issues.
3. User Acceptance Testing (UAT): Allow a small group of users to test the new version.
4. Full System Testing: Perform comprehensive system testing.
5. Collect Feedback: Gather feedback from users and stakeholders.
6. Resolve Issues: Address any issues that arise.
7. Notify Users: Inform users that the new version is live.

8.11.2 Unsolved Lab Activity

1. Develop a patch management plan for a financial application. Include steps for identifying, developing, testing, and deploying patches.
2. Develop a maintenance schedule for a hospital management system. Include regular updates, backups, and performance monitoring activities.

Previous Years Solved Questions

Q 1. Explain various issues involved in software maintenance, with appropriate specific examples. **[IGNOU JUNE, 2010]**

Ans 1. Software maintenance is a critical phase in the software development lifecycle, focusing on modifying and updating software applications after their initial deployment. Various issues arise during software maintenance, each impacting the system's effectiveness, efficiency, and user satisfaction. Here are some of the key issues involved, along with specific examples:

1. Corrective Maintenance
Issue: Fixing bugs and errors discovered after the software is deployed.
Example: A study center's Assignments Management System crashes when students submit large file attachments. The maintenance team needs to debug and correct the file handling process to prevent such crashes.

2. Adaptive Maintenance
Issue: Updating software to work in new or changed environments, such as new operating systems, hardware, or external services.
Example: The system was originally designed to work with a specific version of a database. After an upgrade to the database system, the software needs to be updated to ensure compatibility with the new database version.

3. Perfective Maintenance
Issue: Enhancing the system to improve performance or maintainability.
Example: Users find the interface of the Assignments Management System outdated and not user-friendly. The maintenance team needs to redesign the user interface to improve usability and make the system more intuitive.

4. Preventive Maintenance
Issue: Updating software to prevent future problems by addressing potential issues.
Example: The system's codebase is becoming increasingly complex and difficult to manage. The maintenance team undertakes a code refactoring process to simplify the code, making it easier to understand and modify in the future.

5. Documentation Issues
Issue: Lack of proper documentation can make maintenance tasks difficult and time-consuming.
Example: The original developers of the Assignments Management System did not thoroughly document the system's architecture and code. New developers struggle to understand the system's inner workings, leading to increased time and effort for maintenance activities.

6. Dependency Management
Issue: Managing dependencies with other software components or systems.
Example: The Assignments Management System relies on a third-party library for PDF generation. If this library is updated or deprecated, the maintenance team needs to ensure the system continues to function correctly with the new library version.

7. Resource Constraints
Issue: Limited budget, time, or human resources for maintenance activities.
Example: The study center has allocated limited funds for maintaining the Assignments Management System. The maintenance team must prioritize critical issues and postpone less urgent enhancements due to budget constraints.

8. Security Vulnerabilities
Issue: Identifying and fixing security vulnerabilities to protect the system from threats.
Example: A security audit reveals that the system's user authentication mechanism is weak and susceptible to attacks. The maintenance team needs to implement stronger security measures, such as multi-factor authentication, to secure the system.

9. User Feedback and Satisfaction
Issue: Addressing user feedback to improve the system and maintain user satisfaction.
Example: Students and teachers report that the assignment submission process is slow during peak times. The maintenance team needs to optimize the system's performance to handle high traffic volumes and improve user experience.

10. Regulatory and Compliance Issues
Issue: Ensuring the system complies with new regulations and standards.
Example: New data protection regulations require changes to how the system stores and manages personal data. The maintenance team must update the system to comply with these regulations and avoid legal penalties.

11. Technological Advancements
Issue: Keeping up with technological advancements and integrating new technologies.
Example: Emerging technologies such as cloud computing offer better scalability and cost-effectiveness. The maintenance team needs to migrate the Assignments Management System to a cloud-based infrastructure to leverage these benefits.

12. Performance Degradation
Issue: Over time, software can become slow or less responsive due to various factors such as data growth and inefficient algorithms.
Example: The Assignments Management System's database grows significantly, causing slower query responses. The maintenance team must optimize database queries and possibly archive old data to restore performance.

Previous Years Unsolved Questions

Q 1. What is need of software testing? Describe the objectives of the following testing techniques:
1. Stress Testing Performance Testing
2. Recovery Testing
3. Security Testing. **[IGNOU JUNE, 2012]**

Exercises

Exercise 1 – Multiple Choice Questions

1. Which phase of software development primarily involves breaking down the code into smaller units to ensure each component functions correctly?

A) Integration Testing

B) User Training
C) Coding and Unit Testing
D) Deployment Strategies

2. What activity involves combining individual software modules to verify they work together as expected?

A) Bug Fixes and Patch Management
B) Enhancements and Upgrades
C) Integration Testing
D) Help Desk and User Support

3. Which process focuses on the methods and procedures for rolling out software to end-users or production environments?

A) User Training and Acceptance Testing
B) Deployment Strategies
C) Software Maintenance Activities
D) Enhancements and Upgrades

4. During which phase do end-users verify that the software meets their requirements and expectations?

A) Software Maintenance Activities
B) Bug Fixes and Patch Management
C) User Training and Acceptance Testing
D) Help Desk and User Support

5. Which activity involves improving software based on user feedback and changing requirements?

A) Enhancements and Upgrades
B) Help Desk and User Support
C) Coding and Unit Testing
D) Integration Testing

Exercise 2 – True/False

1. Unit testing ensures that individual components of the software work correctly in isolation.
2. Integration testing focuses on testing the interaction between different modules or components of the software.
3. Deployment strategies involve the process of releasing the software to end-users without any prior training or acceptance testing.

Exercise 3 – Fill in the blanks

1. ____________ involves writing code and conducting tests on individual components or units of software.
2. ____________ involves ongoing activities to keep the software functioning optimally.
3. ____________ are crucial for addressing issues and improving the software's performance.

Exercise 4- Fill in the blanks with two options

1. _____ testing is a method used to verify that different software modules or components operate together correctly, which is crucial in _____.
2. _____ are systematic efforts to prepare users to operate new software effectively and ensure the software meets their needs through rigorous validation, commonly employed in _____.
3. To address and manage reported software problems effectively, one would engage in _____, which is essential in _____.

Exercise 5- Give two answers for the following:

1. Coding and Unit Testing
2. Integration Testing
3. Deployment Strategies
4. User Training Methods
5. Software Maintenance Activities

Exercise 6- Rearrange the sentence

1. Coding unit and testing.
2. Integration strategies various testing uses.
3. Deployment methods different explore.

Exercise 7- Choose the Odd One Out

1. Coding and Unit Testing, Integration Testing, Deployment Strategies, User Training
2. Software Maintenance Activities, Enhancements and Upgrades, Bug Fixes and Patch Management, Integration Testing
3. Help Desk and User Support, Enhancements and Upgrades, Bug Fixes and Patch Management, Deployment Strategies

Exercise 8- Jumble words

1. tsnitgetni
2. ymdloepnet
3. aneantncem

Exercise 9- Match case

Column 1	Column 2
1. What involves correcting program faults?	A. Coding and initial program testing
2. Which stage includes preparing the final build for production?	B. System components assembly and initial testing
3. What focuses on providing continuous support after deployment?	C. Updates and additional features development
4. During which phase do users get trained on the new system?	D. Correction of defects and applying updates
5. What involves the combination of modules and verification of their interactions?	E. Providing ongoing support and troubleshooting

Exercise 10- Assertion – Reason

1. Assertion (A): The implementation and testing phase is essential for the reliability and functionality of software systems.

Reason (R): This phase encompasses activities from coding and unit testing to deployment and user acceptance, ensuring the software meets its design specifications and user requirements.

Options:

1. Assertion (A) is true and Reason (R) is the correct reason for Assertion (A).
2. Assertion (A) is true, but Reason (R) is not the correct reason for Assertion (A).
3. Assertion (A) is false, but Reason (R) is true.
4. Assertion (A) is false and Reason (R) is also false.

Exercise 11- One- word

1. What type of testing ensures individual units of the source code work as intended?

2. What is deployed to correct identified defects in software after its release?
3. Which process involves teaching end-users how to use new software?

Exercise 12- Small Answers

1. Describe the primary goal of integration testing in the context of software development.
2. Explain two common strategies used for deploying software applications and discuss one advantage of each.
3. What are two key activities involved in software maintenance? Explain the importance of each in ensuring the longevity and efficiency of a software system.

Exercise 13- Long Answers

1. What are various deployment strategies that can be utilized for releasing software, and how do they impact the overall stability and scalability of the application in a production environment?
2. What are the best practices for effective coding and unit testing to ensure that individual components of the software function correctly before they are integrated into the larger system?

Answers

Exercise 1- 1) C, 2) C, 3) B, 4) C, 5) A
Exercise 2- 1) True, 2) True, 3) False
Exercise 3- 1) Coding and Unit Testing, 2) Software Maintenance Activities, 3) Bug Fixes and Patch Management
Exercise 4- 1) Integration, software development, 2) User Training and Acceptance Testing, user readiness, 3) Bug Fixes and Patch Management, software lifecycle management
Exercise 5- 1) Writing Functions, Creating Unit Test Cases, 2) Top-Down Integration, Bottom-Up Integration , 3) Blue-Green Deployment, Canary Deployment , 4) Workshops, E-Learning Modules, 5) Bug Fixes, Performance Improvements
Exercise 6- 1) Unit testing and coding, 2) Integration testing uses various strategies, 3) Explore different deployment methods
Exercise 7- 1) User Training, 2) Integration Testing, 3) Deployment Strategies
Exercise 8- 1) Integration, 2) Deployment, 3) Maintenance
Exercise 9- 1 D, 2 B, 3 C, 4 A, 5 E
Exercise 10- a) Assertion (A) is true and Reason (R) is the correct reason for Assertion (A).
Exercise 11- 1) Unit, 2) Patch, 3) Training

Online Resources

Online Exam paper

URL https://forms.gle/rYKWCPr1cGatXLs17
QR Code

YouTube Video

URL https://www.youtube.com/playlist?list=PLzlh_31VWEFrF5voCE1_QwQFqHbPgACLk

QR Code

More Test Papers Practices

Test Paper-1

URL https://forms.gle/fHT1mtn7WCJ6L4QG9

QR Code

Test Paper-2

URL https://forms.gle/b1DGaiu5GeDJfzTb9

QR Code

System analysis and design Test Paper
Chapter- 8
Implementation and Testing

Time Duration: 30 Minutes **Maximum Marks: 25**

General Instructions:
1. The question paper consists of answer any 12 questions out of the given 19 questions and is divided into four sections, A, B, C and D.
2. All questions are compulsory.
3. Section A comprises question numbers 1 to 8. These are MCQs and one liner of one mark each. You are to select one most appropriate response out of the four provided options.
4. Section B comprises question numbers 1 to 5. These are SAQs carrying two marks each.
5. Section C comprises question numbers 1 to 4. These are SAQs carrying four marks each.
6. Section D comprises question numbers 1& 2. These are LAQs carrying five marks each.

SECTION-A

I. <u>Answer any 6 questions out of the given 8 questions</u> **(1*6=6)**

1. What is the primary objective of unit testing during the coding phase?
    A) To test the entire system as a whole
    B) To test individual components or functions in isolation
    C) To deploy the system to production
    D) To perform usability testing
2. Which type of testing ensures that integrated components of a system function together correctly?
    A) Unit Testing
    B) System Testing
    C) Integration Testing
    D) Acceptance Testing
3. What is a key goal of user training and acceptance testing?
    A) To identify bugs in the code
    B) To ensure users are comfortable with the system and that it meets their needs
    C) To deploy the software to a live environment
    D) To write code for the application
4. Which activity involves applying small fixes and updates to improve a software system after its initial release?
    A) Deployment
    B) Integration Testing
    C) Patch Management
    D) User Training
5. What is the purpose of help desk and user support in software maintenance?
    A) To design the user interface
    B) To assist users with issues and questions they have about the software
    C) To develop new features
    D) To test the software
6. What type of testing is performed to check individual components in isolation?
7. What is the process of releasing software updates to fix bugs called?
8. What is the term for training users and ensuring the system meets their requirements before final acceptance?

SECTION-B

II. <u>Answer any 3 questions out of the given 5 questions</u> **(2*3=6)**

1. Define 'unit testing' in software development.
2. What is the main objective of integration testing?
3. List two key activities involved in software maintenance.
4. What is the purpose of deployment strategies in software implementation?
5. Why is user training important in the implementation phase?

SECTION-C

II. Answer any 2 questions out of the given 4 questions **(4*2=8)**

1. Explain the difference between unit testing and integration testing.
2. Describe the steps involved in a typical software deployment strategy.
3. What are the key components of a successful user training program?
4. Discuss the role of help desk support in software maintenance.

SECTION-D

III. Answer any 1 question out of the given 2 questions **(5*1=5)**

1. Analyze the importance of patch management in maintaining software systems. Discuss the challenges and best practices associated with patch management.
2. Explain the process of user acceptance testing (UAT) and its significance in the software development lifecycle. How does UAT contribute to the overall success of a software project?

Chapter 9: Planning and Management

- Understand Project Planning and Scheduling
- Master Resource Management
- Gain Proficiency in Risk Management
- Enhance Project Communication Skills
- Implement Project Planning Techniques

9.1 Project Planning and Scheduling

What is project planning?

Project planning is a discipline addressing how to complete a project in a certain timeframe, usually with defined stages and designated resources. One view of project planning divides the activity into these steps:
1. setting measurable objectives
2. identifying deliverables
3. scheduling
4. planning tasks

Supporting plans may encompass human resources, communication methods and risk management.
Enterprises often have an information technology project planning guide that identifies the processes used. Tools used for the scheduling parts of a plan include Gantt charts and PERT charts.

Why is project planning important?

Project planning is important at every phase of a project. It lays out the basics of a project, including the following:
1. scope
2. objectives
3. goals
4. schedule

Planning enables project managers to turn an intangible idea into reality. Key purposes of planning include the following:
1. facilitate communication and provide a central source of information for project personnel;
2. help the project sponsor and other key stakeholders know what is required;
3. identify who will perform certain tasks, and when and how those tasks will happen;
4. facilitate project management and control as the project progresses;
5. enable effective monitoring and control of a project;
6. manage project risk; and
7. generate feedback useful for the next project planning phase.

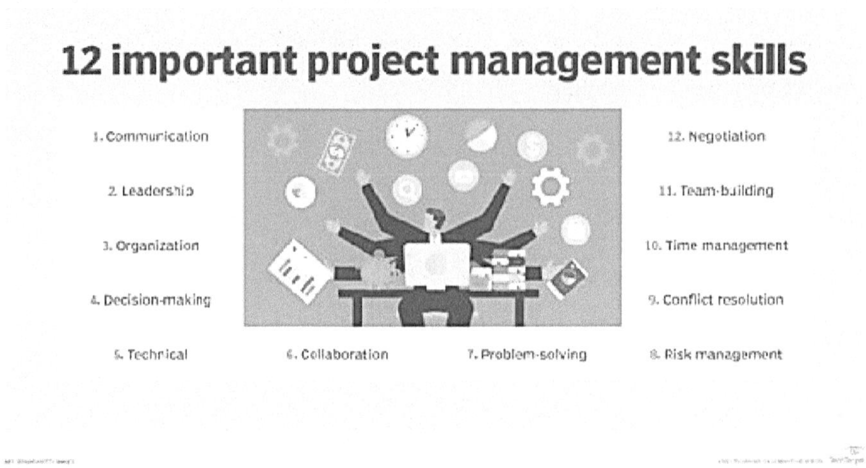

Project managers must have a variety of skills. See the dozen that really matter.

What are the components of a project plan?

The three major parts of a project plan are the scope, budget and timeline. They involve the following aspects:
1. Scope. The scope determines what a project team will and will not do. It takes the team's vision, what stakeholders want and the customer's requirements and then determines what's possible. As part of defining the project scope, the project manager must set performance goals.
2. Budget. Project managers look at what manpower and other resources will be required to meet the project goals to estimate the project's cost.
3. Timeline. This reveals the length of time expected to complete each phase of the project and includes a schedule of milestones that will be met.

How do you create a project plan?

Project planning includes the following 10 steps:
1. Define stakeholders. Stakeholders include anyone with an interest in the project. They can include the customer or end user, members of the project team, other people in the organization the project will affect and outside organizations or individuals with an interest.
2. Define roles. Each stakeholder's role should be clearly defined. Some people will fill multiple roles, however.
3. Introduce stakeholders. Hold a meeting to bring stakeholders together and unify the vision behind the project. The topics covered should include scope, goals, budget, schedule and roles.
4. Set goals. Take what is gleaned from the meeting and refine it into a project plan. It should include goals and deliverables that define what the product or service will result in.
5. Prioritize tasks. List tasks necessary to meet goals and prioritize them based on importance and interdependencies. A Gantt chart can be helpful for mapping project dependencies.
6. Create a schedule. Establish a timeline that considers the resources needed for all the tasks.
7. Assess risks. Identify project risks and develop strategies for mitigating them.
8. Communicate. Share the plan with all stakeholders and provide communications updates in the format and frequency stakeholders expect.
9. Reassess. As milestones are met, revisit the project plan and revise any areas that are not meeting expectations.
10. Final evaluation. Once the project is completed, performance should be evaluated to learn from the experience and identify areas to improve.

What are the 5 phases of a project?

Projects typically pass through five phases. The project lifecycle includes the following:
1. Initiation defines project goals and objectives. It also is when feasibility is considered, along with how to measure project objectives.
2. Planning sets out the project scope. It establishes what tasks need to get done and who will do them.

3. Execution is when the deliverables are created. This is the longest phase of a project. During execution, the plan is set into motion and augmented, if necessary.
4. Monitoring and management occur during the execution phase and may be considered part of the same step. This phase ensures that the project is going according to plan.
5. Closing and review is the final Contracts are closed out and the final deliverables are given to the client. Successes and failures are evaluated.

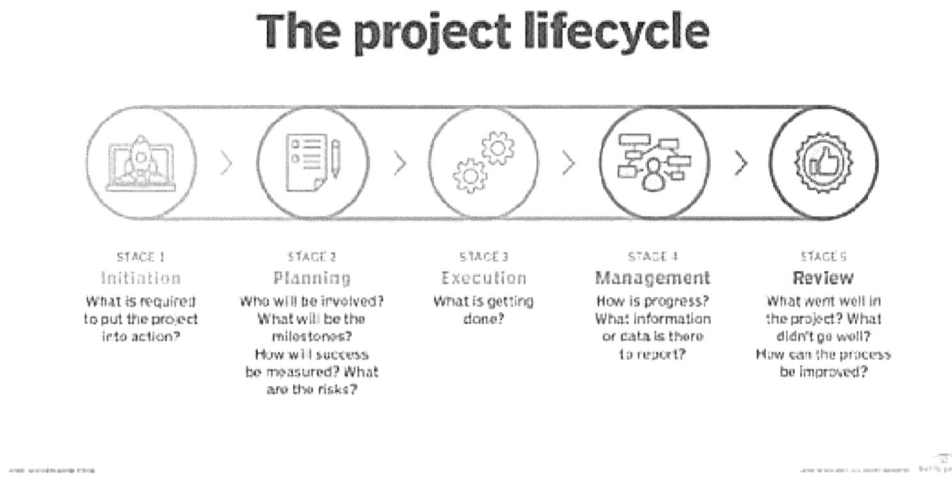

Planning is the second step in the project lifecycle, but it affects all of the phases of the project lifecycle.

What is some project planning tools and software?

Project planning and project management software facilitate the project planning process. The best tools support collaboration among stakeholders, have intuitive user interfaces and provide built-in time tracking and invoicing.
Some project planning software tools include the following:
1. Asana offers different project views to suit a team's preferences.
2. ClickUp comes with several Agile-based features, including a custom automation builder that lets users create reusable task templates.
3. Freedcamp lets users organize their projects using a Gantt chart or Kanban
4. Hive has a template creation tool in the task management feature that speeds up task creation.
5. Scoro is a combination of tools and includes customer relationship management
6. Trello provides Kanban features, budget management, resource management and progress tracking features.
7. Wrike integrates with tools like Jira, Slack and Dropbox.

Project Scheduling

Project-task scheduling is a significant project planning activity. It comprises deciding which functions would be taken up when. To schedule the project plan, a software project manager wants to do the following:
1. Identify all the functions required to complete the project.
2. Break down large functions into small activities.
3. Determine the dependency among various activities.
4. Establish the most likely size for the time duration required to complete the activities.
5. Allocate resources to activities.
6. Plan the beginning and ending dates for different activities.
7. Determine the critical path. A critical way is the group of activities that decide the duration of the project.

The first method in scheduling a software plan involves identifying all the functions required to complete the project. A good judgment of the intricacies of the project and the development process helps the supervisor to identify the critical role of the project effectively. Next, the large functions are broken down into a valid set of small activities which would be assigned to various engineers. The work breakdown structure formalism supports the manager to breakdown the function systematically after the project manager has broken down the purpose and constructs the work breakdown structure; he must find the dependency among the activities. Dependency among the various activities determines the order in which the various events would be carried out. If an activity A necessary the results of another activity B, then activity A must be scheduled after activity B. In general, the function dependencies describe a partial ordering among functions, i.e., each service may precede a subset of other functions, but some functions might not have any precedence ordering describe between them (called concurrent function). The dependency among the activities is defined in the pattern of an activity network.

Once the activity network representation has been processed out, resources are allocated to every activity. Resource allocation is usually done using a Gantt chart. After resource allocation is completed, a PERT chart representation is developed. The PERT chart representation is useful for program monitoring and control. For task scheduling, the project plan needs to decompose the project functions into a set of activities. The time frame when every activity is to be performed is to be determined. The end of every action is called a milestone. The project manager tracks the function of a project by audit the timely completion of the milestones. If he examines that the milestones start getting delayed, then he must handle the activities carefully so that the complete deadline can still be met.

9.2 Resource Management

What Is Resource Management in Software Projects?

By resources, we usually mean people, their time and sets of skills. However, resources also include tools and equipment, money and services. Although types of resources are universal, the management approaches differ across the industries and depend on the needs of projects. Let's see what you need to keep in mind when managing resources in software projects.

Defining Your Project's Constraint

Ideally, successful software projects should meet 3 criteria: software is delivered on time, costs don't exceed the budget, customer's expectations are met. According to **triple constraint theory**, to determine which types of resources are right for your project, you need to focus on one of the three priorities – cost, scope or time.

1. **Time/Schedule** – time frames required for the project to reach completion.
2. **Budget/Cost** – financial constraints of a project. These include the cost of your team members with different skills and experience levels, the cost of contract workers and outsourcing.
3. **Scope/Performance** – tasks required to finish the project. Typically, as the project unfolds, the project scope either grows or shrinks to meet the changing client expectations.

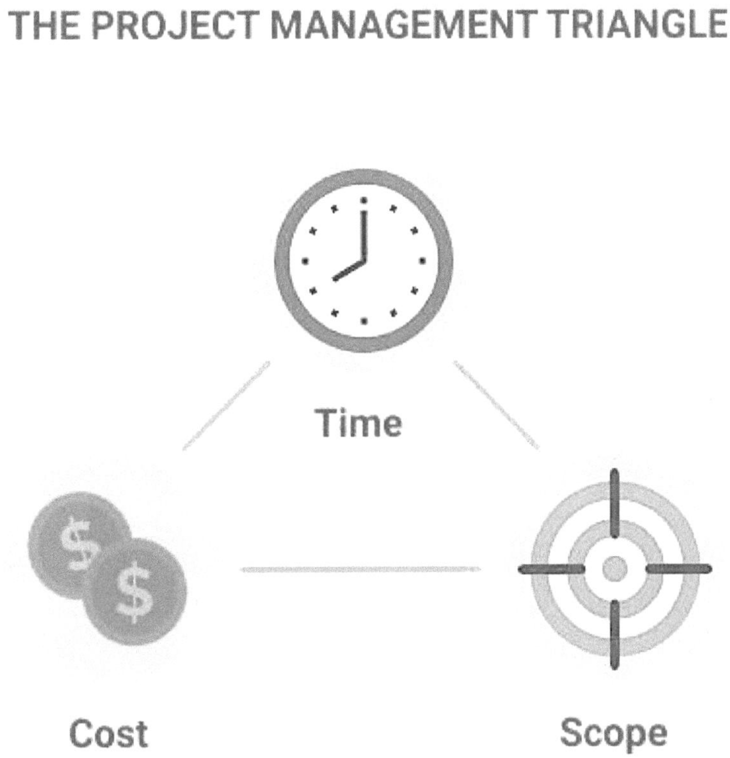

Let's see how it works. If you focus on one of these priorities, the other two will suffer. Sometimes you need to adjust elements to achieve more balance, but sometimes you need to completely switch the priorities to attain maximum results in the given circumstances.
Let's say, your client asked to develop a few more features for the software. It means that Scope becomes the focus of your project management efforts, which, in turn, requires more time and budget for development. In this case, you may assign more staff to the project or look for contractors and third-party services that would cost less than the efforts of your team members. This way, you will achieve a more balanced picture: more human resources will reduce development time, while lower costs of the outsourced workforce will, most likely, allow you to stay within the budget.

How to Manage Resources in Software Projects

To manage resources in software projects effectively, you need to have a clear understanding of its development stages known as **Software Development Life Cycle** (SDLC).It refers to the process for requirement collection, planning, designing, creating, testing, and deploying the software. What makes it stand out from other types of projects is that its final stage is product maintenance that is never over. When a product requires updates, new features and bug fixes, the development process must take a few steps back over and over.

In this section, we are going to give you a quick recap of resource management stages as listed in A Guide to the Project Management Body of Knowledge (PMBOK Guide®).

According to Project Management Institute, resource management includes the following six stages.

Step 1: Plan Resource Management

Goal: Define how to estimate, acquire, manage and utilize all resources.
First, you need to make sure that you have enough available resources to successfully complete the project. It is essential to identify scarce resources and whether you should obtain them from the company's assets or from third parties. You should also keep in mind that other projects may also compete for internal assets, which, in turn, may impact project costs, schedules, risks, quality, and other project areas.

At this step, you need to build a project management plan that defines how project resources should be categorized, allocated, managed, and released. It usually includes but is not limited to acquiring resources, roles and responsibilities, scope baseline, quality specifications, resource control throughout the project life cycle – everything you need to complete the project and meet the quality standards.

Step 2: Estimate Activity Resources

Goal: Estimate necessary human resources, equipment and supplies for the project.
After you decide on the types of resources, it's time that you estimate your team resources and quantities of materials, equipment and supplies necessary to perform project work. As the project development unfolds, its scope, time frames and costs may change. To adjust to the changing circumstances, you may be required to review your resources, which means that you may go back to this stage any time throughout the project to make new estimations.

Estimated vs. Actual Time Report

Custom date | Aug 18, 2022 | Edit Configuration | Export

Clients / Projects / Tasks	Spent Time	Estimated Time	Variance (Estimated Time - Spent)	
			mh	%
Total:	48:26	68:00	19:34	28.8%
Howard Construction	48:26	68:00	19:34	28.8%
Construction	0:55	18:00	17:05	94.9%
Site work	0:55	18:00	17:05	94.9%
Contracts	8:09	8:00	-0:09	-1.9%
Documents review	6:39	6:00	-0:39	-10.8%
Proposals	1:30	2:00	0:30	25.0%
Design	21:36	16:00	-5:36	-35.0%
Apply for permits	8:48	6:00	-2:48	-46.7%
Feasibility study	12:48	10:00	-2:48	-28.0%
Procurement	17:46	26:00	8:14	31.7%
Order equipment	14:57	12:00	-2:57	-24.6%
Order materials	2:49	14:00	11:11	79.9%

Estimated vs. Actual Time report in actiTIME displaying the variance between the estimated time and the actual time expenses

To make accurate estimations, you need to develop a **resource management plan** that defines how to identify a lack of resources and quantify the right resource amounts for each activity. At this stage, you may want to develop cost estimates, resource calendars, weigh up the risks that can impact resource selection and availability.

Step 3: Acquire Resources

Goal: Obtain the necessary resources.
When you know what types and amounts of resources you need to successfully deliver the product, it's time to obtain necessary internal and external to the project-performing organization resources, such as team members, facilities, equipment, materials, supplies. Failure to acquire these resources may affect project schedules, budgets, customer satisfaction, quality, and risks. This process can be performed periodically throughout the project as the client makes changes to desired time frames, project scope or costs.

When acquiring resources, you may rely on the following criteria:
1. **Availability** – the resource is available throughout the whole project period.
2. **Cost** – the cost of the resource is within the budget.
3. **Ability** – the resource provides the capability needed by the project.
Some criteria are unique for team resources:

1. Experience – the employee has relevant experience for the project's success.
2. Knowledge – the employee is experienced in similar projects and understands the nuances of the project environment.
3. Skills – the employee has relevant skills to use a project tool.
4. Attitude – the employee has solid teamwork and communication skills.
5. International factors – employee location, time zone, and communication capabilities.

Step 4: Develop Team

Goal: Train your team members, establish communication inside the team, and prepare the environment for effective collaboration.
At this stage, you prepare your team for effective work and communication in the project environment: identify, build, maintain, motivate, lead, and inspire employees to achieve high performance and meet the project's objectives. The project environment should encourage teamwork and motivate your team by offering challenges and opportunities, providing timely feedback and support, recognizing and rewarding good performance.
One of the models that describe this stage in more detail is known as the **Tuckman ladder**.

It includes five stages of team development, which usually occur in order:
1. Forming – team members learn about the project, their roles and responsibilities.
2. Storming – team addresses the project work, technical decisions, and the project management approach.
3. Norming – team members begin to work together, adjust their behaviors and learn to trust each other.
4. Performing – team works as a stable and well-organized unit.
5. Adjourning – team completes the work and moves on from the project.

If team members have never worked together before, the team may get stuck and have to get back to the earlier stages. On the contrary, experienced teams may skip some of the stages.

Step 5: Manage Team

Goal: Track team member performance, provide feedback, resolve issues, and manage team changes to optimize project performance.
- At the team management stage, project managers need to apply their leadership, communication, conflict management and negotiation skills, provide challenging tasks and recognition to build high-performance teams. At the same time, managers should be sensitive to the skills and motivation of their team members and choose appropriate leadership approaches.
- To keep track of performance and generate data-based decisions, project managers build **work performance reports**. They can contain trends and forecasts, risk summaries, contract performance information, earned value graphs and more. Managers can review schedule, cost and quality control data, use it to predict future team resource requirements and update the resource management plan.

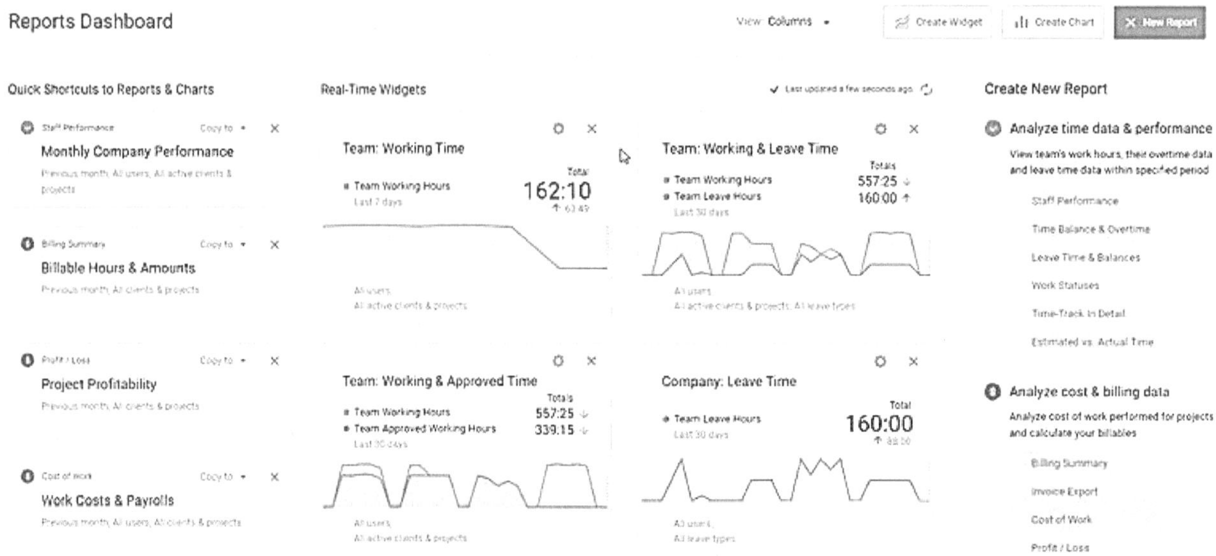

Reports dashboard in actiTIME – set up real-time data widgets and add report shortcuts for quick access

Step 6: Control Resources

Goal: Ensure that project resources are available as planned, monitor the planned versus actual use of resources, and perform corrective action if necessary.
Resource control is performed continuously throughout the project life cycle to ensure that resources are assigned at the right time and the right amount to eliminate blockers and delays. This stage is concerned with physical resources such as equipment and infrastructure, while human resources are addressed in Step 5: Manage Team.

Improve Your Resource Management

The importance of efficient resource planning cannot be undermined. It ensures that the project will be delivered on time, with minimum expenditure and maximum profit. But what are other benefits of effective resource management?
1. Measures efficiency. Resource management provides a bird's eye view on your project trends and needs, allowing you to track and manage resources in the best possible way.
2. Eliminates blockers and delays. When you are focused on planning and monitoring your resources, you can prevent and troubleshoot gaps and problems early on.
3. Prevents burnout. If you keep track of your team's workload, you can notice overallocation cases, productivity trends and respond in a timely manner.
4. Provides transparency. Transparency increases the client's trust and employee engagement, prevents miscommunication between team members and managers.

9.3 Risk Management

A risk is a probable problem; it might happen, or it might not. There is main two characteristics of risk.
1. Uncertainty: the risk may or may not happen which means there are no 100% risks.
2. Loss: If the risk occurs, undesirable results or losses will occur.

What is Risk Management?

Risk Management is a systematic process of recognizing, evaluating, and handling threats or risks that influence the finances, capital, and overall operations of an organization. These risks can come from different areas, such as financial instability, legal issues, errors in strategic planning, accidents, and natural disasters.
The main goal of risk management is to predict possible risks and find solutions to deal with them successfully.

Why is risk management important?

Risk management is important because it helps organizations to prepare for unexpected circumstances that can vary from small issues to major crises. By actively understanding, evaluating, and planning for potential risks, organizations can protect their financial health, continued operation, and overall survival.
Let's Understand why risk management important with an example.
Suppose In a software development project, one of the key developers unexpectedly falls ill and is unable to contribute to the product for an extended period.
One of the solutions that organization may have, the team uses collaborative tools and procedures, such as shared work boards or project management software, to make sure that each member of the team is aware of all tasks and responsibilities, including those of their teammates.
An organization must focus on providing resources to minimize the negative effects of possible events and maximize positive results to reduce risk effectively. Organizations can more effectively identify, assess, and mitigate major risks by implementing a consistent, systematic, and integrated approach to risk management.

The risk management process

Risk management is a sequence of steps that help a software team to understand, analyze, and manage uncertainty. Risk management process consists of
1. Risks Identification.
2. Risk Assessment.
3. Risks Planning.
4. Risk Monitoring

- Risk Identification

  Risk identification refers to the systematic process of recognizing and evaluating potential threats or hazards that could negatively impact an organization, its operations, or its workforce. This involves identifying various types of risks, ranging from IT security threats like viruses and phishing attacks to unforeseen events such as equipment failures and extreme weather conditions.
- Risk analysis

  Risk analysis is the process of evaluating and understanding the potential impact and likelihood of identified risks on an organization. It helps determine how serious a risk is and how to best manage or mitigate it. Risk Analysis involves evaluating each risk's probability and potential consequences to prioritize and manage them effectively.
- Risk Planning

  Risk planning involves developing strategies and actions to manage and mitigate identified risks effectively. It outlines how to respond to potential risks, including prevention, mitigation, and contingency measures, to protect the organization's objectives and assets.
- Risk Monitoring

  Risk monitoring involves continuously tracking and overseeing identified risks to assess their status, changes, and effectiveness of mitigation strategies. It ensures that risks are regularly reviewed and managed to maintain alignment with organizational objectives and adapt to new developments or challenges.

Understanding Risks in Software Projects

A computer code project may be laid low with an outsized sort of risk. To be ready to consistently establish the necessary risks that could affect a computer code project, it's necessary to group risks into completely different categories. The project manager will then examine the risks from every category square measure relevant to the project.
There are mainly 3 classes of risks that may affect a computer code project:
- Project Risks:
Project risks concern various sorts of monetary funds, schedules, personnel, resources, and customer-related issues.
A vital project risk is schedule slippage. Since computer code is intangible, it's tough to observe and manage a computer code project. It's tough to manage one thing that cannot be seen. For any producing project, like producing cars, the project manager will see the merchandise taking form.

For example, see that the engine is fitted, now the area of the door unit is fitted, the automotive is being painted, etc. so he will simply assess the progress of the work and manage it. The physical property of the merchandise being developed is a vital reason why several computer codes come to suffer from the danger of schedule slippage.

- Technical Risks:
Technical risks concern potential style, implementation, interfacing, testing, and maintenance issues. Technical risks conjointly embody ambiguous specifications, incomplete specifications, dynamic specifications, technical uncertainty, and technical degeneration. Most technical risks occur thanks to the event team's lean information concerning the project.
- Business Risks:
This type of risk embodies the risks of building a superb product that nobody needs, losing monetary funds or personal commitments, etc.

Classification of Risk in a project

Example: Let us consider a satellite-based mobile communication project. The project manager can identify many risks in this project. Let us classify them appropriately.
1. What if the project cost escalates and overshoots what was estimated? – **Project Risk**
2. What if the mobile phones that are developed become too bulky to conveniently carry? **Business Risk**
3. What if call hand-off between satellites becomes too difficult to implement? **Technical Risk**

Risk management standards and frameworks

Risk management standards and frameworks give organizations guidelines on how to find, evaluate, and handle risks effectively. They provide a structured way to manage risks, making sure that everyone follows consistent and reliable practices. Here are some well-known risk management standards and frameworks:
1. COSO ERM Framework:
COSO ERM Framework was introduce in 2004 and updated in 2017. Its main purpose is to addresses the growing complexity of Enterprise Risk Management (ERM).
1. Key Features:
2. 20 principles grouped into five components: Governance and culture, Strategy and objective-setting, Performance, Review and revision, Information, communication, and reporting.
3. It promotes integrating risk into business strategies and operations.
2. **ISO 31000**:
ISO 31000 was introduced in 2009, revised in 2018. It provides principles and a framework for ERM.
1. Key Features:
2. It offers guidance on applying risk management to operations.
3. It focuses on identifying, evaluating, and mitigating risks.
4. It promotes senior management's role and integrating risk management across the organization.
3. **BS 31100**:
This framework is British Standard for Risk Management and latest version issued in 2001. It offers a structured approach to applying the principles outlined in ISO 31000:2018, covering tasks like identifying, evaluating, and addressing risks, followed by reporting and reviewing risk management efforts.

Benefits of risk management

Here are some benefits of risk management:
1. Helps protect against potential losses.
2. Improves decision-making by considering risks.
3. Reduces unexpected expenses.
4. Ensures adherence to laws and regulations.
5. Builds resilience against unexpected challenges.
6. Safeguards company reputation.

Limitation of Risk Management

Here are Some Limitation of Risk Management
1. Too much focus on risk can lead to missed opportunities.
2. Implementing risk management can be expensive.
3. Risk models can be overly complex and hard to understand.
4. Having risk controls might make people feel too safe.
5. Relies on accurate human judgment and can be prone to mistakes.

6. Some risks are hard to predict or quantify.
7. Managing risks can take a lot of time and resources.

9.4 Project Communication

Effective project communication is crucial in system design, as it facilitates seamless collaboration among team members and ensures that all stakeholders are aligned with the project's objectives. The complexity of system design projects often requires comprehensive communication strategies to manage diverse groups, handle interdisciplinary tasks, and ensure that the final system meets the predefined requirements. This chapter delves into the best practices for project communication within the context of system design, covering tools, methods, and cultural considerations.

9.4.1. Establishing Communication Protocols

The first step in setting up efficient communication for a system design project is establishing clear communication protocols. This includes determining how information will be shared, who will be responsible for various types of communication, the frequency of updates, and the platforms used for communication. These protocols should be documented and agreed upon at the beginning of the project to avoid misunderstandings.

9.4.1.1 Communication Channels

Choose appropriate communication channels based on the complexity of the project and the distribution of the team. Common channels include:

1. Email: Best for formal communication and documentation.
2. Instant Messaging: Useful for quick, informal interactions.
3. Video Conferences: Ideal for detailed discussions and remote collaboration.
4. Project Management Tools: Essential for tracking tasks, deadlines, and dependencies.

9.4.1.2 Regular Updates

Schedule regular meetings and updates to keep all stakeholders informed. These should include daily stand-ups for operational teams, weekly team meetings for tactical discussions, and monthly strategic review meetings with senior stakeholders.

9.4..2. Communication for Collaboration

Effective collaboration in system design requires that team members have the ability to share ideas, give feedback, and make decisions efficiently.

9.4. 2.1 Tools for Collaborative Communication

Leverage tools that enhance collaboration:

1. Collaborative Document Editing: Tools like Google Docs or Microsoft Teams allow multiple users to work on the same document simultaneously.
2. Design and Prototyping Tools: Software like Figma or Sketch, which include real-time collaboration features, are invaluable for design teams.
3. Code Repositories: Platforms like GitHub or Bitbucket facilitate collaborative coding with features for code review and version control.

9.4. 2.2 Creating a Collaborative Culture

Foster a culture where open communication, sharing of knowledge, and constructive feedback are encouraged. This can be facilitated by regular team-building activities and creating spaces where team members feel safe to express their thoughts without fear of negative repercussions.

9.4. 3. Managing Stakeholder Engagement

System design projects typically have multiple stakeholders with varying interests and levels of influence. Managing these stakeholders effectively is crucial for the success of the project.

9.4. 3.1 Identifying Stakeholders

Start by identifying all stakeholders, understanding their interests, and their influence on the project. This includes end-users, project sponsors, technical teams, and external partners.

9.4. 3.2 Communication Strategies for Stakeholders

Develop tailored communication strategies for different stakeholder groups:
1. **Technical Briefs:** For technical stakeholders who need to understand the system's architecture and integration points.
2. **Executive Summaries:** For business stakeholders interested in the project's progress, costs, and benefits.
3. **User Updates:** For end-users, focusing on how the system will address their needs and any required changes in their workflow.

9.4. 4. Documentation and Reporting

Accurate documentation and reporting are pivotal in ensuring that the project's progress is communicated effectively to all parties involved.

9.4. 4.1 Project Documentation

Maintain thorough documentation, including:
1. **Project Plans:** Outlining objectives, timelines, and resources.
2. **Design Documents:** Detailing system architecture and design decisions.
3. **Meeting Minutes:** Recording decisions and action items from meetings.

9.4. 4.2 Reporting

Develop regular reporting mechanisms to keep stakeholders informed about the project status. This can include:
1. **Progress Reports:** Highlighting completed milestones and upcoming tasks.
2. **Risk Reports:** Identifying potential risks and mitigation strategies.
3. **Change Logs:** Documenting changes in the project scope or design.

Conclusion

Effective communication is the backbone of successful system design projects. By establishing clear communication protocols, fostering a culture of collaboration, managing stakeholder relationships, and maintaining rigorous documentation and reporting, teams can ensure that their projects are completed efficiently and meet all stated objectives. This chapter serves as a guide for system design professionals seeking to enhance their project communication strategies, ultimately leading to better project outcomes.

Summary

1. **Project Planning**: The process of outlining how to complete a project within a certain timeframe, including setting measurable objectives, identifying deliverables, scheduling tasks, and allocating resources.
2. **Scope**: Defines what a project team will and will not do, considering the vision, stakeholder requirements, and what is feasible.
3. **Gantt Chart**: A visual project management tool that helps map project dependencies and schedules by showing tasks, durations, and timelines.
4. **PERT Chart**: A project management tool used to schedule, organize, and coordinate tasks within a project, highlighting task dependencies and critical paths.
5. **Stakeholders**: Individuals or groups with an interest in the project, including customers, end-users, team members, and external organizations.
6. **Triple Constraint Theory**: A project management concept that focuses on balancing time, budget, and scope to achieve project success.
7. **Software Development Life Cycle (SDLC)**: A process for planning, creating, testing, and deploying software, including stages such as requirement collection, design, development, testing, deployment, and maintenance.
8. **Resource Management**: The process of planning, allocating, and managing resources (people, equipment, money, and services) to complete a project successfully.
9. **Risk Management**: The systematic process of identifying, assessing, and mitigating potential risks that could impact a project's success, including project, technical, and business risks.
10. **COSO ERM Framework**: A widely recognized framework for Enterprise Risk Management, providing principles and components to integrate risk management into business strategies and operations.
11. **Project Communication**: Strategies and tools used to facilitate seamless communication among project team members and stakeholders, ensuring alignment with project objectives.
12. **Collaborative Tools**: Software and platforms (e.g., Google Docs, Figma, GitHub) that enable team members to work together in real-time, share ideas, and manage tasks efficiently.
13. **Stakeholder Engagement**: The process of identifying stakeholders, understanding their interests, and developing tailored communication strategies to keep them informed and involved in the project.

14. Documentation and Reporting: Maintaining thorough records of project plans, design documents, meeting minutes, and regular progress reports to ensure transparency and effective communication among all parties involved.
15. Critical Path: The sequence of tasks that determines the minimum time needed to complete a project, highlighting dependencies and crucial activities that must be managed carefully.
16. Team Development: The process of preparing the project team for effective collaboration, including training, establishing communication protocols, and fostering a collaborative culture.

Glossary

1. Big Bang Deployment: A deployment strategy where all system components are released simultaneously, suitable for small projects with straightforward requirements.
2. Blue-Green Deployment: A technique using two identical environments (Blue and Green) where one environment is live while the other serves as a staging area for testing updates before switching over.
3. Canary Deployment: A method of gradually deploying changes to a small subset of users before rolling them out more broadly, reducing the impact of potential issues.
4. Phased Deployment: Rolling out the application in stages to different user groups or regions, allowing gradual exposure and minimizing risk.
5. Work Breakdown Structure (WBS): A hierarchical decomposition of the total scope of work to accomplish project objectives, breaking down larger tasks into manageable activities.
6. Risk Identification: The process of systematically recognizing potential threats or hazards that could negatively impact a project or organization.
7. Tuckman Ladder: A model describing five stages of team development (Forming, Storming, Norming, Performing, Adjourning) to help understand team dynamics.
8. PERT Chart (Program Evaluation and Review Technique): A project management tool used to schedule, organize, and coordinate tasks, highlighting task dependencies and critical paths.
9. Triple Constraint: The concept in project management that balances three critical project constraints: time, budget, and scope.
10. COSO ERM Framework: A framework providing principles and components to integrate risk management into business strategies and operations, promoting a comprehensive approach to managing enterprise risks.

9.5 Project

9.5.1 Solved Project

You are leading a project to develop, deploy, and maintain an Enterprise Resource Planning (ERP) system for a large organization. The project encompasses comprehensive planning and management, including project planning and scheduling, resource management, risk management, and project communication.

Approach:

Phase 1: Project Planning and Scheduling

1. Objectives:
2. Key Activities:
3. Scope Definition
4. Work Breakdown Structure (WBS)
5. Schedule Development
6. Milestones and Deadlines
7. Outcome:

Phase 2: Resource Management

1. Objectives:
2. Key Activities:
3. Resource Identification
4. Skills Assessment
5. Resource Allocation
6. Resource Management Tools
7. Outcome:

Phase 3: Risk Management
1. Objectives:
2. Key Activities:
3. Risk Identification
4. Risk Assessment
5. Mitigation Strategies
6. Risk Management Tools
7. Outcome:

Phase 4: Project Communication
1. Objectives:
2. Key Activities:
3. Stakeholder Identification
4. Communication Plan
5. Communication Tools
6. Feedback Mechanisms
7. Outcome:

Deliverables:
1. Project Plan and Schedule
2. Resource Management Plan
3. Risk Management Plan
4. Communication Plan

9.5.2 Unsolved Project

Suppose you are managing a new software development project. Before starting, review the principles of project planning and scheduling, ensure that you have a clear understanding of the project scope and timelines, verify the availability of key resources, explore different project management tools, and ask for expert advice on best practices. This ensures a well-structured project plan that aligns with the project goals.

9.6 Case Study

9.6.1 Solved Case Study

Implementing and testing are crucial phases in software development to ensure the final product is effective and reliable. Initially, coding and unit testing are performed where developers create the software's source code and test individual components to ensure they function correctly. Integration testing follows, combining these units to verify their interaction and detect any integration issues. Deployment strategies, such as phased rollouts, blue-green deployments, or continuous deployment, are then employed to move the software from development to production efficiently and with minimal disruption. User training and acceptance testing are essential to familiarize end-users with the new software and confirm it meets their requirements. This phase includes training sessions and allowing users to test the software before its full deployment. Regular software maintenance activities, such as performance tuning and compatibility updates, are conducted to keep the software running smoothly. Enhancements and upgrades are made to add new features or improve existing ones based on feedback and technological advancements. Bug fixes and patch management address and resolve software errors and vulnerabilities, ensuring stability and security. Additionally, an effective help desk and user support system is established to provide users with assistance, troubleshoot issues, and offer guidance, ensuring a smooth user experience and long-term software success.

Questions:

1. What is the goal of unit testing in the software development process?
   Answer: To ensure individual components of the software function correctly.
2. What is the purpose of integration testing?
   Answer: To verify the interaction of combined units and detect any integration issues.
3. Mention one deployment strategy described in the passage.
   Answer: Phased rollouts.
4. What two key activities are involved in user training and acceptance testing?

Answer: Familiarizing end-users with the new software and confirming it meets their requirements.

5. What do bug fixes and patch management aim to resolve?

Answer: Software errors and vulnerabilities.

9.6.2 Unsolved Case Study

The process of implementing and testing in software development is essential to ensure a reliable and efficient product. Coding and unit testing form the foundation, where developers write the software's source code and perform unit tests to validate individual components' functionality. Following this, integration testing combines these units to ensure they work together seamlessly, highlighting any issues from their interactions. Effective deployment strategies, such as phased rollouts, blue-green deployments, or continuous deployment, transition the software from development to production with minimal disruption. User training and acceptance testing are critical for preparing end-users and ensuring the software meets their needs, involving instructing users and allowing them to test the software before full deployment. Software maintenance activities include performance tuning, code optimization, and compatibility updates. Enhancements and upgrades add new features or improve existing ones based on user feedback and technological advancements. Bug fixes and patch management address errors and vulnerabilities, maintaining the software's stability and security. Lastly, a comprehensive help desk and user support system assists users, resolves issues, and provides necessary guidance, ensuring a positive user experience and the software's continued success.

Questions:

1. What is the purpose of unit testing?
2. What does integration testing ensure?
3. Name one deployment strategy mentioned in the passage.
4. Why are user training and acceptance testing critical?
5. What do bug fixes and patch management address?

Previous Years Solved Questions

Q 1. With reference to Risk Assessment and management, write short notes on the following: Quantitative Risk analysis Qualitative Risk analysis. **[IGNOU JUNE, 2010]**

Ans 1. Quantitative Risk Analysis is a numerical approach to risk assessment that involves quantifying the potential impacts of identified risks on project objectives, such as cost, schedule, and performance. This method uses statistical techniques and mathematical models to determine the probability and potential impact of risks.

Key Components

1. Probability Distribution: Estimating the likelihood of different outcomes for each risk. Common distributions used include normal, lognormal, triangular, and beta distributions.

2. Impact Analysis: Measuring the potential impact of each risk in numerical terms, such as cost (e.g., financial loss) or time (e.g., project delay).

3. Risk Exposure Calculation: Combining the probability and impact to calculate the risk exposure, often expressed as Expected Monetary Value (EMV), which is the product of risk probability and impact.

Techniques and Tools

1. Monte Carlo Simulation: A computational algorithm that uses random sampling to estimate the probability distribution of different outcomes.

2. Decision Tree Analysis: A graphical representation of decisions and their possible consequences, including risks, probabilities, and impacts.

3. Sensitivity Analysis: Identifying how changes in one part of the project (e.g., cost, schedule) affect the overall risk exposure.

Example

In a software development project, a Quantitative Risk Analysis might identify a risk of a key component failing during testing. The probability of this failure is estimated at 20%, and the impact is calculated as a $50,000 cost to fix the issue and a two-week project delay. The Expected Monetary Value (EMV) of this risk would be: EMV=0.20×50,000=$10,000\text{EMV} = 0.20 \times 50,000 = \$10,000EMV=0.20×50,000=$10,000

Qualitative Risk Analysis
Definition
Qualitative Risk Analysis is a subjective approach to risk assessment that prioritizes and categorizes risks based on their probability of occurrence and potential impact, using descriptive scales rather than numerical values. This method is often used as a preliminary step to identify significant risks that require further analysis.

Key Components
1. **Risk Identification**: Gathering a list of potential risks from project stakeholders, historical data, and expert judgment.
2. **Risk Probability and Impact Assessment**: Assessing the likelihood and consequences of each risk using predefined qualitative scales (e.g., high, medium, low).
3. **Risk Ranking**: Prioritizing risks based on their assessed probability and impact, often using a risk matrix.

Techniques and Tools
1. **Risk Matrix**: A two-dimensional grid that maps the probability of risks against their impact to prioritize which risks need attention.
2. **SWOT Analysis**: Identifying strengths, weaknesses, opportunities, and threats related to the project.
3. **Expert Judgment**: Leveraging the experience and insights of project stakeholders and experts to assess risks.

Example
In the same software development project, a Qualitative Risk Analysis might identify the risk of team members lacking necessary skills. The probability of this risk is rated as "medium," and the impact on the project is rated as "high." This risk would be placed in the high-priority quadrant of the risk matrix, indicating that it needs to be addressed through actions such as training or hiring skilled personnel.

Comparison and Use
1. **Quantitative Risk Analysis** provides a detailed and precise assessment, useful for making informed decisions about risk mitigation strategies and resource allocation. It is typically performed after Qualitative Risk Analysis for high-priority risks.
2. **Qualitative Risk Analysis** is quicker and less resource-intensive, suitable for initial risk assessment and prioritization. It helps to identify which risks need further quantitative analysis.

Previous Years Unsolved Questions

Q 1. What is project Scheduling? **[Chaudhary Charan Singh University BCA, May 2019]**
Q 2. What is the purpose of Project Scheduling? **[Udaipur University, 2018]**
Q 3. Explain the purpose of Disaster Recovery management. **[Udaipur University, 2018]**

Exercise

Exercise 1 – Multiple Choice Questions
1. Which of the following tools are commonly used for project scheduling?

a) Microsoft Word
b) Gantt Charts
c) Excel Spreadsheets
d) PowerPoint

2. What does resource management primarily focus on?

a) Designing user interfaces
b) Allocating and optimizing resources
c) Writing project documentation
d) Developing software code

3. Which of the following is a key activity in risk management?

a) Creating marketing plans
b) Risk assessment
c) Hiring project staff
d) Conducting product testing

4. Effective project communication includes which of the following?

a) Regular Status Meetings
b) Writing code
c) Creating project designs
d) Conducting user acceptance testing

5. Which software tool is often used for project planning and scheduling?

a) Photoshop
b) Microsoft Project
c) AutoCAD
d) SAP

Exercise 2 – True/False

1. Resource management involves allocating and optimizing resources to ensure project success.
2. Risk management is only concerned with financial risks.
3. Gantt charts and PERT charts are commonly used tools for project scheduling.

Exercise 3 – Fill in the blanks

1. Effective project planning includes defining the project ________, budget, and timeline.
2. ________ management involves continuously tracking and overseeing identified risks to assess their status and effectiveness of mitigation strategies.
3. Project ________ ensures that all stakeholders are aligned with the project's objectives and receive regular updates on the project's progress.

Exercise 4- Fill in the blanks with two options

1. Effective __________ management involves estimating, acquiring, managing, and utilizing resources to ensure project __________.
2. __________ charts and PERT charts are tools commonly used in project __________ to visualize schedules and timelines.
3. Identifying potential project risks and developing strategies for __________ them is an essential part of __________ management.

Exercise 5- Give two answers for the following:

1. Project Planning and Scheduling
2. Resource Management
3. Risk Management
4. Project Communication
5. Tools for Project Planning

Exercise 6- Rearrange the sentence

1. and/plans/timelines/include/project/budgets.
2. project/managers/tasks/and/ resources/allocate.
3. communication/is/key/project/effective/to.

Exercise 7- Choose the Odd One Out

1. Scheduling, Resource Allocation, Risk Mitigation, Budgeting
2. Resource Allocation, Communication Plan, Risk Identification, Test Execution
3. Project Scope, Risk Identification, Stakeholder Involvement, Code Review

Exercise 8- Jumble words

1. cerdlasehouing
2. cesourre
3. mkiatinnogia

Exercise 9- Match case

Column 1	Column 2
1. What is the process of estimating the duration of project activities and determining the dates for their completion?	**A.** Resource Management
2. Which involves the effective allocation and utilization of resources such as people, equipment, and materials?	**B.** Project Planning and Scheduling
3. What is the systematic process of identifying, assessing, and managing project risks?	**C.** Project Communication
4. What ensures the effective exchange of information among stakeholders?	**D.** Risk Management

Exercise 10- Assertion – Reason

1. Assertion (A): Effective project planning and scheduling are crucial for the successful completion of a project within the defined timeframe and budget.

Reason (R): Project planning and scheduling help in identifying the scope, setting measurable objectives, and outlining tasks and resources required for the project.

Options:

1. Assertion (A) is true, and Reason (R) is the correct reason for Assertion (A).
2. Assertion (A) is true, but Reason (R) is not the correct reason for Assertion (A).
3. Assertion (A) is false, but Reason (R) is true.
4. Assertion (A) is false, and Reason (R) is also false.

Exercise 11- One- word

1. What is the initial phase of the System Development Lifecycle (SDLC) where requirements are gathered and analyzed?
2. Which diagram is used to model the interactions between users and systems in System Modelling?
3. What process involves continuously tracking and overseeing identified risks to assess their status and effectiveness of mitigation strategies?

Exercise 12- Small Answers

1. What is the primary purpose of project planning in system development?
2. Define 'risk management' in the context of system development projects.
3. Why is effective communication crucial in project management?

Exercise 13- Long Answers

1. Discuss the various aspects of resource management in system development, and how they contribute to project success.
2. Explain the different stages of risk management in system development projects, providing examples of techniques used at each stage.

Answers

Exercise 1- 1) B, 2) B, 3) B, 4) A, 5) B
Exercise 2- 1) True, 2) False, 3) True
Exercise 3- 1) scope, 2) Risk, 3) communication

Exercise 4- 1) resource, success, 2) Gantt, planning, 3) mitigating risk
Exercise 5- 1) Gantt Charts, PERT Charts, 2) Resource Allocation, Resource Optimization, 3) Risk Assessment, Risk Mitigation, 4) Regular Status Meetings, Project Newsletters, 5) Microsoft Project, Asana
Exercise 6- 1) Project plans include budgets and timelines, 2) Project managers allocate tasks and resources, 3) Effective communication is key to project
Exercise 7- 1) Risk Mitigation, 2) Test Execution, 3) Code Review
Exercise 8- 1) Scheduling, 2) Resource, 3) Mitigation
Exercise 9- 1 B, 2. A, 3. D, 4. C
Exercise 10- a) Assertion (A) is true and Reason (R) is the correct reason for Assertion (A).
Exercise 11- 1) Analysis, 2) Use Case, 3) Monitoring

Online Resources

Online Exam paper
URL https://forms.gle/wPRkhT5iY1BBKwrM7
QR Code

YouTube Video
URL https://www.youtube.com/playlist?list=PLzlh_31VWEFpwwqH6iqI3Bu8I6UBnLhaX

QR Code

More Test Papers Practices

Test Paper-1
URL https://forms.gle/oGsQuRn8UiY2Nbru8
QR Code

Test Paper-2
URL https://forms.gle/2xe1ogtnBCzr5jhKA
QR Code

System analysis and design Test Paper
Chapter- 9
Planning and Management

Time Duration: 30 Minutes **Maximum Marks: 25**

General Instructions:

1. The question paper consists of answer any 12 questions out of the given 19 questions and is divided into four sections, A, B, C and D.
2. All questions are compulsory.
3. Section A comprises question numbers 1 to 8. These are MCQs and one liner of one mark each. You are to select one most appropriate response out of the four provided options.
4. Section B comprises question numbers 1 to 5. These are SAQs carrying two marks each.
5. Section C comprises question numbers 1 to 4. These are SAQs carrying four marks each.
6. Section D comprises question numbers 1& 2. These are LAQs carrying five marks each.

SECTION-A

I. <u>Answer any 6 questions out of the given 8 questions</u> **(1*6=6)**

1. What is the primary goal of project planning and scheduling?
    A) To increase project costs
    B) To define the project scope, timelines, and deliverables
    C) To conduct risk assessments
    D) To assign project resources randomly
2. Which of the following is a key aspect of resource management in project planning?
    A) Ignoring team member skills
    B) Allocating resources based on project needs and availability
    C) Avoiding resource allocation to save costs
    D) Assigning the same resources to all tasks

3. What is the main purpose of risk management in project planning?

    A) To eliminate all project risks
    B) To identify, assess, and mitigate potential risks
    C) To create a project schedule
    D) To ignore potential risks
4. Which method is commonly used to ensure effective project communication?
    A) Random team meetings
    B) Ad-hoc email updates
    C) Regular status meetings and communication plans
    D) Avoiding stakeholder engagement
5. What is a critical component of effective project communication?
    A) Ignoring feedback
    B) Ensuring all stakeholders are informed and engaged
    C) Limiting information sharing to upper management
    D) Reducing the number of communication channels
6. What term describes the allocation of team members and equipment to a project?
7. What is the process of identifying and addressing potential project issues called?
8. What document outlines how project information will be shared?

SECTION-B

II. Answer any 3 questions out of the given 5 questions **(2*3=6)**

1. Define 'project scheduling' in the context of project planning.
2. What is the main objective of resource management in projects?
3. List two techniques used in risk management.
4. Why is effective communication important in project management?
5. What is the role of a project communication plan?

SECTION-C

II. Answer any 2 questions out of the given 4 questions **(4*2=8)**

1. Explain the key steps involved in project planning and scheduling.
2. Describe the importance of resource allocation and how it impacts project success.
3. Discuss the process of risk management and its significance in project planning.
4. What are the main components of an effective project communication strategy?

SECTION-D

III. Answer any 1 question out of the given 2 questions **(5*1=5)**

1. Analyze the challenges and best practices in project planning and scheduling. Provide examples to illustrate how effective planning can influence project outcomes.
2. Discuss the role of risk management in project success. Explain how identifying and mitigating risks can help avoid project failures, using real-world examples.

Chapter- 10: Quality Assurance

- Understanding Testing Fundamentals
- Developing Test Planning and Strategy
- Exploring Various Types of Testing
- Implementing Test Automation
- Ensuring Continuous Quality Improvement

10.1 Testing Fundamentals

Testing is a crucial phase in the system design process, serving not only to verify that the system meets the specified requirements but also to ensure that it functions effectively in its intended environment. This chapter delves into the fundamentals of testing in system design, covering strategies, types, and methodologies to ensure robust and reliable system performance.

1. Understanding the Purpose of Testing

Testing in system design is essential for several reasons:
1. **Validation**: Ensuring that the system meets the user's needs and requirements.
2. **Verification**: Confirming that the system complies with specifications and is correctly implemented.
3. **Reliability**: Establishing that the system performs under expected and unexpected conditions.
4. **Usability**: Checking that the system is user-friendly and intuitive.

2. Types of Testing

Several types of testing are integral to the system design process:
1. **Unit Testing**: Focuses on the smallest unit of software design, such as a module or component, to ensure that each unit functions correctly as an independent entity.
2. **Integration Testing**: After unit testing, integration testing evaluates the interfaces between components to detect faults in the interactions.
3. **System Testing**: Tests the entire system's compliance with the specified requirements. It is often performed in an environment that mimics the production setting.
4. **Acceptance Testing**: Conducted by the end-users, this testing ensures the system meets their requirements and is ready for deployment.

3. Test Planning

Effective test planning is foundational to successful testing. It involves defining the objectives, scope, approach, resources, and schedule of testing activities. Key components include:
1. **Test Strategy**: Outlines the high-level testing objectives and methods.
2. **Test Plan**: A detailed document that guides the testing process; it specifies what will be tested, how the testing will be conducted, who will perform each test, and when testing will occur.
3. **Test Cases**: Specific conditions under which the system will be analysed to determine if it meets the requirements.

4. Test Design Techniques

The design of tests is critical in uncovering different kinds of errors or bugs. Techniques include:
1. **Black-box Testing**: The tester has no knowledge of the internal workings of the system. Testing is based on requirements and functionality.
2. **White-box Testing**: Also known as clear box testing, it involves testing internal structures or workings of an application as opposed to its functionality.
3. **Gray-box Testing**: A combination of black-box and white-box testing methodologies. Testing is based on knowledge of the code structure and algorithms.

5. Testing Tools and Automation

Advancements in technology have facilitated the development of tools that automate many testing tasks. Automation helps in performing repetitive but necessary tests which might be cumbersome and time-consuming if done manually. Popular tools include Selenium, QTP, and LoadRunner. These tools can significantly increase efficiency, accuracy, and coverage of testing.

6. Managing Test Data

Test data management is critical for ensuring the effectiveness and efficiency of the testing process. It involves creating, maintaining, and managing data necessary for executing the test processes. Proper management helps in maintaining the integrity of the test environment and results.

7. Monitoring and Controlling Testing

Effective monitoring and controlling of the testing process are vital for:
1. Tracking Progress: Assessing the status of planned tests.
2. Issue Management: Identifying, logging, and tracking issues found during testing.
3. Test Reporting: Communicating testing progress, outcomes, and metrics to stakeholders.

8. Challenges in Testing

Despite its critical importance, testing can present numerous challenges:
1. Environment Mimicry: Creating a test environment that closely resembles the production environment.
2. Time Constraints: Balancing thorough testing with the pressure to deploy on schedule.
3. Resource Allocation: Ensuring adequate resources are available for testing.

Conclusion

Testing is an integral part of the system design that ensures the final product is robust, reliable, and meets all specified requirements. By implementing comprehensive testing strategies and utilizing modern tools and methodologies, organizations can significantly enhance the quality of their systems. This chapter aims to provide a solid foundation for understanding and applying testing principles effectively within the system design framework.

10.2 Test Planning and Strategy

A test plan is a detailed document which describes software testing areas and activities. It outlines the test strategy, objectives, test schedule, required resources (human resources, software, and hardware), test estimation and test deliverables.

The test plan is a base of every software's testing. It is the most crucial activity which ensures availability of all the lists of planned activities in an appropriate sequence.

The test plan is a template for conducting software testing activities as a defined process that is fully monitored and controlled by the testing manager. The test plan is prepared by the Test Lead (60%), Test Manager (20%), and by the test engineer (20%).

Types of Test Plan

There are three types of the test plan
- Master Test Plan
- Phase Test Plan
- Testing Type Specific Test Plans

1. Master Test Plan
   Master Test Plan is a type of test plan that has multiple levels of testing. It includes a complete test strategy.
1. Phase Test Plan
   A phase test plan is a type of test plan that addresses any one phase of the testing strategy. For example, a list of tools, a list of test cases, etc.
1. Specific Test Plans
   Specific test plan designed for major types of testing like security testing, load testing, performance testing, etc. In other words, a specific test plan designed for non-functional testing.

How to write a Test Plan

Making a test plan is the most crucial task of the test management process. According to IEEE 829, follow the following seven steps to prepare a test plan.
- First, analyse product structure and architecture.
- Now design the test strategy.
- Define all the test objectives.
- Define the testing area.
- Define all the useable resources.
- Schedule all activities in an appropriate manner.
- Determine all the Test Deliverables.

Test plan components or attributes

The test plan consists of various parts, which help us to derive the entire testing activity.

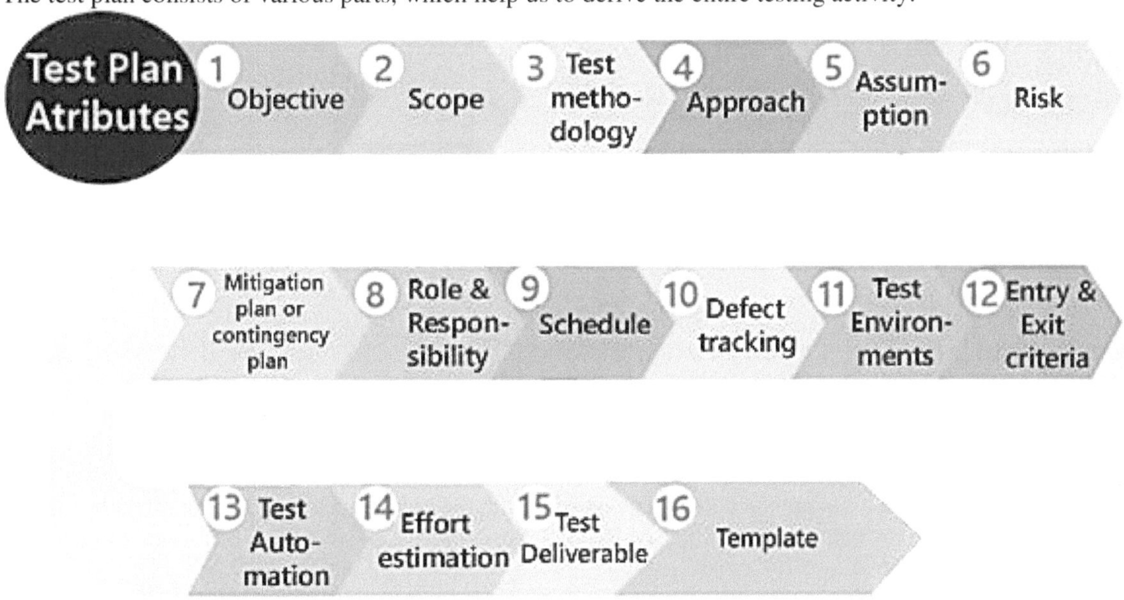

Objectives: It consists of information about modules, features, test data etc., which indicate the aim of the application means the application behaviour, goal, etc.
Scope: It contains information that needs to be tested with respective of an application. The Scope can be further divided into two parts:
- In scope
- Out scope

In scope: These are the modules that need to be tested rigorously (in-detail).
Out scope: These are the modules, which need not be tested rigorously.
For example, Suppose we have a Gmail application to test, where **features to be tested** such as **Compose mail, Sent Items, Inbox, Drafts** and the **features which not be tested** such as **Help**, and so on which means that in the planning stage, we will decide that which functionality has to be checked or not based on the time limit given in the product.

Now **how we decide which features not to be tested?**
We have the following aspects where we can decide which feature not to be tested:
- As we see above that **Help** features is not going to be tested, as it is written and developed by the technical writer and reviewed by another professional writer.
- Let us assume that we have one application that have **P, Q, R, and S** features, which need to be developed based on the requirements. But here, the S feature has already been designed and used by some other company. So the development team will purchase S from that company and integrate with additional features such as P, Q, and R.

Now, we will not perform functional testing on the S feature because it has already been used in real-time. But we will do the integration testing, and system testing between P, Q, R, and S features because the new features might not work correctly with S feature as we can see in the below image:

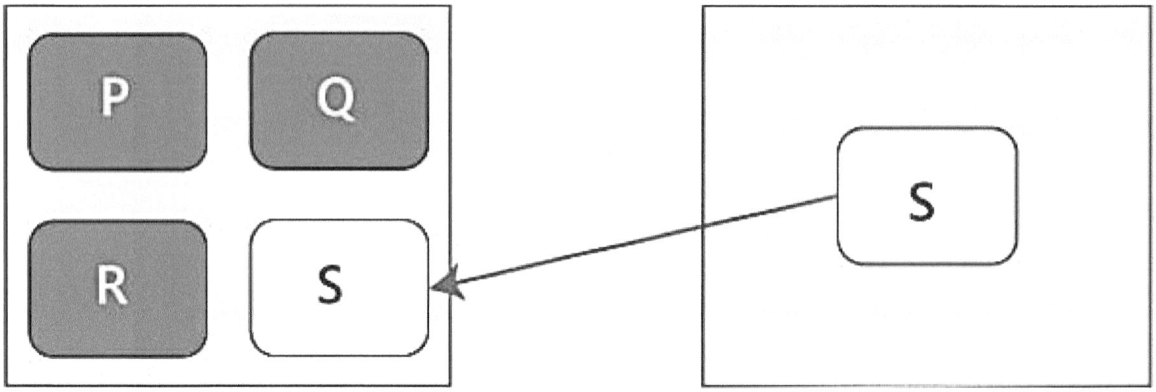

- Suppose in the first release of the product, the elements that have been developed, such as **P, Q, R, S, T, U, V, W….X, Y, Z**. Now the client will provide the requirements for the new features which improve the product in the second release and the new features are **A1, B2, C3, D4, and E5.**

After that, we will write the scope during the test plan as

Scope

Features to be tested

A1, B2, C3, D4, E5 (new features)

P, Q, R, S, T

Features not to be tested

W…..X, Y, Z

Therefore, we will check the new features first and then continue with the old features because that might be affected after adding the new features, which means it will also affect the impact areas, so we will do one round of regressing testing for P, Q, R…, T features.

Test methodology:

It contains information about performing a different kind of testing like Functional testing, Integration testing, and System testing, etc. on the application. In this, we will decide what type of testing; we will perform on the various features based on the application requirement. And here, we should also define that what kind of testing we will use in the testing methodologies so that everyone, like the management, the development team, and the testing team can understand easily because the testing terms are not standard.

For example, for standalone application such as **Adobe Photoshop**, we will perform the following types of testing: Smoke testing→ Functional testing → Integration testing →System testing →Adhoc testing → Compatibility testing → Regression testing→ Globalization testing → Accessibility testing → Usability testing → Reliability testing → Recovery testing → Installation or Uninstallation testing

And suppose we must test the https://www.jeevansathi.com/ application, so we will perform following types of testing:

Smoke testing	Functional testing	Integration testing
System testing	Adhoc testing	Compatibility testing
Regression testing	Globalization testing	Accessibility testing
Usability testing	Performance testing	

Approach

This attribute is used to describe the flow of the application while performing testing and for the future reference. We can understand the flow of the application with the help of below aspects:

- By writing the high-level scenarios

- By writing the flow graph

By writing the high-level scenarios

For example, suppose we are testing the **Gmail** application:

- Login to Gmail- sends an email and check whether it is in the Sent Items page
- Login to …….
- ……
- …....

We are writing this to describe the approaches which must be taken for testing the product and only for the critical features where we will write the high-level scenarios. Here, we will not be focusing on covering all the scenarios because it can be decided by the test engineer that which features must be tested or not.

By writing the flow graph

The flow graph is written because writing the high-level scenarios are bit time taking process, as we can see in the below image:

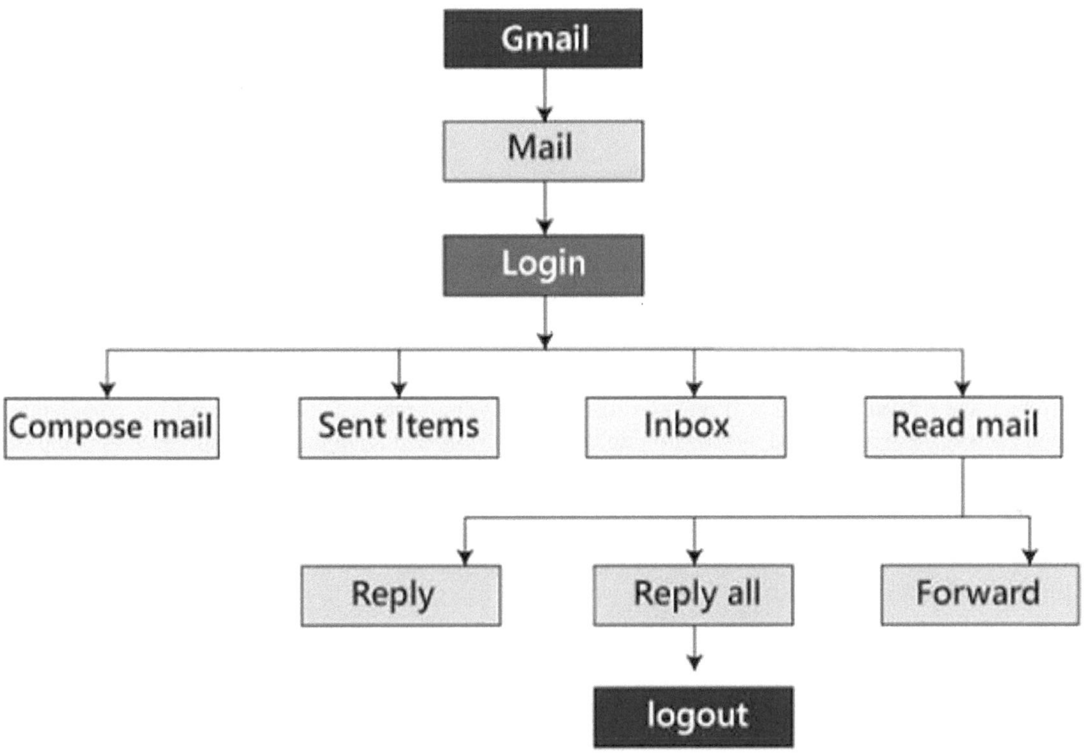

We are creating flow graphs to make the following benefits such as:

- Coverage is easy
- Merging is easy

The approach can be classified into two parts which are as following:

- Top to bottom approach
- Bottom to top approach

Assumption

It contains information about a problem or issue which maybe occurred during the testing process and when we are writing the test plans, the assured assumptions would be made like resources and technologies, etc.

Risk

These are the challenges which we need to face to test the application in the current release and if the assumptions will fail then the risks are involved.
For example, the effect for an application, release date becomes postponed.

Mitigation Plan or Contingency Plan

It is a back-up plan which is prepared to overcome the risks or issues.
Let us see one example for assumption, risk, and the contingency plan together because they are co-related to each other.

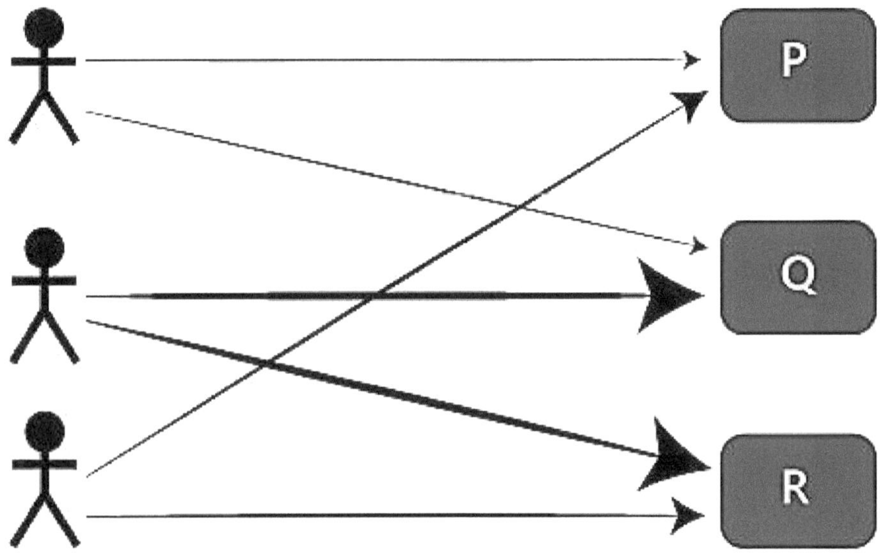

In any product, the **assumption** we will make is that all 3 test engineers will be there until the completion of the product and each of them is assigned different modules such as P, Q, and R. In this scenario, the **risk** could be that if the test engineer left the project in the middle of it.

Therefore, the **contingency plan** will be assigned a primary and subordinate owner to each feature. So, if the one test engineer will leave, the subordinate owner takes over that specific feature and helps the new test engineer, so he/she can understand their assigned modules.

The assumptions, risk, and mitigation or contingency plan are always precise on the product itself. The various types of risks are as follows:
- Customer perspective
- Resource approach
- Technical opinion

Role & Responsibility

It defines the complete task which needs to be performed by the entire testing team. When a large project comes, then the **Test Manager** is a person who writes the test plan. If there are 3-4 small projects, then the test manager will assign each project to each Test Lead. And then, the test lead writes the test plan for the project, which he/she is assigned.

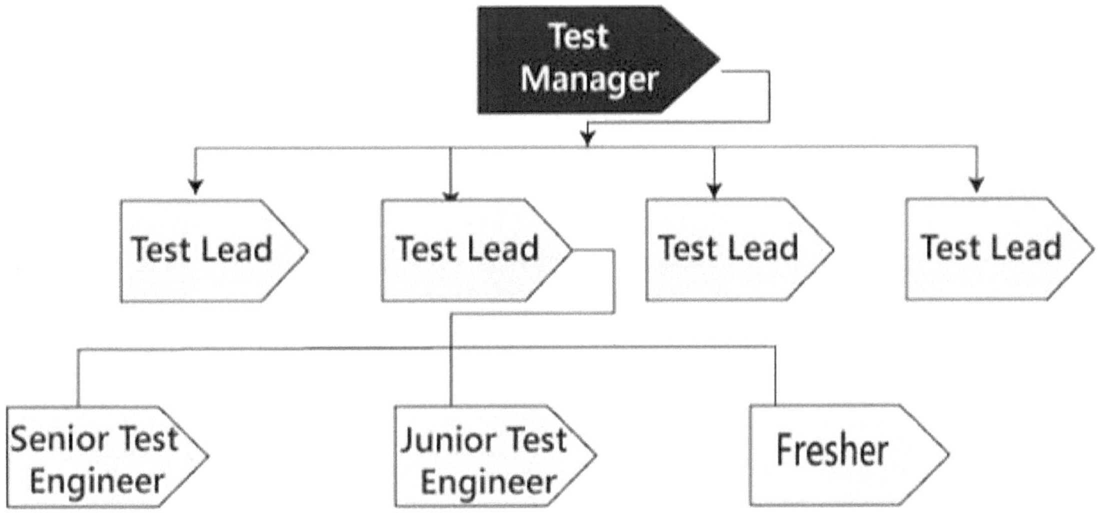

Let see one example where we will understand the roles and responsibility of the Test manager, test lead, and the test engineers.

Role: Test Manager
Name: Ryan
Responsibility:
- Prepare (write and review) the test plan
- Conduct the meeting with the development team
- Conduct the meeting with the testing team
- Conduct the meeting with the customer
- Conduct one monthly stand-up meeting
- Sign off release note
- Handling Escalations and issues

Role: Test Lead
Name: Harvey
Responsibility:
- Prepare (write and review) the test plan
- Conduct daily stand-up meeting
- Review and approve the test case
- Prepare the RTM and Reports
- Assign modules
- Handling schedule

Role: Test Engineer 1, Test Engineer 2 and Test Engineer 3
Name: Louis, Jessica, Donna
Assign modules: M1, M2, and M3
Responsibility:
- Write, Review, and Execute the test documents which consists of test case and test scenarios
- Read, review, understand and analysis the requirement
- Write the flow of the application
- Execute the test case
- RTM for respective modules
- Defect tracking
- Prepare the test execution report and communicate it to the Test Lead.

Schedule

It is used to explain the timing to work, which needs to be done or this attribute covers when exactly each testing activity should start and end? And the exact data is also mentioned for every testing activity for the particular date.

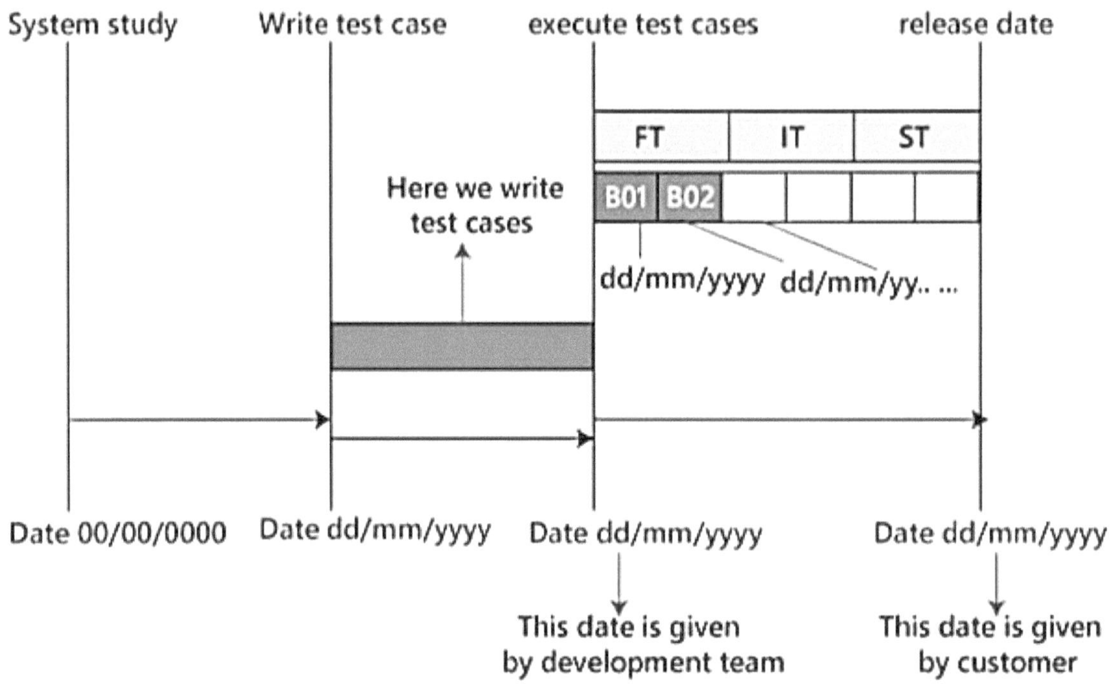

Therefore, as we can see in the below image that for the activity, there will be a starting date and ending date; for each testing to a specific build, there will be the specified date.

For example,

- Writing test cases
- Execution process

Defect tracking

It is generally done with the help of tools because we cannot track the status of each bug manually. And we also comment about how we communicate the bugs which are identified during the testing process and send it back to the development team and how the development team will reply. Here we also mention the priority of the bugs such as high, medium, and low.

Following are various aspects of the defect tracking:

- Techniques to track the bug

.....
......
......
......

- Bug tracking tools

We can comment on the name of the tool, which we will use for tracking the bugs. Some of the most commonly used bug tracking tools are Jira, Bugzilla, Mantis, and Trac, etc.<

- Severity

The severity could be as following:

Blocker or showstopper

.....
..... (Explain it with an example in the test plan)

For example, there will be a defect in the module; we cannot go further to test other modules because if the bug is blocked, we can proceed to check other modules.

Critical

……

…. (Explain it with an example in the test plan)

In this situation, the defects will affect the business.

Major

….

…. (Explain it with an example in the test plan)

Minor

….

…. (Explain it with an example in the test plan)

These defects are those, which affect the look and feel of the application.

- Priority

High-P1

….

Medium-P2

…..

Low-P3

….

….

P4

Therefore, based on the priority of bugs like high, medium, and low, we will categorize it as P1, P2, P3, and P4.

Test Environments

- These are the environments where we will test the application, and here we have two types of environments, which are of **software** and **hardware** configuration.
- The software configuration means the details about different Operating Systems such as Windows, Linux, UNIX, and Mac and various Browsers like Google Chrome, Firefox, Opera, Internet Explorer, and so on.
- And the **hardware configuration** means the information about different sizes of **RAM, ROM, and the Processors**.

For example,

- The **Software** includes the following:

Server

Operating system	Linux
Webserver	Apache Tomcat
Application server	WebSphere
Database server	Oracle or MS-SQL Server

Client

Operating System	Window XP, Vista 7
Browsers	Mozilla Firefox, Google Chrome, Internet Explorer, Internet Explorer 7, and Internet Explorer 8

- The **Hardware** includes the following:

Server: Sun StarCat 1500
This particular server can be used by the testing team to test their application.
Client:
It has the following configuration, which is as follows:

Processor	Intal2GHz
RAM	2GB
....	....

The development team will provide the configuration of how to install the software. If the development team will not yet provide the process, then we will write it as Task-Based Development (TBD) in the test plan.

Entry and Exit criteria

It is a necessary condition, which needs to be satisfied before starting and stopping the testing process.

Entry Criteria

The entry criteria contain the following conditions:
- White box testing should be finished.
- Understand and analyze the requirement and prepare the test documents or when the test documents are ready.
- Test data should be ready.
- Build or the application must be prepared
- Modules or features need to be assigned to the different test engineers.
- The necessary resource must be ready.

Exit Criteria

The exit criteria contain the following conditions:
- When all the test cases are executed.
- Most of the test cases must be **passed**.
- Depends on severity of the bugs which means that there must not be any blocker or major bug, whereas some minor bugs exist.

Effort estimation

In this, we will plan the effort need to be applied by every team member.

Test Deliverable

These are the documents which are the output from the testing team, which we handed over to the customer along with the product. It includes the following:
- Test plan
- Test Cases
- Test Scripts
- RTM (Requirement Traceability Matrix)
- Defect Report
- Test Execution Report
- Graphs and metrics
- Release Notes

Graphs and Metrics

Graph

In this, we will discuss about the types of **graphs** we will send, and we will also provide a sample of each graph.
As we can see, we have five different graphs that show the various aspects of the testing process.

Graph1: In this, we will show how many defects have been identified and how many defects have been fixed in every module.

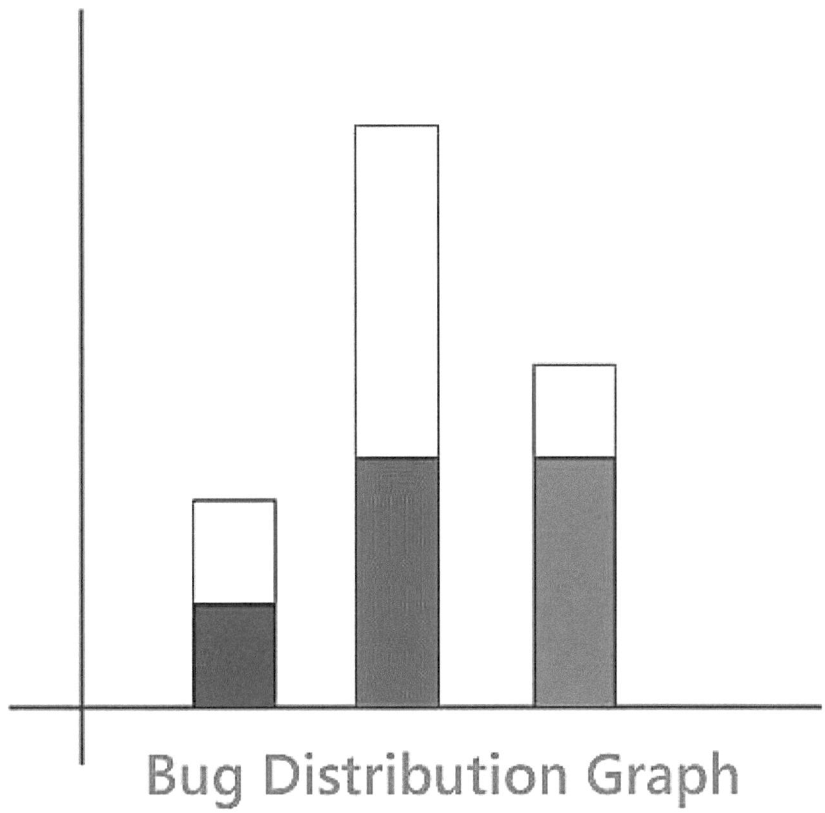

Graph 2: Figure one shows how many critical, major, and minor defects have been identified for every module and how many have been fixed for their respective modules.

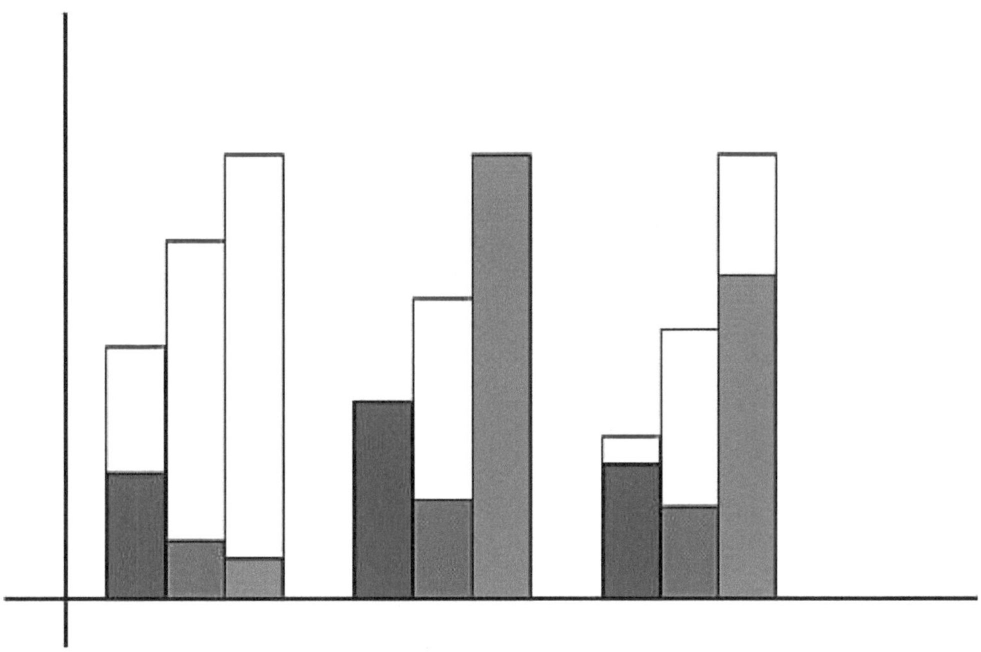

Graph3: In this graph, we represent the **build wise graph**, which means that in every builds how many defects have been identified and fixed for every module. Based on the module, we have determined the bugs. We will add **R** to show the number of defects in P and Q, and we also add **S** to show the defects in P, Q, and R.

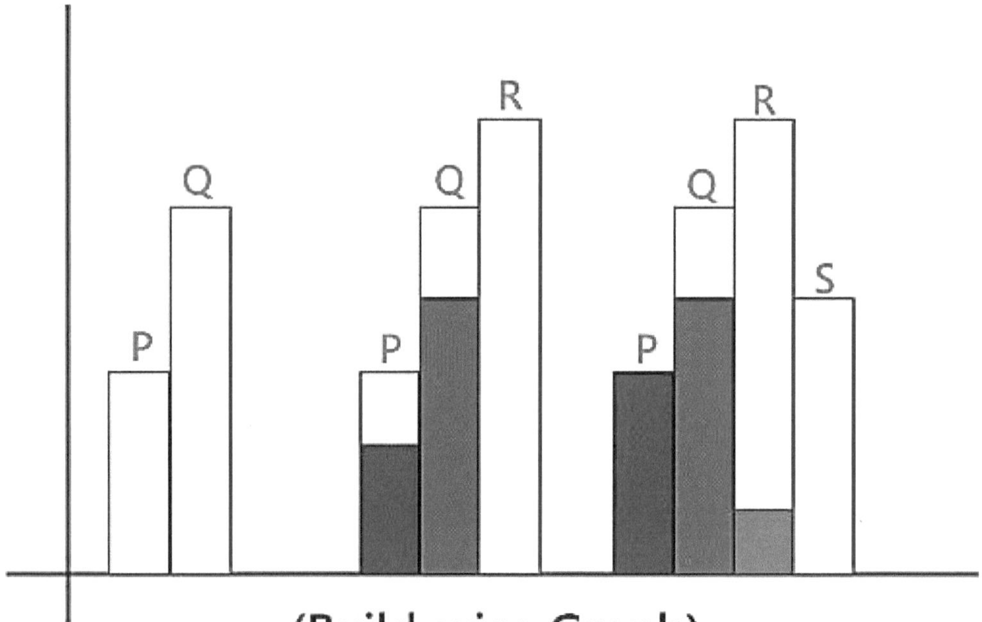

(Build-wise Graph)

Graph4: The test lead will design the **Bug Trend analysis** graph which is created every month and send it to the Management as well. And it is just like prediction which is done at the end of the product. And here, we can also **rate the bug fixes** as we can observe that **arc** has an **upward tendency** in the below image.

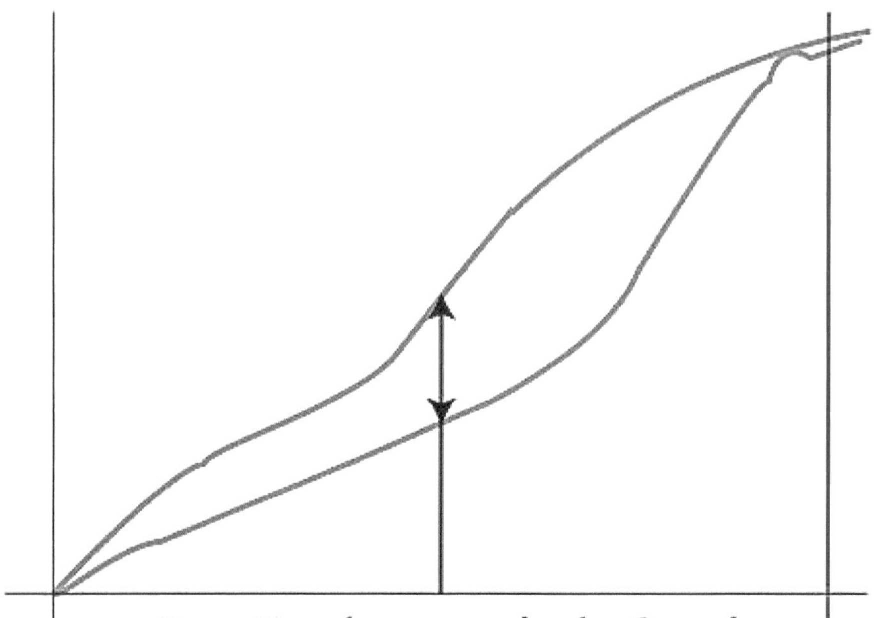

Bug Tendecy analysis Graph

Graph5: The **Test Manager** has designed this type of graph. This graph is intended to understand the gap in the assessment of bugs and the actual bugs which have been occurred, and this graph also helps to improve the evaluation of bugs in the future.

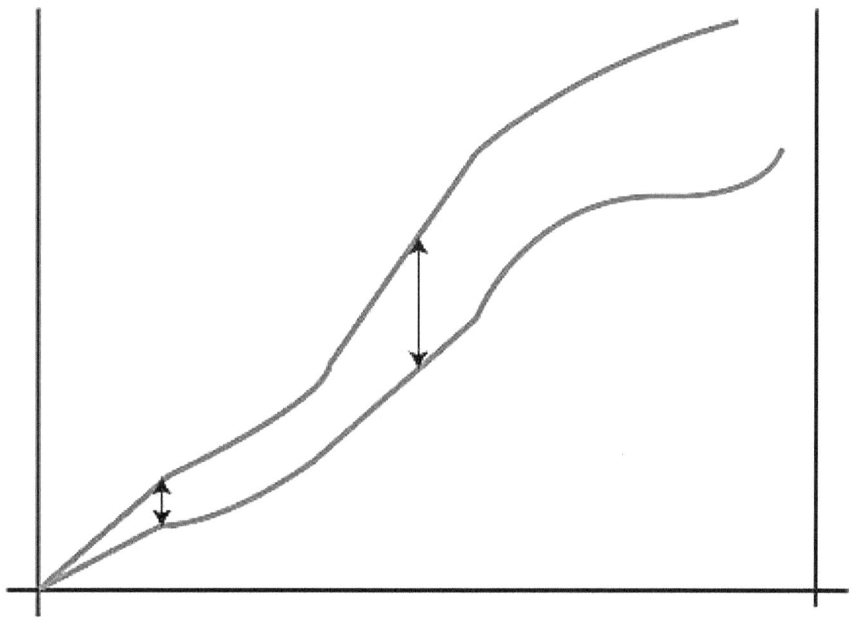

Metrics

Module Name	Critical		Major		Minor	
	Found	Fixed	Found	Fixed	Found	Fixed
Purchase	50	46	60	20	80	10
Sales	..	...	...	...	...	...
Asset Survey	...	...	...	...	...	...

As above, we create the bug distribution graph, which is in the figure 1, and with the help of above mention data, we will design the metrics as well.

For example,

Test Engineer Names	Critical		Major		Minor	
	Found	Fixed	Found	Fixed	Found	Fixed
John	50	46	60	20	80	10
James	..	...	...	...	...	...
Sophia	...	...	...	...	...	...

In the above figure, we retain the records of all the test engineers in a particular project and how many defects have been identified and fixed. We can also use this data for future analysis. When a new requirement comes, we can decide whom to provide the challenging feature for testing based on the number of defects they have found earlier according to the above metrics. And we will be in a better situation to know who can handle the problematic features very well and find maximum numbers of defects.

Release Note: It is a document that is prepared during the release of the product and signed by the Test Manager.

In the below image, we can see that the final product is developed and deployed to the customer, and the latest release name is **Beta**.

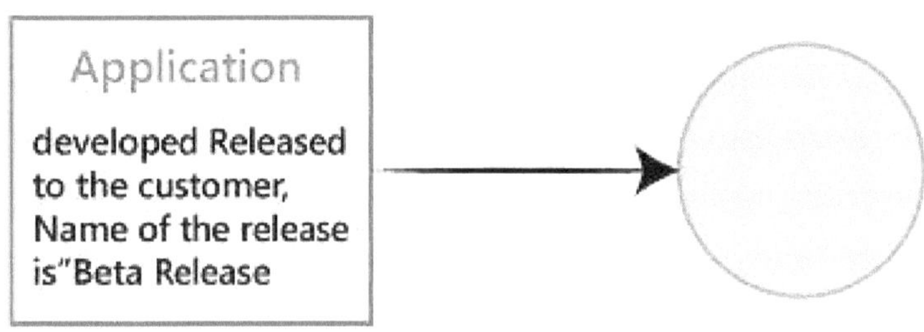

The **Release note** consists of the following:
- User manual.
- List of pending and open defects.
- List of added, modified, and deleted features.
- List of the platform (Operating System, Hardware, Browsers) on which the product is tested.
- Platform in which the product is not tested.
- List of bugs fixed in the current release, and the list of fixed bugs in the previous release.
- Installation process
- Versions of the software

For Example

Suppose that **Beta** is the second release of the application after the first release **Alpha** is released. Some of the defect identified in the first released and that has been fixed in the later released. And here, we will also point out the list of newly added, modified, and deleted features from alpha release to the beta release.

Template

This part contains all the templates for the documents that will be used in the product, and all the test engineers will use only these templates in the project to maintain the consistency of the product. Here, we have different types of the template which are used during the entire testing process such as:

- Test case template
- Test case review template
- RTM Template
- Bug Report Template
- Test execution Report

Let us see one sample of test plan document

Page-1

Testplan

Version	Author	Reviewed By	Approved By	Comments	Approval date
1	...	...	Name of manager	Version 1.0 is developed	dd/mm/yyyy
1.1	...	..	..	Version 1.1 is developed. PQR feature is added	dd/mm/yyyy
.....	.....	.....	.....	.....	.....
.....	.....	.....	.....	.....	.....

Page3-page18

TABLE OF CONTENTS

- Objective pg 1
- Scope pg 2
- Approach pg 3

..
...
...
...

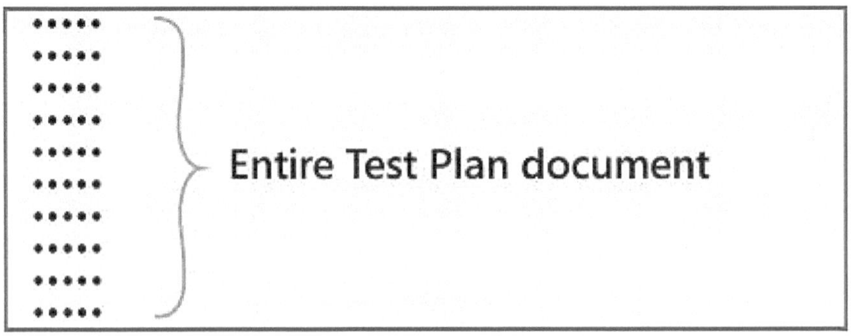

Page-20

REFERENCES

1) Customer requirement specification(CRS)
2) Software requirement specification(SRS)
3) Functional specification(FS)
4) Design Documents

....
....
....

In-Page 1, we primarily fill only the **Versions, Author, Comments, and Reviewed By** fields, and after the manager approves it, we will mention the details in the **Approved By and Approval Date** fields.
Mostly the test plan is approved by the Test Manager, and the test engineers only reviews it. And when the new features come, we will modify the test plan and do the necessary modification in **Version** field, and then it will be sent again for further review, update, and approval of the manager. The test plan must be updated whenever any changes have occurred. On page 20, the **References** specify the details about all the documents which we are going to use to write the test plan document.

Note: Who writes the test plan?
- Test Lead→60%
- Test Manager→20%
- Test Engineer→20%

Therefore, as we can see from above that in 60% of the product, the test plan is written by the Test Lead.

Who reviews the Test Plan?
- Test Lead
- Test Manager
- Test engineer

- Customer
- Development team

The Test Engineer review the Test plan for their module perspective and the test manager review the Test plan based on the customer opinion.

Who approve the test Plan?

- Customer
- Test Manager

Who writes the test case?

- Test Lead
- Test Engineer

Who review the test case?

- Test Engineer
- Test Lead
- Customer
- Development Team

Who approves the Test cases?

- Test Manager
- Test Lead
- Customer

Test Plan Guidelines

- Collapse your test plan.
- Avoid overlapping and redundancy.
- If you think that you do not need a section that is already mentioned above, then delete that section and proceed ahead.
- Be specific. For example, when you specify a software system as the part of the test environment, then mention the software version instead of only name.
- Avoid lengthy paragraphs.
- Use lists and tables wherever possible.
- Update plan when needed.
- Do not use an outdated and unused document.

Importance of Test Plan

- The test plan gives direction to our thinking. This is like a rule book, which must be followed.
- The test plan helps in determining the necessary efforts to validate the quality of the software application under the test.
- The test plan helps those people to understand the test details that are related to the outside like developers, business managers, customers, etc.
- Important aspects like test schedule, test strategy, test scope etc are documented in the test plan so that the management team can review them and reuse them for other similar projects.

10.3 Types of Testing

In this section, we are going to understand the various types of software testing, which can be used at the time of the Software Development Life Cycle.

As we know, **software testing** is a process of analyzing an application's functionality as per the customer prerequisite. If we want to ensure that our software is bug-free or stable, we must perform the various types of software testing because testing is the only method that makes our application bug-free.

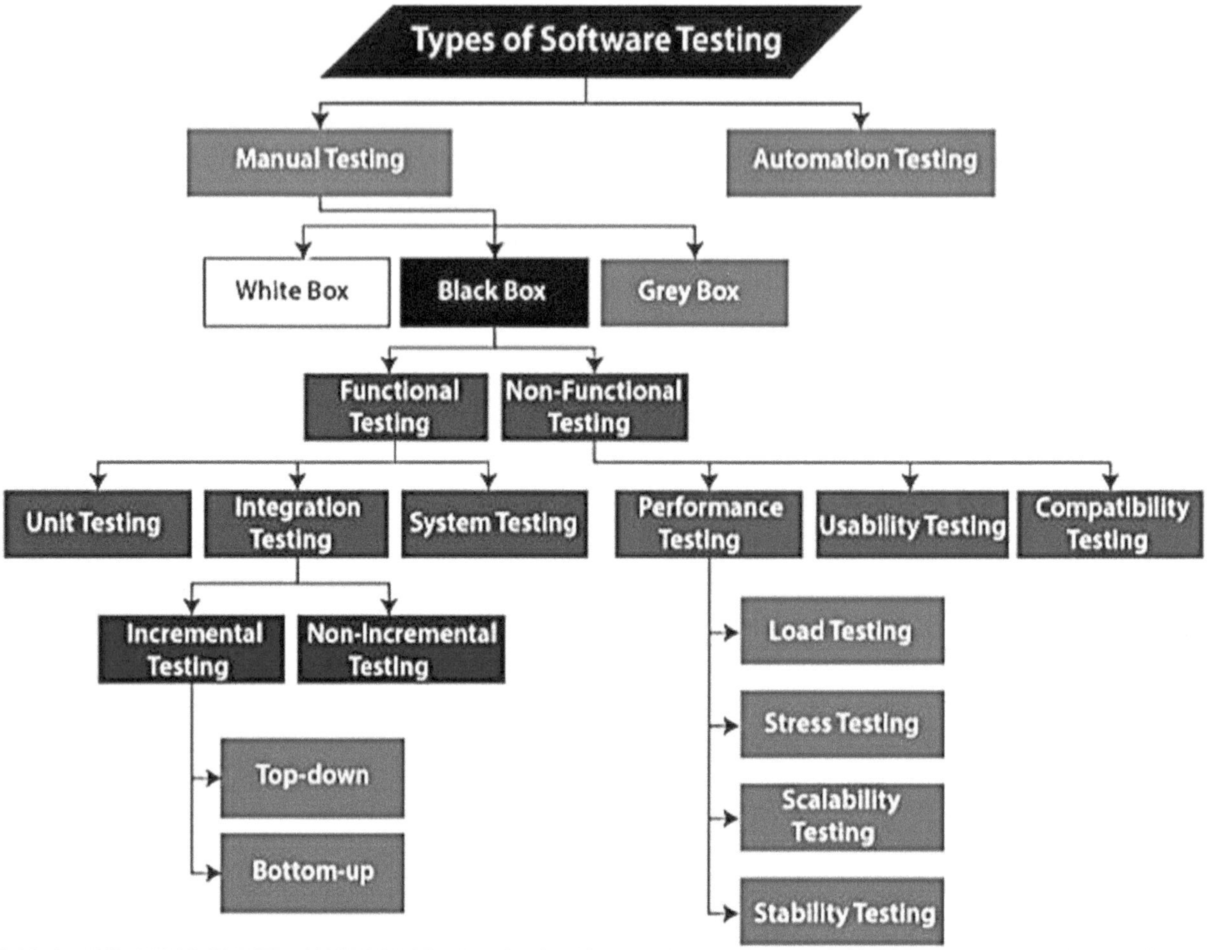

The different types of Software Testing
The categorization of software testing is a part of diverse testing activities, such as **test strategy, test deliverables, a defined test objective, etc**. And software testing is the execution of the software to find defects.

The purpose of having a testing type is to confirm the AUT (Application Under Test).
To start testing, we should have a **requirement, application-ready, necessary resources available**. To maintain accountability, we should assign a respective module to different test engineers.

The software testing mainly divided into two parts, which are as follows:
- Manual Testing
- Automation Testing

What is Manual Testing?

Testing any software or an application according to the client's needs without using any automation tool is known as **manual testing**.

In other words, we can say that it is a procedure of **verification and validation**. Manual testing is used to verify the behavior of an application or software in contradiction of requirements specification.

We do not require any precise knowledge of any testing tool to execute the manual test cases. We can easily prepare the test document while performing manual testing on any application.

Classification of Manual Testing

In software testing, manual testing can be further classified into **three different types of testing**, which are as follows:

- White Box Testing
- Black Box Testing
- Grey Box Testing

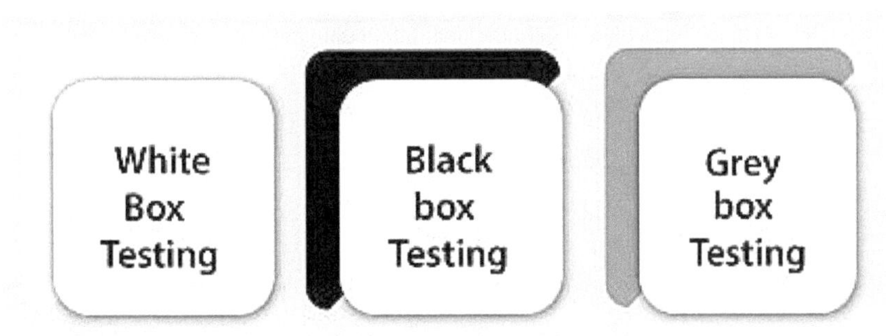

For our better understanding let's see them one by one:

White Box Testing

In white-box testing, the developer will inspect every line of code before handing it over to the testing team or the concerned test engineers.

Subsequently, the code is noticeable for developers throughout testing; that's why this process is known as **WBT (White Box Testing)**.

In other words, we can say that the **developer** will execute the complete white box testing for the software and send the specific application to the testing team.

The purpose of implementing the white box testing is to emphasize the flow of inputs and outputs over the software and enhance the security of an application.

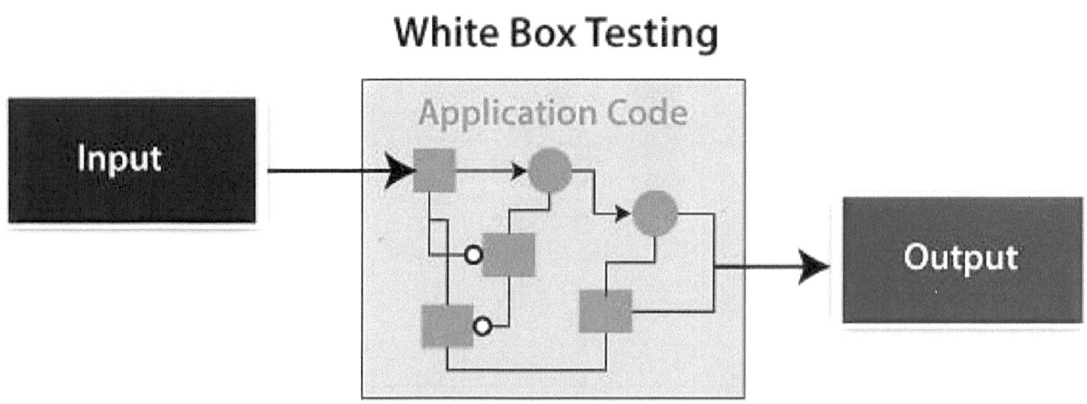

White box testing is also known as **open box testing, glass box testing, structural testing, clear box testing, and transparent box testing**.

Black Box Testing

Another type of manual testing is **black-box testing**. In this testing, the test engineer will analyze the software against requirements, identify the defects or bug, and sends it back to the development team.

Then, the developers will fix those defects, do one round of White box testing, and send it to the testing team.
Here, fixing the bugs means the defect is resolved, and the feature is working according to the given requirement.

The main objective of implementing the black box testing is to specify the business needs or the customer's requirements.
In other words, we can say that black box testing is a process of checking the functionality of an application as per the customer requirement. The source code is not visible in this testing; that's why it is known as **black-box testing**.

Types of Black Box Testing

Black box testing further categorizes into two parts, which are as discussed below:
- Functional Testing
- Non-function Testing

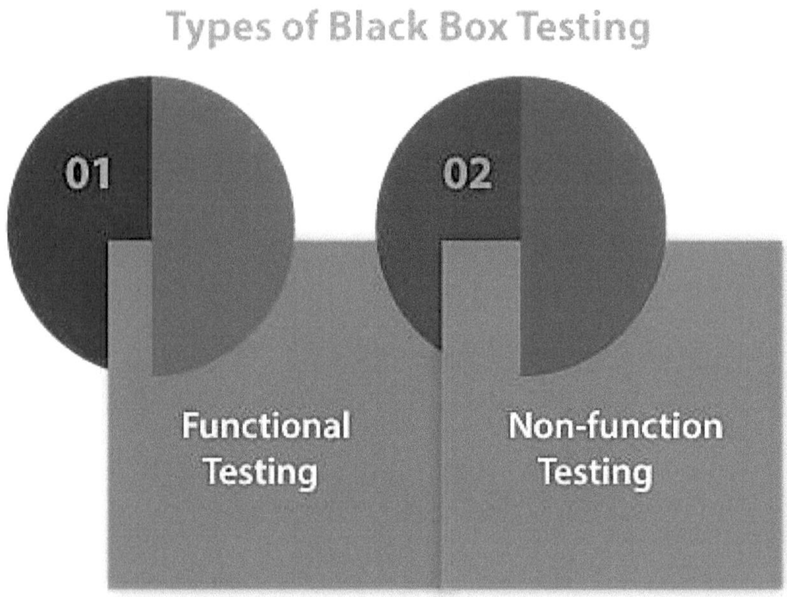

Functional Testing

- The test engineer will check all the components systematically against requirement specifications is known as **functional testing**. Functional testing is also known as **Component testing**.
- In functional testing, all the components are tested by giving the value, defining the output, and validating the actual output with the expected value.
- Functional testing is a part of black box testing as its emphases on application requirement rather than actual code. The test engineer must test only the program instead of the system.

Types of Functional Testing

Just like another type of testing is divided into several parts, functional testing is also classified into various categories. The diverse **types of Functional Testing** contain the following:
- Unit Testing
- Integration Testing
- System Testing

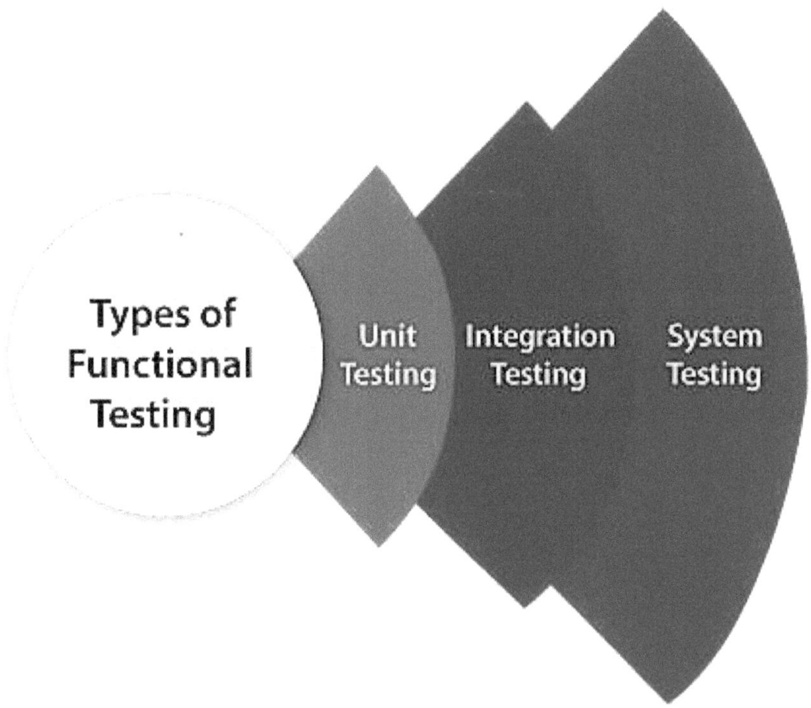

Now, Let's understand them one by one:

1. Unit Testing

Unit testing is the first level of functional testing to test any software. In this, the test engineer will test the module of an application independently or test all the module functionality is called **unit testing**.

The primary objective of executing the unit testing is to confirm the unit components with their performance. Here, a unit is defined as a single testable function of a software or an application. And it is verified throughout the specified application development phase.

2. Integration Testing

Once we are successfully implementing the unit testing, we will go integration testing. It is the second level of functional testing, where we test the data flow between dependent modules or interface between two features is called **integration testing**.

The purpose of executing the integration testing is to test the statement's accuracy between each module.

Types of Integration Testing

Integration testing is also further divided into the following parts:
- Incremental Testing
- Non-Incremental Testing

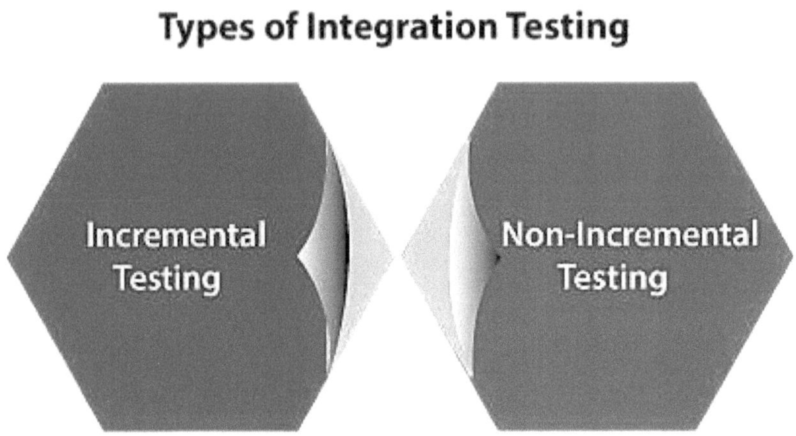

Incremental Integration Testing

Whenever there is a clear relationship between modules, we go for incremental integration testing. Suppose we take two modules and analysis the data flow between them if they are working fine or not.

If these modules are working fine, then we can add one more module and test again. And we can continue with the same process to get better results.

In other words, we can say that incrementally adding up the modules and test the data flow between the modules is known as **Incremental integration testing**.

Types of Incremental Integration Testing

Incremental integration testing can further classify into two parts, which are as follows:
1. Top-down Incremental Integration Testing
2. Bottom-up Incremental Integration Testing

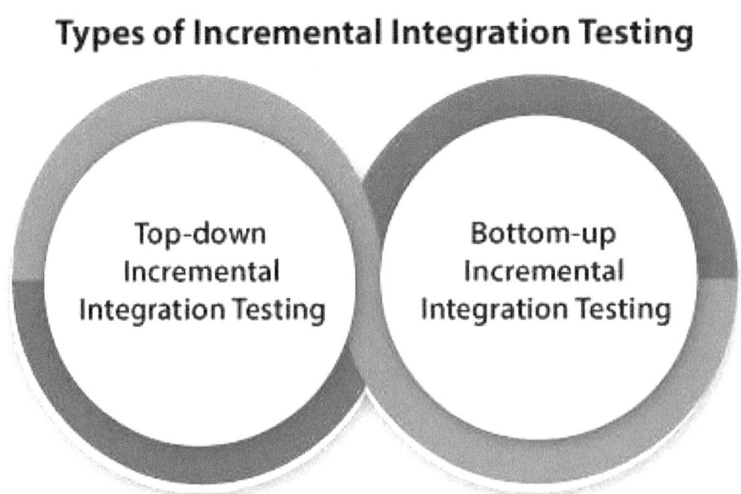

Let's see a brief introduction of these types of integration testing:

1. Top-down Incremental Integration Testing
In this approach, we will add the modules step by step or incrementally and test the data flow between them. We must ensure that the modules we are adding are the **child of the earlier ones**.

2. Bottom-up Incremental Integration Testing

In the bottom-up approach, we will add the modules incrementally and check the data flow between modules. And, ensure that the module we are adding is the **parent of the earlier ones**.

Non-Incremental Integration Testing/ Big Bang Method

Whenever the data flow is complex and very difficult to classify a parent and a child, we will go for the non-incremental integration approach. The non-incremental method is also known as **the Big Bang method**.

3. System Testing

- Whenever we are done with the unit and integration testing, we can proceed with the system testing.
- In system testing, the test environment is parallel to the production environment. It is also known as end-to-end testing.
- In this type of testing, we will undergo each attribute of the software and test if the end feature works according to the business requirement. And analysis the software product as a complete system.

Non-function Testing

- The next part of black-box testing is non-functional testing. It provides detailed information on software product performance and used technologies.
- Non-functional testing will help us minimize the risk of production and related costs of the software.
- Non-functional testing is a combination of performance, load, stress, usability and compatibility testing.

Types of Non-functional Testing

Non-functional testing categorized into different parts of testing, which we are going to discuss further:
- Performance Testing
- Usability Testing
- Compatibility Testing

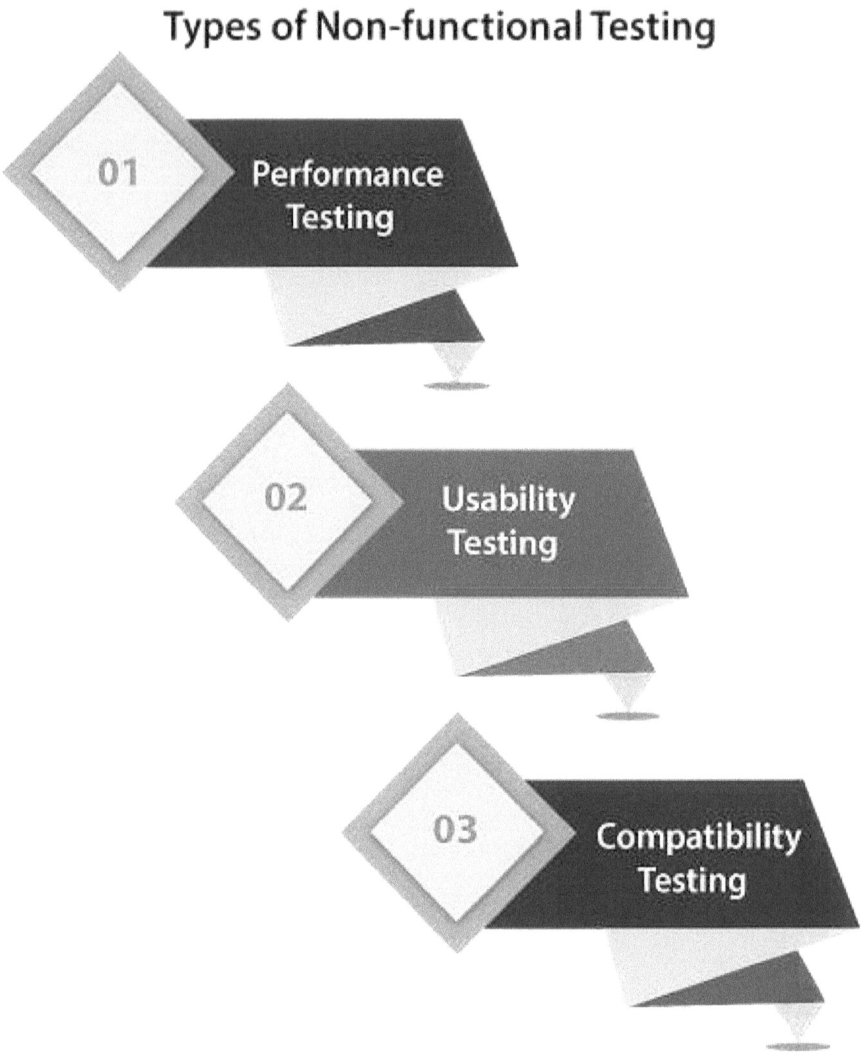

1. Performance Testing

- In performance testing, the test engineer will test the working of an application by applying some load.
- In this type of non-functional testing, the test engineer will only focus on several aspects, such as Response time, Load, scalability, and Stability of the software or an application.

Classification of Performance Testing

Performance testing includes the various types of testing, which are as follows:

- Load Testing
- Stress Testing
- Scalability Testing
- Stability Testing

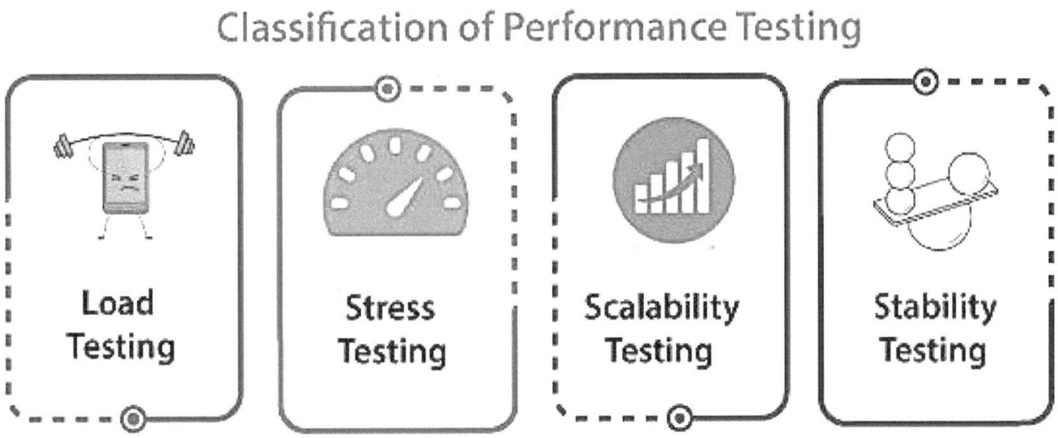

- Load Testing
While executing the performance testing, we will apply some load on the particular application to check the application's performance, known as **load testing**. Here, the load could be less than or equal to the desired load.
It will help us to detect the highest operating volume of the software and bottlenecks.

- Stress Testing
It is used to analyze the user-friendliness and robustness of the software beyond the common functional limits.
Primarily, stress testing is used for critical software, but it can also be used for all types of software applications.

- Scalability Testing
To analysis, the application's performance by enhancing or reducing the load in particular balances is known as **scalability testing**.
In scalability testing, we can also check the **system, processes, or database's ability** to meet an upward need. And in this, the **Test Cases** are designed and implemented efficiently.

- Stability Testing
Stability testing is a procedure where we evaluate the application's performance by applying the load for a precise time.
It mainly checks the constancy problems of the application and the efficiency of a developed product. In this type of testing, we can rapidly find the system's defect even in a stressful situation.

2. Usability Testing

Another type of **non-functional testing** is **usability testing**. In usability testing, we will analyze the user-friendliness of an application and detect the bugs in the software's end-user interface.

Here, the term user-friendliness defines the following aspects of an application:

- The application should be easy to understand, which means that all the features must be visible to end-users.
- The application's look and feel should be good that means the application should be pleasant looking and make a feel to the end-user to use it.

3. Compatibility Testing

- In compatibility testing, we will check the functionality of an application in specific hardware and software environments.
- Once the application is functionally stable then only, we go for compatibility testing.

Here, **software** means we can test the application on the different operating systems and other browsers, and **hardware** means we can test the application on different sizes.

Grey Box Testing

Another part of **manual testing** is **Grey box testing**. It is a **collaboration of black box and white box testing**. Since, the grey box testing includes access to internal coding for designing test cases. Grey box testing is performed by a person who knows coding as well as testing.

In other words, we can say that if a single-person team done both **white box and black-box testing**, it is considered **grey box testing**.

Automation Testing

- The most significant part of Software testing is Automation testing. It uses specific tools to automate manual design test cases without any human interference.
- Automation testing is the best way to enhance the efficiency, productivity, and coverage of Software testing.
- It is used to re-run the test scenarios, which were executed manually, quickly, and repeatedly.

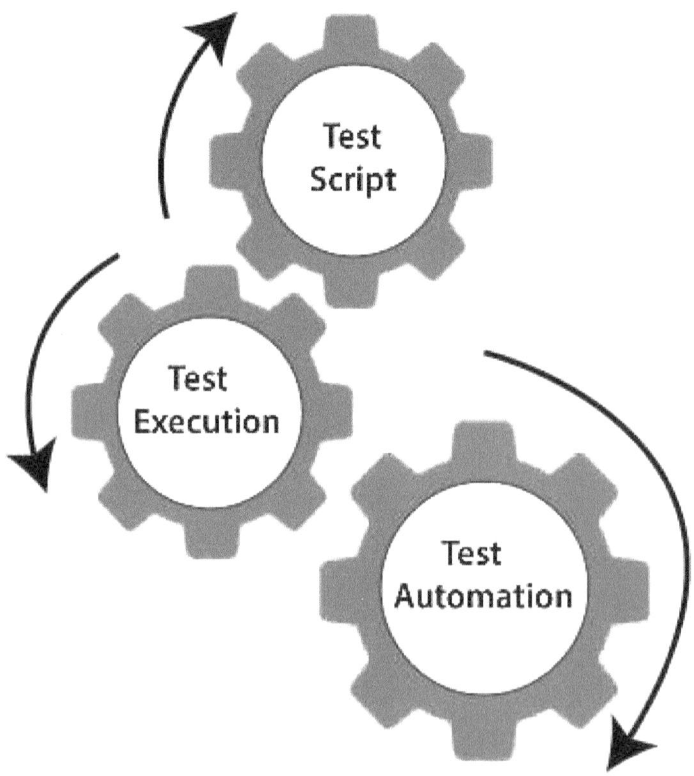

In other words, we can say that whenever we are testing an application by using some tools is known as **automation testing**.

We will go for automation testing when various releases or several regression cycles goes on the application or software. We cannot write the test script or perform the automation testing without understanding the programming language.

Some other types of Software Testing

In software testing, we also have some other types of testing that are not part of any above discussed testing, but those testing are required while testing any software or an application.

- Smoke Testing
- Sanity Testing
- Regression Testing
- User Acceptance Testing
- Exploratory Testing
- Adhoc Testing
- Security Testing
- Globalization Testing

Let's understand those types of testing one by one:

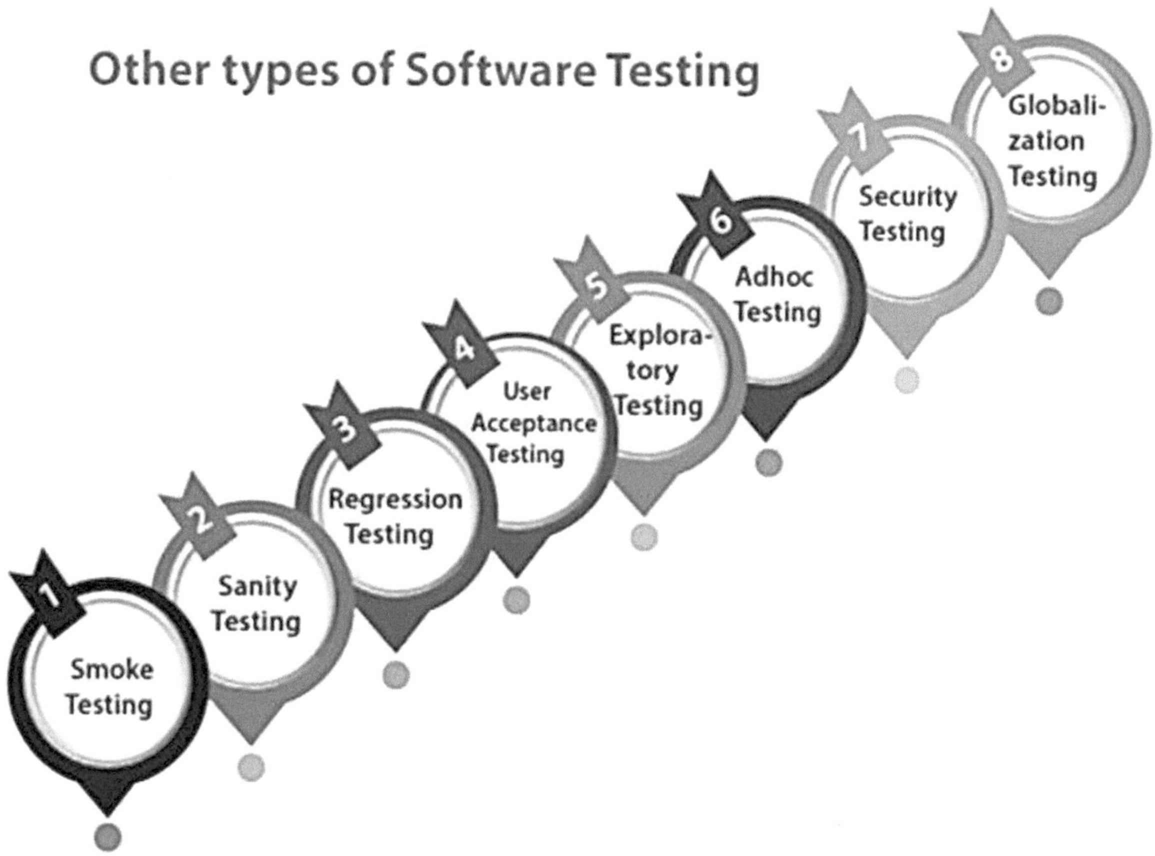

- In smoke testing, we will test an application's basic and critical features before doing one round of deep and rigorous testing.
- Or before checking all possible positive and negative values is known as smoke testing. Analyzing the workflow of the application's core and main functions is the main objective of performing the smoke testing.

Sanity Testing

- It is used to ensure that all the bugs have been fixed and no added issues come into existence due to these changes.
- Sanity testing is unscripted, which means we cannot document it. It checks the correctness of the newly added features and components.

Regression Testing

- Regression testing is the most used type of software testing. Here, the term regression implies that we have to re-test those parts of an unaffected application.
- Regression testing is the most suitable testing for automation tools. As per the project type and accessibility of resources, regression testing can be like Retesting.
- Whenever a bug is fixed by the developers and then testing the other features of the applications that might be simulated because of the bug fixing is known as regression testing.
- In other words, we can say that whenever there is a new release for some project, then we can perform Regression Testing, and due to a new feature may affect the old features in the earlier releases.

User Acceptance Testing

- The User acceptance testing (UAT) is done by the individual team known as domain expert/customer or the client. And knowing the application before accepting the final product is called as user acceptance testing.
- In user acceptance testing, we analyze the business scenarios, and real-time scenarios on the distinct environment called the UAT environment. In this testing, we will test the application before UAI for customer approval.

Exploratory Testing

- Whenever the requirement is missing, early iteration is required, and the testing team has experienced testers when we have a critical application. New test engineer entered the team then we go for the **exploratory testing**.
- To execute the exploratory testing, we will first go through the application in all possible ways, make a test document, understand the flow of the application, and then test the application.

Adhoc Testing

- Testing the application randomly as soon as the build is in the checked sequence is known as **Adhoc testing**.
- It is also called **Monkey testing and Gorilla testing**. In Adhoc testing, we will check the application in contradiction of the client's requirements; that's why it is also known as **negative testing**.
- When the end-user using the application casually, and he/she may detect a bug. Still, the specialized test engineer uses the software thoroughly, so he/she may not identify a similar detection.

Security Testing

- It is an essential part of software testing, used to determine the weakness, risks, or threats in the software application.
- The execution of security testing will help us to avoid the nasty attack from outsiders and ensure our software applications' security.
- In other words, we can say that security testing is mainly used to define that the data will be safe and endure the software's working process.

10.4 Test Automation

Test automation is a crucial aspect of modern system design, essential for ensuring both the efficiency and effectiveness of testing processes. It involves the use of specialized software tools to automatically execute test cases, manage testing data, and compare expected and actual outcomes. This section provides a detailed exploration of test automation within the context of system design, discussing its benefits, strategies, tools, and best practices.

1. Introduction to Test Automation

Test automation refers to the process of utilizing software to perform testing tasks which traditionally would be executed manually by a test engineer. This approach is particularly beneficial in repetitive and extensive testing scenarios where manual testing becomes time-consuming and prone to errors. Automation is not only about executing tests but also encompasses the setup of test preconditions, the selection of what to test, the comparison of expected outcomes with actual outcomes, and the reporting of results.

2. Benefits of Test Automation

Test automation offers several key benefits:

1. **Efficiency**: Automates tedious and repetitive tasks, reducing the time required for test execution.
2. **Accuracy**: Minimizes human errors in test execution and results interpretation.

3. Coverage: Increases the depth and scope of tests, improving the quality of the software.
4. Reusability: Allows test scripts to be reused in different versions of the software, even if some features change.
5. Cost-Effectiveness: Reduces the long-term costs of testing due to decreased manual effort and increased reliability.

3. Developing an Automation Strategy

Creating an effective test automation strategy involves several steps:
1. Scope Definition: Identifying which tests to automate based on their return on investment. Typically, high-volume regression tests, tests that are prone to human error, and tests that are critical for performance are automated.
2. Tool Selection: Choosing the right tools is critical. Factors to consider include the technology stack of the application, the expertise of the team, the quality of support from the tool vendor, and the overall cost of tools.
3. Framework Setup: Developing a test automation framework that supports scalability, maintainability, and ease of integration. Common frameworks include data-driven, keyword-driven, and hybrid approaches.
4. Test Development: Writing test scripts using the chosen tools and frameworks. This includes defining clear and concise test cases, scripting, and ensuring that tests are maintainable and scalable.
5. Maintenance: Continuously updating test scripts to adapt to changes in the system design and ensuring that the automation suite remains robust over time.

4. Tools and Technologies

The choice of tools is pivotal in test automation. Some popular tools include:
1. Selenium: An open-source tool for automating web browsers. It supports multiple languages and platforms.
2. QTP/UFT: A commercial tool from Micro Focus that offers advanced features for test automation.
3. TestComplete: Provides a comprehensive set of features for desktop, mobile, and web application testing.
4. Jenkins: An open-source CI/CD tool that helps automate the different stages of your delivery pipeline.
5. Appium: An open-source tool for automating mobile applications, both Android and iOS.

5. Test Automation Best Practices

To maximize the effectiveness of test automation, several best practices should be followed:
1. Prioritize Tests for Automation: Focus on tests that offer the greatest return on investment. Frequent, repetitive, and high-complexity tests are usually good candidates.
2. Keep Tests Simple and Transparent: Each test case should be simple, performing a single function or test scenario.
3. Ensure Good Test Data Management: Automating the management of test data can significantly enhance the effectiveness of testing by ensuring data variability and maintaining data integrity.
4. Regularly Review and Update Test Cases: As the system evolves, so should the automated tests. Regular updates are necessary to keep tests relevant and effective.
5. Integrate with the CI/CD Pipeline: Automating the execution of tests within the CI/CD pipeline ensures that tests are run regularly and consistently, which helps in identifying defects early in the development cycle.

6. Challenges in Test Automation

While test automation can provide numerous benefits, it also comes with challenges:
1. High Initial Setup Cost: Initial costs can be significant due to tool costs, training, and the time required to establish effective automation.
2. Skill Requirements: Effective test automation requires a certain level of technical skill from the team, including programming skills and an understanding of the tools and frameworks.
3. Maintaining Tests: As the system under test changes, maintaining and updating test scripts can become a substantial effort.

Conclusion

Test automation is an integral part of system design that enhances the efficiency, effectiveness, and coverage of testing efforts. By understanding and implementing a solid test automation strategy, leveraging the right tools, and following best practices, organizations can ensure higher quality systems while reducing manual effort and overall testing costs. This approach not only streamlines the testing process but also supports continuous integration and delivery practices, making it a valuable investment for any software development project.

Summary

1. Validation: Ensuring that the system meets the user's needs and requirements during testing.
2. Verification: Confirming that the system complies with specified requirements and is correctly implemented.
3. Unit Testing: Testing the smallest units of software design, such as modules or components, to ensure each function correctly independently.
4. Integration Testing: Evaluating the interfaces between integrated components to detect faults in their interactions.
5. System Testing: Testing the entire system's compliance with specified requirements in an environment that mimics the production setting.
6. Acceptance Testing: Conducted by end-users to ensure the system meets their requirements and is ready for deployment.
7. Black-box Testing: A testing technique where the tester has no knowledge of the internal workings of the system, focusing on requirements and functionality.
8. White-box Testing: Testing internal structures or workings of an application, also known as clear box testing.
9. Test Automation: The use of software tools to automatically execute test cases, manage testing data, and compare expected and actual outcomes.
10. Regression Testing: Testing conducted to ensure that changes in the code do not adversely affect the existing functionality.
11. Smoke Testing: Testing basic and critical features of an application before performing detailed and rigorous testing.
12. Security Testing: Testing to determine the security of the software application by identifying vulnerabilities and ensuring data protection.

Glossary

1. Gantt Chart: A visual project management tool used for scheduling tasks and tracking project dependencies, often used in project planning.
2. PERT Chart: A project management tool used for scheduling, organizing, and coordinating tasks within a project, particularly useful for identifying the critical path.
3. Test Strategy: The high-level approach and objectives of testing, detailing how testing will be conducted and the overall goals.
4. Test Plan: A comprehensive document outlining the test strategy, objectives, schedule, required resources, and deliverables for a testing project.
5. Test Cases: Specific conditions or variables under which the system will be tested to determine if it meets the requirements.
6. Defect Tracking: The process of identifying, logging, and tracking defects found during testing, often using specialized tools like Jira or Bugzilla.
7. Risk Management: The systematic process of identifying, evaluating, and addressing potential risks that could impact the project's success.
8. Resource Allocation: The process of assigning resources, such as personnel and equipment, to specific tasks within a project.
9. Continuous Integration (CI): A DevOps practice where code changes are frequently merged into a central repository and tested automatically to detect and address bugs early.
10. Smoke Testing: A preliminary test to check the basic functionality of an application before conducting more detailed testing.
11. Regression Testing: Testing existing software functionality to ensure that new code changes do not negatively affect the existing features.

10.5 Project

10.5.1 Solved Project

The "My App" project involves comprehensive quality assurance processes, including testing fundamentals, test planning and strategy, various types of testing, and test automation. Describe the activities undertaken during the testing fundamentals phase and explain why a comprehensive test plan and strategy are crucial for this project. Additionally, identify two types of testing mentioned in the project and their purposes, and discuss the role and benefits of test automation in the "My App" project.

Approach:

Phase 1: Testing Fundamentals

Activities:

1. Understand requirements
2. Set up test environment
3. Prepare test data
4. Define test objectives
5. Train QA team

Outcome:

1. Solid QA foundation, prepared environment, and trained team.

Phase 2: Test Planning and Strategy

Activities:

1. Conduct risk analysis
2. Define test scope
3. Allocate resources
4. Develop test schedule
5. Design test cases
6. Review and approve plan

Outcome:

1. Comprehensive test plan and strategy.

Phase 3: Types of Testing

Functional Testing:

1. Purpose: Verify application functions as expected.
2. Activities: Execute test cases covering all functionalities.

Performance Testing:

1. Purpose: Ensure application performs under load.
2. Activities: Conduct load, stress, and endurance tests.

Outcome:

1. Validated functionality and performance.

Phase 4: Test Automation

Activities:

1. Select automation tools
2. Develop automation framework
3. Write automated test scripts
4. Integrate with CI/CD pipeline
5. Maintain scripts

Benefits:

1. Increased efficiency, coverage, consistency, and early defect detection.

Outcome:

1. Robust test automation process.

10.5.2 Unsolved Project

You are responsible for ensuring the quality of a new College Management System (CMS) designed to streamline administrative and academic processes. The project involves various aspects of quality assurance, including testing fundamentals, test planning and strategy, different types of testing, and test automation. Describe the activities involved in establishing testing fundamentals for the CMS. Explain why developing a comprehensive test plan and strategy is crucial for this project. Identify two types of testing mentioned in the project, their objectives, and how they contribute to validating the CMS. Lastly, discuss the role and benefits of implementing test automation in the testing process of the CMS.

10.6 Case Study

10.6.1 Solved Case Study

Quality assurance (QA) is a critical aspect of software development, ensuring the final product is both reliable and efficient. The QA process includes several key components: testing fundamentals, test planning and strategy, various types of testing, and test automation. Testing fundamentals involve designing detailed test cases and scripts, establishing realistic testing environments, and logging defects through a defect tracking system. A thorough test plan and strategy are essential to cover all critical functionalities, set clear objectives, choose suitable testing tools, and create a structured testing schedule. Various types of testing, such as unit testing, integration testing, system testing, acceptance testing, performance testing, and security testing, each serve specific purposes to comprehensively validate the software. Test automation leverages tools to automate repetitive and regression tests, enhancing efficiency and accuracy. Integrating automated tests into the continuous integration/continuous deployment (CI/CD) pipeline ensures tests are run automatically with each code change, providing immediate feedback and facilitating rapid defect resolution.

Questions:

1. What does testing fundamentals involve in QA?
   Answer: Designing detailed test cases and scripts, establishing realistic testing environments, and logging defects through a defect tracking system.
2. How does a comprehensive test plan and strategy contribute to QA?
   Answer: It ensures all critical functionalities are tested, sets clear objectives, chooses suitable testing tools, and creates a structured testing schedule.
3. Mention one type of testing from the passage and its purpose.
   Answer: Unit testing, which tests individual components to ensure they function correctly.
4. What is the benefit of test automation in QA?
   Answer: It enhances efficiency and accuracy by automating repetitive and regression tests.
5. What is the role of integrating automated tests into the CI/CD pipeline?
   Answer: It ensures tests are run automatically with each code change, providing immediate feedback and facilitating rapid defect resolution.

10.6.2 Unsolved Case Study

Quality assurance (QA) in software development is essential for delivering reliable and efficient software products. This process involves several key components, including testing fundamentals, test planning and strategy, various types of testing, and test automation. Testing fundamentals involve creating detailed test cases and test scripts, setting up realistic testing environments, and identifying and logging defects using a defect tracking system. Developing a comprehensive test plan and strategy ensures all critical functionalities are tested, with clear objectives, appropriate tools, and a structured schedule. Different types of testing, such as unit testing, integration testing, system testing, acceptance testing, performance testing, and security testing, validate various aspects of the software to ensure it meets the required standards. Test automation uses tools to automate repetitive and regression tests, saving time and increasing accuracy. Integrating automated tests into the CI/CD pipeline allows tests to run automatically with each code change, providing immediate feedback and helping to quickly identify and address defects.

Questions:

1. What are the key components of testing fundamentals?
2. Why is a comprehensive test plan and strategy important in QA?
3. Name and describe the purpose of one type of testing mentioned in the passage.
4. How does test automation benefit the QA process?
5. What advantage does integrating automated tests into the CI/CD pipeline offer?

10.7 Lab Activity

10.7.1 Solved Lab Activity

Develop a test plan for a mobile banking application, including objectives, scope, resources, schedule, and risk management strategies.

Solution:

Test Plan for Mobile Banking Application

1. Objectives

1. Ensure Functionality: Verify that all banking features (e.g., account management, fund transfers, bill payments) work as expected.
2. Ensure Security: Test for vulnerabilities to ensure the application is secure from threats.
3. Ensure Usability: Confirm that the application is user-friendly and provides a good user experience.
4. Ensure Performance: Validate that the application performs well under various conditions (e.g., high load, low network connectivity).

2. Scope

1. Features to be Tested:
2. User Registration and Login
3. Account Management
4. Fund Transfers
5. Bill Payments
6. Transaction History
7. Notifications
8. Security Features (e.g., Two-Factor Authentication)
9. Features not to be Tested:
10. Backend Database Performance
11. Third-party Integrations (beyond initial connectivity tests)

3. Resources

1. Team Members:
2. Test Manager
3. Test Engineers
4. Security Experts
5. Usability Analysts
6. Tools:
7. Automated Testing Tools (e.g., Appium)
8. Security Testing Tools (e.g., OWASP ZAP)
9. Performance Testing Tools (e.g., JMeter)
10. Bug Tracking System (e.g., Jira)
11. Devices:
12. A range of mobile devices (iOS and Android) with different screen sizes and OS versions

4. Schedule

1. Planning Phase: 2 weeks
2. Test Case Development: 3 weeks
3. Test Execution: 4 weeks
4. Bug Fixing and Re-testing: 2 weeks
5. Final Testing and Sign-off: 1 week

5. Risk Management Strategies

1. Identify Potential Risks: List possible risks (e.g., security vulnerabilities, performance issues).
2. Risk Assessment: Evaluate the likelihood and impact of each risk.
3. Mitigation Plans: Develop strategies to mitigate identified risks (e.g., regular security audits, performance optimization).

4. Contingency Plans: Prepare fallback plans in case mitigation strategies fail.

Diagram

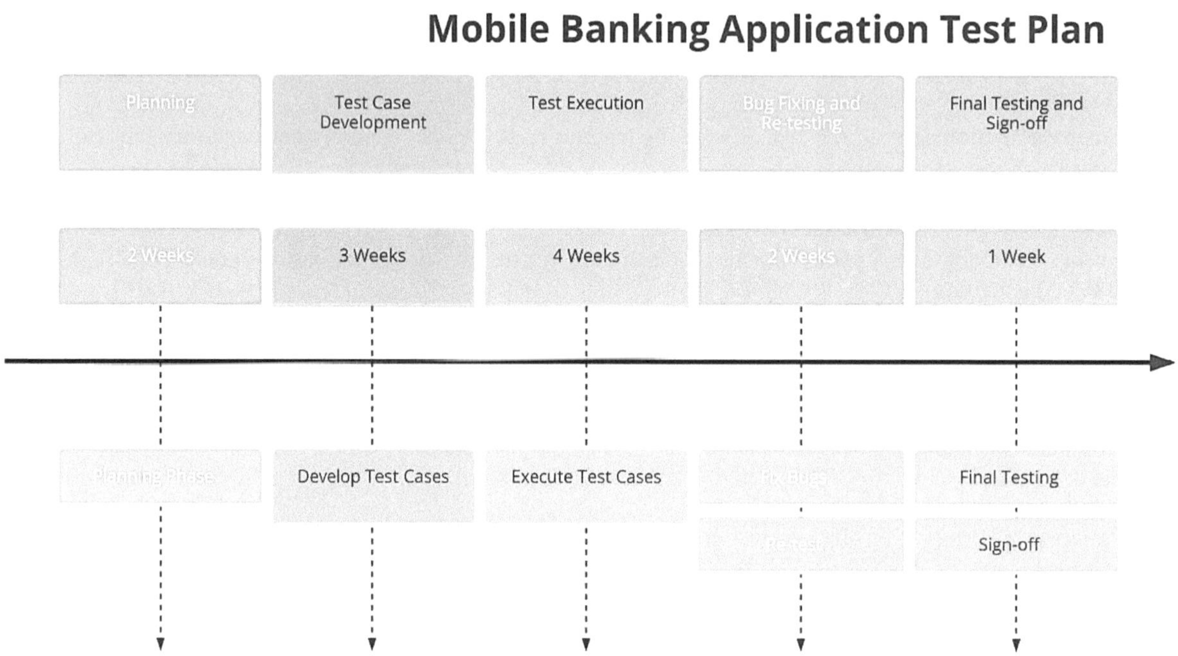

Explanation

Test Plan Stages:

1. Planning Phase (2 Weeks):
2. Define objectives, scope, resources, schedule, and risk management strategies.
3. Identify potential risks and develop mitigation and contingency plans.
4. Test Case Development (3 Weeks):
5. Develop detailed test cases covering all functional, security, usability, and performance aspects.
6. Prepare necessary testing materials and environments.
7. Test Execution (4 Weeks):
8. Execute test cases on various devices and environments.
9. Perform functional, security, usability, and performance testing.
10. Record and report any issues found during testing.
11. Bug Fixing and Re-testing (2 Weeks):
12. Address and fix identified bugs.
13. Re-test to ensure issues are resolved and no new issues have been introduced.
14. Final Testing and Sign-off (1 Week):
15. Conduct final testing to validate the overall functionality and stability of the application.
16. Obtain sign-off from stakeholders confirming the application's readiness for deployment.

10.7.2 Unsolved Lab Activity

Develop a simple automated test script using Selenium WebDriver for testing the login functionality of a web application.

Previous Years Solved Questions

Q 1. Write the importance of quality in software development. List specifications of various quality factors. **[IGNOU MCA, June 2013]**

Ans 1. Quality in software development is crucial as it directly affects the software's performance, reliability, and user satisfaction. High-quality software meets or exceeds customer expectations, operates efficiently, and is maintainable, scalable, and secure.

The importance of quality in software development includes:

1. Customer Satisfaction: High-quality software provides a positive user experience, leading to higher customer satisfaction and loyalty.

2. Reliability: Quality software operates consistently without failures, ensuring users can rely on it for their tasks.

3. Efficiency: Quality software performs tasks quickly and uses resources optimally, providing better performance.

4. Maintainability: High-quality software is easier to maintain and update, reducing the cost and effort required for future changes.

5. Security: Quality software is less vulnerable to security threats, protecting sensitive data and maintaining user trust.

6. Compliance: High-quality software adheres to industry standards and regulations, avoiding legal and financial repercussions.

7. Cost Savings: Investing in quality reduces the likelihood of costly post-release fixes and decreases the total cost of ownership.

Specifications of Various Quality Factors

Quality factors in software development can be classified into different categories, often referred to as software quality attributes. Here are the key quality factors with their specifications:

1. Functionality

1. Suitability: The software's ability to provide an appropriate set of functions for specified tasks.

2. Accuracy: The correctness of the software in performing tasks and producing results.

3. Interoperability: The ability of the software to interact with other systems or components.

4. Compliance: Adherence to standards, regulations, and laws.

5. Security: The capability of the software to protect data and resources from unauthorized access and breaches.

2. Reliability

1. Maturity: The frequency of software failures due to defects.

2. Fault Tolerance: The ability of the software to operate correctly in the presence of hardware or software faults.

3. Recoverability: The capability of the software to recover from failures and restore normal operations.

3. Usability

1. Learnability: How easy it is for users to learn to use the software.

2. Understandability: The clarity and comprehensibility of the software's functions and interface.

3. Operability: The ease of operation and control over the software.

4. Efficiency

1. Time Behavior: The software's response times and throughput rates under specified conditions.

2. Resource Utilization: The efficiency of the software in using resources such as memory, CPU, and disk space.

5. Maintainability

1. Analyzability: The ease with which the software can be diagnosed for defects or causes of failure.

2. Changeability: The capability of the software to be modified without introducing defects.

3. Stability: The software's ability to avoid unexpected effects from modifications.

4. Testability: The ease with which the software can be tested to ensure it works correctly.

6. Portability

1. Adaptability: The capability of the software to be adapted to different environments without significant changes.

2. Installability: The ease with which the software can be installed in a target environment.

3. Co-existence: The software's ability to operate efficiently alongside other software.

4. Replaceability: The capability of the software to be replaced by another software product for the same purpose.

Example Quality Models
1. ISO/IEC 25010: An international standard for software product quality, defining a set of quality characteristics and sub-characteristics.
2. CMMI (Capability Maturity Model Integration): A process level improvement training and appraisal program, defining practices that lead to improved performance.

Previous Years Unsolved Questions

Q 1. Explain the software, product and process quality with example. **[Chaudhary Charan Singh University BCA, May 2019]**
Q 2. Define Quality Assurance. Briefly describe the factors that affect the quality of the system. **[Udaipur University, 2018]**

Exercise

Exercise 1 – Multiple Choice Questions

1. Which of the following is the primary goal of testing in system development?
    - A. To increase the complexity of the system
    - B. To ensure that the system meets user requirements and functions correctly
    - C. To reduce the cost of the project
    - D. To eliminate the need for documentation
2. What is the main purpose of a test plan in software testing?
    - A. To design the software
    - B. To guide the testing process and define the testing scope, approach, resources, and schedule
    - C. To write the user manual
    - D. To estimate the project budget
3. Which type of testing focuses on verifying that individual components of the system work correctly?
    - A. Integration Testing
    - B. System Testing
    - C. Unit Testing
    - D. Acceptance Testing
4. In which phase of testing is the system tested in an environment that closely resembles the production environment?
    - A. Unit Testing
    - B. Integration Testing
    - C. System Testing
    - D. Acceptance Testing
5. Which tool is commonly used for automating web application testing?
    - A. GitHub
    - B. Selenium
    - C. Jenkins
    - D. Visual Studio

Exercise 2 – True/False

1. Test planning is an ongoing activity that starts at the beginning of the project and continues throughout the software development lifecycle.
2. Acceptance testing is conducted by the developers to ensure that each unit of the software performs as expected.
3. Test automation is only beneficial for small projects with minimal repetitive tasks.

Exercise 3 – Fill in the blanks

1. The primary goal of __________ is to ensure that the software meets the specified requirements and functions correctly in its intended environment.
2. __________ testing focuses on testing individual components or units of the software to verify that each unit functions correctly as an independent entity.
3. Test automation tools, such as __________, help in performing repetitive testing tasks automatically, improving efficiency and accuracy.

Exercise 4- Fill in the blanks with two options

1. __________ testing is designed to ensure that a system can handle the expected __________ of data or users under normal conditions.
2. In __________ testing, the internal structure of the application is known and tested, while in __________ testing, the functionality is tested without knowledge of the internal workings.
3. The purpose of __________ planning is to outline the objectives, scope, and strategy for the testing activities, ensuring that the testing process is __________ and thorough.

Exercise 5- Give two answers for the following:

1. Types of Testing
2. Benefits of Test Automation
3. Types of Test Automation Tools
4. Testing Strategies
5. Testing Fundamentals Concepts

Exercise 6- Rearrange the sentence

1. ensures Testing system reliability the of.
2. tests Unit individual test components.
3. approach strategy testing plan.

Exercise 7- Choose the Odd One Out

1. Unit Testing, Integration Testing, System Testing, Selenium
2. Efficiency, Accuracy, Coverage, Waterfall
3. Black-box Testing, White-box Testing, Gray-box Testing, Jenkins

Exercise 8- Jumble words

1. mutoatinota
2. tgenirtaiotn
3. surcoye

Exercise 9- Match case

Column 1	Column 2
1. What type of testing focuses on evaluating the smallest parts of an application, such as functions or methods?	**A.** System Testing
2. Which document outlines the objectives, resources, schedule, and scope for testing activities?	**B.** Unit Testing
3. What is the primary goal of performance testing?	**C.** Test Plan
4. What type of testing is conducted to ensure the entire system meets specified requirements?	**D.** Black-box Testing
5. Which testing strategy involves the tester having no knowledge of the internal workings of the application?	**E.** Performance Testing

Exercise 10- Assertion – Reason

1. Assertion (A): Unit Testing focuses on testing individual components or functions of a system.
Reason (R): Unit Testing is performed to ensure that each component of the system works as intended.
Options:

1. Assertion (A) is true and Reason (R) is the correct reason for Assertion (A).
2. Assertion (A) is true, but Reason (R) is not the correct reason for Assertion (A).
3. Assertion (A) is false, but Reason (R) is true.
4. Assertion (A) is false and Reason (R) is also false.

Exercise 11- One- word

1. What is the process of verifying that a system meets its specifications?
2. Which type of testing focuses on individual components or functions?
3. What is the name for testing that assesses the system's performance under load?

Exercise 12- Small Answers

1. What are the main objectives of test planning and strategy in software development?

2. Explain the importance of unit testing in the software development lifecycle.
3. What is the role of test automation in improving software quality assurance?

Exercise 13- Long Answers

1. Explain the strategies for effective resource management in test automation projects.
2. Analyze the benefits and challenges of using a hybrid testing approach that combines manual and automated testing.

Answers

Exercise 1- 1) B, 2) B, 3) C, 4) C, 5) B
Exercise 2- 1) True, 2) False, 3) False
Exercise 3- 1) testing, 2) Unit, 3) Selenium
Exercise 4- 1) Performance, load, 2) White-box, black-box, 3) test, systematic
Exercise 5- 1) Unit Testing, Integration Testing, 2) Efficiency, Accuracy, 3) Selenium, QTP/UFT, 4) Black-box Testing, White-box Testing, 5) Validation, Verification
Exercise 6- 1) Testing ensures the reliability of system, 2) Unit tests individual components, 3) Testing strategy plan approach
Exercise 7- 1) Selenium, 2) Waterfall, 3) Jenkins
Exercise 8- 1) automation, 2) integration, 3) resource
Exercise 9-1 B, 2 C, 3 E, 4 A, 5 D
Exercise 10- a) Assertion (A) is true and Reason (R) is the correct reason for Assertion (A).
Exercise 11- 1) Verification, 2) Unit, 3) Performance

Online Resources

Online Exam paper
URL https://forms.gle/ntTU2DsaX1f3Mqs88
QR Code

YouTube Video
URL https://www.youtube.com/playlist?list=PLzlh_31VWEFqCtiBC60DnQ-qJIwGpbHlv
QR Code

More Test Papers Practices

Test Paper-1
URL https://forms.gle/G71XPT1CJDRkunKE8
QR Code

Test Paper-2
URL https://forms.gle/2idUjkRjyoVLfAWY7

QR Code

System analysis and design Test Paper
Chapter- 10
Quality Assurance

Time Duration: 30 Minutes **Maximum Marks: 25**

General Instructions:

1. The question paper consists of answer any 12 questions out of the given 19 questions and is divided into four sections, A, B, C and D.
2. All questions are compulsory.
3. Section A comprises question numbers 1 to 8. These are MCQs and one liner of one mark each. You are to select one most appropriate response out of the four provided options.
4. Section B comprises question numbers 1 to 5. These are SAQs carrying two marks each.
5. Section C comprises question numbers 1 to 4. These are SAQs carrying four marks each.
6. Section D comprises question numbers 1& 2. These are LAQs carrying five marks each.

SECTION-A

I. <u>Answer any 6 questions out of the given 8 questions</u> **(1*6=6)**

1. What is the primary goal of quality assurance in software development?
   A) To write code for new features
   B) To ensure the software meets specified requirements and is free of defects
   C) To deploy the software to production
   D) To design the user interface
2. Which of the following is a key component of test planning?
   A) Writing user manuals
   B) Identifying test objectives and criteria for success
   C) Coding new features
   D) Conducting user training
3. Which type of testing focuses on validating individual components of the software?
   A) Integration Testing
   B) System Testing
   C) Unit Testing
   D) Acceptance Testing
4. What is the purpose of test automation in software testing?
   A) To perform manual testing
   B) To automate repetitive testing tasks and increase testing efficiency
   C) To write new code for the application
   D) To document user requirements
5. Which testing type is typically performed last before the software is released to users?
   A) Unit Testing
   B) Integration Testing
   C) System Testing
   D) User Acceptance Testing (UAT)
6. What type of testing validates the integration of different modules?
7. What document outlines the testing objectives and strategies?
8. What is the process of using software tools to execute tests automatically called?

SECTION-B

II. <u>Answer any 3 questions out of the given 5 questions</u> **(2*3=6)**

1. Define 'quality assurance' in the context of software development.
2. What is the main objective of a test plan?
3. List two types of testing commonly used in software quality assurance.
4. Why is unit testing important in the software development process?
5. What are the benefits of test automation in quality assurance?

SECTION-C

II. <u>Answer any 2 questions out of the given 4 questions</u> **(4*2=8)**

1. Explain the key elements that should be included in a test plan.
2. Describe the differences between unit testing and integration testing.
3. Discuss the role of system testing in the software testing lifecycle.
4. What are the advantages and challenges of implementing test automation in software projects?

SECTION-D

III. <u>Answer any 1 question out of the given 2 questions</u> **(5*1=5)**

1. Analyze the impact of effective quality assurance practices on software development. Provide examples of how rigorous testing can improve software quality and user satisfaction.
2. Explain the process and significance of user acceptance testing (UAT) in the software development lifecycle. How does UAT contribute to the overall success of a software project?

System analysis and design
Annual Exam paper
Sample Paper

Time Duration: 3hrs **Maximum Marks: 80**

General Instructions:
1. The question paper consists of answer any 34 questions out of the given 40 questions and is divided into four sections, A, B, C and D.
2. All questions are compulsory.
3. Section A comprises question numbers 1 to 17. These are MCQs and one liner of one mark each. You are to select one most appropriate response out of the four provided options.
4. Section B comprises question numbers 1 to 9. These are SAQs carrying two marks each.
5. Section C comprises question numbers 1 to 10. These are SAQs carrying four marks each.
6. Section D comprises question numbers 1& 4. These are LAQs carrying five marks each.

SECTION-A

I. <u>Answer any 15 questions out of the given 17 questions</u> **(1*15=15)**

1. What is the primary objective of system analysis and design?
   A) To develop software quickly
   B) To understand and specify in detail what an information system should do and how the components should work together
   C) To write user manuals
   D) To test the system
2. Which phase of the System Development Lifecycle (SDLC) involves determining the detailed requirements of the system?
   A) Design
   B) Implementation
   C) Analysis
   D) Maintenance
3. In systems theory, what term describes the interconnections and relationships between system components?
   A) Solving Principles
   B) Boundaries
   C) Interfaces
   D) Interrelationships
4. What is the primary goal of gathering user requirements?
   A) To deploy the system
   B) To understand user needs and document them for system design
   C) To write code
   D) To test the system
5. Which diagram is used to show the relationships between entities in a database?
   A) Activity Diagram
   B) Use Case Diagram
   C) Entity-Relationship Diagram
   D) Data Flow Diagram
6. What is the purpose of normalization in databases?
   A) To speed up data retrieval
   B) To eliminate redundancy and ensure data integrity
   C) To create more tables
   D) To simplify user queries

7. Which design pattern encapsulates database access logic?
   A) Singleton Pattern
   B) Observer Pattern
   C) Factory Pattern
   D) Repository Pattern
8. What is a key characteristic of Agile Methodologies?
   A) Rigid structure
   B) Sequential development
   C) Iterative and incremental development
   D) Long development cycles
9. Which testing phase focuses on testing individual components of the software in isolation?
   A) Integration Testing
   B) System Testing
   C) Unit Testing
   D) Acceptance Testing
10. What is the main goal of user training and acceptance testing?
   A) To identify bugs
   B) To ensure users are comfortable with the system and that it meets their needs
   C) To write documentation
   D) To finalize coding
11. Which project management activity involves determining project tasks and their dependencies?
   A) Risk Management
   B) Resource Management
   C) Project Planning and Scheduling
   D) Project Communication
12. What is the primary focus of quality assurance in software development?
   A) Writing code
   B) Ensuring the software meets specified requirements and is free of defects
   C) Designing user interfaces
   D) Deploying the software
13. What term describes the iterative enhancement of processes within an organization?
14. What document outlines the project scope, objectives, and deliverables?
15. Which type of diagram shows the flow of data within a system?
16. What type of testing verifies that the system meets business requirements?
17. What design pattern provides a simplified interface to a complex subsystem?

SECTION-B

II. <u>Answer any 7 questions out of the given 9 questions</u> **(2*7=14)**

1. Define 'system modelling' in the context of software development.
2. What is the purpose of an activity diagram?
3. List two key principles of Agile Methodologies.
4. What is a Gantt chart used for in project scheduling?
5. Why is resource management important in project planning?
6. What is the role of a test plan in quality assurance?
7. Describe one advantage of using test automation in software testing.
8. What is the main objective of risk management in project planning?
9. Why is user acceptance testing critical before software deployment?

SECTION-C

II. <u>Answer any 9 questions out of the given 10 questions</u> **(4*9=36)**

1. Explain the concept of 'systems thinking' and its importance in problem-solving.
2. Describe the key steps involved in gathering and documenting user requirements.
3. How does normalization improve the quality of a database?

4. What are the benefits of using Entity-Relationship Diagrams (ERDs) in database design?
5. Discuss the advantages and disadvantages of the Waterfall Model.
6. How does DevOps practice enhance software development and operations?
7. Explain the importance of integration testing in the software development lifecycle.
8. What are the key components of an effective deployment strategy?
9. How does effective project communication contribute to project success?
10. What are the main types of testing in software quality assurance and their purposes?

SECTION-D

III. <u>Answer any 3 questions out of the given 4 questions</u> **(5*3=15)**

1. Analyse the impact of effective quality assurance practices on software development. Provide examples of how rigorous testing can improve software quality and user satisfaction.
2. Explain the role of user training and acceptance testing (UAT) in ensuring successful software implementation. How do these activities contribute to overall project success?
3. Discuss the significance of project planning and scheduling in managing project timelines and resources. Provide examples to illustrate your points.
4. Evaluate the benefits and challenges of implementing Agile Methodologies in a software development project. Include examples of how Agile can enhance project outcomes.

Practical Test Paper

Time Duration: 1 Hour 30 Minutes **Maximum Marks: 20**

General Instructions:
1. Each question carries 5 marks.
2. Marks will be awarded based on clarity of explanation, accuracy, and understanding demonstrated.
3. Write your answers neatly and legibly.

Answer any 4 out of 5 questions. Answer each question in 100-150 words.

1. Create a use case diagram for an online shopping system. Include key factors such as Customer, Admin, and Payment Gateway, and describe their interactions with the system. Explain the importance of use case modelling in system design. **[5]**
2. Consider a software development project you are familiar with. Describe the different phases it went through according to the System Development Lifecycle (SDLC) and mention the key activities and deliverables for each phase. **[5]**
3. Design an Entity-Relationship Diagram (ERD) for a small library system, including entities such as Books, Members, and Loans. Explain the relationships between these entities and how the ERD helps in organizing the database structure. **[5]**
4. Given a database table for student grades with redundant data, normalize it to the Third Normal Form (3NF). Describe the steps you took and explain the benefits of normalization in database design. **[5]**
5. Create a project plan for organizing a college event. Include a Gantt chart that outlines the key activities, their durations, and dependencies. Explain the importance of project planning and scheduling in ensuring the event's success. **[5]**

Viva Voce Questions

Q 1: What is the importance of the System Development Lifecycle (SDLC)?
Answer: The SDLC is critical as it provides a structured approach for developing information systems, ensuring quality, efficiency, and the successful implementation of a system. It includes stages such as planning, analysis, design, implementation, and maintenance, allowing for thorough documentation, testing, and evaluation at each step.

Q 2: Explain the concept of systems thinking and its relevance to problem-solving.
Answer: Systems thinking involves understanding a system by examining the linkages and interactions between the components that comprise the entirety of that system. It is relevant to problem-solving as it helps in viewing problems in a holistic manner, identifying root causes, and devising solutions that address the entire system rather than just individual parts.

Q 3: How do you gather user requirements, and why is this step crucial in system development?
Answer: User requirements can be gathered through interviews, surveys, observations, and workshops. This step is crucial because it ensures that the final system meets the users' needs and expectations, leading to higher user satisfaction and successful adoption of the system.

Q 4: What are use case diagrams, and why are they important in system modeling?
Answer: Use case diagrams visually represent the interactions between users (actors) and the system, depicting the functional requirements. They are important because they help in understanding the system's functionality from the user's perspective, ensuring that all user requirements are captured and addressed.

Q 5: Can you describe the process of normalization in database design?
Answer: Normalization is the process of organizing database tables to reduce redundancy and improve data integrity. It involves decomposing tables into smaller tables and defining relationships between them according to rules (normal forms) to ensure that data dependencies are logical and stored efficiently.

Q 6: What are design patterns, and how do they benefit software development?
Answer: Design patterns are general reusable solutions to common problems in software design. They benefit software development by providing proven strategies to solve design issues, promoting best practices, improving code readability, and facilitating maintenance and scalability.

Q 7: Explain the differences between the Waterfall model and Agile methodologies.
Answer: The Waterfall model is a linear and sequential approach where each phase must be completed before the next begins, making it suitable for projects with well-defined requirements. Agile methodologies are iterative and incremental, promoting flexibility and continuous feedback, making them ideal for projects with evolving requirements and a need for frequent updates.

Q 8: What is DevOps, and how does it integrate into system design?
Answer: DevOps is a set of practices that combine software development (Dev) and IT operations (Ops) to shorten the development lifecycle and deliver high-quality software continuously. In system design, DevOps integrates through continuous integration, continuous deployment, automated testing, and monitoring, enhancing collaboration and efficiency.

Q 9: Why is user training and acceptance testing essential in the implementation phase?
Answer: User training ensures that end-users are familiar with the system, reducing resistance and increasing productivity. Acceptance testing validates that the system meets user requirements and is ready for deployment, ensuring that any issues are addressed before full-scale implementation.

Q 10: What are some common strategies for deploying a new system?
Answer: Common deployment strategies include big bang deployment, phased deployment, blue-green deployment, and canary deployment. Each strategy has its own advantages and risks, and the choice depends on the project's requirements, risk tolerance, and resource availability.

Q 11: Describe the role of integration testing in system development.
Answer: Integration testing focuses on verifying the interactions and data flow between integrated units or components of a system. It ensures that combined parts of the system work together correctly and helps identify interface-related issues early in the development cycle.

Q 12: What are the primary objectives of project planning and scheduling in system development?
Answer: The primary objectives include defining the project scope, setting measurable goals, allocating resources, establishing a timeline with milestones, managing risks, and ensuring effective communication among stakeholders. This planning ensures that the project progresses smoothly and meets its deadlines and budget constraints.

Q 13: How do you manage changes to requirements during a project?

Answer: Managing requirements changes involves a structured process of evaluating the impact of changes, obtaining stakeholder approval, updating documentation, and communicating changes to the project team. Tools like change control boards and version control systems help in tracking and managing these changes efficiently.

Q 14: What are the key considerations in designing a secure database?

Answer: Key considerations include implementing access controls, encrypting sensitive data, ensuring data integrity through validation and constraints, regularly updating software to patch vulnerabilities, and conducting regular security audits to identify and address potential threats.

Q 15: Explain the concept of risk management in project planning.

Answer: Risk management involves identifying potential risks, assessing their likelihood and impact, developing strategies to mitigate them, and monitoring risks throughout the project. Effective risk management ensures that risks are proactively managed, reducing their impact on the project's success.

Q 16: What is the purpose of a test plan in the testing phase?

Answer: A test plan outlines the scope, objectives, resources, schedule, and procedures for testing activities. It serves as a roadmap for the testing process, ensuring that all aspects of the system are tested systematically, and that testing is conducted efficiently and effectively.

Q 17: Describe the role of test automation in system design.

Answer: Test automation involves using tools to execute test cases automatically, reducing manual effort and increasing test coverage. It enhances testing efficiency, accuracy, and consistency, making it possible to run large numbers of tests quickly and repeatedly, especially useful in regression testing.

Q 18: What is the significance of entity-relationship (ER) diagrams in database design?

Answer: ER diagrams visually represent the data and relationships between entities in a database. They are significant because they provide a clear and organized way to model the database structure, ensuring that data dependencies are properly defined and facilitating database normalization.

Q 19: How do you ensure effective communication in a project team?

Answer: Effective communication can be ensured by establishing clear communication protocols, using appropriate communication channels (e.g., email, instant messaging, video conferencing), scheduling regular updates and meetings, and fostering a collaborative culture where team members feel comfortable sharing ideas and feedback.

Q 20: What are the challenges of implementing a new system, and how can they be addressed?

Answer: Challenges include user resistance, technical issues, data migration complexities, and integration with existing systems. These can be addressed through comprehensive planning, user training, involving stakeholders early in the process, conducting thorough testing, and having a robust support and maintenance plan in place.

Q 21: Explain the concept of business process modelling notation (BPMN).

Answer: BPMN is a graphical representation for specifying business processes in a workflow. It provides a standard way to visualize the steps and interactions in a business process, helping stakeholders understand and analyse the process for improvements and optimization.

Q 22: What are the benefits of using design patterns in software development?

Answer: Benefits include providing proven solutions to common design problems, promoting code reuse and best practices, enhancing code readability and maintainability, and facilitating communication among developers by providing a shared vocabulary for design concepts.

Q 23: How does the agile methodology differ from traditional methodologies in system development?

Answer: Agile methodology is iterative and incremental, emphasizing flexibility, customer collaboration, and responsiveness to change. Traditional methodologies, like Waterfall, follow a linear and sequential approach, with each phase completed before the next begins, making them less adaptable to changes during the project lifecycle.

Q 24: Describe the process and importance of user acceptance testing (UAT).

Answer: UAT involves testing the system by the end-users to ensure it meets their requirements and is ready for deployment. It is important because it validates that the system functions as intended in a real-world environment, ensuring user satisfaction and reducing the risk of post-deployment issues.

Q 25: What is the role of help desk and user support in system maintenance?

Answer: The help desk provides ongoing support to users, addressing technical issues, answering queries, and providing guidance on using the system. Effective user support ensures that users can efficiently use the system, reducing downtime and increasing overall user satisfaction and productivity.

YouTube Link for Viva Voce Questions:
https://www.youtube.com/playlist?list=PLzlh_31VWEFpoXqf9ap0Pw8Rs-sf8fgyx

QR Code:

ADDITIONAL RESOURCES

System analysis and design Videos Playlist-

Link: https://www.youtube.com/playlist?list=PLzlh_31VWEFpLboxt8lzDzlLBEM-V4h0L

QR Code:

In this book

Welcome to the world of System Analysis and Design, where technology meets problem-solving to create powerful solutions. This comprehensive book blends theory with practice, incorporating real-world examples, case studies, and practical exercises. Explore the system development life cycle (SDLC) step-by-step, with a strong emphasis on modern methodologies like Agile, Scrum, and DevOps, alongside traditional approaches. Gain hands-on experience with essential tools and technologies and foster your analytical thinking and problem-solving skills to tackle real-life challenges confidently.

YouTube Videos Playlists for all Chapters

CHAPTER 1
Link
https://www.youtube.com/playlist?list=PLzlh_31VWEFo5X5g8rflHjgs6Nbhwq22w
QR Code

CHAPTER 2
Link https://www.youtube.com/playlist?list=PLzlh_31VWEFryOILzjHNPE757pir-7S8L
QR Code

CHAPTER 3
Link https://www.youtube.com/playlist?list=PLzlh_31VWEFrog74q_3hWqr80zSeU__6V
QR Code

CHAPTER 4

Link https://www.youtube.com/playlist?list=PLzlh_31VWEFpa7PV3GpfX2YOKVcRdoDSR

QR Code

CHAPTER 5
Link https://www.youtube.com/playlist?list=PLzlh_31VWEFqy0Sa33JI5TpTakUDAario
QR Code

CHAPTER 6
Link https://www.youtube.com/playlist?list=PLzlh_31VWEFpeMWLB8G-vjDj96lUvxwh-
QR Code

CHAPTER 7
Link https://www.youtube.com/playlist?list=PLzlh_31VWEFomrD2VyjpfRPx5Ye6Z3fT9
QR Code

CHAPTER 8
Link https://www.youtube.com/playlist?list=PLzlh_31VWEFrF5voCE1_QwQFqHbPgACLk
QR Code

CHAPTER 9
Link https://www.youtube.com/playlist?list=PLzlh_31VWEFpwwqH6iqI3Bu8I6UBnLhaX
QR Code

CHAPTER 10
Link https://www.youtube.com/playlist?list=PLzlh_31VWEFqCtiBC60DnQ-qJIwGpbHlv
QR Code